Praise for Peter Wyden's *Stella*

"Fascinating . . . a truly unique work in the vast Holocaust literature . . . an unforgettable book."
  —*Library Journal*

"With voluminous and impeccable research, Wyden skillfully presents a surreal portrait of a woman on the horns of a *Sophie's Choice*."
  —*Hadassah Magazine*

"Remarkable detective work, full of personal and political drama."
  —Alexander Dallin, Stanford University, author of *German Rule in Russia*

"Truly stranger than fiction."
  —*Miami Jewish Tribune*

"A chilling exploration of the moral complexities of survival in an insane world . . . [an] unusual and deeply disturbing Holocaust tale. . . . Wyden goes beyond the dismal facts to probe the limits of culpability when faced with 'the final choice: to die or join the devil.' . . . A provocative and haunting work, worthy of the attention—and soul-searching—of a wide readership."
  —*Kirkus Reviews*

"Gripping . . . affecting."
  —*Forward*

"*Stella* distinguishes itself as a work of historical scholarship. . . . penetrating."
  —*Los Angeles Times Book Review*

"Very vivid and exciting . . . I read it with increasing fascination."
  —Gerhart M. Riegner, World Jewish Congress

"Wyden's largest achievement . . . is nothing less than the staring down of evil. For the Devil, Wyden reminds us, may come even in the form of old friends—or ourselves."
  —*Washington Post*

"One of the most fascinating (and sickening) affairs of the second world war. I always wanted to write about it one day; I congratulate Peter Wyden, who did some incredible detective work and found out more than I ever did."
  —Walter Laqueur, Center for Strategic and International Studies

STELLA

PETER WYDEN

ANCHOR BOOKS
DOUBLEDAY
New York London Toronto Sydney Auckland

AN ANCHOR BOOK

PUBLISHED BY DOUBLEDAY

a division of Bantam Doubleday Dell Publishing Group, Inc.
1540 Broadway, New York, New York 10036

ANCHOR BOOKS, DOUBLEDAY, and the portrayal of an anchor
are trademarks of Doubleday, a division of Bantam Doubleday Dell
Publishing Group, Inc.

Stella was originally published in hardcover by Simon & Schuster
in 1992. The Anchor Books edition is
published by arrangement with Simon & Schuster.

Designed by Eve Metz

Library of Congress Cataloging-in-Publication Data

Wyden, Peter.
Stella/Peter Wyden.
p. cm.
Originally published: New York: Simon & Schuster, © 1992.
With additional material.
Includes bibliographical references and index.
1. Goldschlag, Stella.   2. Jews—Germany—Berlin—Biography.
3. Holocaust, Jewish (1939–1945)—Germany—Berlin.   4. World War,
1939–1945—Collaborationists—Germany—Berlin—Biography.
5. Wyden, Peter—Childhood and youth.   6. Berlin (Germany)—Biography.
I. Title.
DS135.G5G55979   1993
940.53'163'092—dc20
[B]   93-24079
CIP

ISBN 0-385-47179-3
Copyright © 1992 by Peter H. Wyden, Inc.
All Rights Reserved
Printed in the United States of America
First Anchor Books Edition: November 1993

1   3   5   7   9   10   8   6   4   2

Contents

Contents

It is neither easy nor agreeable to dredge this abyss of viciousness, and yet I think it needs to be done, because what could be perpetrated yesterday could be attempted again tomorrow, could overwhelm us and our children.

—PRIMO LEVI
The Drowned and the Saved (1988)

BOOK 1

GROWING UP WITH HITLER

1. The Memory

STELLA'S DAUGHTER is a public health nurse in Israel, nearly fifty, wiry, tense, alert to hints of danger in the wind, like a doe. She moves quickly. Incessant smoking has left her chronically hoarse. She subsists on one meal a day and rivers of coffee; sleeps only four hours a night, sometimes two; and admits to being a perfectionist. She wishes she could stop striving for flawlessness and understands that she is trying to make up for Stella's terrible taint.

Her yearning to expunge the mother's shadow is intense. She cannot shake it. After nearly thirty-five years of physical separation, Yvonne has the recurring fantasy of seizing a rifle, trying to find Stella back in Germany, and shooting her dead, wiping out the memory so she can stop atoning.

Stella will not die—not that Yvonne hasn't tried everything short of acting out the fantasized murder. Knowing that her "biological manufacturer" profited from her sex appeal, the daughter does her best to cultivate precisely opposite traits. Her graying hair is close-cropped, her skin windswept. She lives in jeans, shuns makeup and —disregarding the high forehead and blue eyes she inherited from Stella—insists she looks like "the other side," the father she does not know, "probably one of Stella's kind," a male, servicing women in one-night stands.

Emotionally, the separation will not work. The stain stays. "Nothing can help me," Yvonne is convinced. "I will live with it and die with it. I am Yvonne, who had better not have been born."

It was natural that Stella Goldschlag and Lieselotte Streszak, having so much in common, became friends during that year of bloodshed unleashed. Stella was seventeen, Lilo was sixteen. Both were pretty, popular with boys, Jewish, the children of doting bourgeois parents. Both were growing up in the comfortably middle-class Wilmersdorf district of Berlin.

The times, however, were anything but congenial. It was the fall of 1939 and Hitler had just set off World War II. The Jews headed his enemies list, and the social life of Jewish youngsters took place only in their last refuges, the private homes of their mothers and fathers.

And so, on Sunday afternoons, a group of teenagers would assemble in the Wilmersdorf residence of a Jewish businessman, Kurt Kübler, on Mommsen Strasse, to dance, flirt, and engage in small talk. Manfred Kübler, the son of the house, became Stella's steady boyfriend. Lilo and Stella met there and quickly took to each other too.

As the fortunes of war turned slowly against Hitler and his drive to stamp out all Jews exploded in the death camps, both girls acquired false papers and lived furtive illegal lives in hiding; they lost touch with one another until February 1944, when they happened to meet while standing in line to buy milk at a dairy store in their old neighborhood.

Lilo was instantly frightened. Berlin's "U-boats"—illegally subsisting Jews—still communicated by *Mundfunk,* or "mouth radio," carrying life-and-death news, and Lilo had heard of a shattering development. Her old friend Stella was reported to have been "turned" by the Gestapo. Word was that she had agreed to betray fellow Jews, to hunt them down, actually to arrest them.

This sounded so farfetched to Lilo that she was readily reassured in the milk store when Stella smiled and seemed interested only in enjoying a friendly reunion. The young women chatted pleasantly, agreed to remain in contact, and Lilo dismissed the monstrous possibility that her crony might have traded colors and become one of the enemy.

Ten days later, Stella appeared at Lilo's apartment door, no longer smiling. A young male civilian stood menacingly behind her, but Stella did the talking.

"I'm sorry, Lilo," she said. "I have orders from the Gestapo to arrest you. Don't try any nonsense and don't try to escape. If you do, I'll have to use my pistol!"

I too had been friendly with Stella in the Hitler years, and like a recurrent dream, an abiding mental picture of her flashed into my consciousness moments after I spotted the headline in *The New York Times:* "Reunion Recalls School for Jews in Nazi Germany." Her image appeared as soon as I scanned to the fifth paragraph. There I was startled to discover that a get-together had taken place in New York of my old bunch, alumni of the Goldschmidt School in Berlin, which I had attended from late 1935 until early 1937, when my parents and I emigrated to the United States.

Remarkable! I had lost all contact with this interlude of my past. I had been thirteen when I left Frau Dr. Leonore Goldschmidt's little oasis within Adolf Hitler's craziness. It had been a turbulent time, so my memories were mostly of the transition from my Berlin incarnation to my New York self; my recollections of the old German teachers and fellow students were sketchy.

Only Stella was different. While I don't possess a photographic memory, certain people and scenes from my adolescence left a lasting imprint on my brain. One of these is Stella Goldschlag at fourteen, on her way to gym class at Goldschmidt's in her ruffled black gym shorts.

Stella was the school's Marilyn Monroe: tall, slim, leggy, cool, with light blue eyes, teeth out of a toothpaste ad, and pale satin skin. She wore her glowing blond hair in a pageboy bob that seemed to dance whenever she moved. Her posture was so perfect that it required little imagination to picture her atop a pedestal, a monument to beauty, albeit distant up there, silent, sequestered in her private heights—a masterpiece, untouchable, a fantasy for a pubescent boy, and a vision I could never forget.

I spoke frequently with my idol during my time in the Goldschmidt School. Or I tried to. It should have been easy because we had quite a bit in common: our tyrannical homeroom teacher, for one, and most especially Dr. Bandmann's Select Chorus, where we sang standing next to each other. I had seen to that.

The singing could have made for an intimate bond. The excitable Dr. Bandmann was everybody's favorite instructor (he also taught algebra), and Stella and I were among just a handful of kids with good voices who were picked for the Select Chorus, the singers of choice. I had inherited something of my mother's musical talent, and since my voice had not yet changed, I was the only boy singing with the girl sopranos, a heady privilege.

Stella too came to Dr. Bandmann with a musical inheritance; her father was a composer and her mother was also a singer of classical music.

Furthermore, the substance of our music making should have brought Stella and me together. Goldschmidt's curriculum was tailored to prepare potential refugees for life uprooted, abroad. Fellow students were constantly leaving for places like Shanghai and Cochabamba (Bolivia), and Dr. Bandmann had us singing our farewells to them when they departed. These were tearful occasions and we singers furnished appropriate accompaniment. I remember having to hold back a choking feeling whenever Stella and I sang:

> *When fortune smiles at last*
> *Remember us, your past. . . .*

And still, Stella invariably twisted my tongue in knots when I faced her nonsinging self. Once I spent well over half an hour blissfully alone with her—in the heavy Berlin traffic. She let me ride home with her to her apartment house on Xantnerstrasse in Wilmersdorf.

She rode her bicycle; I was on mine, which was bright blue and came with the desirable balloon-type tires. I was enchanted but mired in inconsequential school gossip. Thereafter, having learned where she lived, I often rode past her place, slowing down or stopping briefly, hoping for an "accidental" encounter with my beloved. Romeo never did connect with this Juliet.

Now it was 1988, time for the next Goldschmidt School reunion, and one raw fall evening I stood nibbling hors d'oeuvres and balancing my glass of white wine in an overheated meeting room of the German Club at New York University, near Washington Square in Greenwich Village. Crowding around was my bunch, fellow refugees with German accents, gray-haired survivors of Hitler's Third Reich. An old school link of half a century united us, yet our true sponsor was not really Frau Dr. Leonore Goldschmidt, charismatic and supercharged. It was Hitler. For an insane moment I considered that one of his scowling old portraits in a brown storm trooper shirt should have been hanging on the walls of the German Club at N.Y.U.

The room was heavy with memories. I was talking to the president of a Westchester County, New York, engineering company and suddenly he pulled from the bottom of his wallet a crumpled little yellow cloth bearing a black Star of David. I could guess then that he had survived the war hiding in Berlin, because the star was introduced and had to be worn after September 1941 and at that time the Nazis had ruled emigration illegal. There was no longer a legal way to escape, as there had been earlier for my parents and myself.

Out of sight had not been out of mind for me and Stella in her gym shorts. I knew that she had been trapped in Berlin like the Westchester engineering executive. But what had happened to her? In school we used to gossip a lot of about the spectacular Stella. We still did. The women envied her charm, her looks, and her ability to attract friends. The men exchanged meaningful glances.

Was she alive? If so, where? Rumors buzzed around our reunion party. No one had seen her since before the war, our war, World War II. Yet people seemed to know that something unusual had happened to this schoolmate. Someone had heard that she had become a spy. Someone else said that she had been executed by the Russians. Several said they'd heard that Stella, though Jewish like the rest of us, had, incredibly, become a Nazi collaborator.

A happenstance—my U.S. Army assignment in Berlin right after the war—had made me the only alumnus who knew the secret: the unspeakable crimes Stella had committed in order to survive. In three trials she had been found guilty of aiding and abetting multiple murders. How many? No one could specify, because nearly all her potential accusers were silenced in the extermination camps, but she was evidently responsible for the death of several dozen Jews, more likely several hundred, and one police guess ran to 2,300! And these were not serial murders of the conventional kind, violence rooted in passion or irrationality or greed for financial gain.

Stella had stalked fellow Jews throughout Berlin and betrayed them to the Gestapo, which deported them to die in concentration camps. She functioned much like an executioner on behalf of the Führer's "final solution" of "the Jewish problem." How could she—when she was a Jew like the rest of us? It was an unholy role reversal —the hunted turned hunter, the victim transformed into perpetrator.

There was much that I still didn't know. What had become of Stella? And why, why, why had she chosen to agree to her Faustian pact with Hitler? I had always wanted to solve these mysteries of the beauty I had once worshiped. It was time to pursue my obsession.

Why at this late date? Perhaps I had been immobilized by an emotional overload: too many accounts of horrors, pictures of the ovens, the emaciated bodies, so much to be faced. For decades I couldn't watch a film about the Holocaust. Only the passage of time let my curiosity become energized.

Perhaps because I'm getting older, I was also beginning to take more interest in the art of survival, especially survival in the face of what authorities on stress call "extreme experiences." It was logical for someone from my time and place to turn to the most extreme experience of my lifetime, the Holocaust. Why had I survived? Why could some of my relatives and friends save themselves while others couldn't? What were some of the trapped victims compelled to do to stay alive? Stella, for instance?

I had to find out.

I began with Sophie of William Styron's novel *Sophie's Choice.*

"You may keep one of your children," the drunken, nose-picking SS physician told her during the selection process in her fictional Auschwitz. "The other one will have to go. Which one will you keep?"

Sophie screamed, "I can't choose! I can't choose!"

"Shut up!" the doctor commanded, getting impatient. "Hurry now and choose. Choose, goddamnit, or I'll send them both over there. Quick!"

Sophie chose one of her children and was never able to come to terms with her sin.

I knew that such choices were also forced upon human beings in real life. In 1964, a Swedish psychiatrist, Dr. Snorre Wohlfahrt, reported on a thirty-two-year-old Jewish mother from Poland who was asked by an SS doctor in Auschwitz to decide whether to send her seven-year-old daughter to the gas chambers or to go herself. Convinced that she was about to be gassed anyway, the mother told the doctor to take her daughter so that the child would not be left alone. Decades later, this mother was in psychiatric treatment, could not bear to look at any children, could not tolerate being alone, and believed that strangers peered at her accusingly on streetcars.

I also knew about survivors who remained numb over the decades, finding the scars of their memories too painful to touch—survivors like my silent cousin Lottchen in Amsterdam, ten years old when she left the Bergen-Belsen camp shortly after her friend Anne Frank, the diarist, had died of typhus.

I reread *The Diary of Anne Frank,* that most poignant record by the teenager from Frankfurt, trapped with her family in an attic hiding place for which, strangely, they had failed to provide a second exit. She would have been sixty years old on June 12, 1989, and her memory was still alive. People were still going to see the play based on the diary. Books about it were still being published. Witnesses were still coming forward, testifying to Anne's last days, starved, naked, wrapped in a blanket, "with no tears left to cry."

The collaborator who had betrayed Anne to the Dutch police was never found. Why did he or she do it? Why did Stella track down Jews so they, too, would be murdered? Was she the gentle Anne Frank's opposite, her negative image, the evil Mr. Hyde to the benign Dr. Jekyll? Standing that day amidst my fellow survivors, I determined to find out about my schoolmate, the traitor of the Goldschmidt School. Perhaps she was still alive. If she was, perhaps she was imagining that strangers stared at her on streetcars, her conscience shattered.

Even if she was dead, perhaps there was an explanation, a key to her crimes and similar deeds of others. It seemed unlikely that she was the only Jew who had betrayed Jews. I had to find out. I *had* to know about Stella and these incestuous murders, my war's last taboo.

2. Stella

THE BERLIN OF STELLA'S EARLY YEARS was the frenzied metropolis of *The Threepenny Opera* and Marlene Dietrich's *Blue Angel;* the insistently exhibitionistic homosexuals and the garishly made up transvestites in Christopher Isherwood's *Berlin Stories* and the musical *Cabaret;* the triumph of black Josephine Baker, shimmying in a costume strung together from a few banana peels; uninhibited nudity and cocaine sniffing; hordes of begging boy prostitutes; the boom in psychoanalysis, taking over the fashionable new art from Sigmund Freud in the backwater of Vienna; the stark functionality of Bauhaus architecture.

Stella's home was no part of this turbulence. She grew up as a coddled, overprotected only child in the staid formality and affluence of the West End, a little princess. It exasperated her that other children enjoyed small freedoms that were denied her, presumably because she was loved so possessively. Her parents called her Pünktchen, meaning "little dot," because to them she seemed so small and fragile.

"She certainly was *treated* like a princess," said Jutta Feig, who grew up in Stella's neighborhood and visited the Goldschlags often with her own parents. "Her clothes were the latest styles and the mother carried on about 'my daughter this' and 'my daughter that' and combed those blond curls by the hour. *Ja, ja*, she was a princess, and did she ever know it!"

Stella was, moreover, a product of the assimilation—all but the absorption—of Jews, about 173,000 of them in Berlin out of 500,000 in the entire country, into the fabric of gentile life in the Reich capital. If she was royalty, she was no Jewish Princess as this term is understood in America, but rather one of the snobbish tribe who called themselves "Germans of Jewish origin." They would have blended in even more completely if so many of them had not stood out like neon billboards.

They were too successful, too visible with their distinctively ethnic names, too vulnerable to envy by gentiles. They had preempted too many very public places. All the major Berlin department stores—Wertheim, Hermann Tietz, N. Israel, KaDeWe—were the properties of Jews. All the principal newspaper publishers and thirteen of the drama critics were Jews. Garment manufacturing, a major industry, was generally known to be in Jewish hands.

And so, to an astonishing degree, was the yeasty intellectual life. In the rest of Germany, few Jews enjoyed influence. True, Hamburg was home to the powerful Warburg banking family; elsewhere, Jews were mostly anonymous shopkeepers. Berlin was altogether different. Even the shortest list of the city's cerebral giants resounded like a roll call from a Mount Olympus of culture, German-*Jewish* culture. The roster dazzled.

Arnold Schoenberg, Kurt Weill, and Bruno Walter were among the musicians. Max Liebermann was a revered Impressionist among resident painters. Fritz Lang filmed *M* and Ernst Lubitsch made dozens of movies for the UFA company before moving to Hollywood for successes like *Ninotchka* with Greta Garbo. Max Reinhardt mounted theatrical spectaculars, and at the acclaimed Kaiser Wilhelm Institute, Albert Einstein came to be "the creator of worlds" and ruled the universe of physics.

Rumpled, the quintessential forgetful professor who found it "too complicated" to drive a car, his trademark face topped by chronically messy hair, Einstein made Berlin his home from 1914 to 1933. Here he perfected his relativity theory, won his Nobel Prize, relished his beloved cigars (his wife rationed him to one per day), sailed on the Havel, and entertained friends with his screechy fiddle playing. And here, in 1932, the year before Hitler assumed power, this supposedly impractical academic proved politically prescient.

He liked what he called his "Berlinization," but he was a pacifist, and having grown up in Italy and Switzerland, he was no German. Convinced that Hitler was a barbarous dictator, not to be dealt with, he accepted a post at the Institute for Advanced Study and departed for Princeton, New Jersey.

. . .

Gerhard Goldschlag, Stella's father, was no Einstein. Not in any respect. To Germanized Jews like him and his family, anti-Semitism seemed targeted principally, and in their view deservedly, at Berlin's physically much more obvious minority of 40,000 *Ostjuden*. These very different Jews, despised by gentiles as well as by the likes of the Goldschlags, made convenient scapegoats.

The Eastern Jews were turn-of-the-century refugees from the pogroms of the czars and the cossack terror riders. Self-segregated, they lived a ghettolike existence behind the Alexanderplatz, in the slums of the city's core known as the Scheunenviertel, once a district of barns and cows. They called attention to themselves by their tall, wide-brimmed black hats, their bushy beards and long sideburns, their Yiddish, which sounded like low-class German to us. Their poverty made them rapacious, often unscrupulous. They had been outcasts before they came to Germany. They were outcasts still.

Almost-goyim like the Goldschlags acknowledged their heritage to the extent of celebrating Passover, Chanukah, and the highest holidays of Rosh Hashanah and Yom Kippur—that was about all. They would not think of going near the Scheunenviertel. But Hitler did not discriminate. To start with, like most Austrians, he hated all Berliners. They were Prussian sows, stuck up, cynical, too quick-witted and therefore too slow to knuckle under to Nazi rule. And of course, he had hated all Jews since adolescence as profiteers, Bolsheviks, aliens, untouchables, and, in his parlance, "vermin" to be stamped out.

Despite centuries of greater or lesser discrimination, Jews like the Goldschlags felt immune among the 67 million Germans. They did not read *Mein Kampf*—nobody did. Hitler was a temporary aberration, everyone said so. He would rant himself out of slogans and out of power, as he had ranted himself in. He, not the Jews, was alien, having nothing in common with Goethe, Beethoven, and the other immortal Germans.

"The Jews were pathologically patriotic," recalled Rabbi Joachim Prinz.* "My father served in the war and my grandfather was wounded in 1866, in the war against the Austrians. He was enor-

---

* Although I heard the late Rabbi Prinz preach when I was a boy in Berlin, I never met him. For the interview cited here I am indebted to my old friend Otto Friedrich, who spoke with the rabbi in New Jersey in the 1970s, for his marvelous book about Berlin in the 1920s, *Before the Deluge*.

mously proud of that." The rabbi, who would become president of the American Jewish Congress and head of a large synagogue in Newark, New Jersey, was exceptionally qualified to appraise the Jews of Berlin. He grew up and was trained there. He adored the city, and its Jews adored him. Darkly handsome, a brainy and mellifluous orator, he rose to stardom while still in his twenties. To hear him preach was to be exhilarated. But he knew the Achilles' heel of his congregation, which included Stella and her parents.

"Jews are political idiots," said Rabbi Prinz. "They are too optimistic, too hopeful. They do not understand an enemy."

Although he was hardly a notable name, Papa Gerhard Goldschlag could consider himself a success in the hottest arena of mainstream journalism, both German and worldwide: the newsreels. As the French-speaking chief editor in the Berlin office of Gaumont, with headquarters in Paris, he coolly juggled coverage of catastrophes, elections, coronations, and other headline events; he soothed temperamental daredevil cameramen, and met hairbreadth round-the-clock deadlines monitored by movie theater owners all over the globe.

It was a prestigious calling and often kept him in the office into the night, because newsreels were the public's live tie to the day's events, the television of the age.

Gaumont was one of the first, biggest, and fastest filmmakers. Founded in 1908, it deployed a force of 21,000 before World War I and operated the Gaumont-Palace in Paris, the world's largest theater (6,000 seats). Covering the investiture of the Prince of Wales in 1911, its camera crews hooked two milk wagons onto the royal train, turned them into traveling darkrooms, and showed a thousand feet of film of the event in London the same night.

As a foreign company, Gaumont could restrain the Nazis from purging Goldschlag until 1935, but by then the Propaganda Ministry would no longer tolerate Jews in positions where they might infect the most potent policy medium. The minister himself, Joseph Goebbels, viewed important film clips nightly and approved the week's finished product. Thereafter, Hitler—no less—screened each installment as the ultimate censor.

When Goldschlag had to give up his hectic life's work, he decided to cross a great divide and launched a very different new career in his second love, music—*German* music. Stella heard that the Jewish *Kulturbund* encouraged him to write Jewish music but that he would have nothing to do with Hebrew chanting. He saw himself aiming higher. His vision was to rise to fame as a composer of lieder, the lyric songs of the grand, romantic genre that would make him the rightful successor of his masters, Schubert and Schumann.

Goldschlag's vision remained just that. When the war broke out, he was a round, modest, quiet little man, fifty years old and often depressive. His bow ties and unruly mass of curly dark hair made him look like a figure of the creative arts. His diligence, bordering on the obsessive, propelled him into turning out an inventory of more than 200 lieder, a gargantuan output. Almost all remained in his desk unsung, and when he played them himself at an occasional concert, their reception was usually unkind.

"Mere copies of his famous predecessors," judged a typical review in a Jewish weekly. Stella blamed her father's defeats on the Jews wanting to retaliate against him. "They wanted to squeeze him out," she said. The father attributed his failure to the pace and preoccupations of modern times; he chose to believe that the critics were ridiculing the lieder genre as a whole, not his work.

"Maybe I was born eighty years too late," he told a reporter sadly.

And so he and his family were reduced to the penury and obscurity that would eventually cost them their lives. Goldschlag gave piano lessons. He trudged from recital to recital, acting as accompanist to soloists. He wrote learned reviews for Jewish periodicals that paid next to nothing but were the only outlets open to him. His income barely stretched to cover food and rent for the family's tiny apartment at Xantnerstrasse 2 in Wilmersdorf, just off Kurfürstendamm. At times, they had to live on welfare.

Rarely, a psychic dividend came along to rekindle his longing for recognition as a future Schubert. He would be invited to play his songs at a recital of several Jewish composers. As late as March 1941, shortly before Auschwitz became an extermination camp, he traveled east to Breslau to play six of his lieder at a concert sponsored by the local *Kulturbund*.

The compositions of that evening's program carried titles bespeaking Goldschlag's lingering twin hopes for survival as a *German* composer as well as a *German* Jew. One song was called "God Was in a Good Mood," another "You Must Not Turn Impatient."

Although it was Nazi law that confined his audiences and sponsors to his coreligionists, Goldschlag felt demeaned by this restriction. Before Hitler he had declined invitations from Jewish organizations. He was a combat veteran of the Great War, after all, and prized his membership in the Jewish Union of Combat Soldiers. It was all right to be Jewish if the label was linked to service for the fatherland.

Such striving for identification with his persecutors was not at all unusual or considered quixotic. Around the corner from the Gold-schlags lived the Froehlichs. Their son, an ardent soccer fan named Peter,* a year younger than Stella, passed her apartment house almost daily. His father too had been a *Frontkämpfer,* and like so many German Jews, he delighted in telling anti-Semitic jokes. The Froehlichs smilingly called themselves "three-day Jews," who attended synagogue (no German Jew in good standing used the Yiddish word *shul*) only on the highest holidays, Rosh Hashanah and Yom Kippur. Reflecting upon his identity in subsequent years, Peter Froehlich Gay would call his youth "schizophrenic." It was Hitler, he said, who turned him into a Jew.

This was also true of Stella, the transformation dating from the day in 1935 when new Nazi edicts compelled her to leave her public high school and enroll in the private Jewish school of Dr. Leonore Goldschmidt at the Roseneck in the exclusive Grunewald section. This placed her, officially and for the first time, among the mostly dark-haired and sometimes big-nosed children of the hated minority, the persecuted, the leprous. It also stamped her as poor. The Gold-schmidt School was expensive. Stella could attend only on a scholarship. That rankled too.

Her dimply smile of childhood, the very blond curls, then kept stiff, the coquettish little dresses, carefully tended by her adoring mother Toni, the cuddly presence of a Shirley Temple, had given way by that time. With her teenage princess cool went good—if not spectacular—grades and a verbal sophistication that impressed both sexes at Goldschmidt's, where smooth tongues were not uncommon.

"We were all jealous of her," recalled Ursula Tarnowski, who became a college president on Long Island, New York.

The men recalled her as gorgeous and unattainable, the object of carnal fantasies and rumors, possibly false, of forbidden sex with somewhat older boys. With the understatement of an actress, Stella brought off the impression of being untouchable and touchable at the same time. It was a skill she would not lose through life with four husbands, plus the father of an illegitimate daughter, plus countless lovers.

Girlfriends in school knew a less attractive Stella. They recognized her as a show-off, a liar, and, well, different. They snickered when a

---

* He would become Peter Gay, a renowned professor of history at Yale University and author of an authoritative account of the 1920s Weimar Republic.

teacher asked the class what their fathers did for a living and Stella announced, "My father is a Communist!" They knew that Gerhard Goldschlag was not a lawyer, doctor, or businessman like the others. He was also no Communist. By 1935, Communists were in prison or in hiding. Her father was that henpecked piano player, an unknown composer, oblivious to politics, and chronically poor.

Stella resented her family's pauperism. She hated their small apartment and her inexpensive if stylish clothes. Some of the girls knew that she attended school on the scholarship arranged by Dr. Goldschmidt. Stella knew that they knew, and it embittered her. She was keenly aware of her spectacular appearance and craved the attention it created. She wanted to be a star, not a charity case, and tried to exploit her blondness to help her escape her heritage.

Stella detested being Jewish. Her "Aryan looks" had not kept her public school from expelling her because of her religion. Other Jewish youngsters knew this was part of a general Hitler crackdown. She considered it an unjust personal slight. She wished to rise above being Jewish. Jews were losers. So she lied, hoping to shed her Jewish identity. Her girlfriends knew that her mother, a cold, bossy Brünnhilde type, sang in the choir of the synagogue, and they giggled behind Stella's back when she claimed that her mother was Christian.

Stella also loved to appear sophisticated, more experienced than her years. The attention that her looks commanded from boys had given her an early awareness of sex. Eroticism appealed to her, especially because it shocked her peers. Stella got a thrill out of being shocking. People noticed you when you shocked them.

By standards of decades to come, Stella's advances into adult territory were tame indeed. For the period of her adolescence and the innocent environment of our school, they were quite daring. She starred as the unofficial sex educator, courses in sex education not yet having been invented. Stella briefed the other girls on matters anatomical and did not neglect romantic love either. She brought such novels as *All Quiet on the Western Front* to school and titillated her private audiences with readings of sexy passages. It made her interesting.

"We were all Eves and she was the serpent," remembered Lili Baumann, her closest chum.

In the context of the mores prevailing in the school, this was no overstatement. Some of the girls were repelled by Stella's precociousness. Her fascination with verbal sex frightened them. A few girls actively avoided the apprentice serpent as if she were Typhoid Mary.

One very timid girl's parents were asked by Frau Dr. Goldschmidt to keep their daughter away from Stella. But nobody worried about her chum Lili. Lili was strong and full of curiosity about everything, including Stella. She admired Stella's precocious ways and was thrilled to share forbidden knowledge.

Although timidity never restrained Lili's exuberance in her relationships, the Nazis had shaken her faith in friendships. Before she came to the Goldschmidt School, her classrooms had been equipped with twin desks, and Lili became inseparable from her gentile seatmate. One morning she found that the friend had left to share a desk with a gentile girl who often wore the Hitler Youth uniform. Mystified, Lili questioned her defected friend during recess: Why had she shifted loyalties?

"Jewish blood stinks," announced the girl, aged eleven, and turned away. Lili was crushed and ran home crying all the way. The next day her mother registered her at Goldschmidt's.

Her "Aryan" appearance notwithstanding, Stella did not waver in her loyalty to Lili in all their years together at three schools: elementary school on Joachim Friedrich Strasse, the Hohenzollern Lyceum, and then Goldschmidt's. They were opposites and Lili was intrigued by the differences between them.

Lili was well-behaved, the product of a conventional wealthy home and doting parents. Her father was an important lawyer. Stella was a rebel, a good student but perpetually enmeshed in little fibs and protests. Teachers always kept their eye on Stella, watching for trouble. Her parents seemed ill-matched. Lili found that Stella was scared of her loud, domineering mother, and she developed a low opinion of her friend's ineffectual little father. She was sure that Stella's mother dyed her hair as well as Stella's, another deliciously risqué practice, if true. Allegations, accurate and otherwise, trailed Stella for life, like shadows, sinister and unshakable.

In time Lili experienced Stella as a hanger-on, a social climber. Lili's parents had an enormous, richly furnished apartment, and Stella liked to hang out there rather than in her own dingy flat. She wasn't always welcome. One afternoon, while waiting alone for Lili, Stella sneaked into the bedroom of her friend's parents, took a valuable painting of a classic nude figure off the wall, and reproduced its outlines with a crayon on tracing paper. Lili's mother discovered the art work and threw Stella out of the house.

Stella yelled, "Lili did it!"—a transparent lie.

The episode did not split these friends. Kids being kids, Stella became something of a heroine in Lili's eyes. Their bond became a small-time conspiracy of little voyeurs rebelling against a stodgy adult environment.

Stodgy, but not immune to the bitter passions stirred up by Hitler. Stella and Lili's turf, the Wilmersdorf district, was home to many families of middle- and upper-middle-class Jews. Ensconced in the massive, commodious apartment houses typical of the relatively prosperous West End, more Jews had settled in this district than anywhere else: 26,000 of them—13.5 percent of the total population (compared with a Berlin average of 4.3 percent). Street warfare between Hitler's squads and the Communists was constant and bloody in this neighborhood because the Nazis had achieved unusually strong early inroads in the 1920s. Pubs designated as combat bases by the brown-shirted storm troopers were systematically placed throughout the area.

On March 15, 1933, the Wilmersdorf Nazis staged the first book burning since the Middle Ages.* Their target was the Artists Colony, three large apartment complexes on Laubenheimer Platz built jointly by the Authors Society and the Theater Cooperative for 300 of their members. Authors of future best-sellers, such as Arthur Koestler, were among the residents. Heinrich Mann, Lion Feuchtwanger, and the artist George Grosz lived nearby.

Jewish authors were the scapegoats whose purging was most loudly advertised. But they were not alone. Among the writers who witnessed the destruction of their works at the Opernplatz that night —until he was recognized and fled—was Erich Kaestner, a gentile but known to scoff at the Nazis. Like his famous *Emil and the Detectives,* many of his delightful stories were apolitical. That didn't save his books. The man was too irreverent.

Along with militant neighborhood Communists, Wilmersdorf's resident intellectuals had grown accustomed to impromptu street beatings and shootings by the Brownshirts. The raid of March 15 was different. It was official government business. The marauders

---

* The main event had to wait until May 10; by then a government blacklist of more than 125 authors, including Sigmund Freud, Emil Ludwig, and Erich Maria Remarque, had been approved. Beginning at nine p.m., in heavy rain, students staged a torchlight parade to the Opernplatz, across the street from Berlin University. A wood pyre was set aflame on the square. While a band played martial music, some 20,000 "junk books" turned into ashes. Addressing the enthusiastic crowd, Propaganda Minister Joseph Goebbels said it was time to settle accounts with the "Jewish seductors of the people."

were police officers using firemen and storm troopers̶
ments. After surrounding the Colony so no one could̶
ransacked apartments in search of "Marxist" literatu̶
"suspects" whose names appeared on their lists. Some were̶

"Seven heavily armed men beat me up and pushed me down
steps with my face bleeding," one author remembered. "Downstairs
I was pushed on a police truck. It was a literary convention. The
writer Manès Sperber sat in front of me. One of the guards taunted:
'Gotta nosebleed, eh?' "

The raiders had difficulty deciding which books were "Marxist."
They took whatever volumes looked suspicious to them and carried
them in laundry baskets to the large fire burning in the center of the
square. A few storm troopers tossed the books into the flames. A
mob danced around the fire, shouting its approval. Hitler had been
in power only six weeks, but bedlam had been a normal state in
Berlin for years.

As memories dimmed later, they would simplify. Few people recalled
how inexorably the mid-twentieth century became the creation of a
single person, Adolf Hitler, beginning with his exploitation of the
Great Depression for his political ends, and on through the East-
West split of the world that began in the late 1940s and was essentially his work.

And few memories differentiated between Hitler, the warlord who
actually threatened for a time to win World War II, and the earlier
comical madman played by Charlie Chaplin in the film classic *The
Great Dictator*, when it was still possible to poke fun at the Führer.
Of course, Hitler was both, evolving in fairly slow motion from the
lampoonable comic strip character, taken seriously by only a few
fanatical fellow marchers to a Munich beer hall, into the terror of all
the world.

Stella's youth, spanning the twenties, thirties, and early forties,
witnessed the shaky, raucous freedom of the Weimar Republic; then
repressive dictatorship; then genocide. Eventually, she also experienced a quickly maturing democracy, fattened by postwar economic
miracles.

When she grew up, the slaughter of trench warfare in World
War I was still a force in fresh recollection, as the German media
trendsetters discovered to their surprise. Right in Stella's native Wilmersdorf, at Wittelsbacher Strasse 5, an impecunious twenty-nine-
year-old sports editor feared he might be wasting his spare time

dashing off an autobiographical novel of a terrified teenage infantry-man in "the war to end all wars," as it was called. He had changed his name from Erich Maria Remark to Remarque and called his recollections *All Quiet on the Western Front.*

His publisher, the normally canny Samuel Fischer of Fischer Verlag, rejected it disgustedly with a remark that would haunt him. "Who wants to read about that?" he demanded.

Many millions did. Remarque persuaded his newspaper bosses to serialize his work, and it was a phenomenal hit; sales of the book version were exceeded only by the Bible, and not because of the few sexy passages that appealed to Stella.

The war was in people's bones, and that manic, frustrated alumnus of the bloodletting, Corporal Hitler, had, unlike publisher Fischer, sensed it right along. For years the Führer pounded his impotent fatherland with his ranting reminders of the "shame dictate of Versailles," the vengeful peace treaty that dismembered not only the Kaiser's military but the economy as well.

Stella's father was not alone among German Jews to keep reciting his record in the war to document his loyalty and, hopefully, counteract anti-Semitism. Goldschlag's veterans group ran national advertising reminding "German mothers" of the 12,000 Jews who died for their beloved country. A Jewish fighter pilot ace graced magazine covers, and under the demented priorities of the Nazis, Jewish holders of the Iron Cross First Class were shown respect of sorts until near the end. They were not immediately gassed in Auschwitz but "put back" for a time in the Theresienstadt camp, where inmates merely starved, and some were not sent to Auschwitz until the last months of the war.

While Stella's father was purged early from public life by Propaganda Minister Dr. Joseph Goebbels along with the rest of the "traitorous" incorrigibles of the intelligentsia, he was not automatically placed into one of the new concentration camps, along with Communists, Socialists, trade union leaders, and other opposition activists. He merely lost his livelihood and struggled on as a pauper. And yet he wouldn't for a moment consider leaving the country. Just like my own father. We had no interest in politics, and we were Germans, after all.

3. Berlin Boy

I KNEW EARLY that I was not born into a quiet time. My very first memory is of gunfire. We were living in an expensive apartment on Bismarckstrasse in Charlottenburg, an enormous expanse, cavernous as an old railroad station. It was 1928. I was five years old and sick in bed with tonsillitis.

The shooting came from our street, one of the broad, tree-lined boulevards for which Berlin is famous, and the violence was no surprise to me. In the 1920s, before Hitler suppressed dissent in any form, the Communists and the Nazis were fighting it out on the streets, "the Reds and the Browns" beating and knifing each other, heaving hailstorms of the square Berlin cobblestones and often resorting to gunplay. Everyone considered these battles as normal as traffic jams.

Common or not, the crackling of the guns on Bismarckstrasse scared me considerably. I had heard talk about war, and this sounded like it. I could not have explained what the controversy outside was about, but I knew that the issues did not involve me or my family. Or so we were certain at the time. I had never met anybody who fought in one of the street skirmishes. They were conducted by "lower-class" working people. I pulled my thick eiderdown bedcovers over my ears. The street soon turned quiet. It always did. The shooting was no more than an annoying interruption of my remarkably sedate boyhood.

I was an only child. And very German. My birthday, October 2,

31

was also that of Hitler's predecessor, President Paul von Hindenburg, the former field marshal and victor at Tannenberg, a still-celebrated German battle triumph of World War I. He was honored by us all. The flags were always out on October 2. When I was very little, I thought they were for me.

My parents were not poor like the Goldschlags, nor were we wealthy like my maternal grandparents, the principal owners of the family textile business. We did live in great comfort. I had a live-in nanny. My mother had a cook and a cleaning lady. My clothes were selected with elaborate care; in winter they included a broad-brimmed white hat and a fluffy white fur coat, not then considered effeminate. Ever ahead of her time, my tiny but relentless and feisty mother, Helen, called Leni, had even gone through plastic surgery, a dubious science in its shaky infancy. The surgeon reduced her nose and her breasts; she deemed these organs too large to be in good taste. My father was struck speechless at the cost.

My mother's sense of fun was elaborate and I was her delighted straight man. For somebody's wedding she dressed me up as the ring bearer from a Mozart opera. I was a little symphony in snow white: powdered wig, ducktailed frock, thigh-high stockings, buckled pumps. And a big hit with the wedding guests. I ate it up.

For my cousin Martha's wedding, my theatrical mother outdramatized herself. This cousin was her favorite relative, only a few years younger. Her father, my uncle, was the number-two executive in my grandfather's business. Martha's marriage to another senior man in the business was the family gala of my boyhood.

Surprise! My mother and I weren't present. This was remarked upon with bemusement, Leni and Martha being known as bosom cronies. With our continued absence, the buzz among the guests increased. My mother's timing was always exquisite and she knew about making entrances. The ceremony was about to begin without us, when workmen dragged in a large wooden crate and hammered it open.

My mother and I jumped out to great applause. It was one of her finest productions.

Not all of them were frivolous. Leni Stein, as she called herself professionally (Silberstein being her maiden name), was a career woman when no woman in her set would dream of such ambition. She had her own income, her autonomy—unheard of. Blessed with a slightly more than adequate mezzo-soprano voice, she toured provincial outposts, doing her lieder to friendly reviews—Schubert, Schumann, and the other masters who were also the role models for Gerhard Goldschlag.

My mother liked to careen around the countryside, usually in her little cream-colored Opel with a black sunroof, purchased from her professional earnings. This was revolutionary: almost nobody owned a car and few women knew how to drive. My *Mutti* often took me along for company on long trips, and one of our outings, lasting a week or more, was for my special benefit. I was to become acquainted with my roots, at least those on my father's side, although my father was too busy working to come along.

Nobody would have thought of taking me to my roots on my mother's side. They were forgotten in Mislowicz, Upper Silesia, in the coal-mining region soon to become Poland. My maternal grandfather's people were not, for some reason, considered exactly *Ostjuden* and therefore déclassé, but Mislowicz evoked un-German connotations. It was not an appropriate mecca for a pilgrimage.

My father Erich's native village, Edenkoben on the Southern Wine Road in the Rhine Palatinate, was authentically *deutsch*—civilized, colorful, less than an hour's drive from the French border near Strasbourg, which we still called Strassburg. That city had been taken away from us under the shame *Diktat* of Versailles, when they even deprived us of our colonies, places like Deutsch Ost Afrika with fabulous stamps, much prized by collectors like myself.

My uncle Franz Weidenreich, who held doctorates in medicine and physiology, had been a professor of anthropology at the University of Strasbourg. He was by far the most renowned personage Edenkoben or my family ever produced and would be listed in all the big biographical reference books. Pleasant but distant, with an egg-shaped head like most of the males on my father's side, he had been gone from the area for several years when my mother and I reached Edenkoben with its tiny backyard vineyards, driving the creamy Opel, much clucked about by the natives. They knew few creamy Opels, with or without women drivers.

My Uncle Franz was unavailable because the Rockefeller Foundation had dispatched him to the hinterlands of China, where he spent a decade becoming world-famous for digging up the skull of Peking man and other ancestors. He had already taken an interest in the more immediate Weidenreich forebears. I had been shown a pedigree going back, in tiny market towns of southwestern Germany, to the fifteenth century, when the family name was Weil. It was changed because families used to be named for their professions and one of my earliest known antecedents was a weaver of baskets. He produced them from willows and was presumably loaded with huge stocks of them: Hence: "Willow rich" or Weidenreich.

It was all very honorably German, I was pleased to see, even more so than the achievements of the Brahn branch of the family tree. My uncle Max Brahn edited and annotated Schopenhauer, trained fighter pilots in World War I, and advanced to the rank of *Ober-regierungsrat* in his ultimate specialty, a labor mediator for the government, which found him indispensable for two years into the Hitler Reich. We were all proud of this dispensation—who could be more German than our Uncle Max?—but I didn't think that striking coal miners could compete with fossils in rural China.

I went to court after the war to change my honorable German name legally to Wyden because it kept getting mangled and seemed too much of a load to carry around. If I had it to do over again, I wouldn't. I was too timid then, too conformist.

My father, Erich Weidenreich, was the family's entertainment. He was a cherubic, bald, smiling presence whose easy charm and wit enabled him to bring off the coup of his life: he married the boss's daughter, my mother. This was a triumph of upward mobility because my father's father, my paternal grandfather, Max, had done no better than serving as superintendent of the Jewish cemetery in Weissensee, a sinecure handed out by the Berlin Jewish Community authorities after he went broke in his haberdashery shop in Cologne.

This was a blot on the family record of business success, notably the operation of an Edenkoben dry goods store whose long-ago location had been pointed out to my mother and me during our visit. However, Grandpa Max (really Maximilian) made up for his disgrace by achieving status as a military man. He was gruff enough for it with his choleric temper, and he looked the part of a conqueror in the baby-blue uniform and saber of a lieutenant in the Bavarian royal army, making me proud of him.

My father rebelled against paternal tradition by becoming a comic and shunning armed conflict and its appurtenances. A slight case of asthma enabled him to avoid becoming a combat hero in World War I, a deficiency that never troubled him. He stayed behind at Staaken, a tranquil air base in the woods outside Berlin, and did his share for the Kaiser by performing magic tricks in the officers' mess.

Erich had grown up in the superintendent's little yellow brick cottage on the enormous cemetery, always dark under its immense trees. The gloomy atmosphere did not hold him. Starting in boyhood, he entertained in the Weissensee workers' bars, performing card tricks, telling jokes in several German dialects, and singing endless "couplets," amusing cabaret ditties about current events and trends, which he would teach me in later years. Laughter surrounded my father. Half a century later, he would still fold and knot a cloth dinner napkin to look like a mouse and make it hop up his arm from his hand to his shoulder, to the squealed delight of my sons.

My father's cheer and grace made him an immensely popular salesman. Traveling all over Germany for my patrician maternal grandfather's wholesale textile business, he was welcomed by customers as his industry's own Prince Charming. I never knew anybody who didn't fall fast for Erich's gentle appeal, certainly not my mother or her father, who made him a partner in his business, which at its peak employed some 350 people.

That grandfather, Carl Silberstein, whom I called Opi, was known to adult family members as Carlchen, a misleading diminutive. There seemed to be nothing small about this paterfamilias. He was massively built, all dignity. He pierced people with his steel-blue eyes and dominated his environment by a head of brushed-back white hair so immense that one's gaze became fixed upon it, as on a snowy peak.

If my Opi had had a middle name, it should have been Rectitude. He breathed it, and it had paid off, since he started out with the R. (for Rafael) Zernick firm on Kaiser Wilhelm Strasse, founded by my great-grandfather Zernick as a little dry goods shop. To me, however, Opi was not a forbidding figure. I whooped with delight when he picked me up because this was a signal that I was allowed to dive into his mane with both hands and mess it up, which caused him to whoop too.

Opi was also the bearer of our Jewishness. My father and I, like the Froehlichs, were among Berlin's many so-called three-day Jews; we attended Rabbi Joachim Prinz's *Friedenstempel* in Wilmersdorf only on Rosh Hashanah and Yom Kippur. Opi was an elder there and may possibly have known his fellow congregants Stella and her parents.

I was constantly on the lookout for my Stella, so the temple in Wilmersdorf seemed a likely place to run into her and make the encounter seem casual. No luck. The synagogue had 1,500 seats, and Rabbi Prinz was so charismatic that the police sometimes had to cordon off the overflow on the high holidays. I never spotted Stella in the throng, all in their finest black clothes and hats. Maybe she rarely showed up to be counted as a Jew, even on such holy occasions. Since she was eager to escape from her Jewishness—the shame of being different from the "Aryan" in-group, an outsider shunned by the ruling majority—she would have had her reasons for staying away.

My mother was a "no-day Jew" who passed up the temple, but

not because she wanted to deny being Jewish. All religion struck her as too removed from reality. It offended her pragmatic self, her sense of now-is-now. She revered her father, however, my Opi, and would not hurt him. So I had my Bar Mitzvah, mostly to please him, and I didn't mind, mostly for the same reason. Neither my grandfather's values nor his person were to be crossed.

And then there were the parties at his house, the Seders and, especially, the Chanukah parties (we celebrated Christmas, too). At Opi's parties everybody became an enthusiastic Jew. Opi always invited a flock of kids. Many of them I saw only at his house, once a year, but we invariably had a great time with paper hats and noise-makers. I remember making friends with a distant cousin, Ursula Finke, a quiet, pleasant, slightly plump girl of about my age, who lived somewhere inconvenient downtown, which meant that she was inaccessible and that her family was—like Stella's—not well off.

Yes, I knew that there were Jews less affluent than we were. I learned this by way of my Uncle Richard, who worked in my father's business as a bookkeeper, not an accountant, and wore a green celluloid eyeshade and celluloid cuffs. He lived with his gentile wife, my Aunt Marie, and my cousins Siegfried and Walter, who were about ten years older than me, near my father's cemetery, in the old home district of Weissensee, strictly a working-class quarter.

We used to visit Uncle Richard about once a year, in the company car, a Buick my father was occasionally allowed to use on weekends. On the map it was hardly much of a distance. To us, it seemed like a trek to Siberia. To our less fortunate relatives, we must have appeared like a delegation from the court of Marie Antoinette.

I would remember these crossovers to Siberia decades later when the journey to Weissensee required a cumbersome trip east through the Berlin Wall, with its hurdles of security and contraband checks.

My father was always on stage when I was young, even during vacations. Our family summer holidays were formidable events. Eventually they would become my best-loved memories as an adult. When I was little, my nanny would be taken along, usually for several weeks in one of the better hotels in one of the nicer resorts in Switzerland, Wengen, Kandersteg, or Grindelwald. Later, my parents, often accompanied by friends of ours from Berlin, usually the Nomburgs, Georg and Lotte, would take me hiking and picnicking up some of the easier mountains, all of us singing our lungs out.

One August afternoon, after our party, including the Nomburgs and their two sons, piled into the rustic hut atop one of our junior mountains—it was one of the few structures in all Switzerland where no fondue, no sausages, and no hot chocolate were on sale—it began to snow. The women were upset. Catastrophes were envisioned. We would freeze and remain cut off for days without our Swiss feather beds and vacation cuisine. We might be crushed by avalanches, not an uncommon fate. My father quietly produced his deck of cards and set to work showing off his magic. Of course, it worked. As always, the tension dissolved in laughter. Shortly the snow stopped and we marched back to our hotel, singing.

Much of my father's magic was sleight of hand, but like his salesmanship, it was convincing. "No double bottom, no mechanical device!" he shouted, red-faced and beaming, when he demonstrated some nimble and baffling trick. It was reality deceived.

At first, after January 30, 1933, Hitler seemed mostly to have it in for Communists. We didn't know any Communists, but I felt uneasy standing with my parents on the large terrace of our new Grunewald home on the balmy night of February 27, watching the sky turn crimson over downtown. The Reichstag, the parliament maimed by Hitler, was on fire, the radio said. The arson was pinned on a Communist vagrant, who was railroaded through a sham trial and executed. The story sounded fishy to everyone, and since the Reichstag was such a powerful reminder of democratic government, it had been ominous to see the flames turning this symbol into ruins.

By 1935, pressure specifically directed against us Jews became palpable. Signs saying "Jews Not Wanted" appeared in shop windows. Non-Jewish businesses were harassed into dismissing some Jewish employees, but Jewish businesses in Berlin, like my father's and Herr Nomburg's, were hardly affected before 1938. Along with the enactment of new legislation that made racial discrimination legally mandatory, it was the frenzy of Hitler's rhetoric against us, his "Jewish Bolshevist" enemies, that kept mounting.

More and more often, my parents discussed the future of the German Jews with their friends, especially the Nomburgs.

Opinions remained mixed. Many friends still thought that Hitler was a psychotic soon to be unmasked and toppled in disgrace. The Nazis were dismissed as a loony mob that would shortly run out of recruits because most gentiles we knew seemed to have retained their sanity. The Party might even self-destruct—a wishful notion encouraged by scandals that had erupted when ranking storm trooper leaders were unmasked as homosexuals and butchered by their heterosexual comrades.

"It's absurd," sputtered Georg Nomburg, my father's contemporary, who manufactured men's overcoats downtown. The Nazis made no sense to him. He was certain: "They will never last." His wife, Lotte, quiet and retiring, whispered agreement, as she invariably did. How could the Nomburgs be so sure? I wondered, especially because I knew they had fled to Berlin from the small town of Coburg, where Herr Nomburg's business had been burned down by Brownshirts. But that was Coburg, in the sticks, not our Berlin. Hitler did honor to the town's fealty by speaking to his loyalists there as early as 1922, a year before the Party's true birth in the Beer Hall Putsch of Munich and long before the national malaise that propelled him to power—the number of unemployed—hit three million.

I liked the Nomburgs. Their sons, Fredi and Harry, had been my best friends since our happy days together in Grammar School No. 21 on Witzleben Strasse. Both our families, all seven of us, teamed up for vacations and weekend outings, swimming, hiking, picnicking, duly consumed by all the wholesome activities that Germans are passionately bent upon.

There was a gentleness about the elder Nomburgs that I especially appreciated. They were so relaxing in contrast to my mother, the mini-*Walküre*. Herr Nomburg and my mother could not have been less alike. He was a small, easily frightened man and regularly became upset by my mother's driving, which was, like herself, steady but rather brisk. Whenever she pushed the car into a curve with particular élan, Georg Nomburg would cower, murmur the supplication *"Aber Frau Leni, aber Frau Leni!"* and emit a petrified steamlike hiss from between his teeth.

My mother never seemed to hear his sound effects. She knew where she was going and she was damned well going to get there. *"Basta!"* as she often said, since she also spoke Italian.

By the mid-1930s, my mother was determined to embark upon a very long trip indeed. Inadvertently, my father had the words for it. Whenever a car passed us at a dangerously high rate of speed, he would splutter, "That guy still wants to get to America today!" Only gradually did it dawn on him that this happened to be what my *Mutti* had on her mind.

4. School for Refugees

I HEARD THAT VOICE AGAIN. The guttural, hypnotic clamor of Adolf Hitler was cascading from our radio, haranguing, screeching, cajoling, growling, purring, rising in hot fury, in ecstasy. Frequently the voice was interrupted by frenzied choruses, crescendo waves of *"Heil! Heil! Heil!"*

Finally the voice faded and beseeched. Hitler was pleading, crying out for his martyrdom, the agony of the German nation, encircled by enemies abroad, subverted by Jewish-Bolshevist parasites determined to destroy the fatherland from within. I was hearing the sound of the new time in my life.

I froze. It was 1934 in my public high school in the western suburbs of Berlin. I was eleven years old, one of two Jewish boys in a school of about 800. Hitler's presence-by-loudspeaker was nothing unusual. The Führer's speeches interrupted our classes often, and our ensuing routine never varied. When Hitler subsided, everyone rose, extended the right arm in the Hitler salute, and yelled, *"Heil Hitler!"*

That was the law. It was also mechanical, a commonplace, like pledging allegiance to the flag, except that we had to hail Hitler all the livelong day. I had always joined in, feeling foolish to be hailing this crazy person. Foolish, but not guilty. In my family and among my friends, Hitler was tolerated with bemusement. We thought of him as a nut who had, by some inadvertence, been temporarily permitted to ascend to a position of power. Psychotics often imagined

39

that they were powerful. It was best to humor them along quietly. Eventually they were found out. Hitler also would be found out before long. He had only been Führer for a year.

That morning in 1934, some unaccustomed bulb lit up in me. I wanted to resist. Without much thought I leaned against my desk with both arms, as if in need of support. I wanted to appear unable to straighten up sufficiently to give the salute. It worked. I didn't salute Hitler, and felt triumphant. It had been easy.

That afternoon a few rocks flew in my direction as I left school. They didn't hit me. The air had been let out of my bicycle tires, but the tires were intact and I had no trouble pumping them up. Nevertheless, I was very scared. I kept thinking about a recent school camping trip. We were hiking in the Riesengebirge Mountains, and I was the only Jewish student in the group. A cluster of singers in Hitler Youth uniforms formed directly behind me. Lustily they chanted a popular Nazi marching song: *"Und wenn das Judenblut vom Messer spritzt, dann geht's nochmal so gut!"* ("And when Jewish blood spurts from our knives, everything'll go a lot better!")

I said and did nothing. There was no point in complaining to the homeroom teacher, Dr. Volk. He wore a red Nazi Party badge that seemed to me particularly enormous, and instructed my class that Jews were direct descendants of the devil; everyone turned to look at me, presumably to check me out for horns. That seemed pretty silly even under Hitler. The Hitler Youth people did carry good-sized hunting knives, however, and the notion that these blades might be used to draw a little Jewish blood, perhaps mine, was not totally farfetched.

So, thinking of the knives and my bicycle tires, I never again failed to salute in public school. I decided that my "resistance" had been childish and futile, not brave. Later, I wondered whether I had perhaps wanted to conform, that I resumed saluting Hitler in order to be like the others, the accepted, the regular guys who didn't have their bicycle tires tampered with. I suppose it's possible that subconsciously I yearned to be part of the in-group. I don't really think so. I knew I was different. I think I was simply scared stiff of those knives and Hitler's wild voice ranting over the classroom radio.

I was old enough to realize that some violent psychotics do a lot of damage before they are put away. We were growing up fast during the dawn of the Third Reich.

My conscience wasn't burdened much longer. By late 1935, no public school would have me anymore. Jews were being purged from public life, including school benches. Students whose fathers had done front line service during World War I, such as my Stella's little dad, were exempt from this ruling for a short while longer.

I was happy that my father's asthma had kept him safely near home—a "rear echelon pig," as such shirkers were called. I would never have wanted him in Flanders, at the Marne, or before Verdun, the hallowed battlefields I had read so much about, where our valiants bled with such distinction. No, certainly not there. But did he have to loaf like a pig way to the rear of the front? Couldn't he have found himself a little spot both safe and heroic?

The matter being long academic, my mother enrolled me in November in the Jewish Goldschmidt School. The place had been in existence only since May, the last of five such establishments, all founded by women teachers, and for me it was an instant relief.

Frau Dr. Goldschmidt, who admitted me personally, was not like any other educator I had known. She wasn't dignified. She had been purged from her teaching job in a public school in April 1933, and as the mother of two children and two godchildren, she had decided to provide classes for them and also go into business for herself. The opportunity was obvious to her. A lot of Jewish children needed to continue their education; a lot of dismissed Jewish teachers were looking for jobs.

Leonore Goldschmidt, thirty-eight, reminded me of my own mother: she was a steamroller, voluble, quick, bright, forever in a hurry, brimming with energy, never at a loss for answers and improvised solutions to crises. She didn't walk, she stormed; she never talked, she bubbled, always up to something new. When she died in her eighties in London in 1983, she was learning Russian.

The school was a family enterprise. Frau Dr. Goldschmidt's lawyer husband, Ernst, functioned as chief administrator. Class discipline was of the tight German mold and was applied impartially to the Goldschmidt children, although the teachers smiled when their conferences were interrupted by one of the Goldschmidt kids rushing into the room, shouting "Mama!" and demanding to have the school's principal settle a family matter forthwith.

I too did not consider Frau Dr. Goldschmidt's establishment a forbidding shrine to rote learning, like my earlier Prussian institutions. Her mission was to rush immature potential emigrants like me toward sturdy adulthood—abroad.

The school was co-ed, not a revolutionary idea but still uncommon. Religion played no major role, but the outside world was not forgotten. Our graduates were expected to go to college out of the country. Frau Dr. Goldschmidt spoke fluent English and plugged hard for language teaching. Her academic standards were rigorous. Our enrollment grew rapidly to 300, then to over 500, six of the twenty-four teachers having been recruited from England. Our leader's eyes were on the future, and the educational engine she had invented kept buzzing.

Blessedly, the place felt safe. We flourished amidst the Grunewald woods and huge lawns. We went to classes in a cluster of elegant, airy former mansions with wide halls and tall windows.* Nobody threw rocks here. We were among our own, probably too cloistered for our future good. Few of us were ardent Zionists or Orthodox Jews. Almost nobody's parents had come from Poland or other Eastern countries that German Jews (including my own parents) so shamefully disdained. We were the conventional sons and daughters of conventional upper-middle-class and upper-class professional and business people. Mostly we were families who settled in Germany innumerable generations ago, like those tracked by my Uncle Franz, the anthropologist.

Formerly sheltered by the assimilation of our families into German society, my peers and I felt shielded once again by Frau Dr. Goldschmidt's timely creation. The school was an oasis of good times. We composed satirical class poems. The faculty gave musical birthday parties in honor of Leonore Goldschmidt. We reveled in the victories of our athletic teams (which, of course, could only compete against other Jewish institutions). Tentative romances blossomed among the older students. Camaraderie was palpable, and heightened by foreboding. Almost every month, the crazy Hitler voice on the radio ordained more onerous anti-Semitic restrictions. The outside world was closing in. We sensed that our fling at congenial isolation couldn't endure.

We became experienced at saying farewells, and for me these sad occasions were orchestrated by melancholy music and tears. Standing as close to my Stella as I dared, I sang soprano in Dr. Bandmann's Select Choir and watched her reverently. Come to think of it, she always remained dry-eyed. Dr. Bandmann—nobody ever learned his

---

* The neighborhood's real estate became too valuable after the war for such lavish use of the grounds. My school was replaced by a sixteen-story apartment house and the Belvedere Pizzeria bearing a small memorial plaque.

first name—was dreamy, perpetually unpressed, a lock of curly reddish hair bouncing down his forehead as he sat bent and bouncing over the piano. He was enslaved to music, needed merely to read a piece of sheet music in the streetcar and an ecstatic expression would settle behind his black horn-rimmed glasses.*

For him we sang Beethoven's *"Die Himmel Rühmen des Ewigen Ehre,"* we sang Handel and Mendelssohn, but mostly we sang sad songs at graduation and on the increasingly frequent occasions when schoolmates left for New York or London or, often, places we'd never heard of.

Eventually some of my fellow alumni would compare the Goldschmidt peace to that in Bassani's *Garden of the Finzi-Continis,* so movingly captured in the 1970 Vittorio De Sica film. Some similarities do apply. The film's garden did detach its family of aristocratic Italian Jews from the turmoil of Mussolini's rising Fascism. But the final scenes of the Finzi-Contini clan crowding quietly into the school, dispassionately awaiting deportation, did not fit the people I knew. Almost all of us acted, if sometimes too late. With tragic exceptions, almost all escaped. Nobody I knew met disaster standing quietly by once the danger turned palpable. We were not sheep. We were survivors, one way or another, unlike the others, the millions who perished, the placid who lacked the psychological and financial resources.

Not that we were all alike—far from it. The school's most unforgettable personage was my homeroom teacher, the tall, ramrod-upright Dr. Kurt Lewent, grim, forbidding, aloof, feared. Fifty years later, I would still cringe and see him looming over me—pale, dark, his thick black mustache quivering—inflamed over some trifling stupidity perpetrated by me or one of my terrorized classmates, Stella among them.

Dr. Lewent—the *w* was pronounced like a *v*—exploded in his favorite litany upon confronting human frailty. "So," he thundered, "this is what they call the so-called Jewish intelligence! I see no sign of it!"

Although Jewish himself, Lewent was beset by the same identity crisis troubling most of his students, Stella being a striking example. He was, above all, a German, and carried visible physical damage to

---

* It was not until 1992 that I learned of his fate. He was deported in 1943, together with his girlfriend, a Jewish nurse. En route, they had agreed that they would marry.

prove it: a disfigured hand and a severe limp, trophies earned while fighting for the Kaiser's Reich in World War I.

It must have pained and confused this poor soul when fellow Germans (Germans!) erased him like an inappropriate footnote from the rolls of university professors at the eminent Paedagogische Hochschule, reducing him in rank and forcing him to drill little dunces like us. So he hated us and hated Jews, and most of all he hated himself for having failed in life.

We hated him right back: his sarcasm, the swift retribution for every infraction of his iron rules, the pall he cast over his classroom, the *fear* he engendered, as if we didn't have fear enough in our lives, fear so profound that it sometimes moved even older boys to tears.

Discipline and fear ruled the light moments in Lewent's life too. On rare occasions he permitted himself an amusing remark, and the class burst into laughter. Not for long. Within seconds, Lewent commanded, "Enough laughter!" The ensuing silence was instant and total.

Lewent was a knowledgeable teacher, even if his methods differed from those of his humanist Goldschmidt School colleagues. Many of us would remember it was fear of him that pounded into us the conjugations of French verbs; yet he could also exercise imagination, teaching us the English *r* by making us practice saying "gdeen" instead of "green." Lewent's lessons lasted for life. He saw to that.

Attempts to ingratiate ourselves with this stern master did not get far. Once a group collected money and bought him a fancily bound book for his birthday. Lewent asked that it be exchanged; he wanted Louis Fischer's biography of the ascetic Mahatma Gandhi. A delegation delivered the desired volume to the teacher's house. He barely said thank you and did not ask the students in. Perhaps he was moved and didn't want to show it.

Lewent became a survivor too. I never learned when or how the dictator of the Goldschmidt School got away from Hitler, but in 1946, one of our alumni, Eva Isaac-Krieger, en route to her classes at Hunter College in New York, offered her subway seat to a dignified old man with a cane and was treated to a miracle in exchange.

The old man looked at her gratefully and said, "Eva Isaac-Krieger?"

"Dr. Lewent?"

The reunion lasted two subway stops. The old teacher proved recognizable only by the remnants of his once proud exterior. His hate had given way to gentleness. He had tears in his eyes, and his former student found it difficult to accept that this fragile figure had shouted English lessons at her not long ago. His accent was dreadful. But he lived and had become a different person. The times had beaten Lewent into a tenderhearted Jew.

Stella, my Stella, was a survivor of a different sort. I had no way to guess her vulnerability when we were teenagers, for the frustrating truth about "decent" girls of my sheltered Berlin youth was their apparent aloofness. They did not neck, they did not hold hands. The very word "sex" was unspeakable between the sexes, which made Stella's sex education briefings so daring. Even my liberated mother never discussed sex. She informed me of the so-called facts of life by leaving a volume of Krafft-Ebing on prominent display on our bookshelves at home. I did have eyes in my head, and when they glimpsed Stella in those very short ruffled black gym shorts and her tight, thin white top, I didn't need Krafft-Ebing or other middlemen to make the connection with my body.

Although I had many chances to become chummy with the adored one, inexperience kept me from pressing the luck of proximity. On most days I rode to school up Kurfürstendamm on either the No. 76 or the No. 176 streetcar, always picking my departure time with deliberation. My objective was to board the car on which "my" girls were riding. If I didn't spot them, I would wait until their car came along.

My girls were Stella's best friend, Lili Baumann, the tall track star, talkative, with straight coal-black hair; her cousin Renate Baumann, blond and cheerful; Edith Latte, small, dark, and very, very quiet; and my Stella. They formed a clique and were among the prettiest girls in the school. I hoped that some of their glamour might rub off on me if I insinuated myself into their presence during the lengthy ride on their streetcar. The inevitable crowding offered them little opportunity to move away or to ignore me. Alas, even at close range I lacked the nerve to engage the formidable Stella in real conversation.

In later years, I sometimes fantasized how the outcome of Stella's survival and mine might have differed if I had succeeded in engineering a romance between us. What if we had become inseparable? What if I had set off a friendship between my parents and her parents at one of the Parents Nights of the Goldschmidt School, where I used to see all of the Goldschlag family? What if my mother and Stella's father had hit it off, exchanging notes about their favorite lieder? What if my *Mutti*, the great persuader, had pressured the Goldschlags into emigration in time and we had all wound up in New York?

Ridiculous—absurd for any number of reasons assigned by circumstances and those bizarre times. The game of "If . . . if . . . if . . ." was pointless, and my father had an ancient Berlinese gag for it. He used to scoff, "If my aunt had wheels, she'd be a bus." Under pressure, he knew how to make a pact with reality too.

5. Exit

IT WAS NATURAL FOR MY MOTHER, the mini-dynamo, to be the driving force who decided we should emigrate. There was no family discussion. She had no vision of the mass slaughters to come, but her hold on reality brooked no wavering. Even if Hitler would perhaps do no physical harm to the Jews, he was making it increasingly difficult for us to earn a living, much less to enjoy ourselves. Already some Jewish-owned businesses were being pushed toward expropriation. Every year, new kinds of personal harassments began. It was only a question of time until the cozy life with the amenities that were so much a part of my mother's style became impossible. No, thank you. She was leaving, even though her father, my patrician and normally authoritative Opi, advised strongly against a move.

It was not a bit unusual in these go-or-no-go family dilemmas for the women to display more energy and enterprise than the men. "Women's lib" (in those days, it meant mostly that women had been given the right to vote) had little to do with it. Almost no women had a business, a law office, or a medical practice to lose. They were less status-conscious, less money-oriented than the men. They seemed to be less rigid, less cautious, more confident of their ability to flourish on new turf and, if necessary (at least this was true in my cocky mother's case), to find another man who would support them or make an effective partner.

Once my father had acquiesced in my mother's Christopher Columbus mission—he sighed, frowned, and shook his head sadly—he

47

did go into action with Prussian efficiency. Beneath his gracious, childlike smile lurked a relentless administrator: low-key, his files and index cards exquisitely organized, persistent as a termite. We were going to America. That was a given. There was no discussion about that either. It was *the* place to go. A woman of my mother's flair would consider no lesser refuge.

In 1935, emigrating to the United States was already a torturously slow process, but possible as long as you were in good health, had at least one reasonably prosperous relative there, and had enough money to pay off the Nazis. My father, with his salesman's infinite patience, stood in line at the American consulate day after day. Often the lines were so long and moved so slowly that he managed to see no one before the place closed (always in very early afternoon). Sometimes the consular authorities decided to close shop for days at a time to catch up with their paperwork. But inch by inch, while we waited in line for two years, my father moved us toward the journey to New York.

The language around the house changed. Our future had come to depend on three new guideposts: "the quota"—the total number of German refugees permitted to enter the United States under the miserly immigration laws; "the affidavit"—the document from an obscure umpteenth cousin (whom my father had located in the Bronx during a reconnaissance trip to America) guaranteeing that he would support us if we became destitute; and "the visa"—which would be our stamped admission ticket into the promised land.

The Nazis turned the Jewish exodus into a lucrative industry. There was intense negotiation about the amount we had to pay as our "escape tax," the ransom demanded by the German authorities. To the end, Hitler's government was hungry to possess money and property of Jews. In later years, his functionaries just took things: clothing, eyeglasses, gold fillings, whatever. At the time of our emigration, confiscation was more refined. Jews were pressured to leave the country, but the privilege of leaving was expensive.

My father's business sense saved us. When I was born in 1923, at the height of the German inflation—a loaf of bread cost millions of marks—my father had decided to buy a large life insurance policy. Somehow he found an insurance company, the Nordstern, that sold him a policy for which he could pay premiums in marks while benefits would eventually be payable in dollars. The cash value of the policy had grown respectably over the years. The Nazis were desperate for foreign currency—real exchangeable money—but as yet lacked the nerve simply to seize assets. The insurance policy became our ticket to freedom.

With my mother staking out our strategy and my father negotiating our tactics, my parents went about shrinking our household to make us mobile for our move overseas. We would be allowed to ship a small van of possessions, at hideous cost, but much of our bulky furniture, linens, drapes, and memorabilia had to be left behind. I also suspect that without confessing this, even to themselves, my parents were preparing themselves for a much more modest lifestyle to come.

And so we retreated into a tiny apartment in Charlottenburg, Roscherstrasse 16, in the rear court, four flights up. I was delighted because our next-door neighbor was Erich Kaestner, the author. Like kids all over the world, I had giggled my way through *Emil and the Detectives*. But this was not the principal reason for my bliss at Kaestner's proximity. Nor was I terribly impressed by the sad circumstance that this depressed, emaciated celebrity had had his books banned and burned by the Nazis and that he kept getting arrested for questioning by the Gestapo because, in his low-key, sardonic way, he let it be known that he thought the Nazis were crazies.

I was captivated by Kaestner for selfish reasons. He trafficked with publishers and fans in many countries, so he received a lot of mail from abroad.* Some of the envelopes carried stamps of value, and stamps were my thing. I had graduated from the ranks of amateur collectors and become a trader. My operations were modest but serious. They provided excellent pocket money and enabled me to hang around my most cherished haunts: stamp shops. I raided stamps in my father's business and wherever else I had access. Erich Kaestner, glum and of nocturnal habits, was a juicy source.

Kaestner stayed on in Germany as a deliberate gesture of defiance, very brave but not suicidal for most gentiles. He thought of himself as a civilized, hopefully not untypical German and wasn't about to let hooligans run him out of his own *Vaterland*. But why—*why?*—did Jews like the Nomburgs stay behind too long, unwilling to move, docile—waiting in passivity until millions were herded away like proverbial sheep?

Half a century later, psychologists and sociologists would still argue over the reasons and apply such diagnoses as "blindness," "mass delusion," "ghetto mentality," and "denial of reality." They would still be perplexed. But I have always known why the Nomburgs and the rest of the passive majority didn't pull up stakes.

---

* I suspect that his influential foreign friends and his sizable income in international currencies were largely responsible for the survival of this brilliant and principled artist. Kaestner had endurance. *Emil and the Detectives* is still used by German classes in American schools. My current copy (1985) is from the 131st edition.

To begin with, it's a wrench to leave home, no matter how much is wrong with the place. It takes solid inner security to hitch up a covered wagon. Only adventurers can do it.

We German Jews, moreover, felt anchored in safe harbor. Most of us didn't feel that we were different in our generally fairly tolerant environment. We were patriots with dueling scars from the student fraternities and Iron Crosses from World War I. My father's forefathers had been storekeepers in rural Germany forever; should he have felt like an outcast because hoodlums put rude signs into a few shop windows? Ridiculous!

Most of the stay-at-home Jews rationalized their placidity by pleading lack of money and connections. Often that excuse applied. Even at thirteen I knew that not everybody owned a dollar life insurance policy or could afford the 35-mark monthly tuition at the Goldschmidt School. And like virtually all affluent Jews, we had a branch in the family—my Uncle Richard's in Weissensee—that was, by our standards, poor—and never did get away from Hitler's Reich.

Neither did Stella and her kin, the Goldschlags.

My parents were terribly tense about our own visa prospects. The physical examinations at the American consulate were rumored to be booby-trapped. America seemed to want only exemplary bodies, and my mother was especially worried about me. I had barely survived septicemia, a generalized blood poisoning, when I was seven. That had led to a mastoidectomy, which had left me with hearing loss in my right ear. Would America admit someone unable to pick up every decibel of its clamor?

While this failure was unfixable, my parents did keep us from being rejected for "moral turpitude." My mother had picked up this expression somehow, in English, and it presented another hurdle. My parents' marriage had, in effect, broken up. Both wanted a divorce, but wait! According to rumor—my mother called such a wisp an *on dit*—the pious Pilgrims of America frowned on divorce. Divorced persons were said to be guilty of "moral turpitude," and moral turpitude was a capital cause for visa rejection. So my parents postponed their formal separation. They would not even proceed with it in the United States until after they had secured their "first papers" toward permanent citizenship. Moral turpitude lived.

Our relatives, Cousin Martha and her husband and their daughter, Lottchen, were ultimately able to leave Germany, but they couldn't make it far enough. They had applied for American visas when we did, but Martha's husband fell victim to a physical disability no less innocent than mine. Untold years earlier, while he was undergoing treatment for acne, an incompetent radiologist had left him with scars—inactive but red—over his face. The American doctors insisted he was a cancer risk and refused the family their visas.

They fled to Holland and had to spend war years in the Bergen-Belsen death camp. Such were the terrors of the times that they blamed my father for their lot. We had been totally removed from their visa process. Their reaction, unaccountable, led to a lifelong feud. Martha's husband never spoke to any of us again. It was as if he wanted us to hand back our American visas because he couldn't get his.

We did make it out, our bags further weighted with guilt.

It was February 1937, cold, windy, stormy, and I was seasick a good deal of the time and groaning in our family cabin. We traveled second-class on the S.S. *Washington,* but, I thought, in fabulous style. For my convalescence a steward in a starched white coat brought chicken sandwiches to me in bed. Chicken sandwiches! Who had ever heard of such a delicacy? We had had chicken for dinner at home, of course, but that was a Sunday treat. Absolutely nobody put chicken on a sandwich, certainly not on toast with mayonnaise—mayonnaise!—which was how they pampered chickens on our American ocean liner. So maybe American streets weren't paved with gold. Any country that paved sandwiches with chicken had to be paradise!

Our reception in New York was a letdown. Our relatives had rented a furnished apartment for us on the West Side of Manhattan, sight unseen—or so we told ourselves. It was unfit even for the vermin that called it home. On our first morning in the land of the free, we awoke covered with inexplicable itchy bites. We had met bedbugs, some kindly natives told us later. That was news. We were not familiar with bedbugs.

I was not an instant American. I made a bow when I shook hands. The shattering uproar of the Manhattan subway slammed me into panic. Coca-Cola tasted poisonous. I arrived at DeWitt Clinton High School in the Bronx wearing green knickerbockers and carrying the New York *Staatszeitung und Herold,* my English vocabulary running to around a dozen words. Teachers and fellow students smiled at me, however, and I could hear my accent gradually falling away. Optimal purging of one's accent was the wish of every refugee. Nobody wanted to be a greenhorn.

My mother's personality seemed tailored for the New York pace.

She at once remembered the English she had learned in school and quickly picked up singing students. My father, though only fifty, went into collapse. He never learned English, never held another real job. It was perplexing, then frightening, then infuriating, and finally sad to watch him come apart. He wasn't transplantable. Like delicate wines, he didn't "travel." Still, we all were safe, safe, safe, and as I grappled with the news from Europe, by now from *The New York Times*—my most efficient teacher of English, costing only three cents per day—I felt myself thrust on a roller coaster of guilt, elation, rage at Hitler, and depression over the fate of the Goldschlags and the others we had left behind.

What did we know about the Holocaust, we who were safe in New York, and when did we know it?

Our family's last sign of life from Berlin was dated November 22, 1941, two weeks before Pearl Harbor disrupted mail deliveries for the next three and a half years. The neatly typed, single-spaced letter to my parents must have caught about the last boat. It was from a gnomish, bald, and bearded favorite of ours, Dr. Carl Joseph, our family physician, aged sixty-nine. He presided at my birth, and we called him *Onkel Doktor,* an honorary member of the family.

I recalled him fondly as the miracle worker who—clucking softly —rid me of my ingrown toenails and my chronic sore throats. His letter reminisced about "my old young friend Peter" and my trifling ailments: "How dearly I'd love to look down his throat again, which used to cause so much fuss."

The doctor's note left much unsaid that wasn't difficult to fill in. He was cleaning house, he reported, throwing away paintings and papers, getting ready for a move to an unspecified place. He did not mention camps in the East, clearly wishing to stay out of trouble with the censors, but he made his point by way of our friends-in-transit, Georg and Lotte Nomburg, whose recent move was known to him, up to a point.

"About the Nomburgs, whom you asked about, I can't tell you anything good," was the way he phrased it. "I won't be able to give them your regards because they're too far distant and not reachable by phone." That left some details to the imagination, even crucial details, probably not known to Dr. Joseph either. Not then. Not yet.

So his letter looked back to our mutual past, the Berlin I remembered, reminiscing about the great parties and the wine consumption at our home ("How many bottles landed in the wastebasket!"), and he permitted himself a single sigh: "You never know how well off you are until you're doing worse."

Obviously, this was a farewell message anticipating still much worse to come. "This season we're not wishing everyone a good heave-ho into the New Year, but a good move out of it," our *Onkel Doktor* concluded. "To you we say, *'Auf Wiedersehn!'*—no longer as a salutation but as a literal expression of hope."

We were, of course, extremely agitated, though not yet without hope. We equated the aged doctor's news with privation and possibly some primitive medical work in a camp, not with genocide. We never heard a word about what happened to him and his wife.

Suddenly everyone in the refugee world became more acutely concerned about missing relatives and friends. What had happened to Uncle Max Brahn, to Cousin Siegfried and his bunch in Weissensee, my cronies from the Goldschmidt School who had been left behind? And Stella? What about Stella on her pedestal, made more inaccessible than ever by the fury of events?

6. 1938:
The Year the End Began

WILLIAM SHIRER, thirty-four, lately hired by Edward R. Murrow for CBS as one of radio's first foreign correspondents, was present at the creation.

And like so many sweeping innovations, *Untersturmführer* Adolf Eichmann's new ideas—as Shirer would observe at first hand—worked with stunning directness and simplicity. Eichmann charted the lives of millions. Only a handful survived, including Stella Goldschlag when she made her peace with Eichmann's inventiveness.

At thirty-two, looking as meek as the most anonymous and guileless of clerks, he was a failed traveling salesman, a son from near Hitler's hometown in Austria, plodding up the bureaucratic ladder of the SS, making himself the Führer's premier specialist for what Eichmann viewed as a challenging administrative mission: exterminating Europe's Jews.

He never killed a soul. He was the ultimate supervisor, the *Schreibtischtäter,* the desk perpetrator operating strictly within his quiet office. He only *organized* the death of six million.

"Death" was not part of his professional vocabulary. He "evacuated." He "transported." He "resettled." He "processed," he "cleared areas," he "changed domiciles." And thereby he led Jews to the "Final Solution," a phrase he coined himself.

Eichmann also innovated administratively. He created a nearly self-enforcing system that pushed Stella and other Jews to execute, on his behalf, many of the dirtying details of destroying themselves.

Eichmann's dress rehearsal was staged not in Berlin but in Vienna, the waltz capital. It was the week Hitler annexed Austria, the Anschluss of March 1938, and Eichmann was settling in at the Palais Rothschild, the palace of the fugitive Baron Louis de Rothschild, on Prinz Eugen Strasse, making it headquarters of the "Central Office for Jewish Emigration."

Living in an apartment next door, Bill Shirer saw SS men carting paintings, silver, and other loot out of the premises.

Eichmann, anxious to report quick results to Berlin, summoned the imprisoned head of the Jewish Community, Dr. Richard Löwenherz, and began the meeting by demonstrating his authority. He simply slapped the old man's face. Then, keeping the Jewish leader standing for well over an hour, he solicited his counsel for cleansing Vienna of its Jews, to make the city *judenrein* in accordance with Hitler's orders.

It was so easy, an organizer's vision, a breakthrough. At his 1961 trial in Jerusalem, Eichmann would testify: "I gave Dr. Löwenherz paper and pencil and said: 'Please go back for one more night and write up a memo telling me how you would organize the whole thing . . .' "

Löwenherz complied. If he hadn't, he would have faced dreadful choices. It would have meant deportation to one of the huge concentration camps Eichmann was setting up in Poland and elsewhere to the East—and this happened to about half of Vienna's 180,000 Jews. Possibly Löwenherz might have ransomed his way into emigration like the other, wealthier half, assuming he had enough money; or he would have been publicly lampooned, along with still other Jews who were made to scrub streets and toilets on their hands and knees, sometimes with toothbrushes—scenes also witnessed by Bill Shirer.

It all added up to a lot of work for Eichmann. He needed help, and one of his "best men" was a longtime acquaintance, Alois Brunner,* who worked his way up from humble estate as Eichmann's secretary to become his deputy, then Eichmann's successor in the Vienna bureau, eventually to be called by him to Berlin to help with bigger tasks.

Brunner, twenty-six, was another small-town Austrian but of

---

* Internally, he was known as Brunner I to avoid confusion with Anton Brunner, no kin and known as Brunner II, another SS killer but of lesser status. Brunner II was hanged after the war. Brunner I was still living in 1992 as "Herr Fischer" in Damascus, Syria, occasionally giving interviews to German magazines, still spouting anti-Semitic obscenities.

cruder stuff. Like Eichmann, he was a disaster in civilian life, having been fired from a Jewish-owned department store. He too was physically unattractive, and his unhelpful genes set off particular ridicule among Austrians—perhaps, en bloc, the most anti-Semitic people on earth.

"To judge from his features, he could be Jewish," a colleague remembered. Weighing 123 pounds, he was described by other co-workers as "small, dark, nervous, long and pointed nose, slightly bowlegged, slightly hunchbacked." His eyes were "wicked," his visage "expressionless," his voice "monotonous."

His SS cohorts sneered at him as "Jew Süss," the star of a pornographically anti-Semitic film, and they hated Brunner as a snitch because he habitually reported any infractions of bureaucratic rules straight to the big bosses in Berlin.

Unlike Eichmann, Brunner was a flagrant Jew hater and a hands-on operative. When Viennese Jews had to queue up for deportation to Lithuania, Elliot Welles, then a Jewish teenager and later the chief hunter of war criminals for the Anti-Defamation League of B'nai Brith, watched Brunner prowl around the desks of the clerks, helping to hasten the exodus.

Some of the trains east were commanded by Brunner, and his frigid brutality was remembered. A survivor on one transport saw him casually shoot to death the banker Siegmund Bosel because he was irked by the ailing old man's pleas for mercy in the cold. Brunner had kicked him to the floor and accused him of being a "profiteer."

Brunner knew real profiteering. He moved into an ample villa in Vienna's exclusive Hietzing district, after the eviction of its Jewish owners, and furnished it with art and antiques from residences of others he had deported. Additional treasures stolen from the Jews were presented as gifts to ranking Nazis back in the Reich.

Eichmann's faith in Brunner was justified. The enterprising assistant broadened the principle Eichmann had applied to Löwenherz: to enlist the Jews in carrying out their own destruction. "Brunner invented Jewish collaboration," said Simon Wiesenthal, the Nazi hunter. During the trial that resulted in his death, Eichmann would testify that the Nazis regarded Jewish cooperation as "the very cornerstone" of their Jewish policy.

Brunner developed ingenious uses and permutations for his invention. He signed a directive creating a Jewish *Ordner* service, ostensibly to "keep order." Its mercenaries were the forerunners of the dreaded *Kapo* trusties, many of whom regarded themselves as dependable assistants of the Nazi establishment in the concentration camps, which Eichmann belittled jokingly as *Konzertlager,* concert camps.

These collaborators were the civil-service-like creations that led to Stella's elite contingent, carried in Berlin Gestapo files under the never-published name of Jewish Scouting Service *(Jüdischer Fahndungsdienst).* It probably numbered only twenty young men and women, although one postwar estimate ran as high as sixty. Its minions were known officially as scouts or stool pigeons *(Spitzel).* It was the Jews who called them "catchers" *(Greifer).* These renegades bore some resemblance to at least certain of the often pitifully beleaguered Jewish Councils of Elders that had to help run the fenced-in ghettos into which starving Jews would shortly be herded in every Eastern community.*

The Vienna *Ordner,* who also became known as fetchers, raiders, and *Jupo* (Jewish police), were mostly ruffians hoping vainly for preferential treatment. Usually their deportations were merely somewhat delayed. Meanwhile, these mercenaries kept order in the many long, slow-moving queues; prevented escapes at collection points; and tagged along with SS officers to apartments of Jews targeted for transport, staying behind to supervise the minutely detailed property declarations.

From the inception of the self-destruction system in Vienna and for years to come, many *Ordner* and many Jewish leaders cooperated because the Nazi keepers pointed out that SS men would be much harsher disciplinarians if the Jews refused to, as it were, devour themselves. In the end, almost all who helped Hitler's men were indiscriminately gassed (or beaten to death by fellow inmates in the camps). Only the strongest, cleverest, and luckiest survived—and those who managed somehow to anesthetize themselves.**

---

* These still highly controversial councils, working sometimes as rescuers and sometimes as collaborators, were established on September 21, 1939, by an order from the chief of the SS, Reinhardt Heydrich, stating: "1. A Jewish Council of Elders is to be established in every Jewish community . . . It is to be held literally and fully responsible for the precise, on-deadline execution of all past and future instructions. 2. In case such instructions are sabotaged, the most severe measures are to be announced to the councils . . ."
** Almost totally destroyed were the "crematorium ravens," the Jewish *Sonderkommandos* (Special Squads) in the camps. At Auschwitz they numbered between 700 and 1,000 at any one time. Until they were gassed and replaced every few months, they performed the most unspeakable duties of Eichmann's herculean administrative apparatus. They were required to keep the detailed housekeeping of its end phase in German order, *ordnungsgemäss.* "It was their task to maintain order among the new arrivals," recalled Primo Levi, a member of the Italian anti-Fascist resistance incarcerated at Auschwitz. The Special Squads were further deputized to

A few stayed alive through force of personality combined with stealth. "I got along best with Dr. Murmelstein, the rabbi," Eichmann testified in Jerusalem, and his approval was grounded in tragic fact. Rabbi Benjamin Murmelstein had been placed in charge of the *Ordner* and their ilk, and saw to it that these services functioned smoothly.

The rabbi was exceptionally intelligent and resolute. Author of several popular books about Jewish history and the Talmud, he was visibly formidable, weighing 220-plus pounds. His intellectual prowess, together with his uncontrolled temper and ruthlessness, made it difficult to think of him as a potential victim.

"Among all the internal leaders he was the most intelligent and cautious, but also the coldest and most unscrupulous, fighting mainly for his personal survival," concluded H. G. Adler, a fellow prisoner who would write the definitive history of Theresienstadt. "His behavior was far from humane and in his fits he did not even restrain from beating people."

Murmelstein, Eichmann's favorite, forceful and manipulative, had what it took, including luck. Of the Theresienstadt Jewish leadership, he was the only one to emerge alive.*

The belt system pioneered by Eichmann, Brunner and Company disposed of the Vienna Jews efficiently by way of the Holocaust's first life/death "selection." The machinery worked on dual tracks: it fleeced those whose wealth permitted them to pay off for the privilege of emigration, while deporting the majority who lacked assets to finance escape. Baron de Rothschild from Prinz Eugen Strasse purchased his freedom by surrendering his steel mills to the Hermann Göring works;** ordinary mortals had to board Brunner's trains east.

"extract the corpses from the chambers, to pull gold teeth from the jaws, to cut women's hair, to sort and classify clothes, shoes and the contents of luggage, to transport the bodies to the crematoria and oversee the operations of the ovens, to extract and eliminate the ashes." Only a handful of Special Squad recruits escaped the same death that they facilitated daily. And they survived only "because of some unforeseeable whim of fate." So recorded Primo Levi shortly before his own death by suicide or a never-explained accident in 1987.

* The rabbi's winning streak continued after the war. He was arraigned by the Czechoslovak war crimes authorities but freed. He again walked away in 1948 after arraignment in Rome by a civil court of the Organization of Jewish Displaced Persons. Nobody could turn Murmelstein into a loser.

** Rothschild had been arrested at the Vienna airport, Aspern, while trying to flee; his passport was torn up, the fragments tossed in his face. In prison his captors pressured this billionaire into financial surrender quite simply by giving him next to nothing to eat.

There was an increasingly favored third way out. Ed Murrow of CBS became eyewitness to that route when he visited his man in Vienna, Bill Shirer. They dropped in for a chat at a quiet bar on Kärntnerstrasse, where Murrow turned edgy. He suggested they go to another place. Shirer asked why.

"I was here last night," Murrow said. "A Jewish-looking fellow was standing at that bar. After a while he took out an old-fashioned razor from his pocket and slashed his throat."

The vacation warmth of mid-July 1938 found Shirer on an assignment that turned into a French alpine holiday. The scene was cloudless and breathtaking—Evian-les-Bains, spa for the international superrich—and all was becalmed. It was easy to appreciate the unruffled expanse of Lake Geneva, dotted with excursion steamers and sailboats; the picture-postcard shore of the French side, facing Switzerland to the north; the uncarbonated neutrality of the famous Evian mineral water; the enormous white wedding cake of a hotel, the six-story Royal with its exclusive casino, built in the high hills in 1909 by the queen of England.

For the hotel guests in dark suits, dignified gentlemen representing thirty-two nations, assembled to decide the fate of Europe's Jews, the serenity was contagious.

"All the delegates had a nice time," remembered the Royal's aging concierge. "They took pleasure cruises on the lake. They gambled at night at the casino. They took mineral baths and massages at the *Etablissement Thermal*. Some of them took the excursion to Chamonix to go summer skiing. Some went riding. Some played golf. We have a beautiful course overlooking the lake."

What about the meetings?

"Yes," recalled the old man, "some attended the meetings. But, of course, it is difficult to sit indoors hearing speeches when all the pleasures that Evian offers are waiting right outside."

The indoors agenda of the Evian refugee conference would rate no theatrical piece, no film, almost no space in the history books—a curious, possibly an embarrassed omission. By doing nothing, the assembly performed a dramatic act. It doomed Stella Goldschlag and her kind.

"We are not really covering it at all," wrote Bill Shirer in his *Berlin Diary*. Mostly he hung about with his old pal Jimmy Sheehan, who would soon write his best-selling memoirs, *Not Peace but the Sword*. Shirer's diary recorded: "Jimmy broke the bank at the baccarat table while I was winning a couple of thousand francs more laboriously at roulette."

Sheehan did attend two meetings. "Both sessions reached a very high point in stupid, sanctimonious, heartless pomposity and boredom," he would write, venting his disgust. "Delegate after delegate got up and read a long speech saying that his country sympathized deeply with the suffering of the Jews but could do nothing to alleviate them. The chairs were hard and so were the voices. I went to no more of the sessions."

Sheehan was being relatively kind. Not all the assembled nations sympathized. The delegate from underpopulated Australia declared: "As we have no racial problem, we are not desirous of importing one." The Swiss delegate, Dr. H. Rothmund, noted his country's tradition of receiving refugees and failed to mention that he had just concluded talks with the Nazis to stop immigration of Austrian Jews. If the refugee trickle didn't cease, he advised Hitler's negotiators, then "Switzerland, which has as little use for these Jews as Germany, will herself take measures . . ."

Although the conference stretched over twelve days, the pleas of nearly forty Jewish organizations from all over the world were jammed into a single afternoon. The World Jewish Congress, representing seven million, was allotted five minutes. All the groups from Germany and Austria—Jewish elders briefly let out by Eichmann's special dispensation to serve his own ends—stalked about the Hotel Royal like ghosts out of *Hamlet*. They were not allowed to be heard at all in the deluge of words that sealed their fate.

The entire performance had been the idea of the suave, impeccably turned-out Sumner Welles, President Franklin D. Roosevelt's powerful second in command at the State Department, the under secretary. It was a public relations response to the pressures from American liberals and Jews shocked by five years of Hitler's repressions and the recent months of blatant excesses in Austria. Welles counseled the President to "get out in front and attempt to guide the pressure, primarily with a view toward forestalling attempts to have the immigration laws liberalized."

It all came down to one grim word. The word was "quota." Arbitrarily, the immigration quota ruled how many would survive and how many would die. It was an immutable symbol, a paper curtain not to be touched—or so American politicians regarded it. The annual German-and-Austrian entry allotment for the United States stood fixed at 27,730, but even many of these relatively sparse spaces in the lifeboats had been deliberately left unfilled for years.

It was as if the face of the Statue of Liberty had been blinded by the same sign that appeared on more and more Berlin shop windows: *"Juden unerwünscht"*—"Jews not wanted."

Washington's rigidity was policy dictated by the President personally. Shortly before the Evian meeting, a confidential government memo summarized his position: "It would be unwise to put forward any proposal which would occasion public dispute and controversy, such as a change in the immigration quotas or loans from public funds."

Even if Roosevelt had been an unalloyed humanitarian, he could not survive in office unless he was foremost a politician, a realist, a sometimes ruthless practitioner of the art of the possible. Idealistic presidents were not reelected, most emphatically not when they were thinking of running for an unprecedented third term.

FDR had to be preoccupied with the domestic agenda, and liberality toward Jewish foreigners was, even in retrospect, probably unrealistic. The Great Depression was not over. Unemployment remained high. Congressmen were earning votes with outrageously anti-Semitic speeches, their poison based less on ideology than on economics. More Jews would mean more mouths to feed, and this prospect was unacceptable to a majority of taxpayers. Jews were considered unfair competition. In the very month of the conference at Evian, more than two thirds (67.4 percent) of the respondents in a *Fortune* poll agreed with the statement that "with conditions as they are, we should try to keep them out."

Pitiless? Of course. Yet, again in retrospect, not as barbaric as history would brand the quota barrier. The true onset of the Holocaust, the gassings, were still three and more years distant. Absolutely nobody conceived such a thing possible then. No president, no Jew could remotely have predicted events so grisly when the chief American delegate, Myron C. Taylor, rose at Evian to speak on behalf of Roosevelt.

First among equals and first to address the meeting, Taylor had the delegates sitting in suspense. They expected a magnanimous American gesture that would in effect constitute a demand, a hardship, on their countries, some costly scheme offering wholesale relief to the oppressed and threatening employment opportunities at home.

Taylor had been dealt a formidable part and he looked ready to play it: tall, erect, broad shouldered, rimless spectacles glistening, white hair slicked firmly down and back. He was a respected Catholic lay leader, soon to be the first United States ambassador to the

Vatican; an accredited business leader, the recently retired board chairman of United States Steel Corporation. And this lion stunned the delegates by putting forth a whisper.

The United States, Taylor announced, had decided to use up all places in its present quota—no less but also no more. The relief in the conference hall was all but audible, and even Taylor's miserly promise was never kept.

Behind the scenes, in the rooms of the modest Hotel Splendide, a more personal encounter was being enacted, in his customary flamboyant style, by the Geneva correspondent of the *Prager Tagblatt*, Hans Habe.

He was born Jancsi Bekessy in Budapest, Jewish, and no matter what official coloration he would take on over the years—Swiss, Bolivian, French, American, and finally, unbelievably, German—he was always the quintessential Hungarian survivor. Though he was fluent in all major Western European languages, his speech, too, remained essentially Hungarian, and his perpetually tanned face bug-eyed, his trim figure perfectly pressed and tailored through any vicissitude, his hair color in doubt, usually dyed red.

At twenty-eight, he had already dashed off three readable novels between newspaper assignments, and spent most of the large inheritance of his wife—the first of five spouses he would acquire, in addition to countless mistresses. Spending other people's money was one of Habe's passions. Another was journalism, which he practiced with consummate verve and skill. His enterprise had gotten him expelled from Austria for scooping the world with the front-page headline revealing that Hitler's family name was Schickelgruber.

In Evian, Habe was agreeably surprised when he ran into Professor Dr. Heinrich von Neumann on the hotel terrace. They had last seen each other when Hans was fourteen and this Viennese laryngologist had removed his tonsils. Von Neumann enjoyed international repute, having also operated on the Prince of Wales and the king of Spain.

Once known as Hershel, the professor, sixty-five and all dignity in black, ranked high in Vienna's Jewish establishment, and so the Gestapo had released him from prison and dispatched him to Evian as part of the Nazi campaign to cash in on the proceedings.

"You know, I'm here to sell the Jews of Austria," the professor told Habe after swearing the young correspondent to secrecy in the privacy of his hotel room's balcony. The orchestra on the terrace below drowned out the words.

Von Neumann's briefers had encouraged him to engage in the shabby practice of which the Nazis liked to accuse Jewish businessmen: haggling. Eichmann's men did not dicker about the price of mere inanimate merchandise, however. They demanded "head money," a price per Jew—hard currency that they wanted the democratic governments to fork over for the release of Jews from captivity.

Von Neumann said he had been instructed to ask for $400 ransom each. If pressed, he was authorized to reduce the price to a rock-bottom $200. He was happy to undertake this dubious operation. It might help his people. Confiding his secret to Habe, he sounded very disheartened, however.* He had found the democracies in no mood to spend depression dollars on Jews. The professor had gained a private audience with Myron Taylor, who offered no encouragement toward any deal.

The Evian Conference was scuttled by American politics, isolationism, and hard times, by worldwide fear of Jewish brains and energy as economic competition, and by traditional knee-jerk anti-Semitism. Theodore C. Achilles, a young State Department hand and a sympathetic member of the American delegation, put it succinctly: "Nobody wants any more Jews."

Beyond Evian lay silence. A new international committee was appointed, but no country increased its quota, no country eased immigration restrictions, no country even protested formally to the Nazis. In Berlin the Jews, with their hopes raised and quickly deflated, could only agree with their chief rabbi, Leo Baeck. "Nothing is as awful as the silence," he said.

Only the Germans reacted. A Berlin newspaper headlined gleefully: "Jews for Sale—Who Wants Them? No One."

The disgusting truth was out. No government, no person in power, was willing to save the Jews of Germany. They had been declared free game, all of them, Stella and her family included. Now they were left with a single lifeline. Benjamin Franklin, the printer-philosopher, had pointed to it 200 years before: "God helps them that help themselves."

Professor von Neumann returned to Vienna, and later in 1938, he

---

* Habe preserved the professor's confidence until 1966, when he published a fanciful fictionalized account, *The Mission* (Coward McCann). It was a rare case of a novel that wound up listed in bibliographies as a prime historical source. Though belated, it was another of Habe's scoops. The most reliable factual treatment of the farce at Evian, "The Evian Conference on the Refugee Question," by A. Adler-Rudel, a participant, was not published until 1968 (Year Book 13 of the Leo Baeck Institute, New York).

and his wife and his son "Burschi" were released for immigration to New York under a very rarely granted "nonquota" visa. This special privilege, like his invitation to meet with Myron Taylor at Evian, was the result of his acquaintance with presidential adviser Bernard Baruch, who had sought von Neumann's medical counsel. It was also at Evian that the professor received an invitation to lecture at Columbia University.

The favoritism grew out of another practice that resulted in life-preserving immunity for a small handful of Jews. The Austrians had a meaningful local word for it, *Protektion,* their term for connections reserved for persons of prominence. It did not apply to mortals such as the Goldschlag family and other millions.

Important people abroad had to plot and bargain relentlessly to rescue prominent friends. Low-ranking rescuers would not suffice. The British psychoanalyst and biographer Dr. Ernest Jones lobbied in London for another Viennese refugee that year, his close friend and colleague of thirty years, Dr. Sigmund Freud—not simply a Jew but founder of the "Jewish science" loathed by the Nazis, psycho-analysis.

Storm troopers had ransacked Freud's apartment and offices in the Berggasse right after the Anschluss. His daughter Anna, already arrested once and released, was about to be recalled by the Gestapo. The detention of the doctor, eighty-two and long ailing (he died in London the following year) seemed imminent.

'Wouldn't it be better if we all killed ourselves?" Anna asked him.

Ever the analyst, her father answered with a question, "Why? Because they would like us to?"

Freud's defiance never paled, but his network of influentials abroad, in near panic, had to grasp for increasingly exalted *Protektion.* Dr. Jones enlisted Sir Samuel Hoare, the British home secretary. William C. Bullitt, Freud's onetime coauthor, now American ambassador to Paris, pulled the highest strings in Washington. Secretary of State Cordell Hull (who had a Jewish wife) alerted Roosevelt himself. The very next day, "in accordance with the President's instructions," the United States ambassador in Berlin was told "to take this matter up personally" with the Hitler authorities.

Salvation was near; only Freud resisted. "He could not leave his native land," Ernest Jones recorded. "It would be like a soldier leaving his post." Dr. Jones had his retort ready. He reminded Freud of the S.S. *Titanic,* wrecked like Austria. The second officer had been blown to the surface by a boiler explosion as the vessel sank. Asked when he had left his ship, the old sea dog replied, "I never left the ship, sir. She left me."

Grudgingly Freud acceded to this logic, though not without a nose-thumbing dart at his tormentors. When asked to sign an exit paper certifying that he had not been molested, he added slyly after his name, "I can most highly recommend the Gestapo to everyone."

The Nazis failed to recognize the sarcasm, or chose to ignore it, or were too awed by Freud's *Protektion* to take further steps against this incorrigible old Jew.

"Hard to believe there will be war," Bill Shirer of CBS entered in his diary. Yet on the last warm and sunny weekend of September 1938, with half of the Reich capital cavorting about the Wannsee and the Havel, swimming and boating, and most of the other half bent on that great German passion, the vigorous Sunday constitutional, it did seem as if the megalomaniac who would set the twentieth century on fire was about to light the fuse.

On Monday, Shirer covered Hitler "shrieking" before 15,000 of his Party *Bonzen* in his accustomed venue, the ornate Sportpalast with its forest of blood-red banners. The occasion was the Führer's demand for the annexation of big chunks of Czechoslovakia, and so far the Western powers appeared ready to resist.

Hitler was often unable to suppress a nervous facial twitch, and this night he was beside himself, or so it seemed to Shirer. "For the first time in all the years I've observed him he seemed tonight to have completely lost control," the CBS man recorded. The Führer's anxiety was conspicuous. "He's still got that nervous tic," Shirer noted. "All during the speech he kept cocking his shoulder, and the opposite leg from the knee down would bounce up. Audience couldn't see it, but I could."

Three days later, Shirer wrote: "It's all over." Appeasement was born. Led by Neville Chamberlain, the pompous British prime minister with his trademark umbrella, the Western powers had signed the infamous Munich surrender in the Führer's headquarters. Chamberlain crowed, "It is peace in our time."

Shirer was tracking the action. "How different Hitler at two this morning," he told his diary. "After being blocked from the *Fuehrerhaus* all evening, I finally broke in just as he was leaving." A dramatic transformation was visible: "I noticed his swagger. The tic was gone."

7. The Third Fire

STELLA WAS SENT HOME from school early on November 10, 1938. A "pogrom" was said to be in progress, but she didn't know what that meant. On her bicycle route to her house she passed a butcher shop with its windows smashed and its displays picked bare. She knew it was a Jewish-owned store—the place was marked as such in large white paint, as prescribed by law—yet she still did not grasp that any systematic attack against Jews was in progress. That suspicion dawned on her as she passed Fasanenstrasse. Smoke was billowing from the synagogue with its three broad cupolas. Firemen were standing idly by.

At home her father was gone and her mother whispered that they had to be as quiet as possible. The father had rushed into hiding at the apartment of friends, who were safe because they were American citizens. Jewish males were being rounded up all over town. The danger to women appeared to be less, but no one could be certain. Not suspecting that they were training for the years ahead, Stella and her mother practiced the art of nearly soundless living. Nobody was supposed to be able to tell that they were in their Wilmersdorf apartment, so they walked on stocking feet, kept the lights out, didn't flush the toilet, and fixed no hot meals. Even the clattering of dishes had become a danger to their life as shadows. It was an eerie, frightening existence.

The *Aktion* was not local. Throughout Germany, some 30,000 men were marched in formation into concentration camps, where some were beaten to death. More than 8,000 Jewish-owned shops were destroyed or looted. Pianos were heaved out of apartment house windows. In front of a Jewish-owned millinery store, Richard Hottelet of CBS watched men playing soccer with fancy hats. Others pranced down Berlin's fashionable Budapester Strasse gaily waving stolen girdles and brassieres.

The fires were the scariest manifestation of civilization amok, and the blaze that Stella had spotted at the Fasanenstrasse synagogue, one of 197 houses of worship to be torched that night, was already the third in the wave of flames staking out the rise and fall of Hitler's Reich. The arson of the Reichstag had begun the trail. The book burnings came next. Then the synagogues. Until Hitler was cremated seven years later, more landmark conflagrations would envelop Berlin, all infinitely more sweeping. Hitler and his dream of a "Thousand-Year Reich" lived by fire and would die by it, buried under Allied aerial bombs and Soviet artillery.

Peter Prager bicycled off to the Goldschmidt School as usual shortly after seven o'clock that sunny, crisp morning, unaware of unusual occurrences during the night. En route to Grunewald, he saw fire engines racing about but paid little attention. Fire engines were always racing about.

Prager's mind was on his German class and its dreaded taskmaster, Dr. Lewent. A test was scheduled that morning, and Peter was nervous about it. He hated pressure and did poorly on exams.

Like Stella Goldschlag, Prager went to Goldschmidt's on a scholarship. And like all the other students, he had been expelled from public school. He too had shivered when he had to listen to the song about Jewish blood spurting from knives; his music instructor had actually taught these lyrics in class. His biology teacher had announced in "race theory" class that Jewish inferiority came from the genes. To make his case, he measured Prager's forehead in front of the class and pronounced it too short.

"No need to be afraid," he consoled Peter, who was shaking. "It's not your fault that you're inferior."

Prager, twelve, wanted badly to be "Aryan" like his carefree gentile classmates, and Goldschmidt's liberated atmosphere failed to reassure him. His history teacher, Frau Dr. Goldschmidt herself, related how the British statesman Disraeli tried to alter the shape of his nose by pushing up its tip. Every night in bed, Prager pushed up his nose, and was chagrined when no results appeared in the mirror.

Arriving in school well ahead of his eight a.m. German class, Prager quickly learned why he had seen all those fire engines. Many seats in his homeroom remained empty. Some of the girls were crying and reported that their fathers had been arrested and taken to Sachsenhausen, one of the first concentration camps and the one closest to Berlin. Several teachers had also been taken there.

Not Dr. Lewent. Looking no more glum than usual, he limped into the room and announced, without mentioning any reason, that the school would close, though not until after the first period. The scheduled test had to be taken and Lewent began to administer it coolly. Peter Prager and his classmates were working at the task when Frau Dr. Goldschmidt burst in ten minutes later.

"Pens down!" she shouted. "A Hitler Youth mob is outside. They may try to burn the school down. I want everybody to leave immediately by the back door!" Only later did the students learn that her husband and partner, the lawyer Ernst Goldschmidt, had fled for Denmark during the night, en route to England.

With accustomed imagination, she scrambled to cast a protective cover over her domain. She flatly informed one of her imported British teachers, Philip Woolley, twenty-five and on his first job, that she had transferred legal ownership of the institution to him. Then she ordered the Union Jack hoisted atop the building. Woolley, stunned by his promotion, adored the Goldschmidts and was game. The British takeover, while no doubt illegal, gave the Nazis pause for a short time. Formalities invoking the rights of foreigners still impressed them.

Despite the obvious seriousness of events, Frau Dr. Goldschmidt still would not accept that *Kristallnacht* spelled the beginning of the school's end, at least not in front of the students. "Come back in three days, when we hope everything will have quieted down," she told Peter Prager's class. And Dr. Lewent, true to his reputation, refused to adjourn until the German test was completed.

Quietly, in orderly fashion, the youngsters left school in shifts. Peter felt overwhelmingly lucky when he noticed that the Hitler Youth were shouting slogans in the front of the buildings while his group departed through the rear. The youngest children were led out by older ones, who remained stony-eyed. Some jeering Hitler Youth spotted them and wielded rocks, but did not throw them.

Gerd Ehrlich, fourteen, burly and boisterous, was one of the older boys who led out fellow students. Arriving back home, he learned that his lawyer father was among the "*Aktion* Jews" who had been taken to Sachsenhausen, where he developed a heart condition from which he never recovered.

Klaus Scheye was worried about his brother, who had gone to

Goldschmidt's by streetcar that morning. "I remember clearly my dilemma of the hour," he would write. "Do I save my precious bicycle or my little brother?"

On the run, he managed to do both. Some hours later, his father too would be taken to Sachsenhausen, emerging after six weeks as a permanently broken man.

School did reopen, although it was no longer a tranquil retreat. Catcalling Hitler Youth were permanently stationed hecklers around the Roseneck. Wolfgang Edelstein got beaten up regularly when classes let out, and the words of the accompanying Hitler Youth tunes stayed with him always. One ditty, in translation, went about like this: "Jew Itzig Cod Liver Oil has a sled-run up his ass. . . ." Wolfgang could make nothing of these words—not then, when he was ten, not ever. They were word salad, the best that witless Nazi kids could drum up to be insulting.

For Ruth Nussbaum the torching of the synagogues was all but a bodily assault upon herself and her husband. After the lionized Joachim Prinz had left for the United States in 1937, Rabbi Max Nussbaum, twenty-eight, had taken over the *Friedenstempel* off Kurfürstendamm in Wilmersdorf; at five a.m. on November 10, the sexton phoned their apartment a few blocks away on Lietzenburger Strasse and whispered breathlessly into the phone, "Come quickly, Rabbi, our temple is burning."

Rushing to the scene, the Nussbaums found "clouds of black smoke, fringed with red, billowing from broken windows and the skeleton of the roof." Cops and firemen had cordoned off the building and here, too, the keepers of public order were only making certain that adjoining structures wouldn't catch fire. Ruth watched the faces of the citizen spectators—mostly women wrapped in shawls, many holding children—who had assembled despite the early hour.

"They were all simply and honestly delighted, full of glee, thrilled by the spectacular entertainment," she would recall, "radiant with a kind of triumphant vengefulness, approving, applauding, lifting up their children so they would not miss this historic occasion: 'Look here, Karle, look, they're burning down that Jew-church . . . Wake up, Frieda, come, take a good look.' "

Her husband, the rabbi, had run into the fire to save the Torah rolls, but could retrieve only one, the smallest. Then Max and Ruth walked back home down Kurfürstendamm in a drizzle, broken glass crunching under their shoes, leaving behind a scene "for which a Rembrandt might have mixed the colors out of fire and night, with the weird palette of a Hieronymous Bosch supplying the faces."

By no means all gentiles were applauding. Shortly after midnight, police *Oberleutnant* Wilhelm Krützfeld, fifty-eight, the gaunt and laconic chief of Precinct 16 in the city's working-class Central District, had been awakened by a call at home. Collecting a squad of his officers and a document he thought he would need, he rushed to Oranienburger Strasse. Adjoining the office building at No. 28 that housed the main offices of the Jewish Community stood Berlin's most imposing temple, with 3,000 seats. Although completed in 1866, it was still called the New Synagogue.*

Storm troopers had already set several fires, and the flames were spreading quickly from the wedding chapel. Brandishing the document that had designated the temple a historic site decades earlier, Krützfeld ordered the troopers to desist, and they did. Then he phoned the fire department and stood fast while the blazes were extinguished.

That afternoon the temple's chief rabbi, Malwin Warschauer, sixty-nine, was phoned at home.

"This is your police precinct," said an unknown voice. "*Herr Doktor,* the Gestapo is on the way to your house to arrest you! Leave immediately!"

After hiding six weeks under a bogus name in the Jewish Hospital, the rabbi was able to flee to England. Chief Krützfeld, disgusted by anti-Semitic brutalities, took early retirement.

Karola Ruth Siegel, ten years old and always the tiniest in her classes at school, was watching from the window of her apartment on Brahms Strasse in Frankfurt as her father boarded the truck of the men in black uniforms and big boots. Once the owner of a wholesale textile business, Julius Siegel had been eking out a living as a gardener at the Jewish cemetery. On the sidewalk he turned and spotted his daughter upstairs.

"He tried to muster a smile," she remembered, "and waved as if

---

* Partially bombed out in a November 1943 British air raid, the synagogue was scheduled to be rebuilt by 1995 for a princely $50 million, its three blue-and-gold-tinted domes dominating the neighborhood.

to say, 'Things will be all right.' That was the last time I saw my father."

The last time she saw her mother and grandmother, they were running, running frantically along the station platform and waving goodbye as "Rola" and 100 other Jewish children left on a rescue transport for Switzerland. That was on January 5, 1939. Her father was in a camp. Her synagogue was burned down, her school closed.

Rola Siegel became Ruth Westheimer, better known as Dr. Ruth, the New York sexologist and television personality, still the smallest in any group. Her parents were deported to Lodz, Poland (called Litzmannstadt by the Germans), and she believed that they died later in Auschwitz. She could not be certain, however. They disappeared as if they had never existed.

In Edenkoben on the Rhineland's Southern Wine Road, my father's lovely native village, Heinz Mayer, also ten, was awakened by a rain of glass pounding into his bedroom. Outside, men were yelling, cursing, and laughing, happy to be breaking all the windows of his parents' home, and at dawn several local storm troopers burst in—Heinz knew them all—and took his father to the town jail.

The authorities decided not to burn down the synagogue, erected in 1827; too many homes were too close. Instead, Party men ransacked the interior and carted off the Torah rolls and everything else movable. Sturdy young Brownshirts from the Reich Labor Front camp in Edesheim arrived and began to tear down the building brick by brick. Teachers marched entire classes to the scene to watch history in the making. The town band played patriotic tunes.

On the market square the furnishings that had been ripped out of the synagogue were turned into a big bonfire. Young people danced around it. At the nearby monument for the dead of World War I, a group of Party men with chisels were obliterating all Jewish-sounding names.

That afternoon storm troopers instructed Heinz and his mother to pack no more than ten pounds of belongings apiece and to hand over the house keys. Then they were taken to the market square, where all the other Jewish women and children were assembling.* Buses were waiting, festooned with placards bearing slogans: "Jews, Get

* Mistreatment of Jews in small towns tended to begin at an earlier time and turn more violent than in the large cities. During the Crystal Night arrests, few women were molested in the big population centers because the capacity of the concentration camps was still too limited.

Out!" and "Free Trip to Palestine." Heinz wondered whether he was really going to Palestine.

They were joined by a bus bringing the Jewish males from jail, and as a mob yelled its approval, the little convoy containing all of Edenkoben's forty-one remaining Jews and their Party guards moved southward. They were not bound for Palestine, however. After traveling about thirty miles and crossing the Rhine, the convoy stopped on an open field near Karlsruhe and the Jews were told to get out.

Heinz Mayer heard a shrill whistle, and there stood a familiar figure in uniform: Dr. Leibrock, the lawyer and Edenkoben's Party boss. "Listen, Jew mob!" he shouted. "Edenkoben is now free of Jews! Don't any of you dare to set foot in Edenkoben again. If you do, you'll be shot on the spot. Understood?"

Heinz heard the whistle again. The nearly empty buses left. Some of the women and children began to cry.

The next day the city fathers received an expense account marked "Cost of Jew Transport" for 39.52 marks, including 4.39 marks for thirteen beers and two glasses of wine. The bill was paid out of the Jewish Community's welfare fund.

Two days after *Kristallnacht* Ernst Cramer, twenty-three, was fighting for breath among the dazed men jammed into a truck headed from the Weimar railroad station to the Buchenwald concentration camp. The truck normally held twenty-eight. That morning more than sixty Jews aged eighteen to seventy had been herded into the vehicle by SS men swinging truncheons, steel rods, and rifle butts.

Tall and muscular, Cramer was from Augsburg, where his father struggled to eke a living out of a cigar store. His mother's people had lived in Augsburg since the fifteenth century and were distantly related to my "Uncle" Max, my mother's second husband.

For all of November 12, Ernst Cramer, his father, and the other new Buchenwald arrivals stood, immobile as statues, on the muddy parade ground. Whoever moved was beaten by rubber truncheons or hung from posts by the hands, handcuffed in back. When the weak collapsed, other prisoners dragged them to the washhouse, which that day became a mortuary. At nightfall the new prisoners, over 10,000 of them, were driven into five makeshift barracks. Some had to sleep on top of others.

"During the night many went crazy and suffered from fits of raving," Cramer remembered. Two were drowned by guards in the latrine. The next morning Ernst was assigned to the detail that carried the dead into the former washhouse. This continued to be his chore during the month he spent in the camp, famished, thirsty, his head shaved.

When prisoners with emigration papers were discharged, Cramer could produce an affidavit from American relatives guaranteeing he would not become a public charge. He had to sign a paper certifying that he had been "correctly treated," and was put on a crowded train. His shaved head, hollow cheeks, and filthy clothes gave him away. People knew where he came from. A stranger rose and gave Cramer his seat. Later, Ernst found that a sandwich and a shiny Reichsmark had been stuffed into his overcoat pocket.

His mother tried to get his father released by going to see the *Herr Justizrat* who until then had been a friend and the family attorney. *"Frechheit!"* he yelled at her. "Insolence! How dare you come into my office!" Eventually, however, he was released.

In April 1942, the Gestapo came to get the parents and Ernst's younger brother, Erwin. Clothilde, the longtime maid whom they could no longer pay, stayed behind and reported Erwin's farewell: "Pray for us!"

Withal, Crystal Night evolved into a public relations defeat for the Nazis because it turned out that the brutalities triggered revulsion among the majority of rank-and-file Germans. Documentation of this boomerang effect would pile up from eyewitness reports to the *Deutschland Berichte,* published by the exiled Executive Committee of the German Social Democratic Party in Paris, and, more significantly, from massive soundings of the Goebbels Propaganda Ministry's public opinion research.

But all of that emerged later, much later, and never affected events since German public opinion carried no weight in 1938 and was therefore largely irrelevant.

For Stella, her parents, and every other Jew who had still hoped to avoid the pain of uprooting and to come to terms with Hitler's reign, Crystal Night meant the abrupt, unmistakable curtain to an illusion. Since all the destruction had shocked so many Germans, a semblance of normality was allowed to return for a while. Stella's father came out of hiding; hot meals were again prepared in the Wilmersdorf apartment. Still, the stench of smoke seemed to linger, the memory of shattering glass and the frenzy of the looting all bespoke violence, threat to life. *

---

* Although I had left the scene the previous year, the din of glass smashing onto sidewalks somehow left a mark on me. During a research trip to Berlin in 1988, as

They had to get out—fast, at once! And some 160,000 still managed to flee Germany and Austria after November 1938, almost all of them within the year.

Stella's father too was finally jarred into action to save himself and his family. He wrote to his cousin Leo (formally: Leopold Adolphus) Ellenburg on Maple Avenue in St. Louis, Missouri, pleading for the affidavit of support required with his American visa application. He needn't have worried. Leo, who responded at once, wore many hats, all energetically. Once he had been a dentist, then he sold insurance, then stocks, and he often traveled to Europe, uncommon in those days. Having inherited money from his father, he was well-off and generous. He spoke excellent German, visited Germany frequently before Hitler, and so he went to work on behalf of the Goldschlags with his customary verve, assembling documents, calling downtown offices that might help, soliciting advice from St. Louis friends who were trying to rescue relatives of their own.

It was getting late for Stella, very late, and fear for her life settled in her mind as a permanent companion.

I was walking to cash a check at the American Express office off the Kaiser Wilhelm Memorial Church, my ears were assaulted by the distinctive sound of fifty years before. I stopped, terrified. The memory had been triggered: *Kristallnacht!* It was only workmen removing a shop window for replacement.

BOOK 2

THE GREAT DIVIDE: GETTING OUT OR GETTING STRANDED

8. 1939:
Trying to Escape

THE YEAR WAS 1939, Hitler had ignited World War II, and Stella was singing Cole Porter and Hoagy Carmichael. As the chanteuse for a six-piece band of Jewish teenagers, she was their offering of glamour and spice. The group's director was her boyfriend, soon to be her first husband, Manfred Kübler, blond, clean-cut, a Jewish boy from her neighborhood, whose parents knew the Goldschlag family but distrusted Stella. They thought she was too interested in the Kübler wealth.

Manfred was a master at the accordion and also good at the guitar and the saxophone. The group took music seriously. Many weekday nights the players met for rehearsals in the home of a band member, Hans Sonntag, on Wilmersdorfer Strasse. On weekends they played for dancing at parties in Jewish homes. It was risky. The Goebbels propagandists were denouncing American music as decadent, so the Jewish partygoers loved it with extra enthusiasm.

They adored Stella's thin but pretty soprano and admired her magnificent shape. At seventeen, she was a star. Oppression or not, war or not, Goebbels or not, the stranded Jews were still dancing.

Stella, Manfred, and their musicians learned tunes and lyrics from records they had collected at home, and their repertoire was ambitious. They knew "Stardust," "In the Still of the Night," "St. Louis Blues," "Me and My Shadow," "Jeepers Creepers," "September in the Rain," "Toot-toot-Tootsie, Goodbye," and quite a few more.

The cognoscenti could still get illicit records in the locked basement of Alberti's music store, the hangout of a gentile jazz buff named Hans Buthner, known as "Herr Hitman" because he seemed to know every hit there was. Some thirty jazz lovers had been listening to recordings reverently in the back of a café since 1934. They called their dingy meeting place the Blue Room and named themselves The Berlin Hot Club. One member, a Jewish lad named Francis Wolff, was already versed in Jelly Roll Morton, Benny Moten, and McKinney's Cotton Pickers, and would soon cofound Blue Note Records in New York.

For Jewish and gentile jazz fan alike, the passion for this music was a symptom of protest and resistance against the Nazi establishment. "We always said that anybody who liked jazz could never be a Nazi," said Hans Buthner. Even though everyone pronounced it "yutz" (rhymes with "nuts").

For Stella "yutz" meant more than political dissent. She was adopting it as a high-spirited accelerator of the transition toward adulthood, a career move. It still seemed she would emigrate to the United States. She wanted to take Manfred along—Uncle Leo Ellenburg in St. Louis was so informed—and they were going to start a band there, just as at home. She was going to be a smash as a "yutz singer," just as in Berlin but paid in dollars. Music spoke a universal language, and they were *au courant* with Herr Hitman's latest tunes. Even their English pronunciation, mimicked from their 78-rpm recordings, was passable.

And Stella's vision featured a quite specific role model. She was Josephine Baker, the ultimate in yutz and the hugest of hits in the Berlin of the 1920s—she of the banana-peel costumes, fondly remembered for the fabulous voice, the slinky looks. It didn't make much difference that she was black. Since Germans knew almost no blacks, antiblack prejudice was one bigotry that wasn't widespread. Blacks were interesting, even admired. Only Hitler seemed to turn his back on Jesse Owens when he won the 100-meter dash at the 1936 Olympics—a famous victory and a famous snub, unpopular even among Germans. I was present, watching through my father's binoculars.

La Baker was also the perfect model because she was from America, Stella's promised future home. Germans of the twenties and thirties, and especially educated Germans like the Goldschlags, held America in childlike awe. *Amerika!* It was the promised land that everybody talked about, that everyone called "the land of unlimited possibilities."

The streets no doubt were not actually paved with gold, but they seemed to be. Certainly everyone was pretty dazzling; one knew this from the movies of Fred Astaire and Ginger Rogers. Where else did ordinary people have access to skyscrapers and Hollywood? Why would a shrewd and wildly successful Berliner like Marlene Dietrich desert even before Hitler and move to a foreign country? Because it was the country of the future. And also the country of jazz, starting with Al Jolson in *The Jazz Singer,* another American star celebrated among Germans.

The magnetism of Amerika overcame even Gerhard Goldschlag's blanket rejection of jazz. Stella's father hated the stuff. Its rhythms made it the antithesis of the elegiac lieder he composed. Father and daughter squabbled about this difference in taste. It was the traditional generation gap in action, Stella's first trip out from under the parental wing, her budding independence. It was also the last time she was optimistic, really exuberant, about her life, her own seemingly unlimited possibilities.

Her father encouraged her show business talents, and these included dancing. My elementary school crony Harry Nomburg remembered attending an evening's entertainment at the Jewish *Kulturbund* on Kommandanten Strasse shortly before he left town at sixteen on a youth transport bound for England. There stood little Herr Goldschlag, conducting the band and beaming at his Stella in front row center, one of about a dozen trim young women performing in leotards. Harry would not recall the music, just Stella's name and figure.*

Stella's shape also made her a striking attraction at Feige and Strassburger, a suddenly booming art school operated by two Jewish partners on Nürnberger Strasse, behind the big, expensive KaDeWe department store. Not that Berlin needed more artists. The school did instruct students seriously interested in art, though for most of the new enrollees the establishment served as camouflage, a boondoggle to while away time pending emigration.

With so many occupations barred to Jews, many were learning a craft. It was sensible preparation for their future lives as refugees abroad, a status that Stella and many others were still expecting to attain. There weren't going to be ready jobs in Montevideo or Chicago for German-trained bankers and lawyers.

Stella, having always had an eye for stylish clothes, decided to

---

* Notwithstanding her revulsion at the mere mention of anything Jewish, Stella's name, along with the names of her parents, remained registered on old rosters of *Kulturbund* members shown at a Berlin exhibition in 1992.

spend two years at the school ostensibly to learn fashion drawing. Her talent proved to be limited, her interest in learning a trade was nearly nil, and she never worked in fashion. Nevertheless, she called herself a "fashion artist" for thirty years. Early in the war, this cover kept her out of forced factory labor. An aunt paid the tuition.

Actually, her studies earned Stella pocket money—nine marks per hour—for posing as a model in the nude. Her fellow student Regina Gutermann, whose figure did not qualify her for such work, liked and admired Stella. Regina was one of the students who attended the school *pro forma*. She was filling in time while hoping for a visa to Chile or Bolivia.

"I thought she was so beautiful," Regina recalled, "such a Rubens figure! Her walk was sexy and it didn't look posed. She had a sweetness in her speech—she was class."

Sweetness and class were not Stella's principal attractions for her fellow student Guenther Rogoff, also seventeen. He had ambitions of becoming a serious artist. He also hoped he might coax Stella to become the first girl to sleep with him.

This was not an uncommon fantasy among the young men at the Feige and Strassburger School, so Rogoff never got as far as striking up a private conversation with the object of his desires. She seemed permanently blockaded by an impenetrable thicket of admirers. In addition to his classes, Rogoff took private lessons from an elderly male artist, and once he persuaded Stella to pose for him in the master's studio. Alas, she would not take off her clothes and would not be drawn into talk of personal matters.

By the spring of 1939, Berlin's remaining Jews—they still numbered 80,000—were in the grip of naked terror. Hitler's panzer divisions and Stuka dive-bombers were about to tear into Poland. France seemed likely to fall next. The Jews ranked high on the Führer's unfinished agenda, and his man Eichmann was getting ready to seal off all emigration exits. Jews of small means were the most endangered, and that included Stella and her parents in their little apartment on Xantnerstrasse.

Lack of money was not their only obstacle. Cunning, connections, luck, and infinite persistence were also essential, although as yet the gates remained ajar. More than 75,000 Jews* fled Germany that

---

* In 1937, 23,000 Jews had left the Reich; in 1938, 33,000. After 1939, the escapes slowed dramatically. In 1940, there were 15,000. In 1941, the last year of flight, 8,000 still made their way out legally.

year, an all-time record, and the Goldschlags had at last become reconciled to joining the exodus. Nevertheless, they still felt torn, particularly the father, so their decision-making remained slow, much too slow.

For young people like Stella, loopholes were still available. Our school principal, "Lore" Goldschmidt, had once been an exchange teacher in England. Operating with her usual flair and making the most of her breezy manner and competent English, she had acquired enough fans in the stodgy British education establishment to obtain accreditation for her little Berlin school as an admissions center for Cambridge University. Stella felt that this move also enriched her personal status, and told everyone that Goldschmidt's was an "English school." That sounded aristocratic.

Spurred by *Kristallnacht*, Frau Dr. Goldschmidt again leaned on her British connections and persuaded London's Chief Education Officer, as well as that functionary's brother-in-law, a clergyman in Folkstone, Kent, that the Goldschmidts should be rented two villas in the Kentish countryside. Just as war was about to break out, Lore Goldschmidt managed eventually to transfer eighty of her Berlin charges to the new Kent campus.*

When her school invited Stella to come along to the British campus, another series of fierce arguments erupted in the Goldschlag household. As in many Jewish families, it was the wife and mother, Toni, who had been pushing for emigration all along. She could see disaster ahead if they stayed home. The father refused to split up his little family and part from his only child, his beautiful daughter, even when Stella became furious at not being allowed to leave for England.

Affenliebe, monkey love—blind, automatic, reactive, clinging— was what she called her father's possessiveness, though only behind his back. She felt cozied by her parents' love and chafed under it at the same time, unaware of the paradox.

Although he had been persuaded by his Crystal Night experience and the pleas of his women that the *Vaterland* had become an unsafe place, Herr Goldschlag agreed to become a deserter only if all three went together and only if they could gain admission to the United States with the help of Uncle Leo.

. . .

* Kent was still not far enough to get away from Hitler. In May 1940, he followed the Goldschmidts there by bombarding Folkstone from the nearby French coast at Calais. Along with the students of the local British schools, the Goldschmidt refugees were evacuated by the government to emergency quarters in Wales.

"The Americans were guiltier than the goddamned Nazis," Stella was to say, and her indictment was not irrational.

The spirit of Evian, the international strategy that slammed the doors in the face of Jewish emigration, was striking home with more and more families like the Goldschlags as they caught the exodus fever and learned the specialized lingo of the emigration maneuvering.

"Quota" was no longer an impersonal bureaucratic concept for Stella. And "visa" was no longer a piece of paper. They were lifelines. Daily existence focused on their promise, especially the warranty of the visa, the exit permit. And the ticket to the ticket was another magic wand, another term never heard before—"affidavit," the notarized guarantee from an American of documented substance, preferably a close blood relative, that the emigrant-to-be would never, absolutely never become a financial burden to the United States government. All of the sponsor's income and assets had to be set forth as a bond.

Stella's well-to-do uncle in St. Louis had done more. He had gone to Washington, trying to speed up the bureaucracy. And he sent money for three steamship tickets—an uncle worthy of the great Uncle Sam.

It wouldn't do, it wouldn't do at all. The blow fell early in 1940. After standing in line most of the day, little Gerhard Goldschlag had elbowed his way through the mob of supplicants into the American consulate at Hermann Göring Strasse 21, near Unter den Linden, to be given the verdict. He ranked about 52,000 in the waiting line. The registration number currently being processed was about 38,000. His family's turn would come in roughly two years.*

Goldschlag was devastated, but the pleasant, German-speaking American official took time to console him. *"Ach,"* he sympathized, "you'll see, two years pass so quickly."

That was the face of the kindly Uncle Sam. His other, glowering self came in the mail. It was a form certifying every applicant family's number on the registration list, and it concluded with the following "warning" in German: "Make no travel plans! Physical examination will only be administered after many years! Restrictions are very severe! Prospects are extremely slight! Unfortunately, inquiries cannot be considered in the meantime."

---

* Only 21,000 refugees were permitted into the United States from 1940 until mid-1945, which was 10 percent of the number admissible under the immigration quotas.

The word "many," denoting the years of waiting to come, was printed in boldfaced letters.

Of course, the Goldschlags proceeded to make travel plans anyway. After standing in many more lines and experiencing tremendous luck, Stella's father booked passage on the U.S.S. *Escambion* on October 14. The vessel would leave from the last free port of Western Europe, the continent's last little corner of freedom and hope: Lisbon in neutral Portugal.

Realizing that the warning of the American consulate might prove all too real, Gerhard Goldschlag reached out for alternate routes, too. He gave 400 marks as a down payment to a lawyer—a "Jewish lawyer," Stella would note—for a visa to Santo Domingo, but the lawyer never delivered. And Goldschlag stood in line endlessly again, finally getting inside the Palestine Office at Meineke Strasse 10, to face its staff of ardent Berlin Zionists.

These harried ideologues practiced their own brand of inside anti-Semitism. The schism between Zionists and non-Zionists had always been wide and vocal among Berlin Jews, and the pressure for survival had escalated the intramural hostility. The bureaucratic formations on Meineke Strasse—only two of these officials would survive the Holocaust—viewed nationalist German Jews like Gerhard Goldschlag with reservations rivaling his own.

Trekking to Meineke Strasse with strong misgivings, he was received there in the same spirit. As he reported the encounter to Stella, he was asked outright whether he was a Zionist and he snapped, "No!" The Palä Office people were entitled to wonder what this man was doing trying to wheedle a scarce berth for his family to go to the promised land. Fear of death wasn't enough to qualify: everyone had that. Places on ships to Palestine were so few.

They had their own agenda on Meineke Strasse. They had a nation to found and wanted to populate it with energetic pioneers, enthusiasts for labor outdoors. For them, they maintained rural agricultural camps, rugged prep schools only for the young, which the Nazis authorized until 1942 and where furniture and utensils were labeled in Hebrew so the prospective kibbutzim could pick up the language.

The voyages to Palestine, all illegal, for people without visas, were seaborne obstacle courses seeded with fatalities. A Viennese lawyer, William R. Perl, the principal organizer of sixty-two such trips, did manage to rescue an estimated 40,000 Jews, mostly with the help of the Palestine intelligence service, the Mossad.

One such transport, leaving Holland in July 1939, had carried 500

German Jews aboard the barely seaworthy little S.S. *Dora,* but mostly this grossly unsafe fleet carried refugees from Eastern Europe. A listing of their fates would read like pages from an odyssey of Job: sinkings, shipwrecks, captures by the British Royal Navy, explosions, torpedoings followed by machine gunning, vanishings without a word. The miracle was that one refugee would run this gauntlet alive, let alone 40,000.

Excluded from the deadly race to the Holy Land, the Goldschlags remained, in the last analysis, dependent upon the good graces of that flawed Messiah, the politician Franklin D. Roosevelt. He, quite personally, was the source of the two-faced American policy toward Europe's Jews. With one face he flashed his famous smile and expressed sympathy to worried delegations of Jewish leaders who came to plead with him, and he denounced such Hitler outrages as Crystal Night as unprecedentedly "barbaric" and intolerable. Yet five days after he preached this well-publicized piety, he fixed his other face on Congress and the depressed American economy, and refused again to extend the immigration quotas.

For his actual immigration policy the President relied on channels, his State Department. There, in "Foggy Bottom," the paper channels flowed from Assistant Secretary of State Breckinridge Long. Long was no household name. He did better: he was a wealthy aristocrat from Kentucky, a longtime good friend of the President's, a powerful political supporter and campaign contributor.

The President's wife, the peripatetic and influential Eleanor, called Long "anti-Semitic" to the President's face. FDR bristled and told her not to say such things, which didn't cause her to desist, because she was in fact being charitable. Long was no ordinary anti-Semite. He detested Jews and conspired against them mostly because he was convinced that they conspired against America and all that the Breckinridges and the Longs had valued over the centuries.

Like the Nazis, Long linked Jewish internationalism to communism and was hyperfearful of both. In his diary he railed against his hated fantasy, a fancied chain of saboteurs: "the communists, extreme radicals, Jewish professional agitators, refugee enthusiasts." And more. Long poured out his soul against "bleeding hearts" who wanted to infest his America with refugees. These "radical boys" he damned as "Frankfurter's boys," adherents of the Jewish Supreme Court justice Felix Frankfurter, who were "representative of his racial group and philosophy."

If this sounded much like the sentiments of Hitler himself, the kinship was not accidental. As Breckinridge Long saw Judaism,

Hitler was on the right track in *Mein Kampf*. Long called the Füh-rer's work "eloquent in opposition to Jewry and to Jews as expo-nents of Communism and chaos." In Long's view, immigration was an invitation to more chaos: "It is the perfect opening for Germany to load the United States with agents."

So on June 29, 1940, the State Department instructed all embas-sies and consular offices in a circular cablegram to withhold visas from aliens about whom they had "any doubt whatsoever," even though "quotas against which there is a heavy demand will be un-derissued." In his diary, Breckinridge Long recorded: "The cables practically stopping immigration went!"

The impact was swift. On July 16, an Associated Press dispatch from Berlin reported that several refugees who were about to receive visas had suddenly been turned down after encountering "a new line of questioning which was evidently based on fears in America of 'fifth column' operations."

Young Rabbi Max Nussbaum of the *Friedenstempel* and his wife, Ruth, expecting their visas any day, were panic-stricken, not only for themselves but for the many others still in line, including their congregants, the Goldschlag family. The Nussbaums heard that visa applicants suddenly faced written examinations, a new hurdle, and some of the questions were so esoteric that people were "flunking" in large numbers.

Mistakenly, Rabbi Nussbaum blamed one man. He thought that the culprit was a local American official "who sabotaged the entire emigration" and became "the greatest misfortune for the Jews in Berlin."

The rabbi had no way of knowing it, but the American who was laying down the new rules was an emissary dispatched from Wash-ington by his boss, Breckinridge Long. He was another obscure but fearful functionary, Avra M. Warren, forty-seven, director of the State Department's Visa Division, and Berlin was only one stopover on an extraordinary four-month European swing as Long's enforcer.

Broad-shouldered, broad-faced, thin-lipped, and formal, Warren had been consul at posts all over the world for more than twenty years. Most recently he had been inspector of the entire Foreign Service, the perfect representative of a State Department character-ized by a Jewish congressman as having "a heartbeat muffled in protocol." And protocol had finally placed the land of the Statue of Liberty just about out of reach of the "huddled masses yearning to be free."

One afternoon in mid-August, during Warren's stop in Vienna, a refugee worker from the American Friends Service Committee, Margaret E. Jones, was summoned by him to be briefed on the new policy.

"Miss Jones, you Quakers will be doing a straight relief job for the non-Aryans from now on," said the diplomat from Washington. "No more non-Aryans to go to the U.S.?" inquired Jones. Yes, that was it. Was Congress behind this? No, it was the President's doing, said Warren. He "just did not want any more aliens coming to the U.S. and would like to have it closed, especially for aliens coming from Germany."

The President had long been digging in his heels to resist the pressure of Jewish refugees, even reconciling himself to unusually adverse publicity. No details leaked about the Avra Warren mission, but the dramatic fate of the S.S. *St. Louis* had escalated into a worldwide spectacle with nearly two weeks of devastating and suspenseful headlines.

The luxury cruise liner of the Hamburg-Amerika line ("You travel well on Hamburg-Amerika" was its slogan) had departed from Hamburg on May 13, 1939, with more than 1,100 refugees bound for Havana. The Cubans refused to let them land. After days of on-and-off negotiations by Jewish aid organizations in Havana, Washington, and New York, the *St. Louis* stood by east of Bermuda while Jewish leaders pulled every political string they could find in the American capital, hoping that the ship would be allowed to dock in the United States.

The verdict came to the vessel by wire on June 9. The appeal had gone all the way to Roosevelt. He rejected it with the comment that the matter had to go through channels, in this case the immigration authorities. The officials there, in turn, said that they had received no instructions.

The President would not acknowledge two telegrams from the passenger committee of the *St. Louis*. Other telegrams addressed to FDR were routed routinely to the State Department, which responded that the destiny of the wandering vessel was "a matter for the Cuban government." A last-ditch effort by Secretary of State Cordell Hull to intervene with the President personally also failed.

Stella's future was involved. It was shortly afterward, at a party in Berlin, that she would meet Manfred Kübler, her first husband, born five weeks before her. Manfred had been a refugee aboard the *St. Louis* with his mother, Nanette (Netty), forty-two, and his father,

Kurt, forty-six, who held an engineering degree, owned a surveying company, and was partner in a department store operated by relatives.

When the *St. Louis* steamed back to Europe with its despairing passengers, more rounds of negotiations ensued between Jewish aid organizations and any governments that might possibly be persuaded to take on flotsam rejected by Cuba and the United States. The pace was frantic; the Hamburg-Amerika line wanted its ship back from its abortive thirty-seven-day "Voyage of the Damned"—as American filmmakers would call it when they eventually transformed the trip into a soap opera starring Faye Dunaway.

When the paperwork settled, Holland had agreed to accept 181 passengers; Belgium took 215; France took 227; and at the very last moment, following appeals to No. 10 Downing Street, Britain gave shelter to 284. That took care of 907 homeless. The remaining 200-plus, unacceptable to the various governments for one bureaucratic reason or another, were returned to Hamburg and the mercies of the Nazis.

The Kübler family was among this remnant of the damned. They returned to their miraculously still-vacant apartment at Schlüterstrasse 25. (Their travels would continue. In 1943, Manfred was shipped to Auschwitz, where he died within two weeks, on May 5. His father was taken to the Mauthausen concentration camp in Austria and shortly thereafter executed "while trying to escape." The mother was transported to Theresienstadt and then to Auschwitz to be gassed in 1944.)

In Berlin, rumors of alternative havens kept churning through Jewish ranks when the *St. Louis* returned. Paraguay was supposedly opening up. From Mexico it was possible to get smuggled across the U.S. border. New Zealand was said to be worth trying for. And there was always Shanghai, the last resort. No visa was required there, but it was like going to live in a poorhouse on the moon.

Money was sometimes helpful. A Cuban diplomat offered the Jewish *Hilfsverein* 1,000 passports for $1,000 each. The aid society turned down the deal, mostly because it didn't have the funds. The consul general of Uruguay became so affluent from the trade in documents that his government recalled him because word of his greed had spread. Prices kept rising. Someone heard that someone had bought a genuine Panamanian visa for 10,000 marks, and this was probably not idle talk. In September 1939, the author Erich

Maria Remarque, Stella Goldschlag's former neighbor in Wilmersdorf, had arrived in New York aboard the *Queen Mary* on the strength of a Panamanian passport.

The racket in fake promises kept growing. More and more frustrated travelers forked over more and more cash for nonexistent documents whose sellers then disappeared.

Refugees with specialized skills were in demand abroad. "Help Wanted" notes in the bulletin of a counseling service were so selective, however, that they looked like mockery. In the Fiji Islands, a Jewish pastry baker was welcome, also an unmarried watchmaker, no younger than twenty-five and no older than thirty. Paraguay looked for a candy maker. British Bechuanaland had room for a fur repairer. In Central Africa there was a demand for an unmarried butcher specializing in the production of cervelat sausage. And in Manchukuo a cabaret was searching for a Jewish director who would need to double as a ballet dancer and a ballet master.

Stella Goldschlag's new vocabulary kept expanding. Beyond "quota," "visa," and "affidavit," everyone learned about the *"Zertifikat"* from the British authorities to enter Palestine; the Reich Flight Tax that had to be paid to the Nazis as an exit fine, often equal to a family's entire assets; and the "certificate of harmlessness" required before one could cross the border.

Everybody spoke knowledgeably about the alphabet soup that represented the growing list of enemies and friends. Himmler's RSHA *(Reichssicherheitshauptamt),* the national headquarters of the SS, was the villain of villains. HIAS (Hebrew Immigrant Aid Society, pronounced "hee-us" in German) could help at times to clear away some obstacles; so could *"der Yoint,"* the Joint Jewish Distribution Committee. Both organizations were headquartered in New York and maintained offices with American staff in Berlin until the United States entered the war after Pearl Harbor in December 1941.

In many ways the most cheering ally was *"der Lift."* It was not an elevator, and in the transportation industry it was called "Jew crate." Through 1939, refugees were allowed to take along most of their furniture and household goods, shipped in an enormous sealed van, often painted red.

"It is like a big room without windows," reported Bella Fromm, purged as diplomatic correspondent for the *Vossische Zeitung,* Germany's closest equivalent of *The New York Times.* Her lift to New York cost the staggering sum of 2,500 marks, empty, but that included bribes to obtain it at all.

"Three officials of the Foreign Exchange Office are checking and rechecking every item that goes in, down to the last pot," Fromm wrote, and all was subject to a 200 percent ransom.

To pick up her prized visa after the usual waiting, Fromm joined the line in front of the American consulate at seven a.m. The doors opened at nine o'clock. Her turn came at ten minutes to one. Because of her status as a lapsed journalist, she was no stranger.

"I was ushered in to my good friends, DeWitt Warner and Cybe Follmer, who regarded me with astonishment. 'For heaven's sake, Bella! Why didn't you have someone announce you?' "

"I didn't want any special privileges," said Fromm.

The tension dissolved in ecstasy.

"There was a whirlwind of good wishes, hugs, farewell kisses, and back-slapping," Fromm wrote. "When I found myself outside, the American visa in my hand, I had to sit down on the stone steps and cry in my grateful happiness. Again and again I looked at the document. I caressed the red silk cord that secured the pages. I actually kissed the golden seal."

Fromm was a most unusual refugee. She had "special privileges" and knew it, and refrained from using them. This was especially remarkable because, increasingly, privilege was a crucial key to survival as the time drew near when all remaining legal escape hatches would be shut. The other essential element was simply luck, random luck.

Stella and her family had neither. In the immigrants' lottery of winners and losers, their fate was set.

For the lucky ones, the leavetaking was painfully long, uncertain, and laden with Jewish awareness.

On Passover, April 22, 1940, Rabbi Nussbaum presided over the Seder in his apartment. "We were sure it would be our last one there, but not quite so sure where the next one would be—or if there would be a next one," he would write.

The guests managed a smile as each handed over the price of admission, an egg from the black market to celebrate the normally happy hard-boiled-egg ceremony. This year, hearts were heavy and the symbolism of the Seder could not have been more evocative.

"It was an authentic one, closely akin to the first, the original Seder of our forefathers in Egypt," Rabbi Nussbaum reflected. "If ever it was easy to follow the commandment of the Haggadah to feel as if we ourselves had been part of the Exodus, it was then. Each of us had an invisible 'bundle on our backs' and a 'staff in our hands,' not

to speak of the anxiety in the hearts and the tension of the nerves—
the insignia of a Jew marked for the Exodus, that tragically recurring
scourge of a homeless people."

Hanneli, the rabbi's daughter and the youngest at the table,
chanted the *Mah Nishtana,* the prayer of the Four Questions.

Rabbi Nussbaum was very moved. He remembered: "I was
tempted to answer not, 'What makes this night different?' as the
traditional first question goes, but rather, 'What makes this night
similar, so terribly similar to previous nights in our history?' "

And the future? The rabbi looked from guest to guest. "My heart
was heavy when I pronounced the ancient prayer which is more a
sigh than a prayer: *'L'shanah habaah be'Yerushalayim'*—'Next year
in Jerusalem'—to which each one, I am sure, added silently his own
prayer: . . . or in America . . . or anywhere in the world, only away
from Germany!"

9. Last Stopover
to Freedom

"Papers! Papers! Papers!
. . . Occupation: waiting, waiting, waiting . . ."
—Gian Carlo Menotti, *The Consul*

I T WAS A TIME OF FAREWELLS long remembered and goodbyes ardently desired but never consummated, not by forsaken families like the Goldschlags.

When the film *Casablanca* opened on November 26, 1942, at Warner's Hollywood Theater in New York, one scene in particular moved the normally haughty critics to raves. Ingrid Bergman and her resistance hero husband, Paul Henreid, were leaving Casablanca from its dark, deserted airport. Fog and a Gestapo convertible were closing in.

Ingrid's lover, Humphrey Bogart, trench coat tightly belted, snap-brim fedora pulled into his face at a rakish angle, was seeing her off. It was hard not to feel one's eyes moisten when he muttered, "Here's lookin' at ya, kid," and the plane soared into the night to Lisbon and freedom.

Everyone knew about Lisbon and the ships leaving for America. Erich Maria Remarque researched the scene from the transient's perspective he personified, the same fate that Stella's father had instinctively feared, and my father and other fathers: the rootlessness

91

of the refugee, questioning his acceptability, ever poised to move on. Remarque was wealthy, he was not Jewish, he lived in the best hotel in Beverly Hills and made a twosome with Marlene Dietrich. And still, he remained a refugee, melancholic, drinking too much, calling himself homeless.

"I travel with light luggage," he wrote. Nobody understood refugees better. Their vicissitudes obsessed him; they were his own. Until his death in 1970, his novels would deal with little else.

About the vessels casting off from Lisbon during the war he wrote that each was like an ark of biblical times, the great flood rising daily. October 14, 1940, had been the scheduled day of farewell for Stella and her parents. It came and went. Their ark, the *Excambion,* sailed from the port in the Tagus River, leaving the family behind, their precious tickets lapsed.

Their lifesaving papers had not been processed by the American consulate on Hermann Göring Strasse, would never be issued—not to any of the damned with registration numbers in the 52,000 range. The pieces of paper with rubber stamps in English, the life belts held together by red silk cord and kisses, had become the preserve of a new, last-minute aristocracy of the saved.

A new injustice, made in America and worthy of Stella Goldschlag's contempt for American policy, had further narrowed participation in the lottery: Washington had issued a new list for tickets to the refugee ark. It exempted certain personages from the immigration quota, and a mysterious committee of peers in America could secure a place on the list for you if you were an artist or scientist or intellectual of prominence. Prominence was the key.

In his best-seller *The Night of Lisbon,* Remarque, the former newspaperman from Berlin Wilmersdorf, registered indignation by way of Schwarz, his protagonist.

"As if we hadn't all been endangered," Schwarz says bitterly, "and as if a person wasn't a person. Isn't the difference between a valuable and an ordinary person like differentiating between [Nazi] supermen and non-persons?"

Schwarz is talking to a fellow refugee, soul-searching through the night in a bar off the Lisbon docks. They have only one set of husband-and-wife tickets, but there is still time to argue the morality of the new American admissions roster.

"They can't accept everybody," the narrator says reasonably.

Schwarz favors a noble standard for handpicking the selections.

"Why can't they take the most abandoned?" he asks. "Those without name and fame?"

The Goldschlags might have asked the same question in their own behalf. But these were romantic speculations after the fact, and from a novelist spinning stories. In the deadly competition of 1940, Gerhard Goldschlag's lieder didn't count. He was an artist, right enough, but not *prominent,* and therefore unworthy of rescue.

Some privileged travelers didn't need a place on any list. When Bill Shirer of CBS went to the Lisbon office of the American Export Lines some weeks after Stella's ark departed, he was able to speak with a manager who promised him space on the next trip of the same ship. Shirer was saying farewell to his European beat after sixteen years away from home. The shipping line was engulfed in bedlam.

"The office was jammed with a mob of refugees—jittery, desperate, tragic victims of Hitler's fury—begging for a place, any place, on the next ship," he wrote in *Berlin Diary.* The manager explained that 3,000 stranded souls were milling about in Lisbon. The boat carried only 150 and there was just one per week. Shirer did not ask for favors. He didn't have to. He was an American *and* prominent, a star on the radio. You couldn't be better qualified to exit Europe.

Hans Habe, the Hungarian correspondent at the Evian Conference who had unmasked Hitler as Schickelgruber, arrived in Lisbon shortly afterward in a white Talbot sports car with a wide leather strip tied across the hood, a pile of pigskin luggage strapped onto a rack in the rear. A small, bright red Bolivian passport identified him as Juan Becessi.

Habe hounded the aid committees and smuggler headquarters like the rest of the stranded, not bothering to look in on the American consulate until he met an attractive young Frenchwoman at his hotel who headed a Unitarian refugee committee and recognized his name.

"Why are you still here?" she inquired. "A visa is waiting for you at the American consulate."

Habe, shocked by disbelief into rare silence, spent a sleepless night, raced to the consulate, and found his name listed as number 48 on the roster of the prominent. It was explained to him that President Roosevelt had created the "emergency visa" list administered by a committee that included the author Thomas Mann and the physicist Albert Einstein. He did not learn until later that it was Eleanor Roosevelt who had browbeaten the President into this venture, and that the selection—so similar to the life/death selections in the death camps—had been the work of refugee underlings whom Habe had never met but who were evidently familiar with his recent novels. These works had been slight, but weighty enough to classify Habe as "prominent."

He left Lisbon on November 20 aboard the S.S. *Siboney.* The ticket was financed by the *Yoint,* the Joint Jewish Distribution Committee, Habe being broke as usual. Broke but lucky.

Rabbi Max Nussbaum and his wife, Ruth, had arrived from Berlin somewhat earlier, also panicky and also needing the *Yoint* desperately. Nussbaum had been admitted to the ranks of the prominent because he was a man of the cloth, well connected and articulate. The Nussbaums had affidavits and visas, ship tickets, and a little cash from relatives in Switzerland. The rabbi even had a job waiting in Muskogee, Oklahoma; his new congregation was expecting him for the high holidays.

Representatives of the *Yoint* met the Nussbaums at the station. Then: catastrophe! Their visa was no longer valid. It had expired the day before their arrival. Nobody had explained that it was good for exactly four months minus one day—by State Department fiat. The latest regulation required lapsed clients like the Nussbaums to reapply to Washington for renewals, causing weeks and possibly months of delay and uncertainty.

One avenue of appeal existed. The people from the *Yoint* managed to get the Nussbaums an appointment with the American deputy consul, and the despairing couple gained entry into the consulate past crowds that seemed to have been sleeping through the night in front of the door.

"You have to give me ten minutes," pleaded the boyish-looking rabbi when he was ushered in to see the equally young diplomat, Taylor Gannett.

The deputy consul told the rabbi to take his time. He said his father had been a minister and he himself was all in favor of importing more religion into America. He would renew the visa on his own authority. Later, it developed that he was only in Lisbon for ten days of temporary duty.

During their own two weeks in Lisbon, the Nussbaums were jolted by their idyllic environment: the scents of a million flowers, the permanent sunshine, the easygoing flow of the locals across the 3,000-year-old city's hills—not seven bluffs, as legend has it, but two dozen of them—the gentle Mediterranean life that seemed never to release the Portuguese to go to sleep, certainly not until long after midnight. After Berlin, the relaxed Portuguese ambience and the food—the food!—it was all hard to accept as real.

Luck. A refugee needed luck.

More than 10,000 refugees were sluiced through Lisbon by aid organizations, including 1,200 by the Emergency Rescue Committee of New York, whose imaginative amateur organizer, Varian Fry, thirty-three, an editor of scholarly journals, arrived with $3,000 taped to his leg. Under his guidance, such artists as Marc Chagall and Max Ernst, writers Franz Werfel (*Song of Bernadette*) and Lion Feuchtwanger, outfitted with fake papers, hiked across the Pyrenees or were handed from guide to guide through various fragile underground railways, Feuchtwanger disguised as an old woman.

The philosopher Hannah Arendt, who would analyze "the banality of evil" in her classic *Eichmann in Jerusalem*, escaped via German-occupied France and had to wait three months in Lisbon before the HIAS relief organization was able to provide her with a ship ticket to New York. William Perl, the organizer of illegal ships to Palestine, having been taken from a Berlin-bound Nazi deportation train because he tried to commit suicide and almost bled to death, persuaded a priest in Salonika, Greece, to get him a Portuguese visa.

In the humidity of mid-July, new instructions delivered by Avra Warren, the State Department visa chief, still making rounds to lay Washington's heavy hand on local consuls, succeeded in slowing down the Lisbon bureaucracy still further. The representative of the Unitarian Service Committee found Warren's functionaries even more "difficult to deal with," although they acted friendlier toward American gentiles than to Jews.

Bill Shirer and Ed Murrow of CBS were doing the casino in Estoril, on the ocean fifteen miles west of Lisbon. The luxurious spa resort, with its Victorian villas hidden by palms, eucalyptus, and pines, had long been a haven for monarchs who found themselves suddenly unemployed.

"The gaming rooms were full of a weird assortment of human beings," Shirer entered in his *Berlin Diary*, "German and British spies, male and female, wealthy refugees who had mysteriously managed to get a lot of money out and were throwing it about freely, other refugees who were obviously broke and were trying to win their passage money . . ."

The war remained close. Murrow received word from London that his brand-new CBS office had been bombed and destroyed by a German air raid, the old office having been similarly struck only weeks earlier. And on December 13, he and Shirer were saddened at having to say farewell to each other, breaking a bond grown strong in three years of covering the Nazis.

On the quay by the departing *Excambion,* they paced back and forth in the night until the gangway began to be pulled in. A full moon was bathing the wide Tagus as Shirer hurried aboard and Murrow vanished into the darkness.

At about midnight, Shirer wrote the final entry into *Berlin Diary:* "All the million lights of Lisbon and more across the broad river on the hills sparkled brightly as the ship slid down to sea. For how long? Beyond Lisbon over almost all of Europe the lights were out. This little fringe on the southwest corner of the Continent kept them burning . . ."

Berlin and the Continent had been so wonderful, Shirer reflected, "until the war came and the Nazi blight and the hatred and the fraud and the political gangsterism and the murder and the massacre and the incredible intolerance and all the suffering and the starving and the cold and the thud of a bomb blowing the people in a house to pieces, the thud of all the bombs blasting man's hope and decency."

And it was only Christmas 1940, nearly three years before Stella was cornered into making her choice, her survival pact with the devil, even longer until her verdict that "the Americans"—Breckinridge Long, Avra Warren, and yes, the sainted Franklin D. Roosevelt —"were guiltier than the goddamned Nazis."

Were they? Certainly they had kept her away from Lisbon and from her Uncle Leo in St. Louis.

Stella and Author Peter Wyden
Growing Up in Hitler's Berlin

Stella Goldschlag at age 4, snuggling up to a cousin.

1

2

Stella in school, age 7 and already a subject of gossip.

3

Peter Wyden, a very German schoolboy in Berlin, age 11.

4

Hanukkah children's party at grandfather's house, Peter's beloved "Opi."

Hilarity on holiday: Peter with best friends, the Nomburg brothers, and his mother, 5 Leni (in car), clowning.

The Two Families

6

Gerhard Goldschlag, Stella's father, a failed composer.

7

Toni Goldschlag, Stella's mother, a singer who bossed her family.

8 Author Peter Wyden with father, Erich, and mother, Helen (Leni).

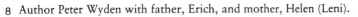

9

Peter and father enjoying
a joke.

10

The
grandparents,
stately on
vacation.

Peter's great-uncle Julius,
honored veteran of the
Kaiser's World War I.

11

12

Georg and Lotte Nomburg,
ill-fated friends of
Peter's family.

School for Refugees

13

14

The Goldschmidt School, oasis for Jewish youngsters within Hitler's madness. [RIGHT] Rudi Goldschmidt, school director's son, rides to sports victory.

15

Dr. Bandmann, the beloved music teacher.

16

Isaak Behar, last Goldschmidt student left in Berlin.

17 Frau Dr. Leonore Goldschmidt, dynamic and much-admired school director.

Manfred Kübler, Stella's
first husband, a boy
from the neighborhood.

19

18

Stella, "the Marilyn Monroe of the Goldschmidt School," relaxing in the
leisure scene at Lake Wannsee.

Way Stations to the "Final Solution"

20

"Clou" night club and theater where Hitler [INSET] made his Berlin debut.

21

23

Royal Hotel at Evian, on Lake Geneva, hosted refugee conference that opened the way for the Holocaust horrors organized by SS Chief Reinhard Heydrich [RIGHT].

25

The Holocaust was administered from here, Kurfürsten Strasse 115, headquarters of *Judenamt* IVB4, bossed by Adolf Eichmann [ABOVE].

24

27

Deportees bound for concentration camps were assembled at former Jewish Home for the Aged, Grosse Hamburger Strasse 26. Eichmann's "best" assistant, Alois Brunner [LEFT], made the rules.

26

28

29

Stella was tortured in basemen of local Gestapo office on Burgstrasse. SS *Sturmbannführer* Erich Mölle [ABOVE] promised her status o honorary Aryan.

31

Pathology building of Jewish
Hospital, Schulstrasse 79, was
Stella's Gestapo base, ruled by
Kommissar Walter Dobberke [ABOVE].

30

Gad Beck and sister Margot, Jewish resistance activists,
got to know Stella all too well.

33

32

Hertha Eichelhardt Wolf
talked Stella out of Gestapo
allegiance.

34

Yellow star designated Jews as outcasts.

36

Rabbi Max Nussbaum longed for "next year in Jerusalem."

35

Synagogues were torched on "Crystal Night."

Trains, thousands of trains, carried Jews to the East and death. Most were herded into freight cars.

37

Stella's War

Stella, then notorious as
"the blonde poison."

38

39

"The beautiful couple,"
Stella and Rolf Isaaksohn,
catchers on the prowl.

40

Grete Moschner
spirited Stella
out of Berlin.

Sergeant Peter Wyden and his adoring *Mutti*, Helen.

Master propagandist Hans Habe [EXTREME LEFT], flanked by author Wyden with "Habe Circus" at Radio Luxembourg.

Stella's Daughter

Heino Meissl, putative father.

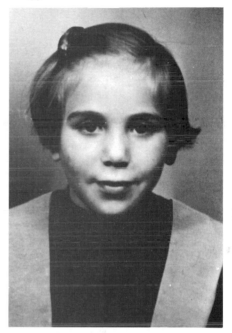

Yvonne, the orphan.

Natan Celnik and wife tried to adopt Yvonne.

Yvonne, Israeli frontline nurse.

47

Branded as collaborator,
her hair shorn.

48

Staatsan_al
fordert für
Stella Kübler
15 Jahre
Zuchthaus

Nr. 147 · 81. Jahr / Berlin, Freitag, 28. Juni 1957

Marching into
court with white
gloves, 1957.

Do. Berlin, 28. Juni
Fünfzehn Jahre Zuchthaus bean-
tragte gestern der Staatsanwalt im
Schwurgerichtsprozeß gegen Stella
Kübler-Isaaksohn. Die auf Grund
des Urteils eines sowjetischen Mili-
tär-Tribunals von ihr verbüßte

With fourth husband,
after the wedding,
hoping for whitewash
and a financial windfall.

49

Stella today,
a bored,
lonely insomniac.

50

"You see, Hitler, you didn't win!"

51

Rabbi Leo Baeck in Theresienstadt camp.

52

Major Pat Dolan, Baeck's rescuer.

54

Author Wyden's cousin Siegfried survived the war in hiding and married Lucia.

Moritz and Esther Zajdmann (Seidman) attending Berlin opera in 1992, nearly half a century after Stella arrested them there.

53

10. On the Brink

SEPTEMBER 19, 1941—Stella and all others who lived through it would never forget the date—was a landmark of segregation and shame, a forerunner of the "selection" process in the concentration camps, the drill that would soon begin to decide, by flick of hand, who would live and who would die.

Starting September 16, no Jew was to be seen, in public or at work, without being marked by a large yellow Star of David as an emblem of identification and blemish. The pariah symbol had to be sewn on, not pinned. It had to be visible high on the left side of the chest. It was *verboten* to cover it up by holding a handbag or a package or anything else over it. Each Jew had to buy a minimum of four stars at the Jewish Welfare Office. Nobody would remember the price except that the stars were not cheap.

"Fair game, fingered!" was the reaction of Klaus Scheurenberg, who remembered Stella from school as a superior athlete like himself. "The star seemed as big as a plate and to weigh a ton." He felt naked—targeted, vulnerable, embarrassed.

Some of his gentile fellow citizens took a kinder view. Each morning at 5:20, Klaus had to take the subway and then walk more than an hour to the Otto Kolshorn factory in the suburb of Niederschönhausen. At eighteen, he had been conscripted to help cut and impregnate wooden railroad ties. (Among the other Jewish laborers were one rabbi, two bank directors, two university professors, and numerous lawyers and engineers.)

In time, he found himself riding every morning with some of the same gentile passengers, and they took to greeting each other with a sleepy *"Guten Morgen"* or, in Berlinese, *"Morjn."* On his first day wearing his star, Klaus, feeling "like a thief," automatically boarded the usual car and dared only to whisper, *"Morjn."* The greeting echoed back in an unusually loud chorus.

Klaus kept standing. "Why don't you sit?" demanded one of the regulars.

"Can't," said Klaus, "it's forbidden for me."

"Ach, Quatsch," snapped the man, annoyed. "Sit down!" *

Inge Deutschkron, who would eventually survive in hiding, received the same command in a more crowded subway full of strangers. "I ask you to sit down immediately!" a little man barked loudly to the star-wearing teenager, rising and pointing to his seat.

Inge had other kinds of experiences as well. Shopping during a winter snowstorm, she and her mother were accosted by a shopkeeper who handed each a broom and demanded: "Sweep the sidewalk!" It was a random impulse to humiliate Jews, any Jews.

As the women began to work, Inge suggested that they sing, and they did. The shopkeeper, furious at this outwardly cheerful form of protest, tore the brooms away and yelled, "Get out of here!"

In a letter home the future American ambassador George Kennan, then at the consulate in Berlin, was indignant at the *Judenstern.* "That is a fantastically barbaric thing," he wrote. "I shall never forget the faces of people in the subway with the great yellow star sewed onto their overcoats, standing, not daring to sit down or brush against anybody, staring straight ahead of them with eyes like terrified beasts . . . As far as I could see, the public was shocked and troubled by the measure . . ."

For Stella, to be branded by the star seemed a particularly traumatic injustice. Why should she be publicly exposed, identified as a Jew, when she didn't look or feel Jewish? Ironically, she and Manfred, also blond and blue-eyed, would occasionally be stopped in the street by passersby who asked why they wore the *Judenstern* when they obviously weren't Jewish.

Manfred and Stella had married that October, both nineteen, both drafted for factory work, drawn together by puppy love, ambition as musicians, and resentment of their Jewishness, and wishing to legitimize their sleeping together so as not to offend their parents. It was a hurried ceremony at Wilmersdorf City Hall. In lieu of a wed-

---

* Scheurenberg would survive Theresienstadt weighing seventy-eight pounds, unrecognizable to his family.

ding trip the pair took the subway downtown to receive the blessings of Manfred's father, who was serving time in the ancient Moabit police prison. He had been arrested on a trumped-up charge involving a black market purchase of some butter.

Eventually, at great risk, Stella stopped wearing the star except at work, freeing herself at least somewhat from the yoke of her detested heritage. It was a liberating act, like shedding handcuffs, and it impressed her that such an effortless gesture of protest empowered her to join the envied Others, the protected, the majority, the in-group; that she could pass and find comfort in the ranks of those who were born lucky—the voluntary gentile Hitler slaves who did not look or act enslaved.

She had converted herself to the status of a Christian for fourteen hours a day. The other ten hours, six days a week, she was a robot, an "armaments Jew," a star-bearing forced laborer. There were still 21,000 Jews toiling for the German war effort in large and small factories all over Berlin, according to the census of Armaments Directorate III. They earned 50 pfennig per hour, more or less, about half the normal pay, and were consigned to segregated toilets like Negroes in the American South.

Stella stood bent over her machine in section 133, one of the two "Jew departments" of the Elmo Works at Siemens, grinding parts for electric motors. Elmo was no mere factory. It too was a cog, a link in a ninety-five-year-old industrial empire, one of the world's great conglomerates, spilling across its own city, Siemensstadt near Spandau, employing more than 80,000 human ants scurrying around the clock on behalf of "final victory" in Hitler's total war.

Work was deadening, hunger on the curtailed Jewish rations was incessant, the cause was despised, and so friendships and cliques formed easily among these toilers. Yet Stella joined no one, keeping to herself for nearly two years. Co-workers like Ernst Fontheim regarded her as stuck-up, on guard against contamination from the rabble. "She wasn't one of us," said Margot Levy.

Section 133 held an ultrasensitive secret. Even the gregarious Fontheim, son of a wealthy attorney, never became aware that among its approximately 100 laborers was the nucleus of an anti-Nazi resistance cell, the Herbert Baum Group of later legend. Mostly passionate Communists, like its leader Baum, who also acted as the section's official "Jew spokesman," these were children of working-class people, about half of them women. The core group that formed at Siemens numbered about thirty, including recruits from other plants. Their average age was twenty-two. In May 1942, they attempted to blow up an anti-Soviet propaganda exhibit in the Lustgarten, and

while the damage was negligible, all were hunted down and immediately executed.

Like Ernst Fontheim, Stella knew none of this. Unlike him, she
would not have wanted to know. "I was never interested in politics,"
she would recall. Keeping to her machine, she was safe, at least for
the time being, while many others were not.

Georg and Lotte Nomburg, parents of my schoolmates Fredi and
Harry and for so long unwilling to follow their sons abroad, could
no longer avoid leaving their beloved Berlin. They reported past the
SS guards to "the Levetzowstrasse," the "Liberal Synagogue" at
Levetzowstrasse 8-9 in the Moabit district, in late October 1941.
Herr Nomburg, the businessman who panicked when a car was
driven a bit too briskly to suit his conservative soul, was filled with
foreboding.

Not that the Nomburgs feared for their lives. The monumental
synagogue with its 2,000 seats, only blackened by the *Kristallnacht*
fire, had been commandeered as the first "collection camp" for Jews
about to be deported. Nobody yet whispered of gassings. They were
going to be used as slave labor somewhere in the East, that was all,
although working conditions would be very grim.

The cold would be bitter in the East, everyone knew. The Nomburgs wore layers of the best and thickest winter clothing they still
owned—furs and fur collars had had to be surrendered by all Jews
some time ago—and they took some solace in the comforting surroundings of a synagogue, though they were not familiar with this
particular temple. It was too far downtown. As an affluent family,
they had attended the synagogues farther out toward home, in the
fashionable West End: on Fasanenstrasse, Pestalozzi Strasse, and
Prinzregenten Strasse.

In the fall of 1941, the Levetzowstrasse house of worship presented a woeful picture. More than 1,000 men, women, and children
had to sleep like animals on straw on the icy marble floor or in the
seats of the women's section upstairs. Still, it was a house of God.

"Come, House of Jacob, let us walk in the light of the Lord," were
the words of the prophet Isaiah chiseled in Hebrew above the four
massive columns out in front.

Deportees walked in darkness, however, usually driven to the
doors in the anonymous closed furniture vans preferred by the Gestapo to hide their efforts from the civilians. The coyness was futile.
The synagogue towered over the corner of Jagow Strasse, an always
busy intersection near the NW 87 post office. Its camp was the first

of the Holocaust's Nazi secrets that were no secrets. Who could overlook the trudging, silent queues of families bent by rucksacks and overstuffed suitcases?

From the outset, any casual passerby knew what was happening. Heino Meissl, a thirty-two-year-old film company publicity man and Lothario-about-town, soon to become enmeshed for life with Stella Goldschlag Kübler, often visited one of his girlfriends, Ingeborg, who lived nearby. He saw the silent people all the time when he went home around midnight.

"I had no doubt they were Jews," he recalled. Ingeborg and her mother told him the whole neighborhood whispered about them. "The loading was almost noiseless," said Meissl. "The entire happening was downright ghostly."

Within, the Nomburgs and their fellow voyagers dozed or squatted on luggage or munched bread-and-butter sandwiches shipped in by the Jewish Community ladies' auxiliaries. And they lined up to pass by long tables behind which clerks had set up large laundry baskets that kept filling rapidly.

"Work papers, bread coupons, tax documents, and money had to be handed over," remembered one of the deportees, Dr. Karl Loesten. "Then came a body search, and after that the luggage was ransacked and shamelessly robbed."

Jewelry was taken, as well as any remaining money, and soap, and chocolate or other bits of food or alcohol. Then came a final bureaucratic stab.

"A court bailiff handed me a document," said Dr. Loesten, "declaring that all my assets had been confiscated because I was an enemy of the State."

The Nomburgs learned that they would leave in two or three days. Their destination would be Litzmannstadt (Lodz), Poland. Word had circulated for some time about wholesale deaths there, mostly from starvation.

The Nazis had a pragmatic motive for putting on pressure to drive as many Jews as possible out of Berlin at that time. Loyal gentile families were being bombed out of their homes and "Jewish apartments" were needed for them. The drive to seize this housing was the responsibility of Hitler's favorite architect, the brilliant Albert Speer, then still Inspector General of Buildings and soon to become Reich Minister for Armaments.*

---

* At the time of Speer's death in 1981, this best-selling author's success at self-rehabilitation stood unique. A Party member and intimate of Hitler since 1932, Speer planned the staging of the giant Nürnberg Party rallies, designed the Führer's

In his office journal Speer kept track of the eviction campaign like a zealous mortgage banker gleefully rubbing his hands at a mounting record of foreclosures. In November 1941, while trains carrying the Nomburgs and hundreds of others were rolling to Lodz, a third major wave of evictions was netting Speer about 3,000 apartments, considered a respectable achievement. Soon his Resettlement Division reported: "A total of 23,765 Jewish apartments have been vacated."

Speer knew that he was seeing the results of this "vacating" as he passed the Grunewald freight station in his limousine en route to his ministry. Crowds of people were milling about under SS guard. While his recollections were generally vivid and would eventually fill two books totaling more than 1,200 pages, Speer's memory of the Grunewald station was less precise than, say, playboy Heino Meissl's impressions of the camp at the Levetzowstrasse synagogue.

"I knew that these must be Berlin Jews who were being evacuated," Speer would write. "I am sure that an oppressive feeling struck me as I drove past. I *presumably* had a sense of somber events." (Emphasis added.)

Waiting in the Levetzowstrasse synagogue for assignment to a train, Georg and Lotte Nomburg faced a single alternative.

"Was there any possibility of evading deportation?" That question was asked at the Eichmann trial. Hildegard Henschel, wife of the Jewish Community chairman, responded as an eyewitness.

"Only suicide," she testified.

"The suicides started immediately before the first transport to Litzmannstadt, and the number increased very rapidly. People took Veronal, some of them took potassium cyanide . . . " About 1,200 killed themselves, just in Berlin, between October 1941 and early 1942.

Barbiturates traded at fantastic prices. Ilse Rewald had a woman friend who sold a Persian rug for 1,000 marks and invested all the proceeds in Veronal. Her suicide attempt was successful. Many were not. The Jewish Hospital set up a special section for the failures, and

---

chancellery, and, as chief of all war production, became Germany's largest employer. Thousands of slave laborers in concentration camps were among his work force. He served all twenty years of his war crimes sentence after the war, yet through artful reconstruction of his record, he died a respected historian, almost a self-made anti-Nazi.

Dr. Hermann Pineas, the head of neuropsychiatry, felt bad for the attending internists.

"They were of a divided mind about whether to try saving these patients or to let them go to sleep quietly," he recalled.

As spirits sank in the Levetzowstrasse synagogue, some normally timorous women decided to end their fears even without pills. They climbed on the balustrade of the upstairs women's section and jumped to the marble below.

Whether this was too easy a way out, or a way too hard, the Nomburgs did not choose to take it. They would brave Litzmann-stadt. It was not an uncommon resolution. A man might get nervous being driven in a car, yet rise above his fear and remain steadfast at the prospect of starving or freezing to death in the Litzmannstadt ghetto.

But first the Nomburgs had to run the gauntlet of their gentile neighbors, the *Volksgenossen*. The deportations had moved into the open. For the most part, only the aged and the smallest children were permitted to ride to the freight stations in covered trucks or furniture vans. The others marched, five and six abreast, through the night for three or four hours, many of the women in tears, all clutching orange-colored paper bags containing farewell sandwiches from the women of the Jewish Community auxiliaries. Ordinary city police escorted the columns. Some of the marchers managed brave smiles.

Hilde Miekley, a gentile secretary, was watching. "Unfortunately, I must report that many people were standing in the doorways and expressed their pleasure at the sight of such a train of misery," she remembered.

"Lookit, those insolent Jews!" she heard someone shouting. "Now they're still laughing, but their last hour has struck!"

At the Puttlitz Street freight station, Herta Pineas, the psychiatrist's wife, wearing a white armband, helped with the boarding of the trains. She was one of eight remaining from the original corps of forty sandwich makers. The others had been deported. Use of public transport having been forbidden for Jews, she had been issued a special permit to ride the subway to her temporary job.

At the trains she saw sick passengers being loaded on their stretchers. A young man with paralyzed legs was riding on the shoulders of his elderly father. Gestapo officers yelled and kicked deportees from the rear to make them move faster. One agent wielded a steel prong that had materialized out of a walking cane at the touch of a button.

Some deportees wore light summer clothing because they had been under "investigative arrest" since summer.

Intimidated by earlier Gestapo instructions, Herta Pineas felt guilty when she refused to accept farewell notes for families being left behind. It would have been too dangerous to perform this last favor. The Gestapo men acted like kleptomaniacs possessed. A mother lost her baby's carriage—deemed an excessive luxury. And when a big down pillow was slit open and some gold pieces were found, clouds of feathers wafted over the station platform. They were still dancing in the wind when the train left for Litzmannstadt.

11. "Everything Is Being Surrounded by the SS!"

THE BOWLEGGED LITTLE SS MAN appeared in the courtyard of the former Jewish Home for the Aged at Grosse Hamburger Strasse 26 one afternoon in October 1942 and told the assembled Jewish *Ordner* that a new regime would take effect in what would shortly become Stella's home. Vienna had shown the way; it was *judenrein.* Berlin was next. The cleansing was moving too slowly. He had his orders. He had done the job in Vienna.

It was Adolf Eichmann's right hand, Alois Brunner. A Viennese accent had once been considered light and amusing in Berlin, along with the equally stereotypical Austrian sloppiness and the kissing of hands. But there was absolutely nothing jolly about this gnomish dignitary, surrounded by several SS types he had imported from Vienna.

Effective at once, all *Ordner* would work around the clock, he announced. Rules at Grosse Hamburger Strasse, converted into a predeportation *Lager* to supplement and eventually supersede the Levetzowstrasse synagogue, were much too lax. All inside doors were now to be locked. The kitchen was to be ripped out to create more sleeping places on the floor. Toilet doors had to go. In fact, all furnishings had to be removed—within twenty-four hours.

There was only one way to meet that deadline. Frantically administrators and *Ordner* labored through the night to heave everything movable out of the windows. It rained beds, chairs, wardrobes, tables, until the place was barren, Brunner-style, fit for sow Jews, and

Prussian sows at that. Austrians detested the arrogant Prussians, a loathing that went back to the old days, along with happier memories of Vienna's thick whipped cream that vanished in Hermann Göring's guns-not-butter campaign.

The *Ordner* corps was also an innovation introduced during what the Jews termed the "Brunner time," and it was patterned after the labor force Brunner had pioneered in Vienna. The *Ordner* helped to cordon off entire blocks and search apartment houses for hidden Jews. Jewish leaders had to rise and remain standing whenever a person "of German blood" entered the room and had to maintain a distance of at least two paces.

Brunner had brought along several Jewish *Ordner* from Vienna. They knew his drill. *Ordner* were to wear red armbands. If they refused to serve or helped anyone escape, they would be summarily shot, Brunner announced, and their families would be loaded onto the deportation trains east.

The Brunner time had begun on Yom Kippur. Berlin's chief rabbi, the revered Leo Baeck, was in the middle of the morning sermon at the small Joachimstaler Strasse synagogue when the phone call came. Moritz Henschel, the chairman of the Jewish Community; Philipp Kozower, the deputy chairman; and Martha Mosse, the director of the housing department, were to report at once to "the Burgstrasse," the feared headquarters of the local Gestapo.

Brunner's "evacuation" scheme was a bit much, even for the SS official who briefed the leaders. "I'm sorry I had to tell you this on the Day of Atonement," he said. And he let them sit down.

A few of the Jewish functionaries found a way to go on strike when faced with having to execute Brunner's orders of self-destruction. They killed themselves, as did Siegfried Falk and his wife because they were supposed to help with the roundups. Most leaders and their deputies, however, went along numbly with the new rules of the Brunner time. Long afterward, some of these unwilling collaborators still defended their acquiescent conduct.

"It appears astonishing to me with what self-possession and stoical calm the [Jewish administrators] let themselves be forced into the deportation work by the National Socialist authorities," one docile participant mused. "I recall clearly the evening in which a hundred of the employees of the Jewish Community and Jewish institutions were called together in the meeting room and given the job of bringing together an orderly list by profession and age from material the Germans gave them. I belonged to those who had to check over these lists. These were the lists for the first group of deportees. The work on these lists lasted deep into the night and another day . . ."

Eichmann, Brunner and Company had done their work well on these pained and honorable Jewish functionaries-turned-collaborators. These deputies saw to it that there would be lists, "orderly" lists, constantly more lists of more prey. They admired the "self-possession and stoical calm" of the doomed. And they followed their leaders. Much as Nazi leaders would excuse themselves after the war, these Elders saw themselves as helpless "little men."

"You can ask, how could you do this work?" said one of the Berlin Jewish leaders when it was all over. "We could not determine whether we had done correctly. But the thought we had was that our doing this would be milder and easier for the Jews being deported than if the Nazis did it."

And so "correctly" too.

Chief rabbi Leo Baeck went along but agonized harder. "When the question arose whether Jewish orderlies could help pick up Jews for deportation," he recalled, "I took the position that it would be better for them to do it, because they could at least be more gentle and helpful than the Gestapo and make the ordeal easier. It was scarcely in our power to oppose the order effectively."

Indeed not, for when Brunner threatened with shootings, he had to be taken literally. In late October, he had ordered a "Community Aktion"; many of the remaining employees of the Jewish Community were to report for deportation. Some failed to appear, so Brunner had eight leaders arrested, and on December 2 all were shot.

As reward for his latest success, Brunner was again promoted and sent off in late January 1943 to repeat his performance, this time to accelerate the roundups in Greece and France. Among his colleagues in Berlin, his example lingered on.

Despite such efforts, the overall execution of the Final Solution remained a vexing assignment for Eichmann and his helpers. It would take three years for the administrative pace to quicken and explode into a flood of gassings.

The administrators had lost interest in emigration during 1940. It was much too slow; the unwelcoming attitude of the nations assembled at the Evian Conference had seen to that. On October 26, 1941, the SS had declared its patience exhausted. A general prohibition of emigration went into effect.

By no coincidence, a faster alternative had just become available.

The first efficient gassings with Zyklon B poison had been administered experimentally the previous month in an extermination camp barely completed near an unheard-of village, Auschwitz, west of Cracow in Poland. The innovation broke the bottleneck.

By March 1943, Berlin's Jewish population was down sharply to 27,250; by April, to 18,300; by June, to 6,800. On June 19, Goebbels, shading the truth only slightly, declared the Reich capital cleansed of Jews.

The Berlin-to-Auschwitz train schedule had hit its stride on January 12, 1943, when 1,210 Jews were "evacuated." On January 29, another 1,000 departed; then another 952 on February 3; 1,000 on February 19; 1,100 on February 26; 1,736 on March 1; 1,758 on March 2; 1,732 on March 3; 1,143 on March 4; 662 on March 6. And so it went until fifty-seven trains had left for Auschwitz. Meanwhile, other trains fanned out to Litzmannstadt (Lodz), Riga, Theresienstadt, Bergen-Belsen, and additional death camps. Some fifty trains went to Riga alone.

The death trains—called "Jew transports" or *PKRs* in the jargon of the railroaders' memos—were the capillaries that pumped out the Final Solution. The heart of the pipeline network was known by the acronym *Gedob,* the Eastern Railway General Directorate in Cracow, where dispatchers joked about the ultimate disposition of their human cargo as "soap distribution."

For the passengers, the hermetic agony of their journey became emblematic of their helplessness, a reflection of their lot. "I was *born* on that train and I *died* on that train," a survivor would summarize in retrospect.

The trains enjoyed distinctive status: exacting timetables of their own and right-of-way priority over all but troop trains. Still, it was obvious that the freight was deemed low-grade. Starting in 1942, the "normal" trainload for some destinations was increased from an average of 1,000 to 2,000 bodies, sometimes 100 per cattle car. The goal was to economize, even though the *Reichsbahn* billed the SS at sweetheart rates for this one-way travel: four pfennig per adult per kilometer; children under the age of four were transported free of charge.

Not one railroad executive would ever be convicted of his contributions to genocide, and the extent of the transporters' enlightenment about the doomed cargo did vary. In the context of wartime movements, the traffic did not stand out. Foreign armaments work-

ers were often shifted en masse. It seemed possible that Jewish families really were being resettled to do work for the war effort, and in
the lower echelons the movers of the Jews were deliberately kept
ignorant of the network's end purpose.

They did wonder about this no-return traffic. Auschwitz, they
speculated in their private gossip, must be a huge and bustling new
metropolis; so many trains went to this out-of-the-mainstream destination and came back empty.

The traffic statistics were carefully compiled and preserved by Eichmann and his helpers to document their administrative success story.
And within this record of population movements—following up the
new pace set in the "Brunner time"—the most spectacular achievement was the "Factory Action," unique and always remembered, of
February 27, 1943, against Berlin's dwindling supply of "armaments
Jews"; some 11,000 had not yet been sent to the trains.

After more than a year at Siemens, Stella had been transferred to
work the early shift, again six days a week, ten hours a day, at the
Erich and Graetz munitions plant in the Treptow district. She
punched a drill press. Her mother worked a press in the same section. Her father usually worked the night shift. Her husband
Manfred labored in a construction outfit in Borsigwalde.

The Jewish rumor mill known as "mouth radio" worked overtime
in late February. Father Gerhard Goldschlag told his wife, Toni, that
some major *Aktion* was said to be brewing. Tense consultations
came to dominate life in the two-and-a-half-room apartment at
Xantnerstrasse 2, which Stella and Manfred by then shared with her
parents, paying 60 marks of the 130-mark monthly rent.

Nothing could be done, the parents decided. To leave Berlin was
impossible; all roads and means of transportation required papers
unavailable to Jews. To live illegally underground, identity and food
ration cards were necessary and also unavailable. More crucially,
what was lacking was the will, as Stella noted in retrospect. Some
Jews were sneaking on foot across the Swiss border. Not Gerhard
Goldschlag.

"My father was a dreamer," she would say. "He refused to believe
that people killed people." Especially Germans who loved Schubert.
They would not harm a lieder writer who lacked all interest in politics and had fought in combat during the Great War. It couldn't
happen. The notion was absurd.

Stella was no longer so sure. Normally she still went along with her parents' views on all important matters except jazz. By then, hardened in more than four years of Total War, she had begun to wonder whether her father was too decent, too trusting to survive. She reconnoitered in the basement at Erich and Graetz and found a potential hiding place behind a pile of construction materials. Just in case.

Saturday, February 27, 1943, was a typically bleak Berlin winter day, although a bit milder than normal, somewhat above freezing. Toward nine a.m., a gentile friend sauntered into Stella's factory workroom, trying to look casual, and whispered, "Everything is being surrounded by the SS!"

Stella peered out of the window toward the main courtyard. Trucks were pulling up. Heavily armed SS men were jumping off. On the sleeves of their black tunics they wore bands identifying their unit: *"Leibstandarte Adolf Hitler,"* an elite outfit.

The gentile forelady was ordering Stella's group to assemble downstairs, and Stella reacted in an instant. Tugging her mother by the sleeve, she motioned her to tarry so they would be last to leave. Once on the stairway, they lagged still farther behind and thus were able to slip into the cellar and vanish in Stella's hiding place. They remained there until shift change and then strode past the sleepy guard at the gate by displaying the wrong sides of their identification cards, the ones not marked with a big purple *J* for *Jude.* That had been part of Stella's escape plan, but essentially the women were saved by something else: their hair.

Both were blondes, and Nazis still believed that Jews could not be blond.

Theirs was an incredibly daring feat, for there were no longer any exceptions to the Final Solution—just one overwhelming spasm whose operative edict was: *"Raus!"*

The remnants of Germany's Jews had fallen prey to a chain of appalling ironies. First, Hitler's obsessive hate had rendered them helpless by cutting off all efforts to flee. Then, their intelligence endeared them to the industrial managers who were starved for workers and became possessive of them as prize labor. At the same time, the enforced presence of the Jews grew increasingly offensive to the apoplectic Führer. They seemed to be mocking him! Again and again he had demanded that Berlin be purified, made *judenrein,* and still tens of thousands of these inferior beings were hanging on in blatant violation of his will. Enough!

So on September 22, 1942, Hitler had issued a sweeping command to another of his executioners, Fritz Sauckel, his labor commissioner, later to be hanged at Nürnberg. All Jews were to be removed from the armaments industry throughout the Reich. As so often, Hitler's spleen had triumphed over common sense. "The mouthings of our economic experts that they can't do without the so-called highly skilled Jewish labor doesn't impress him," gloated Propaganda Minister Joseph Goebbels.

Administrative follow-up came in December: arms factories were advised to prepare for the replacement of Jewish labor by foreign slave workers. What would happen to the Jews was obvious.

Stella's getaway was the more remarkable because the Factory Action, meticulously planned by Alois Brunner, was staffed by thousands of soldiers, cops, SS, and Gestapo men fielding 300 trucks, with every move supposedly coordinated as in an armored blitzkrieg sweep.

None of the targets were given time to retrieve lunch bags or overcoats. Women were hustled—sometimes literally thrown—onto trucks in thin work smocks. Boilermen had to leave bare-chested. Within a few hours the four temporary collection centers set aside for the occasion were bursting.

At that, the operation could have been sabotaged on a major scale, at least in theory. Jewish help was recruited by the Nazis to make all phases mesh, and in keeping with the Eichmann-Brunner policy of letting the Jews destroy themselves, Jewish Community leaders were officially tipped off. They were by then so frightened that they did nothing but follow orders.

On the morning of February 26, Moritz Henschel, the Jewish Community chairman, was summoned to the headquarters of the local Gestapo, Burgstrasse 26, and told to make arrangements for the next day. Five emergency teams of office workers were to be assembled with typewriters at the ready for the preparation of still more lists. The Jewish Hospital was to organize five first-aid teams.

The Jewish assistants were treated to immunity and issued yellow slips to save them from being carted away, too, at least for a time. Henschel did exceed his brief in one detail. The Gestapo had assured him that the deportees would be fed, but he didn't believe it. So he had "an army" of women deputized in the old age homes and in the Jewish Hospital to peel potatoes and clean carrots for the collection centers.

And still chaos erupted because in the end the raiders in their zeal decided not to limit themselves to factories. SS teams marched from house to house yelling, "Any Jews still living here?" and drove victims into trucks at bayonet point. In many apartments children and babies began to cry. Their parents had to leave them locked in while they worked in the arms plants. Now the mothers and fathers were packed for days into places like the huge entertainment hall, the "Clou," where Hitler had once delivered his first Berlin campaign speech, to await deportation once trains became available.

The Clou was emblematic of the Führer's career. When he spoke there in celebration of May Day (May 1) in 1927, his appearances had been sparking so many street battles that the police tried to keep peace by muzzling him with a *Redeverbot,* prohibiting him from speaking in public. So while the assembly in the Clou attracted 5,000 enthusiasts, it had been nominally "closed." Now Hitler was master of all within his reach.

The rear entrance of the Clou opened onto a courtyard overlooked by the offices of the official SS weekly, *Das Schwarze Korps,* Zimmerstrasse 88, and on Wednesday, March 3, 1943, several secretaries, "white with shock," stormed into the office of one of the executives, SS *Hauptsturmführer* Rudolf aus den Ruthen, and asked him to come at once. Down below, Jews were being beaten senseless, without apparent cause, by a man with a dog whip.

Ruthen watched the proceedings for himself with growing indignation and wrote a "Dear Comrade" letter the next day to his superior at Gestapo national headquarters, Prinz Albrecht Strasse 8.

"One truck had just left," he reported. "Another arrived. Jews stormed out of the 'Clou' on the run and tried to board the truck as rapidly as possible. It really couldn't have gone any faster. When half of the Jews were aboard, a civilian, a cigarette in his mouth and swinging a dog whip, came running out of the 'Clou' and beat like a wild man into the Jews who were pushing to get on. I must note that there were Jewish women with small children in their arms. It was a demeaning and embarrassing sight."

And not an isolated incident. As Ruthen told his boss, his secretaries later reported that the man with the cigarette continued to whip Jews boarding other trucks. "In particular, he hit women, and to such a degree that civilians in nearby buildings started shouting down. Whereupon the man with the whip yelled upwards that they were to shut the windows."

Ruthen criticized the procedure as "politically downright insane."

SS men who were more directly involved were enjoying the sights. "When we opened one of the trucks, an older woman fell into our arms, covered with blood and unconscious," recalled a nurse from the Jewish Hospital who had been detailed to a receiving center installed in the horse stables of the military barracks on Rathenower Strasse. "Behind her staggered a perhaps seventeen-year-old girl with blood streaming down her face. There followed a man bleeding from a leg wound. He was supporting his wife, whose dress was totally torn."

One of the SS men handed his rifle to a colleague and took photos. He was laughing.

In the stable, near panic prevailed among deportees separated from family members who had not been working in the same factories with them. "People were half insane with fear for their relatives," the nurse wrote. "They were begging for a place to urinate, for a swallow to drink, for a bit of straw so they could sit down because they had been standing for hours on the filthy, wet mud floor of the horse stable."

Among the elderly who had to entrain for the Theresienstadt camp was chief rabbi Leo Baeck, his heart aching because he had to break a vow. Earlier he had said, "I will go when I am the last Jew alive in Germany." It was not to be.

In the upper hierarchy of the Party, frustration lingered. "The Jewish problem in Berlin is still not entirely solved," Dr. Goebbels complained in his diary in March. Too many Jews had eluded the *Fabrik Aktion* after all. Like Stella.

Not so Stella's husband. Manfred was scooped up while doing his forced labor at a scrapyard in the outskirts of the city. Before he was driven onto an Auschwitz train, he managed to send word to Stella through an *Abholer* (fetcher). His message said he would eventually meet up with her at the Roscherstrasse home of friends, the Feilchenfelds. Nothing further was ever heard from him.

The very week of the Factory Action, I joined the United States Army, aged nineteen, and my feelings toward Adolf Hitler turned personal. The Führer had been Public Enemy No. 1 in my mind, a sort of supergangster guilty of crimes against worthy but faceless victims unconnected with my concerns. When I hit the induction center at Fort Dix, New Jersey, Hitler overnight became my Personal Enemy No. 1.

It was freezing and sleeting at Fort Dix. The cots in the drafty barracks were sardine-packed with unwashed, snoring men, all passing gas. My new uniform itched. The food was insufferably greasy. The inoculations hurt and gave me a fever. If it hadn't been for that bastard Hitler, I would have been snug in my big room in my mother's place above the White Russian colonel's horse stable on East Twentieth Street, doing homework for my night classes at New York's City College (Downtown) while I worked at the *Daily Metal Reporter* by day.

Miraculously, the Army whisked me to the edge of the Civil War battlefield at Gettysburg, Pennsylvania, and a chance to get back at Hitler. There my bloodthirsty feelings had plenty of company, for the destruction of the Führer was the number-one priority of everyone assembled at Camp Sharpe. A more highly motivated group of soldiers may never have existed.

In our muddy cluster of rotting barracks, long abandoned by President Franklin D. Roosevelt's Civilian Conservation Corps, the Army had installed its supposedly secret training center for psychological warfare. What was that again? I was as perplexed as our troops were later on in Normandy. They referred to us as "them psycho boys" and thought we were medics.*

It developed that we were combat propaganda units. Instead of shooting bullets, we were supposed to attack Hitler's armies with words fired via radio, leaflets, and public address loudspeakers. I was enchanted to be back in the word business, and my new company was excellent. These were not the drudges who served time with me on the *Daily Metal Reporter* back in New York. My associates were experienced writers, editors, and radio executives, plus academics from such exalted places as Yale and Stanford. A few had published best-sellers and strolled about lost in thought, looking superior. Most of these soldiers spoke halting and atrociously accented English, but all were at least bilingual.

"I shpeak zix languages," one wit said, "English da best."

Almost all of us were refugees, and since many were Jewish, Camp Sharpe was soon rebaptized "Camp Shapiro." We thought the Army was a nuisance, but we were deadly serious in our dedication to the anti-Hitler cause. Most of us worried about relatives still in German territory, their fates unknown, or about friends left behind, such as Stella.

---

* Until we finally became spectacularly successful at inducing Germans to surrender toward the end of the war, we remained unknown soldiers even at the pinnacle of the government. When one of our ranking propagandists, Wallace Carroll, was summoned to the White House to brief Roosevelt on psychological warfare, the President wanted to talk about censorship instead. Carroll respectfully tried to beg off. He said he knew nothing about censorship and resumed his pitch about psychological warfare. Undeterred, the President cut him off with questions about censorship. He didn't know or care about our esoteric specialty.

My new hero and, I suppose, father figure was our trainer and leader, Lieutenant (later Captain, then Major) Hans Habe, né Bekessy, the same Habe whose passion for bringing down Adolf Schickelgruber enlivened the Evian refugee conference in 1938. In the five years since then, Habe had blossomed into a glamorous international character. Having fought bravely in the French Army and escaped from his prisoner-of-war camp, he wrote one of the first great best-sellers of World War II, the autobiographical *A Thousand Shall Fall.*

His regal bearing suggested royalty. His uniforms adhered to him like a London tailor's fantasy. His numerous decorations included several we had never seen before. We hoped they were French. Habe's Budapest accent and the penetrating croak of his high tenor voice combined into a singular form of communication. One heard in it the commands of ancient Central European field marshals.

Habe was an unexpectedly patient teacher. He tossed off clever headlines like spitballs. He outlined assignments so no idiot could misunderstand. And his revision of scripts and articles taught me a central lesson that I would regularly try to din into other tin-eared writers when this came to be my job.

"Vere iss ze red thread?" Habe shouted in anguish when a manuscript lay festering before him, disorganized, begging for continuity and theme. "I vant to see ze red thread!" We heard that cry often. I hear it admonishing me now.

Our job was to invite desertion—not normally evidence of one's integrity, so we repainted treason as self-defense. Our leaflets showed the Germans phonetically how to call out "ei ssörrender" and encouraged them to come and see us, displaying our impressively designed "passes" signed by General Eisenhower.

War crimes were not part of our curriculum. What did we know and when did we know it? Of course we were aware—and so were most Germans—that Jews, other minorities, and political dissenters were tortured, starved, and sometimes shot in concentration camps. The fact that *millions* were slaughtered was unthinkable, unbelievable.

We *could* have known about the exterminations. The facts were too blatant to remain covered up. Yet even when the news trickled through to large media audiences, it might as well have been whistled into the wind. Jews and gentiles alike wanted to hear no evil, not even among the besieged.

"In November 1942, over the BBC, we heard for the first time about gassings and shootings," Inge Deutschkron, the Jewish writer who survived the war underground in Berlin, reported later. "We couldn't and wouldn't believe it."

I didn't know until the spring of 1945, when the concentration camps were opened, that my Aunt Marie had been deported to the Theresienstadt camp and died there, that my uncle Max Brahn had been gassed in Auschwitz, that my cousin Martha, with her husband and daughter, had made it out of Bergen-Belsen barely alive. And I knew nothing yet of all the others, the deaths, the twists of fate, the compromises of friends, neighbors, classmates left behind like Stella. What had become of them?

12. "To the Bath"

WHEN GEORG AND LOTTE NOMBURG detrained at Litzmann-stadt (Lodz) in October 1941, some 14,000 Jews had died in the fenced-in ghetto during the preceding eighteen months. The population still stood at 163,623; the occupancy rate was almost seven to a room. Keys froze in locks, but many homes were without doors. According to local historians, detainees lived in "huts and holes," waiting for disease and starvation to decimate their ranks further.

Old-timers were stunned and upset at the sight of the first arrivals from Berlin. These Jews were apparitions who might have come from New York or Switzerland. "We were struck by their elegant sports clothes, their exquisite footwear, the many variously colored caps the women wore," wrote one old resident. "They often gave the impression of being people on some sort of vacation, or, rather, engaged in winter sports, for the majority of them wore ski clothes . . . Their layers of fat afforded them excellent protection from the cold. Their attitude toward the extremely unsanitary conditions in which they were quartered was one of unusual disgust . . . They shouted, they were indignant . . ."

Everything being relative, these hated *yekes,* these German Jews, were also rich. Although the Gestapo had stripped them of everything its agents considered valuable, the newcomers still carried enough belongings to explode the entire ghetto economy and further aggravate prevailing hardships. Piece by piece, they sold off what they had. "With what they received, they began to buy up literally everything available on the shelves," recorded one of the ghetto historians. "This caused a shortage in food supply and prices rose with indescribable speed."

To control this madhouse, the Nazis had installed Chaim Rumkowski, sixty-one, a failed businessman and former director of Lodz Jewish charities. Long hated for his authoritarian ways, he used his dictatorial new powers creatively. He had stamps printed bearing his likeness. He recruited 600 club-wielding guards, ostensibly to maintain discipline but really to protect himself. He created a force of spies and mail censors. And he rose to make speech after speech, mostly railing at constituents he considered "destructive."

"Representatives of the new population, I appeal to you again to finally accept the ghetto's conditions of life," he pleaded shortly after the arrival of the Nomburgs. "Aren't you ashamed that I've had to use policemen to force you to work? That I had to resort to confining you to your work crews?"

Stoutly he defended the oppressors. "I am certain that if the ghetto does its work in earnest and does it well, the authorities will not take repressive steps," he promised. "Nothing bad will happen to people of goodwill."

Regardless of performance at forced labor, however, the Nomburgs quickly picked up that for them and other deportees like the parents of the future Dr. Ruth Westheimer, Litzmannstadt was only another way station. Transports to unknown destinations farther east were constantly leaving the station, and Rumkowski saw it as one of his missions to make certain that these further deportations were not dodged.

On January 14, 1942—the Nomburgs had already entrained for "resettlement"—he issued an order stating: "Should persons who are approved for evacuation hide in the homes of other families, not only those persons but also the families who gave them shelter, as well as the house watchmen, will be sent out by force. THIS IS MY LAST WARNING!"

The Nazis helped to spread rumors that the deportees were being dispatched to work in a land reclamation scheme in the Pripet Marshes and in agricultural colonies near Krivoi Rog, in the Ukraine, and Rumkowski authenticated this fiction in his speeches.

"My expectation, based on authoritative information, is that the deportees' fate will not be as tragic as is expected in the ghetto," he said on January 17. "They will not be behind wire, and they will work on farms."

Only the first of these promises came true, because in death the Nomburgs were no longer behind wire.*

The lone SS man who welcomed the trucks full of new arrivals at Chelmno (renamed Kulmhof by the Germans) was a disarming surprise. He was in his sixties, smoked a pipe, and could hardly have been kinder. He helped old people alight from the vehicles. He held babies while their mothers got off. Jolly as a tour guide, he led the newcomers into the big ballroom of the town's only large building, the badly neglected old castle. Here more SS men were in evidence, but they stood about quietly in the background.

Nothing indicated that these Jews, who had come from Litzmannstadt, forty miles to the west, were at that very moment performers in an evil charade. Nothing looked threatening about the sleepy village of Chelmno. It hugged the Ner, a broad, languid river made inviting by flatboats and overhanging willows. No guards or fences were overtly in evidence. The scene was sylvan, worlds away from the war.

It was all sham. On December 8, 1941, the castle at Chelmno had begun functioning as a Nazi extermination center, the very first. When Georg and Lotte Nomburg arrived, its operators, the *Sonderkommando* Lange, were "processing" (the official Nazi term) hundreds of Jews daily. Ultimately, some 300,000 Jews were "processed" at obscure little Chelmno. All newcomers who joined its SS detachment were warned in their orientation lecture to maintain absolute silence about its mission on pain of death and *Sippenhaft*, meaning that their families would face arrest.

Its somnolent atmosphere notwithstanding, the little camp worked quickly and efficiently. The killing sequence was disguised so that the victims would suspect nothing until near the end and could not protest too long, much less resist. Not that the SS commanders were eager to shorten the terror of the victims for humanitarian reasons. They wanted to minimize any undue exertion and psychic burden for their staff of killers. And if the condemned scented danger, they would try to resist. Resistance caused delays. Delays interfered with the inviolable pace of the official schedule.

---

* Their exact fate was never determined. On December 15, 1947, their sons were handed a "decision" of the *Amtsgericht* in Berlin's Schöneberg district certifying that their parents, Georg, fifty-seven, and Charlotte, forty-four, had been "missing" since December 16, 1941, "so that their death is *almost* certain." (Emphasis added.) The date of death was arbitrarily fixed at January 15, 1942.

The elderly SS greeter of the fresh arrivals had a pleasant job. He informed the expectant families that the women could stay home to care for their households and for the children while the men were at work. Sometimes listeners applauded. The greeter said everybody would receive new clothes, but first they must all bathe. They should disrobe and leave their valuables and papers behind, tied into a handkerchief, for later retrieval. His playacting was superb; nobody could tell that he made the same speech up to ten times a day.

Still unsuspecting, the arrivals trudged down a corridor. A sign said "To the Bath." Instead, the naked victims suddenly found themselves in the open, surrounded by numerous SS men who swung whips and drove them into the rear entrances of two gray Saurer delivery vans that were pulled up to a ramp. The people—about fifty per truck—screamed and fought to get away. It was too late.

As the victims shoved in panic, attempting to squeeze their way out of the darkness, clawing at the metal walls and occasionally actually breaking through the doors, the driver turned on the engine. This forced carbon monoxide gas through a special hose attachment into the death chamber. Death was scheduled to come in fifteen minutes. Often it did not, for the performance of the "special cars" or "Kaiser coffee cars" (so called in the official camouflaging terminology) was termed "unreliable" by the operators.

Once the gas worked so promptly that it killed a Polish SS helper named Marian. He had wound up inside the death chamber accidentally during the scuffle to load it. Another time a van skidded on the way to the burial grounds. The doors flew open and some victims tumbled out. A few were still alive and had to be shot on the road by the SS escorts.

One of the drivers, SS *Unterscharführer* Walter Burmeister, testified about these duties at his trial in 1962,* concluding calmly: "Thereafter I drove the car back to the castle and parked it. Here it was cleaned of the secretions from the people who had died in it. . . . What I was thinking, or whether I thought anything at all, I can no longer say today."

Adolf Eichmann, who inspected the proceedings as the responsible Gestapo representative, proved more sensitive. "A doctor in a white smock wanted me to look through a peephole and watch the people

---

* Under the bizarre arithmetic of the West German courts, Burmeister, accused of "aid" in the murder of 150,000 Jews, was sentenced to thirteen years in prison. Of the 160 functionaries of the Chelmno camp who could be identified, 105 had disappeared and were never found. Of the 33 who were actually tried, not one was convicted of murder.

inside the truck," he testified at his trial. "I refused. I couldn't. Couldn't! What I saw and heard was enough. The screaming and . . . the most horrible sight I had seen in all my life. It drove up to a fairly long trench. The doors were opened and corpses were thrown in. The limbs were as supple as if they'd been alive. Just thrown in. I can still see a civilian with pliers pulling out teeth. And then I beat it. . . ."

The secret of Chelmno was no secret. "The place where all perish is called Chelmno," reported the rabbi of Grabow, a nearby community, to his brother-in-law in Lodz on January 19, 1942, "and for the past several days Jews have been brought there from Lodz and the same is done to them. Do not think that I am mad. . . ."

The rabbi had talked to three young gravediggers who had escaped from the Chelmno burial grounds. In February, these eyewitnesses and their grisly accounts arrived in Warsaw, where the ghetto leaders were briefed. Through the remarkably resourceful underground Yiddish press and even through the mails, detailed word quickly reached Jewish organizations and their journals in London and New York. *Jewish Frontier* in New York published an exhaustive report on Chelmno in its September issue and devoted its entire November issue to the murders there and elsewhere, urging that rescue campaigns be launched.

"The world knows," the magazine said. "The evidence is in. The question is what can be done to save the millions still alive."

The news from Chelmno and other killing centers was so totally unbelievable to the outside world, however, even to most of the Jewish world, that they simply could not—or did not wish to—believe.* And this incredulity remained unshakable in the face of continuing eyewitness reports reaching the West for more than three years.

The flat rejection of the facts afflicted the highest places. When Supreme Court justice Felix Frankfurter told President Roosevelt of his concern for the fate of the Jews in the fall of 1942, he was told not to worry, that they were only being deported to build fortifications.

---

* Unbelievable news travels at an unbelievably slow pace. The best-organized accounts in the literature about the world's disbelief and inaction did not make their way out of the archives for forty years or more. They include *The Terrible Secret* by Walter Laqueur (Little, Brown, 1981) and *Were We Our Brothers' Keepers?* by Haskel Lookstein (Random House, 1985).

In July 1943, Frankfurter heard very differently from a unique eyewitness, Jan Karski, a twenty-nine-year-old Catholic lawyer with the Polish Foreign Office, doing secret courier duty between his occupied homeland and the Polish government-in-exile in London. Karski had collected extensive intelligence from the Jewish underground in the dying Warsaw ghetto. Disguised as an Estonian guard, he also penetrated the Belzec extermination camp and saw prisoners stacked, 100 at a time, in freight cars, with floors covered by quicklime that caused the bodies to burn slowly and eventually to decompose.

For forty-five minutes Frankfurter paced and listened to Karski's dispassionately delivered reporting. Finally, he said, "I cannot believe you." The Polish ambassador was in the room and protested. Frankfurter responded: "I did not say that he was lying. I said that I cannot believe him. There is a difference."

Here the historical accounts fade out. Karski's missionary work in Washington, however, did not. On February 28, 1992, this extraordinary courier, now a professor at Georgetown University, told me what happened to him next. Frankfurter, he decided, was being "dramatic" with him for effect. That was the famous justice's manner. Most likely he made a report to his good friend President Roosevelt, because on July 28, 1943, Karski was summoned into the Oval Office and spent an unforgettable hour and twenty minutes with FDR.

Karski was very conscious of his youth and of diplomatic protocol. He and his Polish colleagues made no moves to reach as high as the White House. He emphasized that he was "summoned." Being a highly organized professional, he rehearsed his report to run no more than eighteen to nineteen minutes, devoting only a few minutes to the plight of the Jews. The rest of his time went into questions of concern to his *Polish* principals, such as the postwar borders of Poland and the suspiciousness of Marshal Stalin. Roosevelt gave Karski a series of messages to his leaders. As for the Jews, FDR asked a few questions but registered no reaction to the recitation of horrors: no shock, no disbelief, nothing.

The denials of genocide would not wane for the duration of the war. Thus, in December 1944, Assistant Secretary of War John J. McCloy turned down proposals to bomb the railroad lines into Auschwitz. He said that planes were needed elsewhere. In actuality, McCloy disbelieved the evidence, and confessed his incredulity to a leader of the World Jewish Congress.

"We are alone," McCloy said. "Tell me the truth. Do you really believe that all those horrible things happened?"

In his account of the meeting, the Jewish leader commented: "His sources of information, needless to say, were better than mine. But he could not grasp the terrible destruction."

Of course, the sons of Georg and Lotte Nomburg did not know what was befalling their parents. And Stella Goldschlag had not the faintest notion of what was about to happen to her husband Manfred and other relatives and friends disappearing from Berlin. She was still toiling at forced labor in the Erich and Graetz armaments factory, and when that survival ticket evaporated, she would take refuge within the ranks of a furtive new and unremittingly endangered species, the "U-boats."

Hitler's Final Solution was meanwhile endowed with its official shape by its sponsors, its scale more sweeping than even its chief executioner, Adolf Eichmann, had dreamed possible. It happened at stylish Wannsee and took only an hour and a half. No other event institutionalized the mass killings so explicitly—or stripped the inside operators and their folkways so naked.

Wannsee meant the beach and vast lakeside estates, so when I was a boy, the area was synonymous with outdoors fun. It was also one of Berlin's best addresses. Mere mention of the 640-acre water hole beyond the glorious Grunewald Forest put everybody in a cheery mood. I loved our weekend outings for the tanning in the almost white sand of the largest lakeshore beach in Europe, the swimming, the lunches of freshly caught fish at the packed Schildhorn beer garden with my parents and the Nomburg family. It was the best of life.

Wannsee was so universally favored that I never failed to scan the crowds in search of my Stella, preferably in a bathing suit, even the modest one-piece models of the time. Years afterward, I learned that she had been there often and had paddled along the lake with her husband-to-be Manfred in his little canvas kayak. I never ran into her, which was especially frustrating because I entertained visions of magnanimously inviting her to come along with friends of ours who owned one of the hundreds of little sailboats bobbing in the choppy waters. My largess would not have been without risk since I sometimes got seasick.

Beginning in 1933, the odious winds of Hitler's regime began to blow through the palatial residences along the lake. Max Liebermann, the great Impressionist painter, eighty-six, still lived at No. 42 Am Grossen Wannsee when he was fired as president of the Berlin Academy of Arts because he was a Jew and his art had been classified as "decadent." Worse, he turned his irreverent wit against the Nazis.

"I can't eat as much as I want to vomit," was one of his widely quoted jabs. He was lucky to wind up dying of natural causes in 1935.*

Our happy Wannsee underwent metamorphosis mostly because the killings of Jews were still proceeding much too slowly to suit the Nazi leadership. Many departments were involved and their officials plodded along without orderly plans, without a fully defined overall objective. It was a bureaucratic mess, very un-German.

"There was no coordinated activity and therefore actions were delayed considerably," Adolf Eichmann complained. His associates in the conventional government agencies were not coping efficiently with the innumerable administrative loose ends of carting away and killing such vast numbers of people.

"They wouldn't arrive at any definite solution," Eichmann lamented.

The official in charge of the elusive *solution* was his boss, Reinhard Heydrich, then thirty-seven, *Obergruppenführer* and chief of the Gestapo and the SD, the security service of the SS, its most feared and secret arm. And Heydrich, in turn, had received a no-loopholes written order from *his* boss, the Gestapo's founder, *Reichsmarschall* Hermann Göring, on July 31, 1941, to end the bureaucratic shuffling. He knew the order was foolproof. He had written it.

"I hereby charge you with making all organizational, functional and material preparations for a complete solution of the Jewish question," the document stated. "In so far as the jurisdiction of other central agencies may be touched thereby, they are to be involved." Heydrich was to fashion "an overall plan," Göring demanded in the words ghosted by Heydrich. To avoid any doubt about what he meant by the "complete solution" of the Jews' fate, the last sentence of the three-paragraph order specified that the solution was to be "final." * *

Göring, in his turn, had received *his* signals from Hitler, the supreme architect, whose rabid anti-Semitism dated back to his teen years in Austria. The Führer had publicly threatened the "extermination" of "Jewry" as early as 1939. Such rantings were dismissed

---

* His widow, an invalid, committed suicide at eighty-five. She took Veronal sleeping pills when officers came with a stretcher to carry her to a deportation train.
* * While the euphemism "final solution" is generally credited to Eichmann, its appearance in the ghostwritten Göring order of 1941 may constitute its first use in a major document. Possibly Eichmann ghosted the paper for Heydrich.

as campaign oratory, but among his entourage he expressed himself even more emphatically. At lunch in his field headquarters on October 21, 1941, he described Jews as vermin, telling his intimates: "If we eradicate this pest, we will be performing a great deed for mankind."

By no coincidence, the first deportations of Berlin Jews, including the Nomburgs, began three days earlier.

Yet the Führer was on guard against a counterproductive public relations backfire of the kind that had spoiled Crystal Night for the Nazis. Direct orders from him, actually commanding the specific murder of Jews, were not discovered until 1978. Indeed, every effort was made to keep Hitler separated from his dirty work.

"Under no circumstances may the Führer's office become visible to the outside," his executive assistant said when the "evacuation" of mental patients was first ordered.

"The Final Solution was a masterpiece of secret keeping," said General Alfred Jodl, the Army Chief of Staff, after the war.

Hitler's murder directives were handed down orally by his deputies. Orders for killings were issued by middlemen and were usually preceded by the euphemism "It is the Führer's wish that . . ." *

When necessary, Hitler's personal authority was invoked more firmly, if usually still by indirection. In Minsk, for instance, when the commander of *Einsatzkommando* 8, SS *Obersturmbannführer* Dr. Otto Bradfisch, was told in mid-August 1941 to shoot more than 120 Jewish men and women, he had enough nerve to ask the visiting Heinrich Himmler, chief of the SS, about the origin of the order. Himmler set his executioner straight unequivocally.

Bradfisch recalled: "Himmler replied in a rather sharp tone that these orders came from Hitler as the Führer of the German government, and that they had the force of law."

More than 500,000 Jews had already been shot and gassed by noon on January 20, 1942, five days after Georg and Lotte Nomburg were

---

* Hitler's own hand was not disclosed until February 17, 1978, when a Wehrmacht noncommissioned officer, Werner Isensee, gave a written statement to British researcher Gerald Fleming about a coded order transmitted in late July 1942 from the Führer's headquarters at Vinnitsa to Isensee's radio station at Lutsk in the Ukraine. Signed "Adolf Hitler, Führer's headquarters" and directed to *Gauleiter* Erich Koch in nearby Rovno, it demanded liquidation of all remaining Jews in the Rovno region. As a result, more than 70,000 Jews were shot in massacres between August and November.

assumed to have died, when Heydrich took the chair of the top-secret Wannsee Conference "with brunch to follow."

According to his invitation, the gathering's purpose was to "reach an identical conception" among the participating government agencies. Decoded, this euphemism meant that much more was at stake. Heydrich had multiple goals in mind. He wanted to unify all needed jurisdictions; cement a bond between the uniformed killers and civilian bureaucrats, some of whom had reservations about "radical" Party methods; speed up the killings; and leave no doubt that he, Heydrich, was in command. It was a matter of smooth office politics.

For privacy and class, he picked the perfect spot, removed from the drabness of the downtown ministries: the huge, elegant gray stucco palace with eighteen-foot ceilings at Am Grossen Wannsee 56-58 which he had purchased as a club for his Gestapo hierarchy. The view of the lake was breathtaking; the water seemed almost to lap at the lofty first-floor windows.

He could have done no more to achieve the desired impact. The ambience was superb, the Wannsee address still the best in all Berlin.

The fourteen invited officials were, in the words of his awed principal assistant, Eichmann, "the popes of the Third Reich." Mostly they were state secretaries, the powerful second-echelon functionaries who pushed the action buttons and made sluggish administrative machinery hum in such key ministries as Justice, Interior, and the Foreign Office. Eight held Ph.D. degrees. All sat impressed and silent as Heydrich announced that Göring had directed him to achieve "clarity in essential matters."

Heydrich was, quite simply, the most feared personage in the Reich. His own men called him "the blond beast." Hitler described him as "the man with the iron heart." In the cellars of SS headquarters at Prinz Albrecht Strasse 8, his agents administered unspeakable tortures to suspected opponents of the regime. Heydrich was a collector of women, feared even by prostitutes. They preferred the adjutant who preceded his chief to make arrangements at brothels.

Tall, trim, and agile, Heydrich was no banal apparatchik like Eichmann. The Gestapo chief spoke with a clipped, high, icy voice. His face was shaped like a triangle: high, broad forehead, slightly slanted blue eyes, prominent nose, tight small mouth, startlingly narrow chin. He was a superb fencer, a brave combat pilot, a gifted violinist who was often moved to tears by classical music. But for his audience at the Wannsee Conference, he was a turf-conscious bureaucrat with a history of ordering the murder even of fellow Nazis who got in his way.*

Opening with a formal speech researched and drafted by Eichmann, Heydrich sought to impress the assembled bureaucrats with the breathtaking enormity of their task: "the approaching final solution of the Jewish question." Eleven million European Jews were to be involved, including 330,000 in Great Britain—as yet unconquered—and 18,000 in neutral Switzerland.

Their proposed fate, though described in relatively restrained language in the official top-secret summary of the proceedings, was unmistakable. "Evacuation" to the East was a "temporary" first step. The Jews were to engage in heavy labor "whereby doubtless a large part will fall away through natural reduction." That would not suffice. "The inevitable final remainder," Heydrich lectured, "will have to be dealt with appropriately." **

The formal part of the conference concluded with a relaxed informal discussion that amazed and relieved Eichmann. The representatives of the ministries responded with "unexpected," "extraordinary," indeed "boundless" enthusiasm. Eichmann said later that he had harbored doubts about "such a bloody solution through violence." No longer.

"The most prominent people had spoken," he marveled. "I sensed a kind of Pontius Pilate feeling, for I felt free of all guilt."

Eichmann's formal top-secret report of the meeting was subsequently expurgated "three or four times" by Heydrich.† The ensuing "cozy little social gathering" was not mentioned. As butlers passed cognac, the officials stood about in small groups and made their own brand of cocktail party conversation. They chatted animatedly about technical details, Eichmann recalled, about "methods for killing, about liquidation and extermination," including the inadequacy of

---

* The Wannsee meeting was to be Heydrich's last hurrah. On May 27, 1942, he was fatally wounded by paratroopers of the Czech army in exile.
** The killings of the Final Solution grew into an undertaking so massive and farflung that the ultimate statistics have remained elusive and in dispute. The most exhaustive research effort, comprising 584 pages, was not published until 1991: *Dimension des Völkermords* (Munich: Oldenbourg Verlag), edited by Wolfgang Benz, director of the Center for the Study of Anti-Semitism at the Technical University, Berlin. To compile this accounting, eighteen scholars from seventeen affected nations drew on all sources extant and secured the cooperation of the leading researchers in Israel. This definitive reckoning arrived at a minimum estimate of 5.29 million and a maximum of slightly over 6 million deaths.
† A copy of the sanitized version, belatedly discovered by American document handlers in 1947, was the very first tip-off that such a conference had taken place at all.

the gas vans. In the stillness of Wannsee, no appetites were spoiled and the conferees sat down for a pleasant brunch, lubricated by more cognac.

The third, most private phase of the meeting reflected the satisfaction of the sponsors over the outcome. The guests had departed and Eichmann's joy was unrestrained. For the first time he felt accepted in the ranks of the leadership. Together with Heydrich and another Gestapo boss, he sat "cozily around a fireplace" drinking Stamperl liqueur, smoking, and singing songs. Eichmann had never seen Heydrich smoke or relax before.

The conviviality of the occasion lingered in his mind. "After a while," Eichmann remembered, "we climbed onto the chairs and drank a toast; then onto the table, and traipsed round and round— on the chairs and on the table again."

His Führer's vision, fittingly, was more long-range.

"Mark my words, Bormann," Hitler said over his usual vegetarian dinner one night that same January at the Rastenburg Wolfsschanze, his war headquarters in East Prussia. "I'm going to become very religious."

His deputy, Martin Bormann, misunderstood.

"You've always been very religious," he said, puzzled, failing to comprehend that his Führer was riding a higher flight path. Hitler was being visited, perhaps for the first time, by the mirage of a millennium, the Hitler millennium, the Thousand-Year Reich. Then and there, he stated that he would "put things in order for a thousand years," and this mission would not confine him—as Bormann trivialized the dream—to participating in religious worship. He would become its God.

"I'm going to become a religious figure," he lectured his cronies patiently. "Soon I'll be the great chief of the Tartars. Already Arabs and Moroccans are mingling my name with their prayers. Among the Tartars I shall become Khan . . ."

The sycophants around the dinner table had no reason to doubt their Führer, much less to think him mad. At fifty-two, he had already come closer to ruling the world than any leader in history. From the approaches to Moscow to the U-boat pens in the Atlantic, from the heavy-water plants of Norway to Rommel's panzers chasing Field Marshal Montgomery through the African desert—what better proof could there be that he was the Khan of Khans arrived? The Luftwaffe's V-1 missiles were about to terrorize London. Stalingrad, Hitler's Waterloo, was still a year distant. It was his best of times, time to blueprint more greatness to come.

As soon as the weather warmed up, he would wipe out the Red Army and begin to resettle 20 million German "soldier peasants" in a new Nazi colony. Moscow would be wiped off the map and become an artificial lake. Berlin, renamed Germania, would be the center of the universe. Hitler would rule there from a chancellery of unmistakable proportions and intent.

"One should have the feeling that one is visiting the master of the world," the Führer said.

Master of the world! In Hitler's mind, Europe's 22 million Jews were already shriveling into a footnote. They would simply be "got rid of"—so he told his dinner companions. The machinery was in place. Eichmann would see to the mop-up of remnants like the U-boats, innocents like Stella's father, who would not live to find out about the Gestapo's secret use of cheery Wannsee, who could not believe that, yes, people did kill people, that he and his gentle kind were standing in the way of a vision.

13. Life as a U-boat

THREE YEARS HAD PASSED since Guenther Rogoff had last seen Stella at the Feige and Strassburger art school. She had gotten thinner and was somewhat less fashionably dressed when he ran into her in the anonymity of a busy street, considered by many U-boats to be the safest place to hide. He was enchanted to see her again and found her as delectable as ever. By coincidence, their encounter occurred near mobbed Wittenbergplatz, a short way from their long-closed art school. Although 18,300 Jews were, remarkably, still surviving in Berlin in that spring of 1943, much had changed for them since the roundups of the preceding February, all for the worse.

"What are you doing?" Rogoff asked, showing his delight.

"I'm living illegally," said Stella. "How about you?"

"I'm living illegally too," Rogoff told her, and then, without a pause for breath, he added, "I forge documents for people. Maybe I can help you, too."

It was a wildly audacious disclosure, nearly suicidal, though not for Guenther Rogoff. Danger turned him on and he lived accordingly. "My rule is that I have no rules," he liked to tell friends.

Stella responded with the queenly cool that she liked to affect toward horny men. Acting as if people on the street offered her forged papers all the time, she casually allowed that, yes, perhaps she could use Guenther's help.

Rogoff's mind had already raced ahead.

"I'll do something that I never do," he said. "I'll show you the

130

room where I live." This proposition was about as innocent as taking his pants off in the middle of the street. Naturally, he left himself vulnerable because he saw a heavenly opportunity to get Stella into his bed at last.

Still looking unimpressed, Stella agreed pleasantly. Together they boarded a No. 76 streetcar toward nearby Kantstrasse, where Guenther had found a furnished room under a false name.

"Aren't you worried that you're being foolhardy by taking me to your place?" Stella inquired as the No. 76 moved out.

Rogoff, taken aback, thought this over, and suddenly caution deflated his sex-induced bravado.

"Yes," he said, reddening, and they got out at the next stop.

Why his quick change of mind?

"A miracle," he said, still shaking his head nearly fifty years later, "and totally untypical for me. I wanted to buy her, but to me she always behaved fairly. It was extraordinary."

The encounter also set in motion a chain of events that led Stella into the service of the Gestapo. It happened because the Nazis considered Rogoff a dangerous criminal.

He hardly seemed the type. His father, a chemist, had transferred his skills to the manufacturing of artificially flavored mineral water on a modest scale, and Guenther, since childhood, had dreamed of becoming an artist. He loved to draw and paint people from life and he was good at it. One rarely encountered him without his sketchpad and crayons. His real family name had a solidly German ring,[*] and with his reddish hair, ruddy cheeks, and upturned nose he didn't, as the saying goes, "look Jewish." It was the same genetic good fortune that saved so many other of his coreligionists.

The fate of his family had run the typical tragic course. At seventy-three, his grandmother did not wish to leave the country, and so his father did not commence emigration efforts until 1937. Relatives were found in the United States who owned two pharmacies and furnished the required affidavits guaranteeing to support Guenther's family in case of need. The American authorities rejected the guarantees as inadequate. A lot of time was lost. Additional guarantees were supplied—too late.

---

[*] Rogoff today operates an advertising agency in Europe and requested anonymity. His pseudonym was the name of a dealer in firewood in Minsk, a friend of his grandparents who hailed from that Russian-Jewish city.

The very day the war broke out, Guenther and his father called again at the American embassy on Unter den Linden. En route they had to pass the Nazi Foreign Ministry on Wilhelmstrasse, where generals and diplomats rushed in and out exuding enthusiasm. At the U.S. embassy the atmosphere was relaxed. The two visa applicants were directed to a young man who was sprawled behind a big desk on which his legs rested—an informality unknown in Europe. He checked their registration numbers on a long list, informed them in very bad German that their turn had not yet come, and waved them away.

Though Guenther had landed a good job as a graphic artist, his father was eager to spirit him out of the country even if the rest of the family had to stay behind. A thousand marks were paid to have the boy smuggled into Belgium. It didn't work: Guenther was arrested at the border and returned to Berlin. Next the family tried to obtain an illegal exit for the boy to Palestine, but the crush was much too great; Guenther's turn at the besieged Palestine Office was still a long way off when the Nazis drafted him for forced labor, running a lathe that produced machine pistols.

This would not be his sole employment for long.

As the Nazis' grip on Berlin's Jews tightened and the number of illegally hidden U-boats grew, an underground trade in doctored and forged documents began to flourish. Documents could preserve life, and dozens of Jews and their helpers worked in this new growth industry, some charging little for their artistry, some nothing, and some collecting fortunes.

Passports of deceased foreigners were collected by the Gestapo and could sometimes be bought from a corrupt officer who "forgot" to burn them as ordered. He charged 400 marks apiece—a month's pay for a lot of people. Later on, with the Nazi net tightening further, genuine blank work papers would fetch 3,000 marks, sometimes 4,000.

The market was ravenous, and some of the work was pitifully amateurish. With years of experience and the increasing watchfulness of police and Gestapo patrols prowling for army deserters and other illegals, the quality of the forgeries improved. Much depended on whether the artist needed to produce only a touch-up of an existing document or had to create an official paper from scratch or from stolen blank forms.

Rogoff was dubious when he was first approached about the alteration of a passport. The request came through a young Jewish woman of his acquaintance who worked with a small anti-Nazi resistance group. The man who needed the document was known to

Guenther and was in danger of imminent arrest. He had to leave Germany at once.

"I'll try," said Rogoff, true to his fondness for taking risks.

He was given one of the perfectly authentic passports collected by the resisters from sympathizers, mostly devout members of the Lutheran Church who reported to the police that they had "lost" their papers. All Rogoff had to do was remove the identity photograph and replace it with the picture of the potential escapee. The particular passport had been selected because the written description of its legitimate possessor roughly resembled the photo of the new owner.

For Rogoff's practiced fingers it was easy to loosen the metal eyes that fastened the original photo to the document. The trick was to imitate the portion of the official rubber stamp that partly covered the photo, to transfer that segment onto the new photo, and to make the lettering look worn so that the forged portion would match the rest of the stamp. It was excruciatingly exacting work, because the rubber stamp, any rubber stamp, was accepted as ultimate evidence of legitimacy and authorization by German officialdom and was consequently scrutinized with care. The stamp was a German's supreme totem.

Rogoff took a small blank patch of newsprint from the margins of a newspaper, moistened it, and pressed the passport's stamp against it. Using overlay paper and a tiny paintbrush, he was able to transfer the thus copied piece of rubber stamp onto the altered passport. It worked. The document's new owner made it to Switzerland and eventually to Palestine.

This success marked the start-up of a frantically busy new career for Rogoff. From September 1942 until October 3, 1943, he forged some 200 documents: passports, food ration cards, police identity papers, post office identifications, and *Bombenscheine* certifying that their owners had lost their papers in an air raid. In the end, he graduated to the creation of army identification passes. These bureaucratic extravaganzas required a grand total of thirty-six different rubber stamps.

During his career as a forger, Rogoff's life underwent marked change. His family's deportation to the Maidanek concentration camp hardened his resolve to survive the war and to inflict maximum damage on the Nazis. He forged more often and more rapidly and expertly. His camouflage was foolproof: he rented a corner in a murky sideline business operated by a chauffeur for the Afghan embassy and wore a white laboratory coat to his work, looking like a proud and prim professional man.

As protection against possible traitors, he was never allowed to meet the recipients of his handiwork. He delivered documents in batches, once a week, to the law offices of the resistance ring's leader, who was eventually arrested and shot. During Rogoff's tenure, clients gathered in the leader's waiting room as if to visit a dentist; Rogoff waited quietly next door, gratified to note that he was not the only Berliner to thrive on risks.

Guenther did well financially, too. Indigent customers were supplied by him without fee. Others were usually charged the rather nominal price of 100 marks for a routine job. He could afford to be generous because he was affluent, having discovered a group of gentile housewives who specialized in the private sale of furnishings seized from deported Jews. Often the women procured their merchandise for next to nothing because the owners were unreachable. Rogoff, however, collected a substantial 10,000 marks for his parents' household goods.

He promptly purchased a sailboat for 3,000 marks, kept it docked at a quay near the Pichelsdorf bridge, and used it to entertain his several girlfriends. Nobody questioned his role as a skipper. Like other uppity young Jewish survivors, Rogoff had hit upon the most effective formula for survival: showing off in public with self-assurance, preferably arrogance. People who could bring off such an act —usually very young, perhaps infantile, men—found their twilight existence downright enjoyable. It was like daily cops and robbers.

And so Guenther squired his girls to his boat or for coffee and cake to the famous Café Kranzler. Once, with a Jewish crony and a gentile friend in navy uniform, he dined among the cream of Nazi officialdom at the elite Hotel Kaiserhof itself. It was the height of his foolhardiness and required acting skill. "We held ourselves like the sons of dukes," he recalled.

When he went underground to escape deportation, Rogoff applied similar ingenuity to the hunt for a safe roof over his head. While other U-boats froze through the nights in parks or risked arrest riding endlessly in subways and buses, Rogoff took residence in a succession of comfortable furnished rooms in choice neighborhoods. He found his quarters through the official municipal room-locator service and then negotiated with the landladies. They were required to fill out forms reporting all roomers to the police. Nevertheless, after making five or six inquiries, Rogoff unfailingly discovered a woman who liked his looks, swallowed his cover story that he was an unfortunate draftee soon to depart for army service, and let him stay awhile without her scribbling telltale information onto long forms and taking time to deliver them to the police, who asked still more nosy questions.

Guenther's forgery business worked smoothly because neither the supply nor the demand for documents diminished. By 1943, just about every Jew was finally desperate to leave illegally, at whatever risk. And as Allied air raids at home and military setbacks at the front caused German efficiency to deteriorate, more documents became available to make precarious survival possible in the meantime. People could steal more blanks from unguarded desk drawers. Still, prices went up as in a booming stock market. A set of ration cards for a family had once brought 225 to 250 marks. No longer. Postal identifications could still be had for 800 marks, a full-fledged ID card for 1,500. Slowly the quotations escalated into higher ranges, although some church members could still be persuaded to give up their papers without payment.

All Jews who lived on in Germany for so much as another day had come to appreciate that their dependence on help from gentiles, in tacit or active form, was total. Tragically, many offers of assistance were not legitimate, and the villains couldn't be separated from the heroes.

My own cousin Walter never heard of Guenther Rogoff or his resistance contacts. Blond and blue-eyed, Walter worked as a fashion designer and lived in Weissensee, the working-class district where my father grew up. A man with a foreign accent approached Walter and said he could get him papers for Switzerland. Walter gave him money. The man came back and wanted more money. Walter paid and waited. And waited.

Eventually he realized that there would be no papers, and he took a household poison. He was found dead late one afternoon in 1942 by his older brother, my round, wily little cousin Siegfried, who managed to survive the war in Berlin, mostly because he never slept in the same place two nights in a row and because he had generous gentile friends who owned a grocery store and fed him.

Plus luck, always luck.

True to his word, Guenther Rogoff manufactured a police identification card for Stella, handed it to her by appointment on the street, taking no money and disappearing without a trace. Not until many years after the war would he learn that his forgery would become her undoing and that her fall, shortly after he last saw her, would turn her into the classic Gestapo torpedo against the fraternity of the U-boats.

Rogoff survived Hitler thanks to his cheerful chutzpah and the sharp nose that protected him until Stella's arrest in the summer of

1943 landed him on the "most wanted" list of the Berlin police. That told him it was time to leave the country.

From an old map he arbitrarily picked the picturesque eleventh-century Swiss border hamlet of Stein am Rhein as the likeliest escape hatch. Looking like a vacationer in his Hitler Youth outfit and backpack, he traveled by bicycle, spending nights in comfortable inns, protected by the best papers he could manufacture. In a phone book on the German side of the border he located a man named Schmidt as residing on a farm directly at the frontier. Rogoff bought a bouquet of flowers, placed them on the handlebars of his bicycle, and reported to the local post of the border police.

"I'm visiting Schmidt's," he announced to the guards with a bright smile, and they let him proceed.

Agitated within, he prayed a *Schma Yisroel* when he spotted a Swiss flag in the distance. The frontier followed a brook. Rogoff hid his bicycle in some bushes and waded in. Halfway across, a rustle caused him to dive so only his nose peeked out of the water. The intruder was a deer.

Climbing out on the Swiss side, Rogoff, the forger with a flair, gave the ground a big kiss.

BOOK 3

LIVING WITH
THE GESTAPO

14. The Decision: Making the Deal with the Devil

Iɴ ᴛʜᴇ ʟᴀᴛᴇ sᴘʀɪɴɢ ᴏғ 1943, Stella's luck improved. For the rest of her life she would pick up most of her men in public places, and Rolf Isaaksohn was the first of these fateful linkups. It happened in the queue of a delicatessen shop on Olivaer Platz. The line moved slowly, as usual, so there was opportunity to chat. The mutual attraction was not set off by verbal means, however.

"He was beautiful, she was beautiful," remembered Rolf's cousin Dorothy, then ten. The little cousin also lived underground and spent much of her time with the beautiful couple that spring and summer.

Rolf was twenty-two, darkly handsome—"so Italian," Stella said —tall and lean, immaculate in white shirt, tie, and jacket. But there was more to Isaaksohn—who called himself von Jagow—than his polished exterior. Loaded with cash, cunning, and charisma, he was a protector to be cherished.

"He had such presence," said Dorothy. "His bearing was so secure. And when you're so very handsome, you can get away with a lot. He was a complete actor, an actor who can play roles like a movie star." And like Stella.

Rolf even earned a little money with his acting. He worked as an extra at the famous Staatsoper, the Corinthian-temple-style edifice on Unter den Linden, most often silently carrying a spear in an Italian epic.* Not that he was a verbal slouch.

---

* It was only on August 31, 1944, that Goebbels closed the opera as too wasteful in Total War.

139

How that man could talk! "It's an Isaaksohn trait," said Cousin Dorothy. "We were always charmers who liked to schmooze. And we knew how to adapt."

Adapting—accommodating to the conditions for survival imposed by the Eichmann system—was what Stella and Rolf embarked upon as a team. Whether Rolf was leader or follower, he was the perfect partner because his pleasant appearance and manner were so misleading. He was amoral. His own mother had told Dorothy so.

"Rolf can walk across corpses," said Getrud Isaaksohn, echoing a German folk saying denoting ruthlessness.

Like Rogoff, Isaaksohn trained himself to become a forger and made an excellent income at that trade. His documents enjoyed a good reputation and enabled him to learn the hideouts and surreptitious routines of his clients and their contacts. His forging tricks were ingenious. Rolf knew how to peel an egg and use the skin to create the kind of print impressions that made credentials look properly aged. For Stella he manufactured several additional documents to supplement those made for her by Rogoff.

Almost immediately, the beautiful couple began to live together on Lietzenburger Strasse in the three-room apartment of a Jewish husband who was protected by living with a Christian wife. All told, ten people were housed there. They spent much of their time in bed, and not just for sex. The neighbors could not be made aware that a crowd had found refuge next door. So Stella, Rolf, and their companions worked hard to adhere to rules being followed by U-boats all over town. It was called "noiseless living" and ritualized the art of hiding that Stella had practiced with her mother after her father dodged arrest during Crystal Night.

No more than three people could be on their feet, even bare feet, at any one time—which was why bed was a convenient refuge. Stella and Rolf would snuggle up under the blanket with arms around each other, while some of the others lounged about and tried to keep their whispering to a minimum.

Boredom and Rolf's work, his forging and spear carrying, took the couple and Dorothy out in public, and the trio's favorite hangout was the Café Bollenmüller on Mittelstrasse. It was a short walk from the opera, a favorite of film, music, and media people, and a reasonably safe place to maintain anonymity because it was almost always very crowded. Presumably it would be possible to spot Gestapo agents bursting in wearing their long leather coats and soft-brimmed hats.

At lunchtime on July 2, the strategy failed. A plumpish Jewish acquaintance of Stella's, Inge Lustig, came in, waved to her nervously, and fled. Stella, at a table waiting for Rolf and Dorothy, smiled in recognition. Quickly, several Gestapo men pushed their way into the café. Stella tried to run, but one of the men grabbed her, slapped her hard in the face, and she was taken away.

Inge Lustig was one of the new breed called *Greifer,** and they were Jews who hunted Jews for the Gestapo.

The Lustig woman became a key to Stella's decision-making a few months later. She was living evidence, easy to identify with, that a catcher was a government agent, a new occupation enjoying a measure of respectability, being the creation of the legally constituted authorities. And it was a profession that offered seductive job benefits. Catchers lived very much like ordinary citizens, gentiles! They were not confined to a camp. They did not have to wear a Jewish star. Their hours were their own. They were decently fed and paid. They carried pistols for arrests and their own safety, as well as Gestapo identification cards to certify their authority. Their names came off the deportation lists. Some received incentives: one relative was taken off the lists for every catch brought in, plus 200 marks bonus per head. All were alive, at least for a while.***

When Rolf and Dorothy arrived at the café hand in hand, one of the waitresses whispered: "Listen, the Gestapo was here and took Stella." Stunned, the pair slipped out as slowly and unobtrusively as they could manage.

Rolf was not caught until October and did not start walking across corpses until the following month. The first was the body of his uncle, Dorothy's father. Rolf and the Gestapo came for him on the uncle's birthday, November 19.

"He killed my father, and he did it in his first or second week [working for the Gestapo] to prove how good he'd be at it," Dorothy

* *Greifer*, a somewhat dramatic synonym for "policeman," particularly a detective, literally means a "grabber" or "catcher" who seizes suspects by the collar. Its use in Stella's world probably originated within the Jewish rumor mill, the *Mundfunk* (mouth radio). The Austrian job description was *Häscher*. Jewish collaborators were ranked according to a loose hierarchy. In addition to *Ordner* (order keepers) and *Jupo* (Jewish police), there were *Fahnder* (scouts) and *Spitzel* (stool pigeons). Ranking beyond the *Greifer*, the most aggressive Gestapo workers outside of the concentration camps were the *Kapos* within the *Lager*. The derivation of *Kapo* also is uncertain. Some scholars attribute it to the Italian *capo*, meaning "boss." Others trace it to *Kameradschaftspolizei* ("police of comrades") and believe the expression originated among prisoners.
** The survival benefit rarely lasted long. Almost all catchers were converted into destroyed evidence, gassed in the camps like the "crematorium ravens." After the war, a few did face judgment, which was surprisingly lenient (see pages 273–278).

said. His recruitment as a *Greifer* for the Gestapo was Stella's doing —so Dorothy was convinced: "She led him to the water."

Stella had no way of knowing that since she last saw Guenther Rogoff he had graduated onto the "most wanted" list of the police. All over greater Berlin, officers were looking for him, equipped with his photo as well as samples of his handwriting.

A silly accident had turned him into a priority target. He carried his wallet in a breast pocket of his suit jacket. Although it was stuffed with incriminating papers, he consulted it briefly one day in a crowded streetcar. Intending to return it to his pocket, he let it slip instead between his suit and overcoat; it landed unnoticed on the floor and was duly delivered to the police by an upright *Bürger* as having been lost.

Digging through papers intended for several spurious identities, the delighted officers had no trouble guessing what Rogoff was doing. And when Stella's papers were checked at the Café Bollenmüller, they thought they had finally tracked him down: they recognized his handwriting. This turned her, by association, into a prime target for the Gestapo. They expected to have no trouble beating Rogoff's whereabouts out of this slender young blonde.

On the wartime map of Berlin certain glum, anonymous buildings scattered across the Mitte district, the city's center, were marked in the minds of Jews by neon signs. The mere mention of their street addresses inspired panic.

The Levetzowstrasse synagogue had been the first way station in this geography of terror. Two others were Jewish institutions converted into longer-term prisons by the Gestapo—collection camps where Jews were assembled, sometimes to be held more or less indefinitely, usually to be deported within a few days, sometimes right away. These camps were the Jewish Home for the Aged at Grosse Hamburger Strasse 26 (called "the Grosse Hamburger Strasse") and, a little later, the Jewish Hospital at Schulstrasse 79 ("the Schulstrasse"). Both eventually became home and workplace for Stella.*

* Other infamous locations operated at a more elevated level, and Jews rarely ranked high enough to be taken there. At Kurfürstenstrasse 116, a huge, squat complex, once home to a Jewish Freemason lodge, was Eichmann's *Judenamt* (Jewish Office). The inside was a labyrinth of marble stairways and giant rooms, which Eichmann deplored. "It would be hard to imagine anything more unsuitable for

Stella was first thrust into the Jew-"processing" apparatus at its most widely feared location, the local Gestapo headquarters, Burgstrasse 26—"the Burgstrasse"—on the banks of the Spree River, around the corner from the elevated station Börse and the ancient Circus Busch.* It was a grimy, ornate five-story remnant of another age, defaced by three columns that seemed to have been pasted on the facade. Two cupolas crowned the roof, one of them topped with an onion-shaped dome, the kind seen on Greek Orthodox churches. The street level once held a men's hat shop, a book store, and other humdrum commercial establishments.

The jurisdictions assigned to the various agencies of peril were fixed in every Jew's awareness, and the dark, antiseptic stillness of the Burgstrasse offices ranked as the most menacing. This was the most likely *Büro* one would first experience from the inside, and its rules were the most capricious. When a leader of the Jewish Community offices was ordered to appear at that address, he would strip himself of watch, rings, and other valuables. The reason for the summons might be inconsequential. It could just as easily mean that he would not return.

Ultimately, it would be Stella's looks and intelligence that would elevate her to star rank for the Gestapo. But first, at the Burgstrasse, another asset made her interesting. She was presumed to have information. Her captors thought she could lead them to Rogoff, who, in turn, knew innumerable other illegally living Jews. Hurried as Eichmann's conveyor system was, it could pause to apply pressure on sources of information—potential leaks to help cleanse Germany, as Hitler kept demanding.

---

administrative quarters," he complained. National Gestapo headquarters, Prinz Albrecht Strasse 8, was a more ecumenical operation, where political "criminals" were routinely interrogated by torture. Relatively normal police operations were conducted from "the Alex," the block-sized seven-story red brick police headquarters off Alexanderplatz. Its chief was a volatile aristocrat, the war hero and swashbuckler Wolf Graf von Helldorf, Nazi Party member since 1925, almost before there was a Party. He confiscated passports from Jews and resold them for as much as 250,000 marks, often to the owners. He was no ideologue, however; in 1944, he joined the unsuccessful July 20 assassination bomb plot against his master, Hitler, and was hanged on August 15.

* The Burgstrasse would soon be demolished in an air raid. At about the same time, its chief, *Hauptsturmführer* Franz Wilhelm Prüfer, a bush-league Eichmann who had held court in room 306, died in another bombing attack. He was by then himself imprisoned, accused of embezzlement.

STELLA

Stella spent most of her time at the Burgstrasse in solitary, her cell windowless and stripped of any furnishings. Often she could neither sit nor lie down because the floor was under water. Interrogations proceeded at any hour of day or night, the questioners insisting that she take them to her friend, the notorious forger. She told them she did not know his whereabouts and had never known where he lived, which was true. The agents naturally refused to believe her, and so the physical pressure began, always in the cellars, where the noise of a hydraulic pump muffled screams and protected neighborhood sensibilities.

Rarely were Jewish prisoners tortured by instruments such as the squeezing machine used on Prinz Albrecht Strasse, an iron device into which five fingers would be jammed so they could be mangled or crushed. Instead, Jews were beaten by hand or bludgeoned by sticks or whips. Survivors believed that neither they nor their low-ranking tormentors were considered worthy of technical equipment.

Years later, marshaling her formidable writing skills, Stella described her treatment in the reports she volunteered for the prosecutors at her second trial:

"They kicked both of my shins to the breaking point and kept beating the same spot on my spine. I was bleeding from my mouth, ears, and nose and couldn't eat for days. They wanted to throttle me. Three times they took the safety off a pistol and put it against my temple. Totally shattered, I lay unconscious on the floor. Then they kicked me with their boots and I gave up on my life . . ."

Although Stella's self-pitying recitations were skeptically received, her description of treatment in the Burgstrasse cellars was consistent with testimony of others.

"They insisted on knowing where and with whom I'd last lived," recalled another inmate, Rolf Joseph, a young carpenter's apprentice. "I assured them that I really lived on the streets, but nobody believed me. They absolutely demanded that I name names, but I refused. So they led me into a cellar, bound my hands and feet, and tied me across a wooden crate. Then I was beaten twenty-five times with a bullwhip on my naked behind. I had to count the strokes aloud."

Joseph was strong enough never to break and extricated himself by a psychologically inventive ruse. The Gestapo men were known to fear all contagious diseases like the proverbial plague itself. Running only a slight fever, Joseph systematically scratched his face and had himself transported to the Jewish Hospital as a scarlet fever patient.

An author named Adelberg, who had enraged his keepers by man-

144

aging to escape briefly, rated advanced treatment at the Burgstrasse. He was spotted by a Jewish *Ordner* after a night in the cellars, his mouth, nose, and ears no longer identifiable as such. His arms were fractured. One leg dangled out of joint. His body had been broken all over by a mechanical device that kept hitting him after the Gestapo men had tired and gone to bed.

They had wanted to make Adelberg knuckle under, to "understand," as this victim, barely able to communicate a few words, mumbled to the *Ordner*. A few days later, Adelberg was sent on his stretcher to Auschwitz to be gassed.

Prey like Stella, survivors of torture, were only physically restored to life. "Anyone who has been tortured remains tortured," wrote Jean Améry, an Austrian philosopher who was tortured by the Gestapo because of his resistance activities in Belgium. "Anyone who has suffered torture never again will be able to be at ease with the world, the abomination of the annihilation is never extinguished. Faith in humanity, already cracked by the first slap in the face, then demolished by torture, is never acquired again." *

As for Stella, her treatment in the Burgstrasse cellars demolished her exalted picture of herself. Her prime asset had proved perishable. Having quite consciously relied on her looks since childhood as her way to be outstanding, she suddenly found them ephemeral, meaningless.

All through adolescence, she had lived something of a charmed life. Her beauty had endowed her with power over males, an asset she relished. Tough types like Guenther Rogoff dropped their armor in their eagerness to have sex with her. Her doting parents tried to keep her cocooned by making many life decisions for her even into her twenties.

The Burgstrasse stripped her of all defenses. The males there cared about nothing but Rogoff's whereabouts. The pressure of Eichmann's *Judenamt*, Office IVB4, made them operate with the mindless bloodthirstiness of Genghis Khan. She become a bloody heap on the floor, her identity, her self-esteem shattered.

Eventually, tired of wasting their time on fruitless beatings, the interrogators delivered her to the women's "prison" in a factory area on Bessemer Strasse, near the Tempelhof airport.

---

* Améry was one of the late victims: he killed himself in 1978. His observations on torture were recalled by Primo Levi, a fellow prisoner he befriended at Auschwitz.

This jail was really a cluster of filthy, run-down barracks incarcerating two types of prisoners. One barracks held respectable women, including ladies of the aristocracy, who were accused of *Rassenschande*, sleeping with Jewish men, and were now rooming with a contingent of whores. The other buildings were bursting with foreigners, mostly Polish women, many of them pregnant, who were being held for reasons nobody knew. Stella was kept with the foreigners, though she did not linger for long.

One hot and sleepy midsummer Saturday she reported a dental emergency to her guards. Although her pain was one of the consequences of her mistreatment, it was taken seriously. The Berlin authorities still took pride in handling their victims *ordnungsgemäss*, a beloved term describing official loyalty to orderly procedure. If a prisoner was suspected of withholding information, it was *ordnungsgemäss* to beat her within a millimeter of death. If she had a toothache, she had to be taken to the dentist, even on a weekend.

Benefiting from this surviving remnant of pre-Hitler chivalry, Stella was taken to the police dental station on Scharnhorststrasse. The place was so lightly guarded that she was able to dash out of the waiting room, and there were not enough officers on hand to tail her.

Her immediate concern was for her parents. At the home of friends she learned that they had threatened suicide and were hiding with other friends in Weissensee. Stella knew the apartment. She had long ago stashed away a suitcase there. "When I entered the room, they thought they were looking at a miracle," she would write. Her mother and father examined her injuries and scars and both broke down in tears. It was Stella's birthday.

It was too dangerous for the Weissensee family to continue giving shelter to three illegally living Jews, so Stella and her parents decided to move uptown to a *Pension* on Kaiserallee. Another U-boat had once told them that the place was reasonably safe. They did not know that the source of their information had been misled and recently arrested himself.

After Stella had been free for less than twelve hours, two Gestapo men were at their door. Her parents were taken to the already infamous Grosse Hamburger Strasse.

Stella was beaten again, questioned again about Rogoff's whereabouts, and then returned to the Bessemer Strasse prison barracks. Still considered a possible source of information, she was not yet fodder for shipment eastward and remained on Bessemer Strasse until August 23, 1943, another date that would become historic for deadly reason.

"The Battle of Berlin Has Begun," announced the headline over the front-page article in *The New York Times*. The first of several air raids hit on that Monday night with clear skies, and the details of the air raid were impressive. Some 700 Allied bombers had dropped 1,800 tons of explosives, plus tens of thousands of incendiaries, on the capital. The raid was twice as heavy as any previous attack and losses were fierce on both sides. Nazi flak shot down fifty-eight bombers; 5,680 Berliners died and another 120,000 were made homeless.

Stella's prison barracks for women on Bessemer Strasse were among the hundreds of flattened, burned-out structures, yet she managed to use the ensuing chaos for another narrow escape.

The air raid sirens began to wail at 11:29 p.m. on the preceding Sunday. The first bombs fell precisely at midnight. Streaking west to east, the attackers hit the Steglitz and Charlottenburg districts, set the zoo area aflame, and fanned out over the city center. Stella's neighborhood, Tempelhof, was home to several large war plants, including those of Siemens, AEG Electrical, and Opel Motors. All were severely damaged or wiped out.

Stella's prison became a funeral pyre.

"We were driven back into the flames by carbines," she would write. "Women were on their knees praying. They were burned alive. Some of the cells had not been opened. The wreckage of the Opel Works fell onto the road leading to the prison. In the last minute, before some freight cars exploded and destroyed everything, the gate was opened and I was able to save myself with a Jewish woman from Hungary.

"We crawled through the rubble on all fours. Thick smoke fogged us in. I was almost unconscious when this woman pulled me up and shouted at me. I came somewhat to my senses and we reached the street. The air raid continued. The prison police were trying to round up the women. We got through to Alboin Park . . ."

The attack was among the first of 363 that ultimately destroyed about ten square miles of central Berlin, wrecked about one third of its 1.5 million structures, and killed or seriously injured some 150,000 people. No major capital was ever hit so hard or for so long.

Ed Murrow, the CBS correspondent, witnessed the air campaign that August from 20,000 feet up. Red-eyed and unshaven, he returned to the London studio of the BBC and began his broadcast: "Last night some young men took me to Berlin . . ." The mission in the black Lancaster called *D for Dog* was a night Murrow remembered—from the first flak that made the bomber feel as helpless as "a black bug on a white sheet" to the high explosives, dubbed "cookies," bursting on Berlin "like great sunflowers gone mad."

The flak kept returning ("The lights still held us, and I was very frightened"), and then *D for Dog* finally broke free and Murrow looked out of his window. "The white fires had turned red. They were beginning to merge and spread, just like butter does on a hot plate." Murrow felt ambivalent about the deed done by his plane: "Men die in the sky while others are roasted alive in their cellars."

But always he remained the reporter, the literate, analytical eyewitness.

"Berlin was a kind of orchestrated hell," he concluded. "In about thirty-five minutes over the target it was hit with about three times the amount of stuff that ever came down in a night-long Blitz over London. This is a calculated, remorseless campaign of destruction. . . ."

Remarkably, the devastation never defeated Berlin. Quite the contrary. The gutted armaments factories were patched up with speed unbelievable to the Allied command. Their workers, many made angry and defiant by the threat to their lives and the death of loved ones, actually increased output. Shortly after hostilities ceased, the United States Strategic Bombing Survey, a team of experts appointed by President Harry S Truman to assess damage to industry, found it to have been relatively small.*

That was the big picture. The view from the ground was different.

Gerd Ehrlich, twenty-one, Goldschmidt School student turned U-boat, was sitting out the August 23 raid, disguised in his snappy Hitler Youth uniform, in a big concrete public bomb shelter deep under Bismarckstrasse, close to where I had lived in the late 1920s and had listened to the shooting of street battles.

"The lights went out," Ehrlich was to write. "The shelter wobbled like a ship at sea. The women began to scream and it seemed as if the entire structure was going to tumble down on us . . ."

---

* The defenseless Berlin civilians actually won a hard-to-believe Pyrrhic victory over their aerial tormentors, because fear caused morale to rise. It drove Berliners into working harder. Although the city's population was down from 4.3 to 2.3 million people by the end of the war, production in its surviving armaments factories set an all-time record in 1944.

Gerd was surprised by the ferocity of the attack. There had been innumerable earlier raids that had done little damage. The Berliners dismissed them as "Mosquito attacks" because the bombers were British Mosquito planes and their sting was relatively light. After Propaganda Minister Joseph Goebbels ordered the distribution of handbills to every household on August 1, calling on all "women, children, and pensioners" to leave the city, there was considerable response but as yet little fear.

Some 700,000 of Berlin's 4.3 million people fled to the country. Railroad stations were clogged. People were trying to salvage their valuables in bulging, lead-heavy suitcases. Gerd Ehrlich helped carry some of these burdens on behalf of gentile friends. His thoughts were ambivalent: He applauded and pitied Allied fliers when he saw them under fiery attack from German antiaircraft during the Mosquito raids. He knew that those Allied pilots were friends. Still, he also found himself rooting for the Luftwaffe flak guns that attacked the attackers. The Nazi gunners were protecting his skin.

Other U-boats in other circumstances greeted the raiders recklessly and with untrammeled enthusiasm. Another of my schoolmates, the irrepressible Margot Linczyk, had the excellent fortune for a while to be given access, with her mother, to a luxurious private shelter outfitted by a family of wealthy anti-Nazis. During raids, a butler served champagne. And when bombs began to impact close by, these intended targets of the attackers toasted each other and shouted, "Come on, Tommy, come on!"

As of the early morning hours of August 24—the all-clear sirens didn't sound for three hours—air raids became the central fact of life for all Berliners for almost two years to come.

A red haze hung over the entire city that Tuesday. A heat wave was at its peak. "The central and western districts are nothing but a rubble pile," reported Roland Marti, the representative of the International Red Cross, from his offices in Wannsee to his headquarters in Geneva. "One walks as if it's nighttime . . . Trains are not running . . . We have neither electricity nor gas . . ."

Panic, controlled but permanent, told hold. People went to bed fully dressed because few nights offered uninterrupted sleep. Emerging from their shelters, they found the heat so intense that they wrapped themselves in water-drenched blankets. Dehydration had shrunk the corpses that littered the streets; they looked like charred dolls. Smoke lingered so thickly for so many days that even some men wore veils to avoid having their faces blackened. Armies of rats swarmed through the streets in broad daylight. The worst-hit districts lacked water, electricity, gas, and heat for weeks. Residents stood in line for meals at army soup kitchens *(Gulasch-Kanonen)*.

Many Jews remained in their upstairs hiding places during the raids, facing an ironic paradox. Even as they prayed for their lives during the bombings, they enjoyed a respite from their usual fears. No Gestapo pursuer would be crazy enough to come banging on the door during an air raid.

Gerd Ehrlich had faced danger of still another sort. As bombs scored hits around his shelter that first night, the air raid warden handed him a steel helmet and ordered him to patrol the stairs in search of stray incendiaries. Tapping his way by flashlight, he heard a hissing sound. He happened to come along in time to toss sand on a firebomb before it could torch the building. It was rare luck. On his way home hours later, Gerd felt morally compelled to help carry furniture out of one blazing building after another.

Adrift in the bombed-out city, Stella, still only twenty, was trying to cope with the pain of her injuries and the pull toward her accustomed anchor, her parents, who were still being held in the collection camp on Grosse Hamburger Strasse.

"I had phosphorous poisoning, contusions all over my body, my legs were green and blue, and my shoes fell off my feet like ashes," she would write. "My emotions and my love of my parents caused me to decide to share their lot. I walked for three and a half hours after the raid ended and surrendered at Grosse Hamburger Strasse. . . . I could have run, but I didn't."

Her parents were on the list for shipment to Auschwitz that very day by one of the dreaded cattle car trains to the East. As soon as Stella appeared, her mother, always the family's powerhouse, protested loudly that she would not leave the camp without her child. Since Stella had to be interrogated, this meant that the entire family was temporarily spared.

The Gestapo interrogator quickly got around to demanding that Stella tell him the whereabouts of the elusive forger Guenther Rogoff. Her questioner had several Rogoff forgeries lined up on the desk in front of him, and Stella had already run into fellow prisoners who had been supplied with documents by Rogoff.

Stella didn't know where Guenther was and again she said so. Again the interrogator shouted that she was lying. He placed all three Goldschlags on the next deportation list for Auschwitz but ordered that Stella's case be separated for "handling" by two Jewish catchers who worked for the Gestapo with the Grosse Hamburger Strasse camp as their base. Together they were supposed to hunt up Rogoff. "What advantages will I have?" demanded Stella. No response.

Stella asked her mother what she should do. Toni Goldschlag advised her to fake cooperation, to think of something that would stall the Gestapo past the departure date of the next Auschwitz shipment. The following train would be bound for the Theresienstadt camp, not far from Prague, where conditions were reputed to be more humane.

Mobilizing her acting acumen, Stella told her two catchers that while she truly didn't know where Rogoff lived, she did have an idea what area he hung out in. She invented the story that the master forger was often in the borough of Moabit, usually around Turmstrasse, in the general vicinity of the huge and ornate old courthouse there.

Day after day Stella lurked in hallways and shops around Moabit, supervised by her two catcher shadows, Günther Abrahamson, a big, irrepressible twenty-two-year-old, and his junior partner, Gottschalk, a "half-Jew" lately cashiered from the antiaircraft artillery because of his religious impediment.*

As Stella remembered the outcome of the abortive mission, Abrahamson soon tired of the search, accused Stella of faking, and made a report to this effect to his bosses. Promptly, the names of all three Goldschlags went back onto the list for transport to Auschwitz.

The Gestapo keepers were not yet through with Stella, however. They differed from ordinary thugs in that they were ruled by principles of sorts. They were slaves to orders from their superiors and they were stubbornly goal-oriented. Hitler had issued his final demand to clean out Berlin; he wanted the capital *judenrein* without further delay, and consequently his keepers at the Grosse Hamburger Strasse could lose patience quickly. Habitually, they beat or slapped or kicked their charges, whisked them away on the death trains, or, in the case of occasional *Klärungsfälle* whose racial status was in question, let prisoners anguish for months in uncertainty. Everything still had to run *ordnungsgemäss,* according to the rules.

---

* In 1992, Abrahamson, convicted of "crimes against humanity" forty years earlier in Berlin, conceded to me that he had had frequent contact with Stella as a colleague, but denied that he had ever worked with her directly. Conceivably, two Abraham sons worked for the Gestapo at the same time and place, but circumstances make this unlikely. In the postwar court proceeding against Abrahamson, he testified that he had been teamed by Dobberke with a young collaborator named Gottschalk.

If it suited their mission, the Gestapo keepers could also display the patience of angels, and for Stella they decided to apply their benign treatment. She apparently knew more about Rogoff than anyone else and might yet lead them to the elusive forger. And she held so much other promise as well. Her obvious devotion to her parents made them perfect hostages. Better yet, Stella was in the thrall of Rolf Isaaksohn; she had succumbed to the temptations of Rolf's profitable forgery business and was being led by him, away from the bourgeois values of her family.

Isaaksohn was by that time also on tap at the Grosse Hamburger Strasse camp. He was there for an indefinite stay, having declared himself ready to be of service to avoid deportation. Indeed, he told Dobberke he could personally assemble an entire train of deportees.

Not least, Stella's keepers were impressed by her cleverness, the cool, the agility that had already enabled her to escape twice from the Gestapo. And her trump card was highly visible: she had a talent for exploiting her looks and sex. She was unique, a star waiting to be discovered and put to work! Where would they find another blond, blue-eyed Jewess who could wiggle her way into any male confidence, who knew the habits, contacts, hiding places, and psychology of the U-boats, who could spot these tenacious resisters on the streets and in the cafés, and who was herself so desperate, so greedy to survive, and tough enough to recover from torture with no visible damage?

All this made her sufficiently interesting to be led into the presence of the number-one man on the scene, the camp commander, SS *Hauptsturmführer* Walter Dobberke, the local Hitler, a flick of whose head sufficed to consign an inmate instantly to standing room on the next death train.

Another train was about to leave, a new list of 1,000 death candidates was being completed, everyone had to be ready and fit for transport—it was the climax of Dobberke's busy week. Though pressed for time, he quickly recognized that the sales pitch his staff had given him about this beguiling blonde seemed on target. Gruffly he informed Stella that he would again postpone the deportation of all three Goldschlags if she would do her civic duty and assist in tracking lawbreakers, starting with Guenther Rogoff. Stella shrugged and nodded agreement. The deal was struck.

The meeting proved a fateful match of favorable first impressions. The small, muscular, and crude Dobberke—he always wore civilian clothes and was addressed as *Herr Kommissar*—had started his career as a cop in an unappetizing assignment: the morals squad among the raucous whores of Alexanderplatz; he appreciated a well-spoken female asset when he faced one. Stella, in turn, had an affinity for power and was totally determined to survive. The two made a natural team, and for nearly two years they would enact the classic drama of Mephistopheles enslaving Dr. Faust.

The manipulation of Stella began with Dobberke, in his role as the bad cop, informing his more refined and better educated deputy, SS *Rottenführer* Felix Lachmuth, of the agreement he had reached with her. Lachmuth, acting as the good cop, was to get her working as a catcher on a regular basis. No threats would be necessary. Softened up by her beatings, Stella was a willing recruit who would join the staff and was to be treated like an employee.

The sudden change in her treatment startled and pleased Stella immensely, so soon after the cellars of the Burgstrasse, and she took advantage of it at once, still expecting that she would eventually be deported with her parents, like almost everybody at the Grosse Hamburger Strasse. Lachmuth seemed civilized and a good sort. Could he possibly use his good offices to switch the family to a list for Theresienstadt instead of Auschwitz?

Lachmuth told her not to worry and led her into the kind of get acquainted conversation that bosses strike up with new hired hands who need to be relaxed a bit.

Behold, the two had quite a bit in common. So, her mother was pursuing a career as a singer of classical music? Remarkably, Lachmuth said with a rueful grin, he had harbored similar aspirations in peacetime. With whom was Stella's mother training? *Ach,* Professor Schuetzendorf? What a small world! Schuetzendorf had also been Lachmuth's teacher. Employer and employee laughed, pleased by their newly discovered bond.

"Lachmuth had complete understanding for my predicament," Stella would write. "He wanted to help me. This assistance took the form of a permanent pass that permitted me to leave the Grosse Hamburger Strasse camp at any time, and I didn't have to wear the *Judenstern*." She was also given a private room and, from time to time, money. Her parents would be retained as hostages. It was the bargain she had hoped for.

15. First Blood

S TELLA'S COMPUTERLIKE MEMORY for names, dates, addresses, and other useful minutiae became an instant Gestapo asset. Her colleague Günther Abrahamson was impressed by her competence. Being an easygoing type from the provinces, he marveled at the "intensity" of her work habits. To him, she represented the "elite" of the catcher profession, indeed its very "embodiment."

Sophie Erdberg, an unmarried young U-boat of her acquaintance, recognized the tracks of Stella's footwork when, one by one, some twenty members of a young Jewish social group disappeared. They had belonged to a circle, mostly singles, who met to dance to recordings, preferably the fox-trot, on Sunday afternoons in 1942 at the Wilmersdorfer Strasse home of Ilya Sonntag. Not even tea was served at these socials because nobody could produce such luxury extras, and the group never gathered in the evening because of the eight p.m. curfew for Jews.

After Stella defected, Erdberg discovered that she was the only one who had not been betrayed by her fellow dancer. Sophie attributed her luck to her shyness. "I don't think she caught my name," she said. Sophie, on the other hand, would remember Stella's conspicuous presence without difficulty. The newly hired Gestapo catcher had been the best-dressed dancer in the group.

News of Stella's treachery spread rapidly, at least among those U-boats who hadn't, for safety reasons, cut themselves off from all

Jewish contacts. Ernst Goldstein, once an agent for cigar distributors, heard that fall from an *Ordner* at the Grosse Hamburger Strasse camp about a strikingly beautiful, elegantly dressed blond woman who had been "turned" by the Gestapo, along with her handsome boyfriend.

Late one morning, Goldstein and his wife, Herta, decided to risk having coffee in one of the many cafés on Kurfürstendamm. "We couldn't run in the streets all the time and we had to be away from our furnished room for a while," Herta remembered. "The landlady was getting nosy."

Her husband picked one of the larger places and took a table near the rear exit. Within a few minutes he seized his wife by the arm and hissed, "Here are the head hunters!" Without a doubt, the tall, stylishly outfitted blonde was Stella and the young man with the soft hat and well-tailored suit had to be Rolf Isaaksohn. Their looks and actions matched their descriptions perfectly. A photo of Stella had even circulated in the U-boat community.

They walked in slowly, peering about—a shade more intently than if they had only been looking for a table. Their slow-motion entrance gave Goldstein time to toss a five-mark note on their table and stride out toward the back, arm in arm with Herta, both wildly agitated yet managing to appear casual and thereby avoiding a chase.

Margot Levy, nineteen, nearly panicked on her half-Jewish boyfriend's rented houseboat when Stella showed up one weekend in early fall. Although the two young women recognized each other instantly as former co-workers at Siemens, neither one alluded to these contacts or inquired what the other had been up to since then. Jews had learned to remain carefully circumlocutious in conversation with all but closest intimates. Margot had heard that Stella was working for the Gestapo. And since all armaments Jews were supposed to have been shipped off to the East, Stella had to know that Margot was living illegally.

Luckily, the star catcher was herself out on a risky limb: she was practicing *Rassenschande* for the weekend with a tall, blond Wehrmacht soldier whom she obviously hadn't known long or well but who already knew his way around the boat, which was docked at Schildhorn on the Havel River—a short way north of Wannsee, where the Holocaust was formalized. The soldier had rented the tiny cabin across the gangway from Margot and her friend, Heinz Meyer, and shared the single bed with Stella.

Two other couples also rented cramped quarters and there was enough *Kartoffelschnapps* (potato liquor) to turn the outing into one convivial session of partying. Outwardly merry, Margot found it difficult to hide her fear of possible arrest by Stella; yet nothing happened, and she never saw Stella again. The catcher evidently felt she couldn't risk having the Gestapo find out about her outing with a non-Jewish man. Heinz Meyer saw the handsome soldier again on future weekends, always with a different girl.

Margot's fear was justified, for Stella, long acquainted with the Wannsee vacation territory, was making it part of her hunting ground. On one weekend she led her Gestapo people to cabins housing sixty-two Jews.

Gerd Ehrlich, still in his Hitler Youth getup with its enormous black leather boots, barely eluded Stella when she was still new at her job.

He felt only a light tap on his shoulder that crisp early afternoon in October 1943, the fifth year of the war. He was inching ahead in the food line of a café on Savigny Platz because the place was permitted to sell one daily blue-plate special between noon and two p.m. without ration stamps having to be surrendered.

"Hi, Gerd, how are you?" said a friendly female voice directly behind him.

Gerd was another escape artist, fashioned from the same mold as Guenther Rogoff. He lived in furnished rooms, one night at a time, never once having to stay in a whorehouse, like one of his U-boat chums. Gerd had plenty of money from the sale of his parents' Persian carpets. He bought, sold, and altered identification documents. He courted several girls, mostly Jewish but not all. He went swimming and to the movies. And his naturally exuberant disposition was undimmed by his daily romp on the thinnest of ice, young males being under constant suspicion as likely draft evaders.

"I felt I lived on borrowed time," he recalled. "In a way it was a lark. You got cocky."

Cocky, yet excruciatingly careful. Part of Gerd's secret as a survivor-in-hiding was his almost uncanny olfactory sensitivity. Like a deer, he could scent the slightest hint of danger. And like a deer, he froze at the sound of the female voice behind him in the café.

The voice was not immediately familiar and that was bad. He had been using four different phony names. Only his closest friends knew him as Gerd, his real name, and he knew their voices well. Something was fishy.

Poker-faced, he turned around and recognized the lovely Stella. He knew that she had been Stella Goldschlag in the Goldschmidt School; then he had known her as Stella Kübler in the war plant of Erich and Graetz, known as E. and G., where both had been doing forced labor on artillery shells and *Panzerfäuste* until early in the year. He also knew her, by way of recent gossip among fellow U-boats, as "the blond Lorelei," the Gestapo catcher.

Gerd was instantly aware that his situation was rendered particularly precarious by the man in the black uniform who stood in line in front of him. This was no ordinary SS man. The *"SD"* stitched onto the forearm of his tunic signified that he belonged to the dreaded *Sicherheitsdienst*, the Gestapo. Perhaps this was no coincidence. The man might be working with Stella.

"I'm sorry, miss," Gerd said pleasantly. "I don't know you. You must be mistaking me for someone else."

"No, no," Stella responded, laughing, "I know you're Gerd Ehrlich! Don't you recognize me? We worked together at E. and G.!"

"I'm sure you're wrong—my name is different."

At that moment the SS man, who had been served, turned around and stared at Gerd, who knew he was safe for a few more seconds because of his other camouflage, more convincing than his Hitler Youth costume: his looks, "Aryan" enough to grace a Nazi Party poster. Muscular, blue-eyed, with ash-blond hair and a choirboy face, he looked nothing like the pornographic stereotypes of hook-nosed, swarthy Jews caricatured in Julius Streicher's hate sheet, *Der Stürmer*. "Streicher saved our lives," Gerd would recall, chuckling at the irony. "They never suspected us nice German-looking boys of being Jewish!"

Standing between Stella and the Gestapo man, Gerd had to move fast, and he did. With a rough shove to the chest, he sent Stella sailing to the floor and dashed out at top speed. Track sports were his great love and it showed. He dashed up the steps to the elevated station on the downtown side, down again on the uptown side, barreling out of the station, trying to watch for a departing streetcar. Savigny Platz was a busy intersection, so he at once spotted a tram on the move, jumped aboard, and disappeared among the many standees.

Gerd's father, a lawyer—wary of abandoning all that was familiar, much like Stella's dad and Guenther Rogoff's and my own—had long resisted leaving Germany. "We were doing too well," Gerd said.

When emigration to America was first suggested to his family, the father asked, "What am I going to do there?" Later came the promise of a visa for Trinidad. "We were not that desperate," Gerd remembered.

Not yet. Hope did dwindle after his father was arrested on Crystal Night and later developed heart trouble in the Sachsenhausen concentration camp. The old gentleman died of it the following year— and Gerd was left responsible for his mother and his younger sister, Marion—responsible and accountable, especially in his own mind. It was to become a stone upon his soul for life, a burden never to be discharged, though there was little warning at the time.

On November 19, 1942, with deportation trains operating more and more frequently, Gerd had worked the night shift and was sleeping at four p.m., when his mother woke him with word that the family was to report that night to the Grosse Hamburger Strasse collection camp. The order had been expected and the family had agreed on a plan. Gerd was to try to survive underground by himself; as a quick-witted "Aryan" male, he had a chance to subsist, at least for a while. His mother and sister had no wish even to make such an attempt. At no time was there any argument about these arrangements, so debatable in retrospect.

Like most others, the Ehrlichs had not yet heard of gas chambers and did not scent death. So while Gerd helped his women pack their allowed baggage, two rucksacks, all three were fearful but not despairing. The trivialities of the travel preparations seemed to leave no time for tears.

Toward eight p.m., Gerd and his mother and sister set off to the camp by elevated train to the Mitte district in the eastern part of town. Only the clanking of the train wheels and the occasional shudder of the car suggested that they had embarked upon a passage, a transport to unknown places much farther away to the east.

While it was obviously risky for Gerd to escort the two women to the doors of the camp with its police guards, it was silently taken for granted that he would do so. On a dark and drizzly night the guards would be watching for Jews trying to get out, not headed in. Gerd handed over the rucksacks, gave his sister a kiss, bent his head to receive his mother's last blessing, and turned away fast, greatly upset, not looking back.

He would banish the scene from his mind for years; it was too painful. What eventually came back to him most vividly were the sounds of the elevated car to the Börse station and the camp bathed in floodlights, mingling with the fantasy of rattling freight cars, the cattle train that took his mother and sister to—as it later turned out—the gas of Auschwitz.

For the rest of his days Gerd would be frightened of rail stations and couldn't tolerate the sight or sound of trains.* At the time he was simply drained and, foolishly, went home to sleep. When Gestapo officers came to seal off his parents' apartment, he showed his phony papers and said he was renting his room and knew nothing about the Jews who had cleared out.

The officers left him alone, but after his next encounter with the Gestapo—the collision with Stella at the café—he decided to quit the country, regardless of peril. This time he had undoubtedly made the "wanted" list. Like Rogoff. And like Rogoff, he decided to head for the likeliest nearby neutral country, Switzerland.

Underground contacts brought Gerd to a woman of lofty principles and breathtaking daring, Luise Meier. Frau Meier lived in a villa in the exclusive Grunewald section, but Gerd met her only for furtive rendezvous on the street. Elegantly turned out and well spoken, Frau Meier explained that her two sons had been decorated and had died fighting with the SS on the eastern front. Possibly they had been involved with organized killings of Jews. Her conscience troubled her and she had decided to organize an underground railroad to help Jews escape.

The operation worked through the cooperation of friends in the German border town of Singen whom Frau Meier had met during vacation trips in years past. These helpers were reliable beyond any question, Frau Meier said. Some thirty Jews had already been exfiltrated through the amateur group without a hitch. Gerd Ehrlich knew some of these refugees, so he agreed to take himself, his best friend, and the friend's fiancée to the Singen railroad station at five p.m., October 10, 1943. Frau Meier had requested a substantial payment which she said she would hand on to her helpers. Money being of little use, Gerd delivered several typewriters and bicycles.

Beyond Stuttgart the trio took milk trains south because these were rarely subject to controls. At the Singen station they would be met by "a lady in black with a bicycle." A woman who fit this description was indeed waiting, greeted them warmly, and led them into the woods near the frontier. In a clearing of the trees a man was waiting who led them some distance farther through fields until they

---

* "Phobic reactions to situations that recall memories" are standard symptoms listed in the medical literature for the psychological condition known as posttraumatic stress disorder.

saw a road shimmering in the distance. The road was patrolled by a border guard, the guide said. The frontier was at the quarry just beyond. The three fugitives were to cross between 9:25 and 9:35 p.m., when the guard left to be relieved. They were to clear the last stretch by crawling because troops with searchlights were nearby.

It sounded clear-cut, but it wasn't. Just before they reached the Swiss section of the forest, the day-bright fingers of a searchlight flickered across their bodies and all but pierced them. They froze and the light groped on. They crawled south, reaching a road they knew nothing about. They were lost. Suspecting that they were on friendly territory, Gerd nevertheless proposed that they exercise utmost caution and spend the night where they were. They did, and the next morning it became obvious: they had slept on friendly ground.

Unintentionally, Stella had been the moving force behind Gerd's survival. If he hadn't blundered into her, he might have tried to brazen it out in Berlin against increasingly forbidding odds. Quite possibly, Gerd would eventually have been unmasked and might well have followed his mother and sister into the Grosse Hamburger Strasse, the last stop before the death trains.

If the venturesome Frau Meier was known to Gerd Ehrlich as a shadowy manipulator of distant agents, another of my former Goldschmidt School fellow students experienced her as an adroit hands-on operator.

Margot Linczyk, sixteen, another former singer in Dr. Bandmann's chorus, had managed to subsist with fake papers because her widowed mother's boyfriend worked in the office where deportation lists were prepared. He simply removed their names.

"I thought our life was a great adventure," Margot recalled. "I got us hiding places. I could steal, I could lie—it was fun! I think it was a reaction to my Germanic upbringing, always having to sit up straight and so on. I got my identity card from the post office by yelling 'Heil Hitler!' so loud that they got scared I might report them for not responding fast enough." Silently, she said to herself, "Shit on it!"

Of course, it couldn't last. When two Jewish fetchers came to get Margot and her mother, the mother rushed at them with a kitchen knife. The fetchers fled, but it was time for the Linczyks to leave the country. They too met Frau Meier through the Jewish grapevine and agreed to compensate the border runners with 5,000 marks' worth of family jewelry.

On the train to Singen, Margot sat with her mother and carried the jewels in a gift-wrapped box. Frau Meier traveled in the next compartment. All three wore black armbands of mourning, and at their destination they bought a big wreath, purportedly to decorate a grave in a cemetery near the border. All three proceeded to a forest, where Frau Meier turned over Margot and her mother to a guide who walked them into Switzerland after several scares en route.

(After the war, Margot heard that Frau Meier was eventually betrayed and arrested. Her daughter hired three lawyers who repeatedly managed to obtain delays in the proceedings against her, and just as Frau Meier was about to stand trial before the most notorious of the Nazi tribunals, the People's Court, the war ended and she was released.)

Ismar Reich, seventeen, cocky and classified as an escape risk, was locked up in the basement "bunker" of the Grosse Hamburger Strasse. Windowless and seemingly airless, his *Keller* was reserved for "difficult cases." At night, it was also home for Dobberke's black German shepherd.

Misery being governed by a hierarchy of its own, Reich was better off than the men jammed into the adjoining cell No. 1. Its ceiling was only four feet high, so the prisoners couldn't stand up. Reich had barely space enough to move among the twenty men in his cell, but on his second day he had inched himself into a spot near the door where he could watch the commotion in the murk of the corridor.

Several new prisoners were being herded into the bunker by a figure grossly out of keeping with the surroundings: a beautiful and elegant young blond woman attired in a trim dark green tailored suit and a green Tyrolean hat, which she wore at a jaunty angle. She was clearly very much in charge, acting possessive about the new arrivals.

Reich's cellmates began to mutter.

"That's Stella," someone whispered into his ear. He had heard of her and knew how feared she was. Here was this phenomenon in action, striding through the bunker like a queen bee, a star, commanding attention just as in her time at the Goldschmidt School.

"She owned the place," Reich would conclude.

It no longer shocked him to see that a Jew had turned on other Jews. He knew the breed. When he had been caught trying to pick up some black market food, his arrest was conducted by a pistol-wielding catcher named Bruno Goldstein. And on Reich's arrival in the camp, he was curtly questioned by Max Reschke, an authority of Prussian bearing who commanded a private office next to Dobberke's on the ground floor; he was a fellow inmate who had advanced himself to the rank and immunity of "Jewish camp director."

Shortly afterward, Reich was taken aside by two friendly young men wearing red armbands. They gave their names as Cohn and Abramowitz and said they were helping the authorities in the "Outside Service." Reich needed no details to figure out what that meant.

"Why don't you work with us?" one of the catchers asked. "We're *Kameraden,* we're Jewish too. Let the Gestapo take care of you!" Given the alternative, the logic was seductive.

Not to Reich. "I would never have that on my conscience," he replied.

That ended the recruiting effort. There was no pressure, no punishment for refusing to take refuge on the Gestapo payroll. Many of the newly arriving deportees were propositioned with recruitment deals of one kind or another. Almost all turned down Gestapo employment without serious thought. In fairness, Stella had no way of knowing that it was possible to reject the Gestapo with relative impunity. She did know what it was to lie crumpled on the floor after being tortured, and she knew that her parents were probationers, on the brink of the list for the next Auschwitz train, barely reprieved from the last list at the ultimate moment. Temporarily.

Not many of the current denizens of Grosse Hamburger Strasse remembered or cared that Dobberke was incongruously holding sway over territory at once Jewish and formerly known for Christian altruism. His *Lager* was inaugurated as the Jewish Home for the Aged in 1829. The Jewish High School for Boys was next door. The city's largest synagogue and the Jewish Community office were practically around the corner, at Oranienburger Strasse 28. The *Scheunenviertel* with its Hassidim was in easy walking distance.

And yet, anti-Semitism or not, Grosse Hamburger Strasse had, in another era, been a historical landmark: "the street of tolerance." Next to Moses Mendelssohn's cemetery stood Berlin's most beautiful baroque church, the Lutheran Sophienkirche with its own cemetery adjoining. A short way down the street was the huge St. Hedwig's Krankenhaus, the leading Catholic hospital. Only a few steps farther, Grosse Hamburger Strasse terminated at the Koppenplatz, where in 1704 a councilman donated a little plot of ground to the city for a paupers' burial ground.

The Berlin of the Kaiser and of the Weimar Republic had had no difficulty accommodating Jews alongside Lutherans, Catholics, and paupers.

Bare as a moonscape, stripped of every movable appurtenance of civilization by order of Eichmann's man Alois Brunner, the Grosse Hamburger Strasse became a pitiful universe of its own, actually not one world but two. On the floorboards of the top story, those inmates were bedded down who were condemned to the Auschwitz trains. Suicides by jumping from this floor were not uncommon. Deportees destined for the less dreaded Theresienstadt were quartered on the second floor.

Transfers from the third to the second floor could sometimes be wheedled, so frantic attempts at negotiation and bribery were constant. Illness, real or fake, could stall departures. Dread of an unknown fate gripped everyone, and when *Ordner* made rounds of the rooms at night, reading off names of residents to be shipped out, tears flowed. Few managed to sleep once they were handed cardboard signs, to be hung around the neck, bearing the leprous "T" for imminent transport.

For nimble captives who had managed to tuck away substantial sums of money, the Grosse Hamburger Strasse was the last way station for perhaps, just possibly, striking a deal with the enemy. Dr. Edith Kramer-Freund, forty-two, a widowed physician, ran, by fantastic luck, into two resourceful former patients. The doctor was due for deportation to Auschwitz at six a.m. the next day. The two expatients were horrified. Did the doctor have money? Yes. The patients had bribed a camp functionary to get them exit permits to Sweden. They were to leave that very day.

They took the doctor's bribe, 300 marks and 300 cigarettes, and gave it to a Jewish lawyer with a record for successfully bribing Gestapo men. It was hoped that this negotiator could get Dr. Freund switched to a Theresienstadt train leaving at four a.m.

Remarkably, the bizarre alliance worked. The lawyer appeared at eleven p.m. and when he met with Dr. Freund and the Gestapo coconspirator, *Kommissar* Dobberke himself, the deal was already done. It was luck: there were fifty-nine names on the Theresienstadt list and there was space for sixty. Dr. Freund survived.*

---

* The remarkably efficient lawyer did not. Eventually, together with his wife and two children, he was deported to Theresienstadt, where he appeared, greatly agitated, in Dr. Freund's room, pleading for his life. He had been a Gestapo informer

To another fortunate survivor of the Grosse Hamburger Strasse, Anneliese-Ora Borinski, the camp was like the tuberculosis sanitarium in Thomas Mann's *The Magic Mountain*. The novel's young hero spent seven years on the mountain, buffeted by disease and death, but he made it back to the outside. At the Grosse Hamburger Strasse, Borinski wrote, she was surrounded by hopelessness but also by a "last flickering of the will to live, a greed to taste one more time all that life has to offer."

Borinski was with a group of young Zionist friends who assembled each morning in the yard for exercise and sat close together in a circle every evening to sing Jewish songs ("We fight for liberty, equality, and justice . . ."). Gestapo officers watched, showing their puzzlement over the confidence manifested by the doomed en route to the trains.

At the rate of about 1,000 a week, almost all Jews had to pass through the overcrowded old building sooner or later. Inevitably, Stella, the star catcher, was sometimes confronted by her bourgeois past. When Regina Gutermann was brought in, Stella's good-natured, not so svelte fellow student from the fashion design school spotted her shapely old chum stalking through the second level. There, adult inmates and children of both sexes slept, squeezed together like livestock on the bare floor while Stella kept house with Rolf Isaaksohn in a private room with an inviting couch and soft illumination from a red bulb.

"I'm Regina!" said the old school friend, smiling and stepping up.

Stella marched past, expressionless, in silence.

The same technique didn't work with impudent little Isaak Behar, her chum from the Goldschmidt School. He was too noisy and persistent, and on this occasion guards were watching.

"Stella!" shouted Behar when he encountered her unexpectedly, sauntering through the camp, looking "like a boss."

"You here?" she responded, also taken aback.

"*Ja,* and how do I get out of here?" he demanded, remembering their last encounter on Kurfürstendamm, when she had magnanimously let him run away for old times' sake. It was different this time. She had to make her Nazi loyalty known in front of the staff.

---

guilty of betrayals as terrible as the crimes of any catcher. He would take money from Jews for false passports, and when they appeared to pick them up, the Gestapo would be waiting. In Theresienstadt, he was promptly hauled before the ghetto court. Dr. Freund testified on his behalf, but the tribunal of the inmates sentenced him and his family to immediate deportation to Auschwitz and death.

"You'll get out of here, all right," she snapped, "but as a corpse! And don't you dare try to escape!"

In fact, the Grosse Hamburger Strasse was less than escape-proof, even though the building was surrounded by patrolling police guards, the ground-floor windows had been blocked by bars, and floodlights had been installed to keep front and back day-bright at nighttime.

All such measures served as provocation for big, bluff Kurt Cohn the tailor, recently captured on the run by Stella and Rolf on Rosenthaler Platz. Cohn was one of the irrepressible types who survived through chutzpah. He loved ice cream, and when he was ravenous, he would march into an ice cream parlor and let the personnel believe he was just another burly cop. He looked and acted the part. With a flourish he'd help himself to an ice cream waffle, shout, "Shut up or I'll take you with me," and march off.

In his Grosse Hamburger Strasse basement cell—it faced the cemetery dating to 1627, now vandalized and leveled, where the philosopher Moses Mendelssohn had been buried—Cohn studied the patrol patterns of the guards. They passed his window only every five minutes. Silently he and his six cellmates began to loosen the bars from their cement footings. It took them eight days, chipping in a frenzy, driven on by the possibility that one or more or all of them might be yanked out to an eastbound train.

After enough bars were sufficiently unstuck to be removed, Cohn waited until the night a bad air raid sent the guards scurrying into shelters. He was the first to dash through the bombs into the cemetery and onward, followed by his cellmates, into illegal hiding again.

Such daring paid off only rarely. Moritz Zajdmann's sister wanted to smuggle burglar tools to him, but she lowered them into the wrong manhole outside the building. And Rolf Josef turned out to be worse off than before, at least initially, even though several Jewish *Ordner,* as was not uncommon, decided to help him and his associates to escape.

Josef had spent four weeks caged like a bird in the notoriously confining cell No. 1. The experience failed to dampen his fire. As soon as he was transferred to bunker No. 6, he and his five cellmates launched plans. No. 6 wasn't always locked; sometimes the prisoners could roam the corridor to investigate. The *Ordner* would whistle whenever a Gestapo man came near. Josef and his friends found a door with only a simple lock. Behind it a staircase led to the street.

Remarkably, additional assistance became available. From a

plumber who came to repair the pipes, the gang stole badly needed tools. Then a Jewish nurse agreed to help. Nurses were still employed at the big Jewish Hospital on Iranische and Schul-Strasse. Being very pretty, she had been arrested because she slapped an SS man who propositioned her. As everyone knew, *Kommissar* Dobberke had an eye for attractive females. He permitted the nurse to circulate freely around his camp, and she agreed to slip a sleeping potion into the *Ordner*'s evening coffee. Only Dobberke's dog was of concern.

On the appointed night everything worked. The nurse put the *Ordner* to sleep. The shepherd snored. The lock was easy to pick. Unfortunately, having been kept away from any view of the street, the fugitives weren't aware of the floodlights outside. The moment moving shadows appeared, the guards took up the cry: "They're breaking out!"

Dobberke administered twenty-five wallops of his whip to each escapee—his penalty invariably ran to twenty-five strokes, not twenty, not thirty. Then he ordered the rebellious group, handcuffed, onto a transport at once.

Josef wasn't undone. Surrounded by forty-eight fellow Jews stuffed into a rickety French freight car, the women and children screaming and weeping, he fished out a pair of pliers that he still kept hidden in a shoe, removed the cuffs of his friends from the Grosse Hamburger Strasse camp, and tapped his way along the wall of the rail car. Sure enough, one side lacked reinforcing metal bars. Straining in unison, strengthened by their desperation ("We knew it meant our life or our death"), the group fought for a last chance at freedom before Auschwitz, and actually beat and kicked a hole through the side of the old railcar.

Some eighty kilometers east of Berlin they jumped into the darkness. Guards saw them and started shooting, but the train engineer, no doubt fearing further escapes, didn't stop.*

Learning of this escapade, Dobberke only shrugged. It didn't happen on his watch. He did his thing *ordnungsgemäss*. Indeed, his superiors seemed intent on restricting his attention exclusively to his personal domain, the Grosse Hamburger Strasse. Rarely was he summoned to the Burgstrasse headquarters, and then only briefly to be reprimanded over some slipup. No one had ever heard of him being admitted into the headquarters cellars.

---

* Escape from an Auschwitz train, while infrequent, was not unheard of. Sometimes such a feat was even brought off by a daredevil who would take the risk working solo. Ismar Reich and Isaak Behar saved themselves this way.

On the one occasion when he escorted a transport to the Theresienstadt concentration camp—and the same was true of his subordinates when they commanded a train to Auschwitz—he was politely kept out of the KZ itself. Local personnel took over outside the premises. The jurisdiction of the Berlin Gestapo foot soldiers was circumscribed to curtail gossip, limited to what they needed to know to perform their particular duties in the Eichmann machinery.

16. The Keeper and the Catcher

"LIMITED" WAS THE APPLICABLE WORD to describe Walter Dobberke altogether. He was a man of very few words, most of them barked. Short (less than five feet four), stubby, with close-cropped dark hair and a vacant poker face, he was a rustic from a no-man's-land of farmers far north of the capital—a countryside too lacking in appeal for Berliners even to use it for camping.

Although he had not advanced far in his chosen field by the age of thirty-seven, Dobberke was no robot, nor was he an ideologue. He was a primitive, rut-minded career cop, like his father before him, and he rose to sergeant by way of twelve years of plainclothes service among the whores and pimps of his former beat.

Indifferent to the honors bestowed upon pre-1933 *alte Kämpfer,* the original ramrods of the Party, Dobberke joined up only in 1937, shortly before being assigned to the Gestapo. His Party number was correspondingly high and undistinguished: 5 848 662. Nobody ever heard this rube from rural Pomerania allude to Hitler or politics, one way or another. Such abstractions were not his turf.

If his chief, Adolf Eichmann, represented the banality of evil, then Dobberke exemplified the banality of a cop's mind—base and closed. Escapes, transgressions of the rules turned him, very briefly, into a maniac. Violations of his world stimulated him because they gave him permission to administer a cop's favorite medicine—discipline. And since Jews had been classified by his superiors as criminals or worse, he ranked them accordingly in his life's cast of characters.

His captives sensed nevertheless that when Dobberke cursed them as sow Jews, he wasn't really venting the passionate partisanship of a philosophical anti-Semite. He was pulling rank, having once dealt similarly with the dregs of the underworld—pimps, pickpockets, and other lowlifes. If he had a *Weltanschauung,* it didn't keep him from running drunken skat card parties at two a.m., playing against Jewish prisoners whom he had treated to twenty-five lashes in the line of duty a few hours earlier.

Dobberke stored his bullwhip in his office closet the way executives stash their raincoats. And everybody could see that his orientation was ecumenical: quite openly he squired a Jewish girlfriend, Sister Elli, a young nurse from the Jewish Hospital.

The camp environment seemed to subsist more on its grapevine than on the available diet: bread, watery soup, bitter ersatz coffee, sandwiches passed through the guards by gentile friends outside, and bits bartered by the jailers against watches and rings that some prisoners had managed to keep hidden.

Since life inside was lived at such close quarters and eastbound trains were waiting, tension never let up. Just because your name did not appear on the current list, you were not necessarily safe until the next train. If it happened that a transport was not packed to bursting, you might be called at the last moment as space filler.

The scene was, as Stella later described it, "a volcano." The *Mundfunk* kept bubbling, and speculation about the relationship between Stella and Dobberke made for a popular diversion in the lava of rumors. Opinions varied. Some took for granted that Dobberke's more or less automatic skirt hunting had led to sex with Stella from the start. Most eyewitnesses disagreed. They argued that Dobberke had probably tried his luck but been rebuffed. He was too crude. She was too grand an aspiration for him, and he needed her more as the star of his catcher network than as a sex object—he had plenty of those.

The striking transformation of my fellow singer in the Goldschmidt School's chorus into a zealous cleaning woman for Dobberke entailed a meshing of many elements. Fear for her parents' lives. Fear of her own possible deportation. Fear of more torture in the basement. Fear of a still-likely Hitler victory. Loss of her bourgeois prewar identity. Devaluation of her accustomed armor—her great looks—through the Gestapo's primitivism. Dependency on her protector, Rolf. And the monkey-see-monkey-do echo given off daily by her own new in-group, her Jewish fellow catchers.

Once Stella had won approval in the Gestapo milieu, her primal fear of her keeper began to dissipate. She liked to think that she had risen above him. When she had an opportunity to express herself discreetly about him, she would snicker. It was a good-natured little sneer.

Dobberke? He was a cop who drank.

The banality of Dobberke's duties as chief keeper and thrasher of the Grosse Hamburger Strasse *Lager* bored even this undemanding henchman. More and more, he seemed merely to go through the programmed motions of a persecutor. To Johanna Mühle, twenty-nine, his patient and gregarious secretary, with whom he shared his office and confidences, he remarked that he'd much rather be back doing regular police work. He missed the chase. Investigating lowly whores and their pimps was more rewarding than this monotonous business with Jews. And so he drank and drank, drank anything—including vile-tasting cocktails mixed with medical alcohol stolen from Sister Elli's hospital.

Dobberke was one of banality's dregs. Not even torture instruments were entrusted to him. "He was much too low-ranking for that," said Gad Beck, laughing. Beck was a canny survivor who had made it his business to study his keeper with care.

And yet *Hauptsturmführer* Dobberke was a mini-dictator, the Führer of his little Grosse Hamburger Strasse universe. To underestimate him was to risk one's life. His power was absolute and sometimes it pleased him to use it beneficently. He could place your name on the list that meant the death sentence—departure on the next train. He could also order your name removed if Max Reschke had already written it onto a list, which was the officious Jewish camp director's job.

Dobberke would simply give the name to Reschke, who would place an X next to it, which spelled a temporary reprieve. The name would reappear automatically on the next list. Dobberke could then order it X-ed again. And again. And again. It depended mostly on whether Dobberke, in his cop's brain, believed that you possessed useful information that might still be extracted from you, especially names, names of still-hidden Jews, names and secret addresses. Or perhaps you had mastered a skill he required to administer his fief in an *ordnungsgemäss* manner (be it cook or order keeper, *Abholer* or handyman); or you were a prospect for recruitment as a catcher; or maybe he had taken a shine to you. Dobberke was judge, jury, and train dispatcher. Everything hung on his whim.

Dobberke could even release you from the *Lager* altogether, although the joy of such largess was fleeting. All but inevitably, the Gestapo's Jew-cleansing machinery would locate you, suck you up again, and spew you back into the Grosse Hamburger Strasse, onto a list and onto a train.

Klaus Scheurenberg, twenty, experienced Dobberke's arbitrary power to give life and to take it away. Klaus was one of those "Aryan-looking" young people whom only Hitler had finally turned into Jews and who had perforce come to feel like Jews. As a boy, Klaus would get a light slap across the mouth from his mother whenever a Yiddish word slipped into his speech. Yiddish was so uncouth. Mother would reprimand him: "Don't dirty up our beautiful German mother tongue!"

Now Klaus and his mother were incarcerated in Dobberke's *Lager,* and Klaus—envious and disgusted—was watching Stella march in and out, evidently at will. He and she had attended the same Jewish vocational high school after Stella left Goldschmidt's. Here they did not speak.

Before getting scooped out of their apartment, Klaus and his mother had managed to scribble a note to Klaus's father: "Papa, we've been fetched [*abgeholt*]. Please come quickly to the Grosse Hamburger Strasse. Klaus and Mama."

Papa was away taking Jews to a train east. He had been fired as an executive when the Hermann Tietz department store was "Aryanized" and renamed Hertie. Thereafter he supported his family as the concierge of a *Judenhaus,* a segregated apartment house for Jews. Now he had been drafted as an *Abholer* who helped old deportees with their luggage. Once he had been beaten up by an SS man who caught him sneaking a sandwich to one of his deportee clients. A Gestapo officer had saved him from being pushed onto the train as well, because the elder Scheurenberg still had his uses.

It was this role that saved Klaus and Mama Scheurenberg, at least for a while. The father hurried to see Dobberke, who promptly released wife and son.*

Among innovations introduced by the Dobberke regime in 1943 was *Schleusung* ("sluicing"), a euphemism for theft. It proceeded nonstop, silently, in basement rooms overseen by Party Comrade Prokop

---

* All were eventually dispatched to Theresienstadt, where only young Klaus survived.

and his staff. All prisoner luggage was assembled there to be searched for valuables by the Prokop crew. "Valuables" was an all-embracing term. It included not only money and jewelry but such items as bed linen, assuming it was in good repair. It was generally assumed that choice nuggets wound up in the pockets of the searchers or Dobberke, whose concepts of "thine" and "mine" were known to be interchangeable.

And yet the leader's pleasures remained few. Bombed out of his home, he was nominally jammed with his family into the tiny apartment of his secretary. He rarely seemed to go there, however, and his wife was never mentioned. It did please Dobberke to flaunt his authority by playing favorites. Once he took a liking to the wife of an *Ordner* named Manfred Guttmann. The shapely spouse worked as a cook and served the drinks at Dobberke's nocturnal card parties. The deportation of both Guttmanns was canceled seven times. Eventually Dobberke assured their survival by destroying their name cards in his office file. The lucky Guttmanns thus ceased to exist on paper, and paper still possessed much power under the Nazis.

What Dobberke tolerated poorly was to be crossed. A resistance figure named Zvi Abrahamson had escaped, and Gad Beck was at hand when Zvi was brought before Dobberke after recapture.

"He took Zvi and beat him half dead in my presence," Beck recalled. Appropriate invective accompanied the action. Dobberke yelled: "You pig, you dirt, you filth, you ran away from me!"

Somehow Abrahamson escaped once more. Again he was captured and lived to talk about it: "First thing, Dobberke bashed my teeth to bits. One blow was sufficient."

Sadism was not the Gestapo man's sole motivation. It offended his cop mentality that Abrahamson was keeping information to himself, thereby challenging Dobberke's authority. Again and again, the same questions kept hammering at the prisoner: "Where were you the first night? Where were you the second night? Where did you get your money?" Dobberke drummed away hour after hour in pursuit of such detail.

The trick of exploiting seemingly inconsequential information—a skill acquired during his tenure with the morals squad—had never deserted Dobberke. After a U-boat named Margot Goerke was arrested in an illegal Weissensee apartment, he learned that June 23, 1943, two days hence, was her birthday. This prompted him to anticipate that her Jewish friends would appear at the hideout to congratulate the young Margot. Three women did, which ended their freedom. Dobberke had deputized his sidekick, Felix Lach-muth, to lie in wait for them.

Faced with rank—almost anyone of higher station—Dobberke crumpled. Gerhard Löwenthal, incarcerated in the basement with his father two cells away, watched the Gestapo man dissolve in subser-vience at the appearance of Löwenthal's Uncle Max. The uncle, 100 percent gentile, was a ranking engineer at the Heinkel warplane works. As soon as the uncle dropped the names of associates and party *Bonzen,* Dobberke let the father go—though not young Ger-hard, who was suspected, correctly, of being involved with the fab-rication of fake identity documents.

It turned out that Gerhard merely required the intervention of still-higher rank. A gentile friend turned to a Herr von Holtzbrink, who ran an optician shop that serviced the highest elite. At the moment, indeed, several pince-nez of the SS *Reichsführer,* Heinrich Himmler himself, were waiting to be mended. Young Löwenthal, a qualified optical repairman, was needed at once! At least so Holtzbrink, ap-pearing in SS uniform, was persuaded to yell at Dobberke. Dobberke yelled right back at first, which made Holtzbrink furious. He grabbed Dobberke's phone, called a high SS office, and explained that Löwenthal was needed at once for Himmler's glasses. Then he handed the phone to Dobberke, who received his orders like a trouper. Outranked and intimidated, he discharged Löwenthal on the spot.

Luck, chutzpah, plus a hefty dollop of fear, fear of the worst, had saved Gerhard, as it would so many others.

The fiction that only labor awaited the deportees in the East contin-ued to be carefully nurtured by the Eichmann machine. The Gestapo wanted to minimize resistance from the Jews and avoid a public relations kickback from the population. And so the shipments were executed with the Gestapo brand of discretion.

Nothing moved before ten p.m. or after six a.m. Transport to the trains was again mostly via the notorious furniture vans, except that Dobberke, who provided supervision as far as the train station, moved around under the camouflage of an ambulance. Departures were staged only at out-of-the-way freight stations, and even there the trains were parked on distant tracks. Sometimes the deportees were asked to bring hammers and a supply of nails to suggest that work awaited them abroad.

One of the exit terminals was Grunewald station, stuck away in the most outlying western suburbs, and this was where Ismar Reich was taken, in a van bursting with more than seventy prisoners and several rifle-bearing guards, all standing up, weaving with the van's motion. It was dark inside, but young Reich stood wedged near the two back doors where a crack of light made nearby faces visible. Peering about him, Reich was suddenly dumbstruck. A foot or two away stood a middle-aged man with an instantly familiar face.

It was the once amiable Dr. Jacob, Reich's family physician, who had assisted at his birth. Doctors were not normally deported, not yet. If they accompanied transports as far as the station, they were medical aides—escorts charged with keeping captives moving in case of emergencies en route. They served as more or less willing collaborators.

Reich knew all this. He was also among the few with no illusions about the fate that awaited him. The doctor was one of the expediters of the Final Solution, and Reich couldn't resist challenging the man.

"How come you're here?" he demanded. No reply.

"You brought me into the world," he flung at the doctor, "and now you're bringing me to my death!"

Silence from Dr. Jacob. Silence from the guards. Silence from the other prisoners. The only sounds were the rumblings of the careening van.

Once out of sight, deportees were subjected to every possible cruelty for the sake of speed. When a Jewish doctor came to the aid of an old man who fell and fractured his ankle while boarding another cargo car, the physician was ordered to do kneebends with a brick in each hand. Nobody was to delay this freight.

A vast chasm persisted between trains to Theresienstadt in Czechoslovakia, which was not considered truly "east," versus "East" transports to Auschwitz. Theresienstadt deportees were allowed to carry briefcases and toilet articles. Upon arrival at their camp, they actually received their luggage, at least much of the time. Auschwitz people could take nothing but a blanket.

And still, very few of the Auschwitz group divined what was happening. Wishful thinking prevailed. One of those who caught on was a Dobberke charge named Harry Schnapp; at a war crimes trial this realist would testify: "If you take a toothbrush away from a person, this can only mean that he no longer needs it, and a civilized person doesn't require it only in the event he is no longer living."

Conceivably, Dobberke himself didn't know that his captives were systematically gassed in Auschwitz. His loyal secretary and confidante, Johanna Mühle, clung to this view. Possibly, he did know the truth but was maintaining security silence. Mühle didn't think this was the case. Prisoners often asked her what Auschwitz was like. She questioned her boss about it repeatedly. The most he came out with was: "It can't be very pretty in Auschwitz."

Mühle may have been correct about her boss's innocence because she knew him intimately and their relationship made him open up to her on sensitive matters, including the Orwellian bureau-speak by which the Eichmann machine sought to camouflage organized death.

Shuffling papers in their joint office, Mühle once came across an unusual document. The paper was red onionskin, the subject "special treatment" of a particular Jewish captive. The treatment was to be administered right in Berlin. Johanna was pleased.

"Isn't it nice that Jews get treated better when they get ill," she said.

This made Dobberke crack up with laughter, whereupon he advised Mühle that "special treatment" meant death. He certainly was in no doubt about that.

At the working level within the Gestapo, in the ranks below Dobberke, some were knowledgeable and many still were not, not even as late as 1943. Erwin Sartorius, a staff driver, had assisted a crew of fellow agents with the loading of a Theresienstadt train at the Anhalter station one night. He then repaired to a nearby pub with four of the crew for beer, and the ensuing conversation became an eye-opener for him.

One of the agents, obviously a new man, suddenly took to musing about the destiny of all those thousands of Jews who kept being carried off to the East. He wondered where they were all winding up. There were so many of them! An enormous number of new barracks would have to be put up to accommodate them all.

A more senior officer snickered and told the questioner not to worry. "When those Jews get to their destinations, they'll have no more toothaches," he said euphemistically, still avoiding words like "death" or "killing."

The questioning Gestapo man refused to believe what he was hearing. Why were the Jews carrying luggage if they'd never need their things?

His colleagues joined in explaining that this was a shrewd detail of the official camouflage. If civilians saw the Jews at the railroad without any bags, it would look suspicious.

. . .

By February 1944, the flow of deportees through the Grosse Hamburger Strasse had slowed to a trickle. Few Jews were left to be rounded up, and so the camp was moved into the so-called Pathology Building, actually the rather small morgue, of the block-sized Jewish Hospital. The gate was at Schulstrasse 79, around the corner from the hospital's official entrance at Iranische Strasse 2, in the Wedding district (once the stronghold of a boisterous KPD, the Communist Party of Berlin).

The move was the ultimate milestone for the Berlin Jews in their odyssey from one confinement to the next—their last *Lager*, the final island that still dispensed nothing worse than Dobberke's beatings. An extra-large transport to Theresienstadt had to be assembled to dispose of the excess humanity that couldn't be sandwiched into the smaller new quarters.

For more than half a year Stella's satisfactory service had caused Dobberke to remove her parents' names from one transport list after another. He told Stella that the latest order made it impossible to exempt them yet again.

Stella protested as vigorously as she dared. Dobberke was adamant. Stella didn't let up—whereupon Dobberke colored himself helpless. The orders had come from the *Reichssicherheitshauptamt*, national headquarters of the SS on Prinz Albrecht Strasse, seat of Heinrich Himmler. Only certain types of *Mischlinge* ("mixed" offspring of Jews and non-Jews) and *Klärungsfälle* (cases requiring investigation) could be put back—absolutely no one else, with no exceptions. The exempt categories didn't apply to the Goldschlags. They positively had to leave.

"Ich gehe mit!" shouted Stella impulsively. "I'm going too!"

Dobberke reasoned with her, assured her that she was safe as long as she did her job with Rolf.

"Be glad you don't *have* to go," he pleaded, sounding like a vice president in charge of sales afraid of losing his best salesperson. Whatever Rolf did to keep Stella safe remained private between the two lovers.

Stella's parents cast the decisive vote. She invariably listened to them, and they knew what they wanted. This was one occasion when the father was the stronger partner. The mother could not stop crying. Round little Gerhard Goldschlag was dry-eyed and firm.

"You'll stay, and we're happy about that," he told her. "We go gladly in your stead and we're not afraid."

Stella saw herself released from her obligations to her family, and all three were relieved that the parents were not headed for Auschwitz. None believed that anything worse than forced labor was in store at Theresienstadt, a conviction that Dobberke reinforced, presumably in good conscience.

Stella acquiesced as soon as her boss agreed to final favors. Stella and Rolf were allowed to take her parents to the train. And the Goldschlags would not have to put up with the indignity of going by furniture van; they could depart the camp in Dobberke's ambulance and take along mattresses as well as heavy blankets.

The Goldschlags were leaving aboard an *Ordner-Transport*. The cars of their section of the train were reserved for some fifty *Ordner* and employees of the Jewish Community offices who were no longer needed by the Gestapo as the number of Jews in Berlin diminished. They had been among the relatively privileged who had served the Nazis in the belief that they would be spared deportation or might stall long enough for the Allies to win the war. This expectation did materialize for a small handful. For those leaving with the Goldschlags, their abandoned hopes made the departure a particularly bitter scene.

"I was drained, done for," Stella recalled.

Stella's recollection of her parents' peaceful resignation at their departure sounded questionable to me. Maybe her mother and father were bravely attempting to protect their daughter from as much anguish as possible. More likely Stella was lying to me. Or did the separation perhaps leave her with a memory so painful that it became intolerable and therefore blocked in her mind?

I knew that posttraumatic stress disorder was commonly triggered by physical or emotional disasters. My authoritative *Merck Manual* told me that the condition can start when "availability of social supports" stops and that "impairment of memory" can be the consequence. Certainly her parents had always been Stella's "social supports." But my speculations seemed dubious. Too many facts were simply not obtainable.

Did the parents cling to a belief in the fiction that Stella continued to limit her Gestapo collaboration to a search for Rogoff alone? Given the volume of the arrests she made during the five months she lived under the same roof with them at the gossip-prone Grosse Hamburger Strasse camp—and the fear that her reputation inspired among inmates—it was most likely that the mother and father were knowledgeable. Did they forgive her? Accuse her of unforgivable acts? Argue? Disown her? Choose to believe the daughter's lie to protect their own sanity? Were they simply grateful that they weren't being shipped to Auschwitz?

There was no way to find out, but whatever the facts, the contact between Stella and her parents did not rupture. Several times she sent bread to her parents in the camp. One card came from her father. He reported playing his own beloved lieder at recitals in Theresienstadt. He also accompanied camp orchestra concerts on the piano.

A second and final card came from Stella's mother, and it made clear that Gerhard Goldschlag's music making was more than solace for the other inmates. His playing was keeping the Goldschlags alive, exempt from continuing transports that took Jews from Theresienstadt to Auschwitz to be gassed.

Toni Goldschlag's postcard almost said so outright. "If Vati didn't have his music, we'd be where Netty is," she wrote. Netty Kübler was Stella's former mother-in-law, by that time also known to have been shipped on to Auschwitz to be killed.

The "model" concentration camp Theresienstadt, an hour's drive northwest of Prague, materialized for the Goldschlags as a grotesque tangle of hope and terror, corruption and courage, privation and efforts at a degree of self-rule. Between 1941 and 1945, 140,000 Jews were herded through this dilapidated relic of a former military garrison town dating to the late eighteenth century. Some 33,000 died, mostly of epidemics or starvation; 88,000 were deported on to extermination camps; the remainder clutched somehow to life, a few finding themselves shipped, miraculously, to Switzerland and Sweden late in the war.

No one's fate was predictable from one day to the next.

Gerhard and Toni Goldschlag were afflicted with an additional personal burden: the notoriety of their daughter, based largely on fact but in part on festering legend. Stella's deeds were known throughout the camp, sometimes in grossly exaggerated or false versions. Inmates spread reports of "Kübler transports"—entire trains full of deportees, all allegedly rounded up by Stella. And when Frieda de Klein ran into her old friend Netty Kübler in the Theresienstadt armory, Netty threw herself into Frieda's arms, sobbing. She was inconsolable because she was convinced that her daughter-in-law Stella, "that beast," had betrayed her own young husband, Manfred Kübler, as well as her father-in-law to the Gestapo.

(While Stella's record was an invitation to such charges, she could not have acted against the Küblers because they were deported before she was enlisted by the Gestapo.)

Compelled to move about Theresienstadt branded by the daughter's reputation, the parents were doubtless exposed to much shame, on top of having arrived already "deeply saddened" by Stella's treachery (as recalled by their Jewish camp director back in Berlin, Max Reschke).

No doubt their lot was painful to the most prominent of the Berliners in the camp, chief rabbi Leo Baeck, Theresienstadt's paterfamilias, as saintly a Jewish figure as Germany ever produced. When offered a place on an evacuation train to Holland, he refused, preferring to minister to his people. Emaciated, outwardly serene, he preached, he comforted in the hospital, he lectured on aging, and when the Council of Elders was depleted by deaths, executions, and deportations in the late fall of 1944, he reluctantly became a member and finally, at age seventy-one, the chief Elder. Anguished souls like the Goldschlags were his mission.

Most probably, the Goldschlags sought maximum anonymity in their predicament, for while records, histories, memoirs, and memorial institutions for Theresienstadt exist in profusion, the few remaining traces of Gerhard and Toni Goldschlag reflect a shadow existence for them. Not having been "prominent" enough to pave his family's way to Lisbon and on to America in 1941, the father remained a cipher in the camp, a nobody, by his own choice or because of his insignificance, most likely both.

Records show no more than Gerhard Goldschlag's arrival on February 23, 1944, aboard transport No. I/108-14551 from Berlin, and his departure for Auschwitz October 1 on transport No. EM-677. His wife arrived on the same train and left the same day as her husband, but separated from him, assigned to transport No. EM-1351.

For years it had been feasible, tantalizingly, to evade transport eastward at least temporarily. The Nazis left the composition of death shipments up to Jewish "commissions," so "connections" within the "Transportation Department" could sometimes get one's name expunged from the list for a while. Sickness, real or faked, could be parlayed into delays. Money, food, and tobacco could buy postponement. Barter was tense, lively, constant. A few young women prostituted themselves with members of an inmate "commission."

In the fall of 1944, the Nazis seized their last chance to minimize, however slightly, the enormity of their crimes by wiping out a little of the evidence, some of the victims, in a final frantic rush. The volume of transports grew into a torrent from which escape was impossible. Between September 23 and October 28, 23,500 Jews were whisked east aboard the cattle cars of twelve trains, thereby causing the liquidation of another Theresienstadt anomaly: its rich cultural life, unique in all the Holocaust.

The pool of available scholarship had been organized into a program of almost nightly lectures. A record exists of my uncle Max Brahn, seventy—the former *Oberregierungsrat* and pride of my family—speaking in attics, without notes, about two of his favorite subjects, Schopenhauer and Nietzsche, until the last train of October took him and his wife away.

Theatrical productions drew audiences totaling as many as 40,000 a week. Smetana's *Bartered Bride* was performed thirty-five times; *Carmen, Aïda,* and *Tosca* were popular; and inmates had not lost their sense of humor. An original operetta featured a number sardonically entitled "Theresienstadt, the Most Beautiful Town in the World," and a cabaret convened in the "Potato Peeling Room."

Incongruously, music flourished in most concentration camps. The Nazis wanted an anesthetic and a noise suppressor, and the Jews desperately sought a soporific, no matter how ineffective. In Maidanek, marches and dance music blared through loudspeakers to drown out the cries of the gassed. In Belzec, the SS ordered the six-man prisoner band to play the German pop tune "It'll All Be Over Soon" on the route to the gas chambers, day after day. In Buna, Elie Wiesel was once briefly treated to marches by the inmate band in the "orchestra block."

Auschwitz, as in so many other respects, achieved the most. New arrivals stumbling out of trains were greeted by swing and tangos, but the musical stars, the all-girl band, played mostly for the SS, often including the music-loving head physician, Dr. Josef Mengele. And one sunny afternoon Fania Fénelon, the soloist, sang with her group outdoors from *The Merry Widow* for the visiting Gestapo chief, Heinrich Himmler.*

Rehearsals for this occasion were frenzied, sometimes stretching to twenty hours a day. "You must perform perfectly so as not to offend his ear," the terror-stricken inmate conductor instructed. When someone played off-tune for the great man, she whispered, "He'll gas us all!" But Himmler only looked bored.

In Theresienstadt, musicians played and composed "for time" at the highest professional level. Seven resident composers produced

---

* Fénelon's memoirs, *Playing for Time,* were adapted by Arthur Miller and shown on CBS-TV September 30, 1980, starring Vanessa Redgrave.

such works as Hans Krásas's children's opera *Brundibar*. Seven orchestras flourished. Gerhard Goldschlag was missing from virtually all ranks. I talked with the jazz pianist Martin Roman, the Berliner who led "the Ghetto Swingers"; he never heard of Stella's father. Neither did the musicologist Joža Karas, whose remarkably detailed book *Music in Terezín* lists some 250 names of Theresienstadt musicians.

Searches of three archives turned up only one fragmentary reference to Goldschlag. He was recorded as a member of the *Stadtkapelle*, the town band, not one of the full-fledged orchestras, and from September 11 to 14, 1944, he received extra rations for this modest role. Possibly records of additional music making were lost. Perhaps Goldschlag was indeed active in one of the symphonic ensembles, as Stella believed. No matter. He was a nonentity among his peers, isolated from them even for the final journey. The camp's music fraternity, including all recognized composers, was shipped out together on October 16, more than two weeks after Stella's father.

Among survivors mourning the end of musical life was Dr. Edith Kramer-Freund, the physician from the Grosse Hamburger Strasse camp who had bribed her way out of an Auschwitz transport back in Berlin. She recalled: "One of my deepest impressions was of the children who gave a concert of songs from *Carmen*. The day after the performance, the children were deported to Auschwitz. They were looking forward to the railway trip and sang a chorus while they marched to the station, not knowing that it was their last song." *

Adolf Eichmann was another music fan when he had business in Theresienstadt. Dr. Freund watched him during a rendition of Verdi's Requiem. Although the doctor found the production "unforgettable," it failed to soften Eichmann; the performers were shortly dispatched to Auschwitz.

Along with several other Jewish prisoner physicians, Dr. Freund was regularly detailed to clean the office and quarters used by Eichmann during his visits. The fastidious SS man would not leave this task to unqualified personnel without M.D. degrees.

Once Dr. Freund encountered Eichmann at the railway ramp. She had just counted the number of Jews who had died in the cattle wagons en route from Hungary.

---

* Uncertainty about the destination of the trains was cultivated by the Nazi command and was not always unwarranted. In addition to a few shipments to neutral countries, some transports headed for work camps in Germany and to other camps such as Bergen-Belsen where no facilities for gassings existed.

"How many?" asked Eichmann.

It was a considerable number and the doctor told him.

"Good," said Eichmann.

His machinery was faltering, but the trains still rolled.

17. The Catcher and
the Lover

To the illegally subsisting U-boats, the team of Stella and Rolf, who sometimes also worked separately, seemed to materialize everywhere in the spring and summer of 1944. Moritz Zajdmann and his sister, Esther, were horrified to spot the couple lying in wait —incredibly, lounging on a bench—in the lobby of the quiet Swiss embassy, once the overrun American consulate, on Hermann Göring Strasse near the Brandenburger Tor. Esther recognized Stella at a glance. They had been fellow inmates in the Bessemer Strasse prison.

The catcher pair gave the Zajdmanns a "Gotcha!" smirk.

It was the Zajdmanns' first trip out of their apartment hiding place in more than three months. Frantically, naively, they had decided that the neutral Swiss might take pity, that they might be talked out of an exit visa. Instead, the Zajdmanns were barely given a hearing, and when they darted out of the building, Stella and Rolf were by then strolling outside, waiting to pounce. The Zajdmanns, young, with agility driven by desperation, fleeing for their lives, made a narrow getaway by running faster than the catchers.

The Swiss embassy was one of numerous promising locations patrolled by "the beautiful couple." A string of cafés—Dobrin, Kranzler, the León, the Wien, the Uhlandeck, the Teschendorf, and other West End places that fugitives at times couldn't resist visiting in their loneliness, boredom, and craving for food—were also inviting targets because they functioned as occasional moorings for the U-boats.

Traditionally, a café was second home to many Berliners, an intimate nest to roost in. Habitués attached themselves to one or two preferred places where they were familiarly if brusquely greeted by the help and sheltered according to protocol: you could preempt a tiny marble-topped table without ordering more than the Berliner's Iron Ration—a small can of coffee and a piece of *Kuchen*—and nobody would try to evict you from your turf, not even by a reproving glance.

The *Kaffeehaus* tradition, born in three-quarter time during Kaiser Franz Joseph's Imperial Vienna, held special appeal for gregarious nondrinkers like most Jews. Protocol also required that you didn't order beer in a café. While drinkers perched silently over beer and schnapps in the thousands of small neighborhood *Kneipen*, dark and smelly, Jews flocked to the cheerier expanses of the cafés to gossip, argue politics and art, make deals, and puff cigarettes and cigars as if nicotine were the elixir of life.

By the time of Stella's tenure with the Gestapo, celebrity hangouts like the Romanische Café with its 1,000 seats were fading or gone, the coffee was ersatz, the cake was concocted of unmentionable fillers. But Jewish traditions die hard, and the *Kaffeehaus* lived on as Stella and her kind tore away the social safety net of the survivors.

It took several raids before the circle of Jewish regulars who convened at the little Café Heil on Olivaer Platz would disperse. At the Café Trumpf near the Memorial Church, Stella ferreted out several victims and held them at bay by blocking the revolving exit door until Gestapo men arrived on the run. Occasionally she literally fingered victims by pointing them out to agents from a safe distance.

Coffeehouse congeniality had become an invitation to death. Only fast-paced, crowded eating places like the cafeteria-style, low-priced Aschinger restaurant offered fleeting sanctuary; there the enticement was formidable: not just a snack but a hearty meal, the one-pot blue-plate special, to be had without ration stamps.

Certain movie houses attracted Stella and Rolf. Planning carefully, they would arrive just before the show let out. Then, primed by their wide circle of acquaintances from their youth and by their own surroundings as illegals, as well as a sharp nose for coreligionists, they would accost suspicious-looking film fans, Rolf holding detainees by the arm while Stella burrowed through handbags in search of valuables and address books. Time and again, a well-worn address book was a vault of secrets, crammed with names and hideouts of more quarry. Regina Gutermann, the student in Stella's fashion school, was trapped in her refuge during the very night of a Stella-Rolf movie patrol that yielded such a little telltale book.

In time Rolf became almost as infamous as Stella. He was the more physically aggressive of the two, more likely to flash his Gestapo revolver, and he, too, stood out because of his exceptional good looks. Like the inveterate showman that he was, he couldn't resist swaggering around in an ostentatious costume. Oddly, his getup was bound to be a giveaway. The large, floppy brim of his hat and the length and rich leather of his overcoat gave him, intentionally or not, the look of a Gestapo snooper. It amused Rolf that he had confiscated the coat from a Jewish victim at the time he arrested the man.

Like longtime detective partners muscling through the cops-and-robbers television shootouts of the future, he and Stella meshed smoothly. They moved as one. Working a raid, they rarely spoke. The action came off almost automatically, as if preprogrammed, each self-assigned to perform motions to complement the other; little verbal communication was needed.

The bowlegged Dobberke, in his ill-fitting black civilian suits, was their control. During his prewar duty with the morals squad, he had become accustomed to running networks of stool pigeons—a helpful experience for maximizing the Stella-Rolf team's effectiveness. Dobberke made certain that the couple could operate freely and with official backup certifying legitimacy. They were authorized to keep hours as they pleased and did not have to return nightly to the Grosse Hamburger Strasse or the Schulstrasse camp. Well fed and paid, their morale remained high well into 1944. Freed from wearing the yellow Jewish star, they could roam without its restrictions. When conventional cops took note of them, they had only to flash their green Gestapo identity papers with their photos. The documents specified that they were empowered to act in "Jewish affairs."

Dobberke further supported the pair by applying his cop's habits and sense of system. He supplied lists of Jews still believed to survive in hiding. And he assigned territories so the couple wouldn't fall over the tracks of other *Greifer*. Rolf and Stella received preferential treatment. They were allowed to operate throughout such likely West End hunting grounds as the area around Kurfürstendamm and Joachimstaler Strasse and along streets like Lothringer and Landsberger, as well as Schönhauser Allee, where a few Jews still managed to hold on.

Stella frequently appeared at certain funerals, ostensibly as a mourner, actually in her official capacity. The burials were for "Aryan" spouses in mixed marriages. When such gentiles died, their Jewish partners would automatically lose immunity from deportation. The funeral would confirm such a change of legal status, and Dobberke would have Stella poised on the spot to avoid delays. She made arrests at the cemetery or followed her prey to nab them on the way home.

Her talent for establishing quick, chummy rapport with males was handy. Shortly after starting her Gestapo career, she struck up a conversation with Chaim Horn on Rosenthaler Strasse. In back of No. 39, a gentile couple, Otto and Else Weidt, operated a shop for the blind where brushes and brooms were produced. A number of blind Jews were employed there to give them refuge, plus a few who, like Herr Horn, were taken in by the Weidts although they merely pretended to be sightless.

Returning to her street from an errand, Frau Weidt was horrified to see Horn chatting with the famous "blond ghost." The fellow had a reputation for being softhearted and gabby. Shortly afterward, the Gestapo drove up and the Weidts' shop was out of business.

Whenever a U-boat hadn't caught on that Stella had been turned by the Gestapo, the arrest became a *fait accompli* before the victim knew what was happening.

The moment Edith Ziegler, who had met Stella years before, hurried off the subway at Uhlandstrasse, Stella stepped up and snapped, "Come on, Edith, you're coming with me!"

Ziegler, startled, demanded to know what in the world was going on.

Stella: "Better come along quick! You've got to go to the *Lager*! Otherwise I'm calling the Gestapo!"

Edith Ziegler went with Stella and died in Auschwitz. Her arrest took seconds.

When Rolf occasionally became involved in scuffles and fisticuffs during such busts, Stella stood apart at a safe distance. And if they were working a potentially resourceful opponent, Rolf took the lead.

Josef von Drewitz-Lebenstein, an inmate of the Jewish Hospital camp, had escaped from an outside work detail and succeeded in buying a train ticket to Paris at the KaDeWe department store. But then he got so hungry that he dared to slip into Aschinger's for the daily special. Rolf and Stella jumped him as he left.

"Hold it!" Rolf yelled. "Now we've got you! We've been looking for *you* for two weeks!"

They returned the victim to the camp by subway. En route Rolf relieved him of his money and the Paris ticket.

Even the corruptible Dobberke felt that Rolf's and Stella's habitual thievery was less than *ordnungsgemäss*. He perceived such behavior as insolence and probably due to the youthfulness of his prima donna agent and her consort. As a countermeasure he sometimes asked his senior catcher, the fifty-year-old former social worker Bruno Goldstein, to escort the couple on raids, instructing him to watch the pair's itchy fingers.

It was like entrusting the proverbial fox with the safekeeping of the proverbial henhouse. Goldstein was a thief too. When he was placed on trial after the war—he was given a prison sentence of seven years—an elderly woman testified that he swiped her watch, and that of her husband, while depositing them on a deportation train.

Not every collaborator was as aggressive as Rolf, Stella, and Goldstein, and not all found themselves dealing with docile targets. Manfred Guttmann ranked as a lowly *Ordner* assigned to assist various *Greifer* on raids. With an armed catcher named Heinz Holstein he went to Lothringer Strasse to arrest Irma Schneider in her ground-floor apartment. Frau Schneider scrambled out through a window, Holstein in pursuit. Guttmann was knifed ten times in the groin by her lover. Unconscious, the *Ordner* was taken to the Jewish Hospital. He did poorly for more than a year there and would suffer for life from bladder damage.

Like Stella, Guttmann would serve ten years in Soviet detention camps, and so would the Jewish camp director Max Reschke, extravagantly hated by all—including Stella, who went out of her way to denounce him at her own trial. By coincidence, Reschke had been director of the Jewish boys' school on Kaiser Strasse. By temperament, he was a Prussian ex-soldier and a persnickety crosser of *t*'s and dotter of *i*'s.

Dobberke performed a perfect act of casting when he placed the pedantic Reschke in charge of compiling deportation lists and deputized this collaborator to listen with deaf ears as inmates appeared before him to plead for postponement of their banishment.

Klaus Scheurenberg, once Reschke's student and more lately his prisoner, lived on to observe: "If Auschwitz ordered 1,000 humans, then 1,000 had to be sent—not 1,001, nor, heaven forbid, 999. One could count on Herr Reschke to fix things accordingly."

As the penultimate war year 1944 progressed and the Allied landings in Normandy on June 6 signaled the end of Hitler's winning streak, the Stella-Rolf pairing grew troubled. Stella's close relationships assumed the configuration of triangles, and the first of the quasi-partners was Dobberke.

The three of them functioned at even closer quarters in the Schulstrasse Pathology Building than in the Grosse Hamburger Strasse. The new accommodations were part of the loosely patrolled complex of adjoining buildings on leafy parklike grounds, and yet they were separate, the outlandish arrangement being dictated by the Nazis' view of the two jurisdictions. Jews kept in Pathology were, for the most part, doomed. Those housed in the remaining six sprawling structures lived in effect the unpredictable lives of probationers.

The ivy-covered, three-story Pathology, while looking like a cozy, old-fashioned apartment house, was known as "the police station." It was newly fenced in, tightly guarded, accessible through a private side-entrance gate, and connected with the six other structures by subterranean corridors.

Fittingly, the condemned spent their remaining days in bare rooms once reserved for cadavers and their keepers: the mortuary, autopsy chambers, dissection stations, and bacteriology laboratories. The building's former functions required privacy, and so did the new. Hearses had once come and gone without having to be seen by patients. So now did the trucks hauling off prisoners to the eastbound trains. Death was kept out of sight, if not out of mind.

Remarkably, the hospital itself was still permitted to house more than a thousand Jews: doctors, nurses, patients (genuine and fake), "half-Jews," Jews whose ambiguous status kept them under endless investigation ploddingly pursued, transients, *Ordner* whose services could not yet be dispensed with—flotsam, the leavings of Berlin's Jewry.

All had reason to believe that they were living on borrowed time, yet time even now concerned the Nazis less than *Ordnung*. The men who ran Eichmann's machinery were, above everything, Germans, and even in the chaos of deprivations, shortages, bombings, shootings, hangings, and administrative bedlam, the old saying held true: *"Ordnung muss sein"*—"Order must prevail." The maxim might as well have been: *"Ordnung über alles."* *Ordnung* meant that the law had to be applied in fact and spirit, that every paper for every "case" had to be filled out, stamped, signed by all parties, including the damned, and placed in the correct file. Jews who were seriously ill were rarely classified as *Transportjuden* to be chucked onto trains. They had to be operated on and tended before being sent to their deaths, and since it was strictly *verboten* for gentile medical personnel to treat Jews, a sizable Jewish medical staff had to be maintained for them.

The Jewish physicians, by law, were not to be respected as "doctors." They had been demoted to "treaters." They and the rest of the Jewish residue languished on and on, teetering on the brink, churning in the yeasty, isolated world of the Jewish Hospital, usually for months, sometimes for years. While their terror was overtly reined in by the passage of time, it could never be erased from the mind. The days ground on under the gallows, as on death row, in hope of a pardon through an Allied victory.

In the Pathology Building, life continued without special restrictions for members of the Nazi establishment, including the Jewish *Greifer*. At the same time, the Gestapo prisoners were never off their tightrope, kept in suspended animation, everlastingly subject to immediate deportation. The tight space brought inconvenience. Only Dobberke and Johanna Mühle commanded an office to themselves. Stella and Rolf had to sleep in the basement.

The war intruded more insistently by way of nearby bomb hits and shocking newspaper headlines. Though artfully camouflaged by Dr. Goebbels's *Promi,* the Propaganda Ministry, the geography of one central fact could not be wished away: the Allies kept closing in on Berlin from east and west.

The strain exerted on the Dobberke-Stella-Rolf triangle was profound. All three needed one another. All three felt threatened by the new pressures of the outside world, no longer quite so safely at bay. The Stella-Rolf love life was coming apart. There were fights, wild screaming matches. Rolf was being suggestively cozy with an inmate named Peter, and Stella was suspecting her lover-partner's sexuality. Rolf began beating his woman. Once he threatened her with a knife.

Dobberke, alarmed, sensed that Stella was beginning to slip away from his control. He couldn't be sure why. Was it her troubled relationship with Rolf, or was something else influencing her to change? Regardless, he felt called upon to assert his power. He demanded that Stella and Rolf get married. No excuses were acceptable. He had to have *Ordnung* on his beat, and a husband wielded more authority over a wife than a lover.

Rolf shrugged and agreed. He worried that Stella might decide to turn into a witness against him, either for minor transgressions now or major crimes after the war. Stella agreed reluctantly, feeling overpowered by the two domineering men in her life and burdened by fresh memories: the departure of her parents and so many others on the trains, the trains that never stopped rolling.*

---

* All told, 50,535 Berliners were deported, 35,738 to Auschwitz, the remainder to Theresienstadt. The Auschwitz transports had dwindled to carry between thirty and

So on October 29, 1944, the beautiful couple was duly wed in the marriage bureau of the local borough hall. Later, Stella insisted that she was drummed into Rolf's custody and would trivialize the incriminating match as a sham marriage for the sake of appearances— a shotgun union engineered to accommodate Dobberke's quest for *Ordnung* so that his machinery, Eichmann's machinery, could grind on.

In court after the war, Stella attempted to cling—with barely noticeable lapses, all inferential—to the fabrication that she stalled the Gestapo for a year and a half while she kept up a vain search for the wanted forger Rogoff. If she maintained dealings with her keepers and accepted favors from them—so went her litany time and again —she was doing it only for her parents, the beloved mother and father she so much wanted to keep off the trains.

No one connected with her case, not even her defense attorney, gave the Rogoff story enough credit to warrant comment. The fact of her employment by the Gestapo was undeniable. According to the prosecution, her primary motivation was her "striving after a better life and for power over the lives of her coreligionists." Her desire to help her parents remained unquestioned, but the prosecution kept demanding the obvious: How could she possibly be continuing to protect her parents after they had left for Theresienstadt?

Only a few close friends knew what moved Stella after she suffered the loss of the anchorage of her life so far, her parents.

"She became a tigress," remembered one of her confidants—a tigress clawing for her own survival, given to "outbursts of violent behavior," one of the symptoms of posttraumatic stress disorder, followed by dependence on new "social supports."

Sullen, severely depressed, abandoned, she fell—at least at first— more than ever under the thralldom of Rolf, her sole surviving attachment, the man whose own mother said he walked over corpses.

Rolf, in turn, thought he needed Stella as his partner, his Jew bait, his Dobberke bait. And so he told her that if she didn't stick to the

---

forty deportees by 1944 but did not cease until the sixty-second train left on January 5, 1945. The last train to Theresienstadt, with 117 aboard, left Berlin on March 27, only a little over a month before the Russians conquered the capital. Although few trains of any kind were still operating anywhere, Eichmann's cargo remained subject to Goebbels's slogan-turned-mockery, *"Räder müssen rollen für den Sieg!"* ("Wheels must roll for victory!")

Greifer work with convincing fervor, Dobberke would wonder about her loyalty to the Gestapo, whether her zeal had perhaps dwindled because the loss of her parents had plunged her into depths so profound that she could no longer perform her assignment. Would she have to be dispatched east as well?

Rolf knew how to pose the question: Did Stella want to live, or did she want to commit suicide?

The reply was obvious to a twenty-one-year-old girl-woman of dubious inner resources.

And something further had clicked within her psyche with the departure of her parents. Her friends sensed that Stella suddenly acted like an instrument of the law, *licensed* by the Gestapo—not just ordered—to do away with Jews, authorized to vent her hate for them, to pronounce them guilty for her travail because they were Jews—dirt—declared by her legitimate government to be worthy only of being wiped away so Germany would be *judenrein*.

That couldn't be permitted to become her fate too. If she wanted to live, she could not be identified with this dirt, she had to show that she had steel enough to help clean up, not to be cleaned away, and Dobberke had given her the means.

By autumn of 1944, however, the role of tigress was losing appeal. Rolf, the principal producer of her militancy, had become a disillusionment, disloyal, a sexual fake, a drudge haunting bombed-out streets for fewer and harder-to-find victims. The hunt had exhausted itself and palled. Besides, Stella was hardly thick or unworldly; she heard the radio, sometimes even the forbidden BBC, she knew how to read between the lines of the Goebbels soft soap in the papers. The Allies were coming, and what would she do without character witnesses?

The Germans had an evocative word for what she needed to think about doing: *umsatteln,* resaddle, switch to another horse, but quietly, very, very quietly.

The opportunity materialized unexpectedly, in a shoe store of all unlikely places, where she encountered a stranger who became her partner in a new triangle.

18. The Hertha Triangle

It started with a simple errand. Stella needed shoes. Passing by the Eichelhardt shoe store at Rosenthaler Strasse 45 on a warm September afternoon, she decided to walk in. Hertha, the owner's wife, appearing younger than her forty-two years, smiled behind the counter, ready with the usual excuses dictated by the war. Since Stella possessed no ration ticket, no sale was possible. Besides, Hertha happened to have no size in stock except her own, 35, and as she could tell at a glance, that would be much too small for this customer.

Stella, with *her* first look, observed that this was no ordinary saleswoman. Hertha was petite, her figure trim to perfection. She was elegantly dressed, exuberant, animated as an actress, more emotional than Stella but much like her. And it seemed possible that Hertha was Jewish.

She was. She owed her freedom to the protection of her husband, who wasn't. Hertha was also extraordinarily alert, the type of whom Berliners said, *"klein aber oho"*—"small but sharp." It didn't take her long to recognize from physical and verbal clues that she was confronting the famous "blond poison." Her snap reaction was incisive.

"I was of a mind to kill her," she would recall.

And yet Hertha was, like Stella, skilled at intrigue, a performer with exquisite control, sharpened by the many recent crises in her life. On reflection, her fury waned. Stella could be helpful. Hertha

192

knew a lot about survival, especially about outwitting the Gestapo goons in the *Lager* on Schulstrasse, Dobberke, that bastard Dobberke, that crook and his *Greifer*. And Stella could be exceptionally useful with the management of Hertha's extramarital affair.

She turned on her considerable charm, starting to chat sociably and winding up by inviting Stella for tea at her apartment, Giesebrecht Strasse 15, on the second floor off the back court. Stella felt drawn to the warmth of this woman, so meticulous about her appearance, like herself; so youthful yet old enough to be her mother. She was delighted to accept.

Once the women got together in the quicksilvery Hertha's home, her murderous initial thoughts about the poisonous Stella turned full circle. Hertha began to perceive her intriguing visitor as "a soul who lost her way," a little girl tragically "misled."

Hertha wanted to help and be helped. Moreover, Stella appealed to another unusual side of her personality: Hertha was a meddler, a "buttinsky," as some Jews said, and not of the casual sort. She was a purposeful, aggressive reformer. Her preferred hobby was the make-over of women, almost any new acquaintance who seemed to her to require it. Time and again, on briefest association, she would prescribe new hairdos, new makeup, and new men for startled prospects. To Hertha, newly encountered strangers were talking mannequins, adoptees, the daughters she never had.

Stella was Hertha's meat—a spy to be used and a soul to be saved. Fate and the exigencies of war had fused them in a shoe store.

"I took her into my house like a child," she remembered, "and she looked up to me like a mother, almost like a holy person."

The visits became regular, lively, eventually almost daily sessions. Stella and the new mother she had been craving would sit for hours chatting about music, gossiping about the *Lager*, and reading. They listened to classical records, just as Stella had done as a child at home with her parents. Correctly—and approvingly—Hertha diagnosed Stella as *putzsüchtig*, addicted to primping. Enthralled, the young woman exclaimed long and loud over Hertha's closets, over-stuffed with stylish dresses and coats, all unfortunately much too small for Stella. She went out to stand in line, shopping for Hertha, the grown child fetching for Mama.

Sad but dry-eyed, the catcher of Schulstrasse began a recital of the appalling time she had passed through with her parents, how deeply she adored them and feared for their fate even yet, how they had spoiled her in childhood, a childhood that had been so peaceful, so filled with music, so perfect. Stella's fluid word pictures made wonderful listening, and Hertha was impressed by her new woman-child's "rich" vocabulary. Stella was never boring.

Hertha's secret mission—to give Stella the make-over treatment, to reform her—would have to be pursued on tiptoe, very slowly indeed. It was so obvious that Stella was at pains to cover up not only her crimes but herself from herself. Hertha was *oho* enough, canny enough, to pick up on the essence of her new charge's tortured psyche. The complexity of her reform mission was a challenge—her idea of having a terrific time while her husband minded the shoe store.

Hertha launched her plan by confiding in Stella about Rudolph Wolf, a Jewish inmate of the Schulstrasse *Lager,* first unraveling the tale in small installments to check her young acolyte for any negative reactions. There were none. To the contrary, Stella knew Wolf and liked him and she opened up with her feelings about Dobberke. He was indeed "crafty like a farmer," as Hertha said in the German vernacular, and yes, he was a bastard and a crook, as receptive to payoffs as the whores and pimps on his former beat.

She had met Wolf in 1938, Hertha related. He was her husband's cellmate in the Alex, the Alexanderplatz police prison, where Herr Eichelhardt was serving time for the crime of *Judenbegünstigung,* favoritism toward Jews. He told Wolf, who was first to be released, to seek out Hertha, who would help him.

Hertha adored Wolf instantly. He was so tall and handsome and beautifully dressed, so cosmopolitan, and so perpetually broke (much later, it turned out that Wolf could never hold on to a mark because he was a pathological gambler). Hertha served him dinners and handed him hundreds of marks at a time. The shoe store, which specialized in buying up remainders, had long been a gold mine.

When Herr Eichelhardt got out of prison, the friendship became a threesome. Sex in the Eichelhardt marriage had become virtually "extinguished," Hertha told Stella. The husband preferred younger women. Wolf's appearance proved convenient.

After the war, Wolf and Hertha would marry, but at this instant he hovered in mortal danger of deportation on one of the trains. The Eichelhardts bought him repeated postponements by shoveling massive bribes at Dobberke. They swamped the little Gestapo functionary with shoes, riding boots, and all manner of delicacies, including geese plucked for broiling. The bribes worked until the cocky Wolf, in the Schulstrasse courtyard, spit at a *Greifer* named Neuweck, a collaborator he found particularly hateful.

Neuweck was a loud, corpulent braggart. He went around broadcasting that he had personally sent away 511 Jews, whom he referred to as "my customers"—paying customers from whom he solicited bribes. In effect, Neuweck claimed to be pretty much running the *Lager* behind the scenes. He could get anyone's name placed on the list for Auschwitz, he boasted. Through his bribed crony, a Gestapo officer named Herbert Titze, he claimed he could even get Dobberke transferred any time he chose.

Some of Neuweck's claims were true. When Wolf spit at him, his name promptly went on the Auschwitz list. But Stella, privy to almost everything that transpired in the *Lager,* learned of this acute danger and phoned Hertha, who went into action immediately.

Fortuitously, she had the goods on Neuweck: she knew that he had lately stolen eleven pieces of gold jewelry from a pair of Jewish twins he had arrested. And she also knew that Dobberke worried chronically about maintaining his position. He felt insecure, disliked by his superiors, threatened by a possible transfer. Transfers usually meant the *Ostfront,* the killing fields of Russia.

Hertha phoned Dobberke and aimed at the despicable Neuweck with three barrels. She snitched about the eleven pieces of jewelry and about Neuweck's claim that he could have Dobberke removed, and she passed along the inside news that this loudmouth had in fact placed their protegé Wolf on the Auschwitz list.

"What?" Dobberke shouted when he heard about Wolf. "That can't be!"

The camp boss was beside himself. Stealing from Jews was of course routine and tolerated, although his superiors didn't like such sensitive practices to be bruited about. Headquarters was always fretting about counterproductive gossip in the population, negative public relations. But it was something else for Dobberke's authority to be threatened, to be actively undermined; that went too far!

Hertha assured him that she had her facts straight: Wolf was definitely on the list.

"Just a moment," he said. "I'll have a look."

He looked, curtly thanked Hertha, and had Wolf transferred permanently to the Jewish Hospital for treatment of a stomach ailment, the scourge of just about every starved, tension-ridden inmate of the *Lager.* Wolf was saved, and Hertha had Stella to thank for it.

Instead of Wolf, it was Neuweck and his wife who went on the Auschwitz list. When the detested *Greifer* got the news, he used his connections for the last time. He asked his ally, the SS man Titze, to loan him a pistol and shot first his wife and then himself. Auschwitz was for *Kunden* only, for customers, not insiders who pulled strings.

Dobberke continued as an unknowing partner in the triangle with Hertha and Stella. He often wondered aloud to Hertha where she kept getting such voluminous and meticulous inside information about his own *Lager*. Hertha, the actress, never let on that she knew Stella, and told her blond informant-friend not to come to the shoe store again and run the risk of being observed in Hertha's company.

Once Stella was so anxious to see her soul mate that she went to the store anyway. Hertha was incensed.

"*Raus!*" she yelled. "You absolutely can't be seen here!"

All too aware that rumors raced through the Schulstrasse like the cold virus, she took the trouble of mentioning Stella's forbidden shoe store visit to Dobberke, preventively and in her own actress style. It was the sort of performance and intrigue that Hertha loved to improvise.

"Guess who came to my store," she exclaimed in mock indignation. "Stella! She wanted to buy shoes. The nerve of her!"

Dobberke bit, and he never found out how two women were leading him by his cop's nose, and *Saujuden* women at that.

Dobberke's hospital prison was still holding firm, although bombing raids were becoming more frequent and the younger male prisoners more daring. Which was no coincidence. The noise of the air raids and the ensuing confusion encouraged attempts to break out, and chances of survival on the outside were improving slightly. The administrative chaos among the Nazis helped, and the now clearly approaching Allied victory intensified not only hope for survival but also each prisoner's determination not to be among the last to be shoved aboard the trains, not to wind up one of the last to die, like a final casualty in *All Quiet on the Western Front,* on an otherwise uneventful day.

Hans Faust, incarcerated on the ground floor at the Schulstrasse with more than thirty men, became aware of several young prisoners with stolen tools chipping at the walls toward shafts that led to manholes. Faust considered himself too old and pessimistic to join the resisters. After two weeks of burrowing, the daring young men clambered into the street during a heavy bombing—only to be seized instantly by guards.

"They didn't get to take three steps," Faust remembered.

Dobberke—as usual, enraged because he had been crossed by the would-be runaways, his authority challenged—had about a dozen of the men from Faust's cell herded in handcuffs into a corridor "for questioning" in the middle of the night. Obviously, he had been asleep. One by one, Dobberke beat them with his whip, demanding to know how the escape had been prepared, who participated, where the tools came from. Nobody squealed. Faust played dumb, and one of Dobberke's whip lashings landed in his face.

One of the younger suspects, Eugen Herman-Friede, was in the group rounded up for Dobberke's attention.

"He comes running down the hallway, uniform jacket open, uncombed, pistol in hand," Friede would remember. "He puts the pistol back in the holster, takes his many-tailed leather bullwhip, and then it starts."

After whipping the fifth victim, Dobberke took off his jacket, went into his office, hung the jacket over a chair, blew his nose, took a deep breath, and started up again. Friede was the seventh man to be beaten and noted no diminution of Dobberke's vigor.

Still handcuffed, the suspects were driven into a cellar room, totally dark, freezing in the cold of the war's last winter. The space was bare except for a single chair in the center, and the men kept running in circles, running and running, to ward off the cold. Politely, as if dancing a minuet, they took turns sitting on the chair for brief breaks. Once Faust, while perching exhausted on that chair, dozing, could see himself still running, running in circles, around and around in the icy room. The half-waking nightmare would never leave his memory. Its grind without limit was worse than the whip.

Nobody ever talked.

On their third day in solitary, an *Ordner* came in and tossed a multicolored tin box at their feet, saying, "There, for you, from Dobberke! It's cigarettes, Kyriazi brand."

The old cop had respect for perpetrators who didn't squeal.

Gently, indirectly, Hertha started to close in on Stella's crimes. During their homey talk marathons, she took to pondering about *Greifer,* speaking as one Jewish woman to another. Everyone knew about *Greifer.* Hertha said she was trying to understand these people, these aberrations.

"How can Jews betray Jews?" she mused rhetorically. "I mean, that's dreadful! They've got to be terribly unhappy, pitiable beings!"

Hertha never asked questions, never condemned the *Greifer,* always made clear that one had to feel terribly sorry for these people, that they were bound to feel appallingly sad and, yes, guilty, that their consciences had to be hell itself.

Stella hung on the words, nodded assent, and said nothing. She did not appear embarrassed or otherwise affected and fell in with her deputy Mama's fiction that the conversation was impersonal and dealt only with unknown unfortunates.

Two people with a lesser bent for dramatics could not have brought off this charade. To Hertha and Stella, the born actresses, the game came naturally, and they went through it, in one version or another, for weeks of cozy huddles. Time seemed interminable. Hertha was rarely needed at the store. Stella, mysteriously, seemed to be excused from spending time at the *Lager*.

Sometime in the late fall of 1944 or in the early days of Berlin's raw, dreary, dark winter—neither woman could remember the timing more precisely—the explosion came in Hertha's kitchen. The scene was domestic—in Berlinese parlance "like at Mom's." Hertha was at the stove cooking and sipping cognac from a cup. Stella was peeling potatoes. What finally broke the dam? Neither would know or be able to guess. Perhaps a critical point of overflow was hit in Stella's conscience. No matter: something intangible caused Hertha to become, suddenly, at one outpouring, the mother confessor.

Stella admitted that she was working for the Gestapo. She cried, released at last. She had to do it, she absolutely had to, she had to save her parents, there was no other way!

"But they left months ago," Hertha remonstrated.

"Yes, but by then I was hooked," Stella cried. "I couldn't get out anymore."

She was blooded. The choice was unequivocal, as Dobberke had made plain: it was either his work or his train.

Hertha would never recall hearing a word of guilt or regret. Stella was preoccupied with her future self. She *wanted* out, release from Dobberke, but she didn't know how to get free. She felt lost.

But she wasn't. Hertha's creative imagination was available and was promptly stirred. If she could break through Stella's shell, then Dobberke and Rolf would become available to be maneuvered further.

She asked Stella how it was possible for her to spend so many hours at the Giesebrecht Strasse apartment, instead of chasing more Jews on the street.

Stella said she kept insisting to Dobberke that there were simply no more Jews to be hunted up. But she could tell that the excuse was wearing thin.

Hertha suggested that Stella recruit Rolf as her replacement on their joint beat. Let him work alone, lie to Dobberke about it, and share credit with Stella for his solo catches. "If you still love me a little, you'll do it," Stella was instructed to tell Rolf.

She did and managed to sell the scheme. "The work was fun for him," Hertha would recall.

If Stella had, to a large degree, achieved freedom from further *Aussendienst* for Dobberke, it was mostly Hertha's doing. But not entirely. The continuing pressure of the Allies on the steadily retreating German forces was also compelling Stella's personal withdrawal from the war, causing her to give thought to the fate of Dobberke, her Dr. Faustus, lately doubling as her protector, and the theatrical, no longer reliable Rolf.

Berlin was about to be caught in a giant pincer. By early 1945, Soviet tanks had pushed as far as Posen (Poznan) near the German border. The Americans had forced the collapse of Hitler's final desperate lunge westward, the bloody battle in the snowy hills that he called the *Ardennen Offensive* and that the West named the Battle of the Bulge.

Soon the Americans, the British, and the French would storm across the Rhine and drive into the Reich. The once feared Luftwaffe was grounded, literally out of gas. The air raids on Berlin, formerly confined to the hours of darkness, now hit home around the clock. For Stella the trap was closing. The question was how to break out and with whom.

Rolf had not released Stella from street duty as an act of charity or because he had any feelings of guilt. He had shifted his sexual interests; furthermore, Stella had become a drag. She whined. She had lost her zest for the hunt. She was moody, often depressed.

Rolf also looked ahead to the war's end and the recriminations certain to follow, when the hunters would become the hunted. He had accumulated plenty of money and had his private getaway plan. Stella had no place in it. She had turned into a liability, too well known, too easily recognized. In the imagery of Rolf's mother, she was another corpse to be walked over.

Stella recognized the rejection, of course—her first. Since her parents had left her life, she needed to lean on men. They provided emotional anchorage, sex, and protection from worldly danger. Rolf was hopelessly incriminated. Dobberke's outlook was disastrous. Who next?

19. The Heino Triangle

IN THE SPRAWL of the 370-bed Jewish Hospital, the art of survival was practiced in numerous ways by a remarkable assortment of characters driven by a variety of motives, mostly dread. Quite possibly, no such hospital existed before or since.

Some had to do labor to stay off the trains, temporarily or perhaps permanently—one never knew. In the largest of the halls the Gestapo, mindful of profits to be turned from all its human resources, dead or alive, had installed a maze of machinery where inmates worked day and night shifts without pay to manufacture, of all things, children's clothing.

Wheels were still made to hum for victory envisioned.

Others—no one knew how they were selected—just sat out the days, mostly on the floor, waiting—waiting for a train, an Allied victory, death in an air raid, no one could tell. The system was in charge, and the system seemed to know no system. Meanwhile, a daily walk was allowed in the courtyard, precisely forty-five minutes, exercise being *ordnungsgemäss* for all German prisoners, including those on the list for the next departure east.

Returning from her walk one afternoon, Gad Beck's twin sister, Margot, walked in on her boyfriend. She was a pretty girl of twenty-two, with naturally wavy chestnut hair and a somewhat Oriental-looking face. Her young man was exceptionally handsome, from an affluent family. The young pair had known each other for some time and had belonged to the same small Jewish resistance group. Margot had expected to marry her lover, but here he was in bed with the famous Stella.

"She was one hot number," said Gad Beck in vivid recollection.

Stella was far from the only one seized by the hospital's epidemic of sex—a phenomenon recorded by Bruno Blau. This lawyer-publisher spent more than two years in the hospital because the Nazis accepted the perhaps deliberately erroneous radiological diagnosis that he was dying from cancer of the spine.* Nothing was wrong with his eyes, ears, and mind, however. Very little got by Blau and his detailed note keeping.

"Despite all the dangers—or perhaps just because of them—love played a big role in the lives of the doctors, nurses, workers, and patients," he wrote. "If I discuss this it's not because I'm taking pleasure in gossip but because it is psychologically interesting to see how people react sexually in such a situation. Is it blasphemy or a need to be anesthetized? Or are there people whose sex drive becomes more powerful when they find themselves in such straits? Does that lift all inhibitions?"

Güther Rischowsky, who stayed alive in the hospital for two years because he did well as gardener, roofer, and handyman, recalled: "We were young and there were always love affairs going on. We had a gramophone and held dances and played cards. One couple after another disappeared."

Privacy was rarely at hand. "In the bunker everything went pell-mell, men and women," remembered Eugen Herman-Friede. "At night there was constant rustling and coming and going."

Greta, the blond head nurse of pediatrics, shared the bed of *Oberregierungsrat* and *Obermedizinalrat* Dr. Dr. Walter Lustig, the Jewish Hospital director, who enjoyed immunity because he was married to a gentile physician, conveniently absent in Bavaria.**

If one dared to address Lustig, a big, bluff *Kommandant* type with

---

* Blau, once publisher of the academic journal *Zeitschrift für Demographie und Statistik der Juden,* was one of the radiologist's last patients. Together with his woman assistant, the doctor almost completed a breathless forced march to the Swiss border. At the last moment he noticed that his companion had fallen behind. He went back for her and both were arrested. Returned to the hospital, both took poison and died, the doctor immediately, the assistant a few days later.
** Such exemptions were precarious. One husband of a "mixed marriage" was a prisoner in Dr. Dr. Lustig's hospital: Dr. Arthur Eichengruen, a chemist, illustrious because he was responsible for the development of aspirin, no less, for the Bayer pharmaceutical interests. His crime consisted of having left his official required middle name, Israel, off his aspirin patent application. He did fill it out to benefit his company, not himself.

a big, bluff air, it wasn't necessary to use his titles in full: *Oberreg-ierungsrat* (Superior Government Councillor) and *Obermedizinalrat* (Superior Councillor in Medicine). One did have to call him Dr. Dr. in recognition of his doctorates in medicine and philosophy. Only the doctor doctor's SS boss called him Lustig; he was actually seen shaking the hand of the great Lustig, holder of major decorations from his World War I service as a heroic frontline surgeon.*

Everyone thought Lustig was a Gestapo collaborator, and he did in fact command life-or-death powers. Proof had come as far back as October 20, 1942, when Himmler's headquarters, the almighty RSHA, directed the doctor by phone to select approximately 50 percent of his hospital staff for deportation. With the help of his two Jewish secretaries he prepared a list of some 300 of his personnel. The task was completed by seven a.m. the next day, as ordered, and all of Lustig's nominees were transported to their deaths.

In Dr. Dr. Lustig's anarchic realm, the new prisoner, Heinz (Heino) Meissl, towered like the proverbial gentleman-and-scholar above the anonymous multitude. He did not make his entrance until September 1944, when his streak of luck finally ran out. First he found himself, hoist by the petard of his cleverness and sexual dazzle, in Dobberke's grip. Then, to his surprise and delight, he landed in Stella's welcoming arms. The route was roundabout.

Living illegally in the home of a film director friend, Meissl had become edgy. He needed to get out of the apartment, to make a living, to clear up his ambiguous "racial" status with the Gestapo once and for all. He realized this was at best a dicey undertaking, but years of off-and-on uncertainty had worn him down.

Four times they had had him fetched between mid-1942 and the fall of 1944. Three times he was let go. Once he was accused of *Rassenschande,* racial despoilation. He protested that he happened to be sleeping with three young women at the time, all of them guaranteed "Aryans."

Meissl insisted that his mother was a total "Aryan," his Prague-born father only "half Jewish"; he himself shouldn't ever have been molested, much less be facing a train ride east! The Nazi race research specialists, however, were of divided minds about Heino's

* Gallows humor was still circulating in the Jewish Hospital, even about the greatly feared Dr. Dr. Lustig. His name meant "merry" and *gierig* meant "greedy," in an intricate play on words, he became known as *Oberlustrat Gierig.*

pedigree, and the "Thousand-Year Reich" would pass into history before they could decide upon a verdict.

The Gestapo's hand was also slowed, if not stayed, by a certain reputation that followed Heino, rumors that he did nothing to dispel. The Gestapo was remarkably vulnerable to insider gossip, and according to the rumble along its grapevine, Meissl possessed an enviable asset: connections.

Everybody knew that high-level contacts could be crucial protection. Stella had seen in a desk drawer, as far back as the Grosse Hamburger Strasse *Lager,* a typed list of 300 designated "protected Jews," mostly in the arts, film, and theater, bearing a figurative seal of immunization from Hermann Göring himself. The murmur about Heino was that he had pull reaching as high up as *Reichsleiter* Martin Bormann, Hitler's own deputy. The mere suggestion set off tremors. After the war, it emerged that he was merely acquainted with the press chief of the *Reichsarbeitsführer,* the labor boss Robert Ley. Or so Meissl explained when it was no longer politic to have one's name linked to Bormann, by then a war criminal, defamed and presumed dead.

To extricate himself from the Gestapo race detectives, Heino's film director friend recommended that he enlist the undercover help of a certain Erika Miethling, whom the friend knew "pretty well." She worked as secretary to one of Eichmann's top *Bonzen* in the *Judenamt,* the stately edifice at Kurfürstenstrasse 115, and she sometimes came to visit Meissl's friend.

Miethling's recruitment consisted of Meissl getting to know her at least somewhat better than "pretty well." Heino knew how.

"After abundant consumption of alcohol, I came in closer contact with Fräulein Miethling and she finally declared herself ready to do something for me at her office," he remembered. "She said it might be possible to have my name stricken from the 'wanted' list and have my file placed on ice." Her code word was that his case could be *gebügelt,* flattened with a pressing iron, ironed out, which was Gestapo bureaucratese for getting rid of an annoyance.

A day or two later, Miethling called. Meissl should come to Kurfürstenstrasse at ten the next morning. Her boss would see him. Meissl was worried; this sounded too easy. He decided to ring up Miethling's boss, actually got him on the phone, and asked straight out whether "anything would happen" to him if he came by. The *Bonze* told him not to worry, they'd talk it all out.

Meissl never got to see the fellow. After waiting under guard in Eichmann's palace for three hours, knowing he was "trapped," he was taken in tow by two Jewish *Greifer* from the Schulstrasse camp who warned him they'd shoot if he tried to run.

As he was being led out through the huge lobby, Meissl spotted Fräulein Miethling. She was coming down Eichmann's broad circular marble staircase, blanched when she recognized him, and turned her head away. Meissl called out to her, but she acted as if she didn't see or hear him.

Meissl never blamed her for his arrest. She had been deceived by her boss, so she informed Heino during her one visit to see him in the Schulstrasse camp. And though she did not rate *bügeln* privileges, she appeared to have exerted some influence. Meissl's file in the camp was marked "NR," not registered for transport, which meant at least a temporary commutation of a possible sentence to the trains.

Under these circumstances, it was not so demeaning to be assigned to the "rock command" in the courtyard of the *Lager*, refurbishing bricks piled up after bomb hits.

Stella met Heino through Rudi Wolf, Hertha's love. The two men had quickly become good friends, and Stella took to Heino at once. Several fellow prisoners did warn Meissl about this spectacular blonde's treacheries. Stella assured him she had reformed, however, and Meissl decided to believe her, though he had to overcome some reluctance at first.

While Stella's allegiances remained questionable, Meissl lived in downright terror of Dobberke. In a time and place of horrid risks, all was relative and had to be weighed.

"I was overwhelmed with fear," he would remember. "The transports were still running regularly. Stella got a look at the lists. And she could get me off."

Stella made the overtures. She sneaked food and cigarettes to Meissl, smiled her toothpaste smile, and made it generally obvious that he was her kind of man, that she enjoyed his company. In an emergency, she said, she would spirit him out of the camp through the cellar corridors.

There was a good deal to like in Heino. At thirty-five, he was more mature and cosmopolitan than Rolf. Meissl too was a showman, but he displayed this trait in a much lower-key, seasoned manner. Tall and slender, he was always well groomed and well dressed. He was well-read and well-spoken. Like Stella, he possessed a formidable gift of gab. "Charming" was the word most often used to describe Heino. And he had class—a captivating quality for Stella.

Meissl had launched his career path slowly as a high school drop-out, then a clerk in a book store. Displaying early artistic talent, he enrolled in evening courses in commercial art. While lugging cameras for the UFA film company, he took to moonlighting as a *Pressezeichner*, dashing off drawings for newspapers when they covered fast-breaking trials. It was a highly marketable art form. The Gestapo drafted him to sketch wanted people, and he would continue with portraiture after the war. Heino studied faces instantly and accurately, making him popular as a speedy commercial artist.

Stella valued Meissl more as a *Lebenskünstler,* an evocative expression meaning "artist in the art of living"—code for "operator." He knew his way around women and was a diligent bed partner. He offered glamour-by-association, conversing with some intimacy about highly placed people such as the boxer Max Schmeling and prominent singers and actors; this lent him an air and uplifted the ambience of the *Lager.*

Stella also fell in love with Heino—she would eventually refer to him as "my dream man"—because of another qualification. He had a future. He made a perfect match, not only as potential husband and father but as an escape route—a character witness.

Soon everyone would face marathon *Fragebogen,* questionnaires of reckoning, to be filled out for the Allied authorities, demanding to know precisely who did what to whom and when and why throughout the war years. The questionnaires would determine everybody's status for a long time, and who would present a more exculpating *Fragebogen* than Heino? He was Jewish enough to have been treated as a victim, yet not Jewish enough to be objectionable to Stella. He was nice-looking, good in bed, and he had managed his Gestapo pursuers with virtuosity suggesting that he would get himself, and her, out of Dobberke's reach once the perils of the war's final convulsion arrived.

She never caught on that her fantasy was, among its other flaws, much too late. She was guilty of far, far too much. When the ingenious Hertha Eichelhardt turned this traitor around, some Jews were doubtless saved from Stella, but never Stella from herself. That was impossible.

Appraising his own prospects, Heino was likewise encouraged. Hopefully, Stella was protecting him from Dobberke's lists. She was also another sexy conquest for him, and it didn't trouble him that she still shared a room with Rolf, because she bore witness to the increasingly troubled relationship by having to run around the *Lager* sporting a fat shiner from their battles. On at least one occasion,

Heino and Rudi Wolf had to come on the run to rescue Stella from her husband's rage.

Around Christmas 1944, Heino and Rolf had held a private meeting to discuss their triangle with Stella. It turned into a peace conference. So in 1945, there were no more shiners for Stella and no further fears for Heino that Rolf might denounce him to Dobberke for something, anything. Rolf had his own future to worry about.

And Stella was, as ever, busy. She carried mail and messages for Wolf and smuggled into the *Lager* entire meals lovingly prepared for Rolf by Hertha after he underwent several stomach operations. For Meissl, Stella smuggled out letters to his mother in Munich and fetched clothing from his quarters in the huge apartment complex at Saarländer Strasse 66 near the Anhalter station. Meissl was friendly with his concierge, Grete Moschner, a trim, pleasant-looking woman in her thirties. He gave Stella a note to Grete so there would be no difficulty in removing possessions from his apartment, and Stella made sure to place herself on good terms with Frau Moschner.

For Dobberke she still performed chores regularly. Meissl remembered: "When I met her, she went out every day to check whether Jews were still living at certain addresses. But she was going alone. For 'catching,' it was always two who went together, and they were usually armed. But Stella could no longer go with Rolf. The two were too well known. That's why Stella was sent out only to do research. And there was no big problem when she came back without being able to report successes. She just said she couldn't find any Jews anymore."

So Stella still had not really quit the Gestapo. She had demoted herself to the less active status of a "scout" for Dobberke and had in fact ducked into something like semiretirement.

Stella's triangular existence thus shifted into the final configuration of the war. She was manipulating Heino and Dobberke now, and the Gestapo *Kommissar* showed occasional signs of mellowing. Hammering at his rocks in the courtyard, Meissl once caught Dobberke teaching his lady love, the Jewish nurse Elli, how to ride a bicycle. Eichmann's agent was perhaps not really changing his view of the enemy; Elli's friends suggested that she may have been acceptable to Dobberke because she looked "so blond and Aryan."

Fellow nurses reacted with mixed feelings to Elli's romance, nobody being ready to condemn her strongly. "She did no harm to any of us," mused Inge Lewkowitz, "and it was all quite open." On further thought she wondered whether perhaps Elli's relations with the enemy might in fact have tempered Dobberke's furies. "If it hadn't been for Elli, maybe we would all have been shot," Lewkowitz speculated.*

About Stella, even if she was no longer trapping Jews on the street, there wasn't the slightest doubt. "Her aura was one of complete fear and evil," said nurse Monika Berzel. "If I saw her, I'd dive for cover."

Nurse Edith Friedmann was all but convinced that Stella remained active for the Gestapo. She had an argument about this suspicion with one of the night nurses the evening a new patient, a young musician, was brought in. The night nurse told Friedmann she thought Stella was no longer dangerous. Friedmann felt her colleague was being naive.

"She'll come by and interrogate him," Friedmann warned. "She'll start with something like, 'You poor thing, I hope you didn't have too much trouble when you went illegal. . . .' "

The night nurse tried to dismiss this scenario, but Friedmann made her promise to tell the new patient simply not to answer Stella's questions. "It's no crime not to reply to her," she said.

The next day the night nurse came to see Friedmann. She was agitated and reported, "Edith, I want to apologize. Stella came and asked exactly the questions you told me she would."

Was Stella only going through the motions, for the record, her work record, to demonstrate to Dobberke that she was still useful, still deserved not to be packed off on the next train? If she had drawn information out of the ailing musician, might she have suppressed it or doctored it to prevent peril to Jews still in hiding? Nobody could tell.

Whether she was still active or had lately neutralized herself, there was of course no way for Stella to wipe away her record. There never would be, no matter how trifling the new reports about her were.

"I was warned she was hiding in the bomb ruins, watching us," a nurse recalled. "We would be allowed to go to a café and she was supposed to be watching to see whether we crossed the street in the

---

* When some of the surviving nurses of the Jewish Hospital organized a reunion in New Jersey in 1988, Sister Elli, residing in New York, was in attendance. Feelings about her were still mixed and some former colleagues did not speak to her. Nobody asked her to leave, however.

right way or were jaywalking, whether we were wearing the Jewish star, and she'd report to Dobberke."

Truth? Or rumor? Paranoia wasted on trivia? No matter.

About their boss, the fearful, almighty Dr. Dr. Lustig in his starched and spotless white coat, there never would be any certainty either.

"Those who survived owe it to him," concluded the otherwise suspicious Edith Friedmann emphatically, and many agreed. They would cite case after case of Lustig saving lives by covertly stalling or sabotaging Gestapo orders while he snapped to attention at the commands of his high-ranking SS bosses—he seemed not to deign to have much truck with the lowly Dobberke—and slyly double-crossing them when he spotted an opportunity.

That was one face, the angel-of-mercy face, of the doctor doctor. Wearing his other face, his hangman visage, he apparently did not hesitate to send Jews to the trains whenever his masters turned insistent. In a showdown he became a cog within the system that was in power, and he did his duty, performing *ordnungsgemäss* in the tradition of his rank, simultaneously master and servant, like Adolf Eichmann.

When acting autonomously, Lustig was capable of the worst. He enjoyed administering psychological torture of the most sadistic variety. In sentencing one of his SS bosses to prison after the war, a German court would write about the unindicted coconspirator Lustig: "He even threatened his principal secretary, repeatedly and seriously, with putting her on the 'transport list.' For instance, he said to her, 'If you talk to me about the transports, you'll be the first one on the list!' When she once asked him whether a particular secretarial chore could wait until the next day, he replied cynically, 'If you're trying to get to [the concentration camp at] Lublin, by all means let the work wait until morning.' "

Lustig was, like Stella, anti-Semitic, and the court categorically diagnosed him as such. He had proved his mettle as the Kaiser's frontline surgeon, the iron man with the Iron Cross, loyally *deutsch* to his innermost, unable to come to terms with his Jewishness, and he would die for these sins.

The precise details of Lustig's demise never became known. He vanished in the free-for-all of bloody vengeance rampaging through Berlin the moment the last shot was fired. The German court reported: "Accused, at the end of the war, of having allied himself with the Gestapo and delivered his own people unto the knife, the Soviet occupation forces either shot him or beat him to death."

No grave was ever found, no marker, no document, no list. The sentence passed upon Dr. Dr. Lustig was anything but *ordnungsgemäss,* but it was as unambiguous as if ordered by Eichmann.

A dim trail was unearthed in 1991.* It evaporated in the sprawling barracks of the Rummelsburg police prison in the outer stretches of a desolate East Berlin warehouse-and-railroad district where the doctor was brought following his arrest, most probably by Russians. His denouncer remained unknown. His wife, Annemarie, the gentile doctor in Bavaria, unable to pick up a further trace, had Lustig declared legally deceased. The finding dated the event as of December 31, 1945.

The indignity of such an inglorious finale to his career would have greatly nettled Dr. Dr. Lustig. In the line of his last duties he had learned about burials in unmarked mass graves. Anonymity was not his own style, however.

Whatever the details, knee-jerk justice had finished him, and soon Stella would likewise be shown how the Soviets administered the law.

She already knew of other mortal dangers to herself. As far back as February 1944, she had received a registered letter, dispatched from the Möckernstrasse post office, containing a duly rubber-stamped death sentence from the court of an unnamed locality. It announced that the judgment was punishment for her crimes as a catcher and stated, "The verdict will be executed at the end of the war."

The message, bloodcurdling even if obviously fictitious, was the work of a tiny resistance group, men and women, Jews and non-Jews, operating out of suburban Luckenwalde, where its leader, Hans Winkler, was a clerk of the court and had access to legal forms. Originally the group called itself a "savings association" and went about finding hiding places for Jews and procuring food and fake papers for them. Later, renamed Work Group for Peace and Reconstruction, Winkler's courageous if quixotic band disseminated anti-Nazi leaflets and plotted such visionary feats as a never attempted armed liberation of the Grosse Hamburger Strasse camp.

---

* I am indebted for this information to the tireless Klaus J. Herrmann, professor in the political science department of Concordia University in Montreal, Canada, who persuaded Soviet diplomatic and Red Cross officials to yield what even the German police and their courts could not break loose. The assumption that Lustig died at the hands of the Soviet Army was never questioned. Hildegard Henschel, the wife of the Jewish Community chairman, said: "If it hadn't done the job, the surviving Jews would have had to avenge all those for whose end he was responsible."

The group issued death threats against several collaborators, but Stella inspired its particular fury. No one else was as closely watched. No one else received a verdict as explicit as hers. A group leader also negotiated with a dentist at the Jewish Hospital to poison her. The act was to take place during routine dental treatment. However, the dentist would proceed only if the group could give him a guarantee of an immediate, safe escape abroad. This being impossible, the assassination plot died. While Stella didn't know about it, she was aware that she had made deadly enemies.

More immediate was the daily physical risk she and her hated *Greifer* colleagues assumed. Cornered, the surviving Jews considered them fair game, and the numerous assaults on them were no secret. Stella was present when Moritz Zajdmann attacked Rolf Isaaksohn outside the opera, and everyone was aware that the *Ordner* Manfred Guttmann had been stabbed in the bladder and that *Greifer* Ruth Danziger had had her face bloodied when a prisoner named Inge Grün hit her with the flat of her hand in the Grosse Hamburger Strasse camp. It was hardly an immune peer group Stella had chosen to join.

Worst and always terrifying was the clacking of the trains east. Inge Lustig, the catcher who had betrayed Stella at the Café Bollen-müller, was among the many collaborators who went "on transport" and died when she became useless to Dobberke.

"She couldn't deliver anymore," Stella remarked dryly. The trains were still running at the time when Stella wasn't delivering anymore either.

20. Final Days

WALTER STOROZUM, lately returned from Auschwitz, and on duty at the reception desk of the Jewish Community offices on Oranienburger Strasse, did not recognize the strikingly voluptuous and stylishly attired blonde who was brought before him early in 1946 by some policemen from the nearby provincial town of Liebenwalde.

The blonde was upset at the cops. She said she was Stella Isaaksohn and wanted to be issued an official card certifying that she was a "Victim of Fascism." This meritorious designation was beyond price during that icy and hungry first postwar winter. While ordinary citizens had to survive on rations even skimpier than in the last days of the Nazis, an officially accredited Nazi persecutee was entitled to relatively opulent food parcels supplied from the United States by the *Yoint* and the HIAS relief organizations.

Storozum directed Stella to the upstairs office for Victims, and soon he could hear the rumblings of a commotion. Markus Safirstein, another Auschwitz inmate who had made it back, was working in the office next door and looked inside. Obviously, Stella had been recognized. She was writhing on a chair, her lips tightly clenched. About half a dozen co-workers, normally benign men and women of Safirstein's acquaintance, were holding her down. One man was scrambling about, wielding a pair of scissors. Stella made no sound. The others were shouting, cursing, slapping her, calling her dreadful names, and trying to get her to hold still.

She had narrowly escaped a worse fate. The survivors in the room

211

were so incensed that they were all set to beat her up, hoping to injure her severely. At the last moment, a respected official stepped in, Günther Ruschin, and snapped, "We don't beat up women!" He did not, however, object to the enforced haircut.

Stella wiggled and jerked fiercely; it took nearly half an hour before her trademark, those notorious golden curls, had been snipped so short that she looked plucked, nearly bald. Safirstein had long since left. While he did not interfere, the scene made him uncomfortable because the woman had done nothing to him. The same did not apply to her tormentors. They seemed to know a good deal about Stella. Their involvement in her punishment was clearly personal.

Safirstein was not shocked. The newspapers frequently ran photos of petrified-looking women with their hair shorn off, surrounded by jeering civilians with guns. Usually the victims were French whores or ordinary female citizens who had slept with German soldiers, for money or food, and were getting their comeuppance from vengeful members of the resistance movement. It had become a routine treatment of the time, and for months Stella never let herself be seen without a kerchief. It was a gentler lot than getting shot, hanged, or beaten to death. As before, all suffering was relative.

For their part, the true victims of Fascism, the Jewish Community staff workers recently reprieved from concentration camps, had grown so cynical that they doubted Stella would face further punishment at all. Walter Storozum figured that the German cops, those Nazis who were called to fetch Stella, would let her go right away, en route to police headquarters.

"She'll just take off her pants," he said.

The beginning of the end had started to unfold for Stella in February 1945. She discovered she was pregnant. After the first shock, she was delighted. A child would bind the personable Heino more closely to her, and even Russians were said to shy away from raping pregnant women. She loved Heino and would ever insist that he was also happy about the child, that he promised to marry her.

Heino remembered no such sentiments. He said he was appalled, that he suggested an abortion; Stella wouldn't hear of it.

Meissl felt cornered. He wasn't in love with her and would always insist that she didn't truly love him either. She was attached only to his future role as a character witness and paterfamilias. Heino didn't trust her. "She only saw an alibi in me," he said.

The resolution of their impasse was, they well knew, in the hands of the Americans, closing in on Berlin from the west; the Russians, approaching from the east; and the Allied planes above the city.

The aerial bombings, in a rising crescendo, reduced Dobberke and his henchmen in the Jewish Hospital to much the same miserable level as Heino, Stella, and their other charges. All sat huddled together under the flaking, crumbling ceilings of the bunkers: some 800 from the hospital—patients, staff, forced laborers, *Ordner,* and flotsam—plus about seventy prisoners and *Greifer* from the Pathology Building, plus a handful of Gestapo controllers led by Dobberke.

Gad Beck was amused by the Gestapo man's dilemma. "He crawled in just like us," Beck remembered, snickering.

One big difference remained between the two sides, however. Beck and his people were in great spirits. Liberation was near. Dobberke was glum, although overtly he still clung to his power, knowing that he could even yet consign human beings to the trains at his whim.

"Why are you of such good cheer?" Dobberke asked Beck as they sat in the freezing bunker, where night had become permanent after the electricity failed, and bombs were falling down the block. "You know what awaits you!"

The irony of their lot—the equality of captor and captive—tickled Beck. Chutzpah had been keeping him alive. Once he had considered hanging himself by the necktie that his captors had unaccountably left him ("Neckties are sewn so they withstand an enormous lot," he said). No more. The trains no longer frightened him greatly, and he couldn't resist twitting the once almighty Dobberke. The leveling between them was reaching its end phase. Both were about to fall into the hands of the Russians.

"The same awaits you that awaits me," he reminded Dobberke.

Beck almost felt sorry for him. He had never figured Dobberke for a killer. The fellow was a street cop overpromoted by Adolf Eichmann's system. Years hence one would have called him a victim of the Peter Principle.

Götterdämmerung struck in April. By the sixteenth, Russian tanks had raced across the German border and into the town of Seelow, thirty-two miles east of the capital. General Dwight D. Eisenhower's American troops had stopped fifty miles to the west. Nobody in Berlin knew it, but Ike had decided he couldn't win the competition for the capital ("the main prize," he had once called it) and would leave this plum to the Russian allies.

And still and still . . . Crazily, Wehrmacht soldiers were still stubbornly resisting on both fronts, still in fear of the frantic do-or-die commands from Hitler, who still kept on flinging them out of his last subterranean hiding place, the *Führerbunker*, a quick walk south of the Brandenburger Tor.

A short way to the west, at the railroad-and-subway station Bahnhof Zoo, Stella, Heino—out on a pass—and Rolf convened for a hasty, tearless farewell around midday on the seventeenth. The distant rumbling of cannonading Soviet artillery was clearly audible.

Rolf, carrying a bulging briefcase, disclosed that he had arranged for a diplomatic car to take him along on its flight north to the Baltic port city of Lübeck. Stella's fate was left unmentioned, which did not surprise her. Rolf had already told her he didn't feel responsible for her. No explanations were called for; no one had suggested that he might be the father of her child. Besides, Stella had earlier snooped through her husband's briefcase. It contained several travel permits —she couldn't tell whether they were phony or not—along with marked-up maps and more than 40,000 marks in small bills, a fortune.

From the station, Meissl took her to his apartment house where the concierge, Grete Moschner, was packing to leave for the provincial town of Liebenwalde, twenty miles to the north and still reachable by suburban train. Fearing Russian brutality, Frau Moschner, like many Berliners, had found a refuge with friends in the countryside.

Meissl explained that Stella had to leave Berlin at once. She was an escaped political prisoner from the Schulstrasse camp, three months pregnant, and feared for her life. After some hesitation, Frau Moschner offered to take Stella along to Liebenwalde and to hide her in her place. The two women hurried off for their train, Meissl promising Stella he would come for her. She was not to worry. The apocalyptic swirling around Berlin would only be a passing phase.

In actuality, only the very last was true. Heino was of no mind to return for Stella. He had a future. She had none.

"I must say I wanted to get rid of her," he would confess nearly fifty years later. "I didn't want her clawing at me."

He told himself that Stella's child was not his. Anyway, with her well-documented promiscuity, who could ever be certain? Heino wanted only to get away, to flee to his mother in Munich, to join the frantic migration southward toward the relative safety of Bavaria. It was an exodus of resourceful survivors, including much of Hitler's staff, whose departure was code-named Operation Seraglio.* Pop wits called it "the flight of the golden pheasants."

The Germans had a convenient word for such bolting under pressure: a Goebbels euphemism invented—and lately used cynically— to denote hasty retreat. The expression was *absetzen* and it was everywhere. Literally, it meant to break away, to separate—exactly what was on Heino Meissl's mind. Goebbels employed the word to mean, as everyone recognized, to rescue oneself from danger, to bug out. Which was also on Heino's mind.

"It was not one of my heroic deeds," he recalled dryly.

For the time being, however, he had to return to the Schulstrasse *Lager*. He had only been let out on a brief pass for the purpose of "procuring supplies." Dobberke issued the document from time to time after pocketing more cash from Hertha Eichelhardt. Besides, the camp was safer at this point than the streets. Aerial bombs had become just one ingredient of a mortal mix with more worrisome artillery shells. And SS men were stringing up army deserters from lampposts by way of warning.

In the camp that night, Dobberke questioned Meissl about Stella's whereabouts. Heino disclosed nothing. Fortunately, there was not much time or energy left for the Gestapo man's interrogations. He and everyone else in the hospital were by then spending almost all their time in the bunkers. Heat and water supplies had ceased shortly after the electricity. The Russians were piercing the city limits. Emergency operating rooms had been moved below ground, and wounded were pouring in—civilians, Wehrmacht soldiers, and finally Russians. The blood-splattered Jewish doctors worked around the clock.

Sitting on the bare cellar floor—it had become too crowded to lie down and there was practically no food—Bruno Blau, the lawyer, was still scribbling his notes. He was beginning to suspect he would never make it alive out of the crazy hospital that had sheltered him, however precariously, for more than two years.

Soldiers and SS men had erected barricades nearby, and the sound of machine gun bullets from the street fighting had become a leitmotif of the struggle outside. Snipers were firing from many houses.

---

* The name, an allusion to Mozart's opera *The Abduction from the Seraglio,* was a bit of camouflage within a code. The Nazis were delighted to quit Berlin alive, and the *Führerbunker* was hardly a harem.

Within, the hospital buildings shook with detonations and the wounded were crying out for water. Even the observant lawyer Blau could not remotely discern the full dimension of the battle. Much of it had moved underground. The sewage canals were filling with corpses and wreckage of the subterranean fighting. The Nazis had mined some of the tunnels, and occasionally huge underground explosions cracked the pavements open; spurts of flame spouted upward. The Russians had carted in water tanks that rumbled from one unit to another. Black-faced Soviet soldiers materialized from the sewers for a few gulps from ladles and resubmerged to fight on.

On Friday, April 20, little Rudi, a fourteen-year-old Jewish prisoner whom Dobberke had deputized as a shoeshine boy, was in position to listen to a hurried telephone conversation between the *Lager* chief and his boss at the *Polizeipräsidium* on Alexanderplatz, Gestapo *Sturmbannführer* (Major) Erich Möller. The *Lager* was to be liquidated. Liquidated! At once!

Möller had no time for arguments. He had been ordered to leave for Ahrensfelde, the northeastern suburb where he lived, to organize remnants of a *Volkssturm* band, kids and oldsters, many without arms, for yet another "last" stand—not an impressive assignment for a field-grade officer outranking Sergeant Dobberke by so many notches.

Stella knew Möller. Given her affinity for places where power reposed, she had once been able to get herself received in his Alexanderplatz office to request preferential treatment for her parents. Möller had turned her down, but he was pleasant about it. She was, after all, something of a comrade-in-arms of the outfit he had joined way back in 1925.

As a founding member of the Brownshirts, Möller acquired solid qualifications to become a liquidator of a Jewish camp. During the street battles with Communists in the 1920s, he had repeatedly been beaten and sustained knife wounds. He joined the Gestapo at its founding in 1933. Under "character qualifications," his 1944 personnel evaluation listed: "Go-getter, tenacious, eager to serve, stubborn, impulsive, undemanding, a typical mercenary."

This was not a man to shrink from doing his share to implement Himmler's last-minute spasm against the remaining camps—to eradicate the Jews whom his men had not yet been able to gas, to wipe them out in the hopeless hope of doing away with as much human evidence of genocide as loyal Party men like Möller might still obliterate.

Trembling, little Rudi, the bootblack, hustled to report news of the impending liquidation to Gad Beck, Heino Meissl, Rudi Wolf, and an assembly of other inmates. With nothing left to lose, the desperate group decided to confront Dobberke and demand the impossible: their freedom. They argued that it was simply too late for any other finale to the chronicle of the Jewish Hospital.

Dobberke listened, ashen-faced, surprisingly thoughtful. This was no Erich Möller, no automaton ready to unloose a massacre at thirty seconds before midnight. But would this dogged old cop actually discharge his prisoners? He said he'd think about it.

Unspoken but obvious was the reality that he still held power he could now use to buy insurance for himself. In his hands was the fate of nearly 1,000 future character witnesses who might soon testify that *Hauptsturmführer* Walter Dobberke showed himself merciful when the end was at hand. What testimonials could be more persuasive?

On the twenty-first—Gad Beck and the others could hardly believe their eyes at first—Dobberke actually had the prisoners in Pathology line up and personally signed their discharge papers.* It was a topsy-turvy day in a madcap world—and the end of Dobberke's career as an overpromoted cop.

Overpromoted but not helpless. Before he signed the discharge papers, he extracted signatures from his prisoners. One of his uniformed Gestapo agents made the rounds of all the rooms in Pathology, where prisoners sprawled across the floors. The officer carried lists and everyone signed them to certify that Dobberke had refused Möller's orders to do away with them.

Observing the chaos engulfing Berlin after its capture, Dobberke realized that papers in German would yield nothing if offered to the Russians by a Gestapo man. Since he was dark-haired and swarthy,

---

* Dobberke's action may have been singular for a Gestapo man, but free-lance discharges were not unheard of. To the west, Wehrmacht Lieutenant Jean Reiffenberg had the men of his *Volkssturm* platoon blast open a departed Nazi county leader's safe with an antitank *Panzerfaust*. As Reiffenberg had anticipated, it contained a stack of discharge forms. He sat down on the spot, filled in and rubber-stamped a document for each man, and sent them all home. They had not run off on their own. *Ordnung muss sein*, order had to prevail. Reiffenberg, by then Washington correspondent of the *Frankfurter Allgemeine Zeitung*, was still laughing over the scene when he told me about it at lunch in the 1950s.

he thought he might make his way toward the American lines with identity papers, which he had in readiness, certifying him as a "half-Jew." His girlfriend, nurse Elli, whose papers identified her as Jewish, left the hospital with him.

Dobberke knew he was a walking target, marked by enemies, and one of the fiercest of these was Gerda Lewinnek, caught and delivered to him less than three months earlier and savagely beaten by him. Dobberke insisted that she must know the whereabouts of her friend "Bulli" Schott, thirty. She didn't—not that she would have given the information away if she had known—and so the beatings continued up to the day Dobberke deserted with his Elli.

Bulli, whose real first name was Salomon, was the kind of Jew who goaded Dobberke and his peers into apoplexy. A middleweight champion of the prewar Maccabi (Jewish) boxing team, built like a bull, Bulli had several times muscled his way out of various concentration camps since 1938, the year he met Gerda. After his last getaway, late in 1944, he had made it back to Berlin from Auschwitz, where he had functioned as *Bademeister* in charge of the sparingly available showers and had also starred in exhibition boxing surprisingly tolerated by the guards.

When the European war ended in early May 1945, Bulli emerged from hiding and found his Gerda in her parents' apartment house on Lippehner Strasse, but the joy of their reunion was dimmed by the danger of moving through the city's anarchy without papers. A post of the Soviet secret police (called NKVD before it became the KGB) happened to open shop next door, and Bulli found a Jewish officer who spoke Yiddish and issued documents for him and Gerda. They tried to get him interested in arresting some neighborhood Nazis, but the Russians were only after war criminals of some importance.

On May 6 one of her former fellow prisoners from the Schulstrasse camp had visited Gerda and reported unexpected news. The visitor had seen nurse Elli slipping in and out of an apartment in her building. Gerda became agitated. Elli might lead them to her tormentor, *Kommissar* Dobberke.

Under the vigorous cajoling of four NKVD agents whom Bulli and Gerda took to Elli's place, the nurse broke down in tears, and on May 9—the day after Germany's unconditional surrender was signed at 11:15 p.m. in a school at Soviet-occupied Karlshorst—Bulli's posse appeared in a large refugee camp beyond the western city limits. There Dobberke had hoped to shed his identity in the prevailing bedlam and sit out the weeks until the arrival of American and British occupation troops.

This was a cunning calculation, for the camp was west of Pichels-dorf, a normally sylvan water sports center on the Havel River— ironically, just north of Wannsee, the official launching site of the Holocaust—and relatively secure until lately. This was the marina fun turf where Guenther Rogoff had kept his sailboat. Isaak Behar had shivered many nights trying to sleep under the canvas of boats drydocked there in winter.

Suddenly this resort area had exploded and become the last hoped-for escape hatch away from the Russians. Where once his supreme boss Heydrich danced on the tables to celebrate the impending doom of Europe's Jews, now Dobberke, along with many other culpable comrades, was caught up in the final bloodletting of the final hours of the final battle.

Three were on the run hoping to make history. They were trusted officers, the last contingent to slip out of the *Führerbunker,* dis-patched by Hitler personally to carry two copies of his "political testament" to the outside world. It was Sunday, April 29, and a runner had just reported that the Soviets had been stopped on Wil-helmstrasse, a little over 1,500 feet from the bunker. They were clearly planning to capture Hitler.

"How will you get out of Berlin?" the Führer demanded of the trio.

Captain Gerhard Boldt stepped forward. Pointing at Hitler's map, he traced the proposed route: up the Kurfürstendamm to Adolf Hit-ler Platz, on to the Olympic Stadium, and out over the bridge at Pichelsdorf. There, Boldt said, they would seize a paddleboat at the marina and escape across the Wannsee.

Hitler turned to his deputy. "Bormann," he said, "see that these three are supplied with an electric boat. Otherwise they'll never get through!"

Boldt felt himself redden with frustration and anger. He was eager to get out and it looked as if they might find themselves blocked at the last moment. Hitler's order was ridiculous. How in the world was Bormann supposed to procure an electric boat in all this chaos?

"We'll get another kind of motorboat, *mein Führer,*" Boldt put in hastily, "and we'll be sure to muffle the sound."

And so the couriers in their camouflage jackets and steel helmets hurried along westward with Hitler's last document. He had dictated it from notes probably drafted by Goebbels, who was also about to poison himself, and even now, in their extremity, there was no for-getting the Jews, those damnable Jews. "It is not true that I or any-one else in Germany wanted war back in 1939," Hitler wanted the world to believe after his death. "It was desired and provoked solely by those international politicians who either come from Jewish stock or are agents of Jewish interests. . . ."

The Pichelsdorf escape route ran along Heerstrasse through Spandau, Berlin's westernmost suburb, and across the broad Havel River. For days every inch of pavement was clogged with baby carriages, tanks, horse-drawn wagons, cars, and mobs of desperate civilians and soldiers, most of them on foot. Hours after the surrender was signed, intermittent Soviet shelling continued because some units had not gotten word that all was over. Some 20,000 refugees were killed or wounded in the last melee.

Since the Soviet conquerors were short on transport, Bulli Schott, Gerda, and their search party made their way to Dobberke's camp on foot, like the refugees. Expecting a shoot-out, the NKVD made the couple wait outside. There was no gunplay. The Russians identified Dobberke readily because they had learned the name appearing on his papers, and the party hiked back into town with him in tow.

Stoically concluding that Elli had given him away, Dobberke marched along, meek and depressed, not breaking his silence when Bulli kept taunting him delightedly, daring him to run away, hoping that the Russians would kill him. When the party had to negotiate a badly damaged bridge, the very bridge Hitler's last emissaries had escaped over, Bulli cackled and dared Dobberke to jump off. Dobberke trudged on, the collar of his long overcoat turned up, toting the inevitable overstuffed German briefcase.

Bulli didn't have the last laugh, however. The escapade had taken about twenty-four hours, and when he brought Gerda home on the morning of May 10, her mother was furious and chased him out of the apartment, convinced that he had compromised her daughter's virtue. She could not be mollified until he and Gerda were married in July, eventually to emigrate to Sydney, Australia.*

Dobberke found himself incarcerated in familiar company: two of his former Jewish hirelings. He was sharing a tiny cubicle with Manfred Guttmann, the *Ordner* who had been knifed in the bladder,

---

* For details of Dobberke's capture I thank Sophie Caplan, an old friend of Bulli's and research assistant to a historian who has also been most helpful: Konrad Kwiet, a former Berliner on the staff of the Special Investigations Unit (for war crimes) of the Australian Attorney General's Department.

hospitalized for a year, and was still limping on a cane, and Heinz Holstein, who led that raid.

The small world of this jailbird threesome was tucked into a camp at Posen, near the Polish border. They had walked there most of the way: the Russians had no transport for prisoners. Posen was a transit stop where the three men from the Grosse Hamburger Strasse and the Schulstrasse camps parted company. Holstein later disappeared in the direction of the Soviet Union, presumably to Siberia. Guttmann limped on to Buchenwald but lived to tell that Posen was Dobberke's last stop.

His cot was next to Guttmann's and his Gestapo diet had left him in vigorous health. The rations dished out by the severely pinched Russians kept him ravenous, so he accepted their deal of trading extra bread for hard labor, shoveling coal into boilers during the harrowing winter of 1945–46.

He caught a cold. Guttmann and Holstein could do nothing but watch his fever rise. Eventually it was high enough for the Gestapo man to be taken to the sick bay run by German medics, prisoners of war. The diagnosis was diphtheria. There were no medical supplies, so Dobberke shortly died. Guttmann and Holstein got the word from the German medics.

For years rumors circulated in Berlin that the Russians had shot or hanged Dobberke as retribution for the way he used the power delegated to him by the Eichmann death machine. But his lot, in death as in life, was banality itself. In the end, he was just an over-promoted cop who became victim of a cold that advanced itself to mortal illness.

Most inmates, having nowhere to go, celebrated the advent of peace in the *Lager*. Those who dispersed across the city joined some of the remaining U-boats, also emerging here and there. Eventually nearly 1,400 of these hidden survivors would be counted. At the moment, they faced danger from battle-weary, hypersuspicious Russians unable to separate friend from foe. To them, a German was a German; all Jews had perished. Even the lowliest *tovarich* from behind the Ural Mountains had heard that.

Some Jews only narrowly avoided getting shot—this time by friends—while reveling in their liberation. Occasional fighting was continuing in the Charlottenburg district, so the streets were deserted when Gerhard Löwenthal, having survived in hiding by the grace of his Uncle Max and Herr von Holtzbrink, the optician and honorary SS man, ventured out. He was carrying two pails and was headed to a fountain to fetch water.

A Soviet soldier appeared, pointed his rifle at Löwenthal's stomach, and growled distinctly menacing words. Löwenthal, blond and blue-eyed, was almost scared out of his considerable wits—but not quite. He tried to placate the Russian in German, repeating *"Jude, Jude,"* pointing at himself. It didn't work. The Russian seemed ready to fire. Löwenthal, young and muscular, could have been a Nazi soldier gone underground.

The first Hebrew prayer that the cornered Löwenthal had ever learned flashed into his head and he shouted, *"Schma Yisroel, Adonai Elohaynu"*—"Hear O Israel, the Lord is Good, the Lord is One." By fantastic luck, the Russian was Jewish. He fell on Löwenthal's neck and ran off to get sausages for him and his hidden family.

In Liebenwalde, her hiding place in the woods and heather of Brandenburg, Stella, still convinced that her charming knight Heino Meissl would come to carry her to safety, was looking forward to the birth of her child.

In normal times, Liebenwalde was a pretty little market town that had slumbered for 700 years around a well-kept green common. Only ruins remained of its massive thirteenth-century fortress on the sandy hill above, but within a few miles north and east roosted castles surrounded by enormous estates, the playground of the uppermost upper crust, devoted to hunting—riding to their yelping hounds while horns tooted.

The permutations of German history were in evidence all over. The original aristocrats on horseback had been the *Kurfürsten*, the electors of Brandenburg Province. In Stella's time, fat Hermann Göring pranced in velvet knickerbockers and red silk stockings around his baronial estate, Karinhall, near Eberswalde, wallowing in stolen art—dozens of Rembrandts, Cranachs, Raphaels—and surrounded by his 100,000-acre hunting preserve and its private zoo of African animals.

On April 20, twenty-four Luftwaffe trucks had left loaded with the most priceless possessions, and an engineer officer reported to Göring that all was ready. The *Feldmarschall* ambled across the road, bent across a detonator, blew the place up with a huge roar, and proceeded south to help celebrate Hitler's birthday in the Führer's Berlin bunker, together with Himmler and the other intimates.

The next day Göring fled south and Himmler drove to his headquarters at Ziethen Castle, just north of Stella's Liebenwalde, where the chief of the SS was enmeshed in a bewildering variety of manipulations simultaneously: undercutting Hitler by maneuvering for a separate peace with the West, nodding benevolently at Jewish negotiators from Sweden who were frantically trying to save a last few concentration camp survivors, stampeding his men to wipe out all the Jews under any circumstances.

This countryside, called Schorfheide, was the ringside of the German rulers, and so Stella was present at the collapse of one world and the birth of the next, the era of the Communists.*

When Stella was installed in the center of this uproar by Grete Moschner, the charitable concierge, Liebenwalde was still in German hands and a mass of chaos: fleeing Wehrmacht soldiers, dilapidated trucks full of wounded, the main highway between Neuruppin and Eberswalde nearly gridlocked with the remains of the Hitler Reich's collapse.

If Frau Moschner had lived but a few miles to the south and west, Stella would have been deluged by a last-ditch tragedy vastly more awful: the death march of 33,000 starved prisoners out of the Sachsenhausen concentration camp. Stella was soon to experience the place as a prisoner herself. In the war's last spasms, it was the scene of Himmler's ultimate irrational act before committing suicide.

He had wanted to be neat in disposing of the terrible human evidence of Nazi crimes. "They shall go under with us!" he told intimates. "That is the clear and logical order of the Führer and I will see that it is carried out thoroughly and meticulously."

But time had run out. Himmler could only hope to move the inmates out of the way one day ahead of the conquering Russians. In panic, he had the SS march them north and very slightly west, past Liebenwalde, toward the Baltic. There was no time left to kill so many in the customary well-organized massacres. For thousands, it meant death on the road instead.

Early on the morning of April 21, SS officers divided the prisoners into groups of about 500 and drove them onto the highway toward Neuruppin. Some were given a little bread and 200 grams of sausage; most got nothing. The SS was in a hurry. An elderly Pole staggering

* The area's role as the playground of the ever rotating elite would continue unbroken. The Russians were followed by Erich Honecker, the Communist premier of East Germany. Dour but no proletarian in the realm of perks, he rusticated at Hubertusstock, his hunting castle at Lake Werbellin, presiding at meetings with other heads of state and running veritable massacres of the roaming deer.

along in front of Henry Orenstein fell and twisted his ankle. Unable to keep up, he was motioned toward the roadside by a guard.

"Realizing that he was going to be killed, the man fell on his knees and joined his hands together in a gesture of prayer," Orenstein remembered. "The SS guard, his gun about two feet from the man's head, let loose with a burst of fire, and the Pole keeled over and lay still on the ground."

Organization still prevailed. "The SS men at the rear of the column were *looking* for stragglers and shot them where they fell as if it were the most routine thing in the world," Orenstein would write. "Their faces were blank. There was no hate in them, no pity, just business as usual."

The casualties mounted as more prisoners collapsed from exhaustion and dysentery induced by a diet of roots and grass. "At least 700 in our column were shot to death in two days," Orenstein noted. "We could see hundreds of other corpses alongside the road, left by columns marching ahead of us. The countryside was beautiful, spring was in full bloom. The incongruity of nature around us and the slaughter of innocent people was hard to reconcile."

On the road to Wittstock, a representative of the International Red Cross was able to talk to some of the marchers. "The detainees went down on their knees weeping, stretched out their arms and begged me not to let them die," he reported. The Red Cross man had enough food parcels for only a few of them and was able to give a lift in his car to a small number. Never did the phrase "too little and too late" apply more tragically.

"In the morning of 22 April, on a 7 km stretch between Löwenberg and Lindow, we found the first 20 detainees who had been shot by the roadside," said another Red Cross report. "Each had a bullet in his head. As we advanced, we found an ever increasing number of detainees who had been shot, by the roadside or in ditches . . . some of which had been thrown into camp fires and partly burned . . . We saw several hundred on the way . . . Some of the commandants tried to prove that they had rendered the exhausted and sick detainees a service by shooting them and thereby sparing them further suffering."

Wolfgang Szepansky, another marcher from Sachsenhausen, saw many corpses scattered around farms, usually near potato bins, where the SS killed the desperate foragers.

"More and more dropped from hunger," Szepansky wrote. "More and more shots banged . . . May 1, 1945, showed us a cold shoulder and sent us an awful snow storm! In the distance, but clearly audible, the thunder of [cannons] rolled. In our ears it was the ringing of bells. . . ."

By a stroke of irony, the arguably vilest of the high-ranking Nazi war criminals was fleeing from the Russians through the same chaos: Rudolf Höss, forty-five, once adjutant to the commandant of Sachsenhausen and subsequently responsible for the death of probably more than 1.3 million Jews by the hard-to-grasp estimate of his boss Eichmann. That was the record Höss had compiled when he became commandant of Auschwitz. Now he had returned to Sachsenhausen with orders from Himmler personally. Höss was to direct the final self-contradiction, the forcible exodus from all the still-remaining *Lager*. Frantically he had been attempting to deal with the hopeless task of wiping out Himmler's tracks (and his own) by yelling orders over the fragile phone lines from his old Sachsenhausen home ground.

The last week of April found Höss on the run for his own life, in command of a retreating column of SS trucks, heading west and north with his family through the nights, away from Berlin. Inching along without lights, constantly getting stuck in mud and traffic, Höss kept alighting to boss the pandemonium he and his cohorts had created: defeated soldiers, deserters, fleeing civilians, Allied prisoners of war, and the residues of Jews routed from his camps, together with their guards, all overloading every escape hatch leading away from the Russians.

Berlin was, of course, the ground zero of world history that April. When would it fall? What would be left of it? And most suspenseful: Would Hitler be dead or alive and available to be placed on trial as the greatest war criminal since Genghis Khan?

Some of the most critical of the war's last shooting swirled in the privileged territory north of Berlin, almost within earshot of Stella in Liebenwalde.

Hitler's final fixation was on one obscure SS general. His name was Felix Steiner, and unlike most of his Waffen-SS colleagues, he was an alumnus of the regular army with a reputation for competence and cool. Hitler had bombarded him with order after order to swing his army group from just north of Berlin toward the south to rescue the capital—and the Führer.

Peering through his magnifying glass, hands shaking, head bob-

225

bing, Hitler stabbed at his map—so all his entourage would remember—and kept muttering, "Steiner! Steiner!"

Steiner was in no position to bail the Führer out. His "army group" was nonexistent; his troops were outnumbered by more than ten to one and mostly useless. They had shriveled to what he called "a completely mixed-up heap," including many sailors and pilots who had never fired a rifle. There was almost no ammunition anyway.

At his field headquarters in Nassenheide, a farming hamlet a few minutes by car from Liebenwalde, Steiner faced down his superior, General Alfred Jodl, the same warlord whom Hitler had asked in triumph eons ago: "Jodl, is Paris burning?" Now Jodl was forced to beg Steiner to relieve Berlin. Steiner was having none of it.

A few hours later, Jodl's superior, *Feldmarschall* Wilhelm Keitel, appeared in Nassenheide to repeat the same humiliating plea. Steiner replied: "No, I won't do it. This attack is nonsense—murder!"

The two marshals informed Hitler. The capital's fate had been sealed for a long time; now the Führer knew it too.

A day or two after that, still inching westward at the head of his truck column, Höss spotted a familiar figure as he was wedging his vehicles through Wismar. It was another ranking refugee reduced to the role of traffic cop—Keitel!* The marshal was scurrying along the street, personally trying to untie bottlenecks and round up fleeing Wehrmacht men for still more "last" stands.

And on April 30, still on the road, Höss learned from the radio at a roadside farm that his world had gone up in smoke. The Führer and his wife of one day, Eva Braun, had killed themselves after withdrawing to the private quarters of their Berlin bunker. Eva took poison. Hitler then bit into a cyanide capsule and shot himself in the right temple with his Walther pistol. Both were cremated on the pavement outside, as the Führer had ordered.

Liebenwalde was not the sylvan retreat Stella had hoped for. Like most German communities about to fall into enemy hands in east and west, but especially in places about to come under the sway of

---

* Keitel, commander in chief of the Wehrmacht from 1938 until the end, had been responsible for the "Night and Fog Order" of 1941, permitting summary arrest and disappearance of any presumed "security risk." He was sentenced to death and hanged October 16, 1946, after his trial at Nürnberg. Höss was surrendered to the Polish authorities and was hanged April 16, 1947, in front of his former commandant's home at Auschwitz.

the vengeful Russians, the town had been in an uproar for weeks. Many of the men fled westward with a few possessions, driving their horse-drawn carts, leaving behind only a few of the women and children, whom they did not wish to expose to the ubiquitous dive-bombers howling over the roads. Of the more than 3,000 villagers, only a few hundred remained, badly frightened.

Even the one gesture of support that the civilians could offer the starving Wehrmacht soldiers straggling through town in their head-long retreat led to more misfortune. The women handed out the only available food, raw rhubarb from the local fields, which the soldiers gobbled so hungrily that it caused them diarrhea.

SS men distributed ammunition to the ragtag *Volkssturm* militia-men, warning them to husband each round "as if it's your last piece of bread." After dynamiting the two bridges that were Liebenwalde's main links to the world, the SS men fled west, led by the local Party *Ortsgruppenleiter*, leaving the village in the care of a fanatic *Volkssturm* leader named Fritsche.

When the Russians were reportedly within a few miles of the town, the remaining locals gathered in front of the City Hall and a collective survival instinct pressured them, to their own amazement, into democratic action unknown since the 1930s. Fritsche shouted that all women and children were to leave at once; the town was about to come under artillery fire and his *Volkssturm* would die fighting the Russians.

Mumbling in the crowd gave audible testimony that the people weren't interested in futile heroism at their expense. Someone yelled, "Who's got the guts to raise a white flag?" A *Volkssturm* man, Gerhard Schröder, who had been working at the Kurmark munitions factory in the outskirts and had steeled himself with a few drinks that morning, raised his hand. Frau Müller, the town nurse, called out, "I'll help you."

Together they climbed to the top of the church steeple, took down the black SS flag with its death's-head, and raised their surrender signal, a bed sheet. Fritsche went home and shortly afterward shot his wife and then himself.

Once the Russian troops hit the outskirts, a spontaneous act of individual local enterprise helped them along further. Anxious to protect his father's sawmill on Hammerallee, Wolfgang Linde, twenty-six, also rigged up a makeshift white flag, greeted the con-querors in person, and showed them the way into town.

Some shell fragments landed in Liebenwalde—indentations were still visible in walls half a century later—but it was never clear whether the Russians were trying to hit the town or the fleeing Germans. Thanks to the informal assembly at the City Hall and its two emissaries, Schröder and Müller, as well as the lonely and redundant effort of Linde, the lives of the citizens and refugees like Stella were spared.

Worse was yet to come.

The moment the Russians arrived, a wave of rapes began that would eventually ravage nearly every female, from children to grandmothers. Some who were on the way to the cemetery were pulled into a barn behind the hospital; most were assaulted by (usually drunk) soldiers crashing into homes as if merely hunting for souvenirs. Grete Moschner became one of the victims in her temporary bungalow home at Seestrasse 6, while Stella managed to hide, unharmed but trembling at the nearby screams, behind a wall that had no readily visible door.

There was just time to shunt the several resident children outside before about a dozen Russians stormed in, searching for Wehrmacht soldiers who might be in hiding, then demanding vodka, and then women. They turned down the only available alcohol, eggnog, as too sweet, and privacy was not required for sex.

The appalling rape epidemic was a generic disease, a form of collective punishment both personal to the utmost extreme and impersonal in that the attackers, sometimes lined up one after another to fall upon the same victim, seemed totally indifferent to all but two requirements. The target had to be female and German, that was all —much as Stella and Eichmann had required only that their prey be Jewish.*

The source of the rape disease was likewise universal. Every Soviet private knew that his country had suffered more than 20 million casualties at the hands of the Germans, that the Germans had burned down hundreds of villages, slaughtered millions of Jews, Poles, Russian civilians, and prisoners of war, and that such official propagandists as Ilya Ehrenburg were urging Stalin's men to overcome all scruples and act as avengers without mercy.

"Kill! Kill!" screamed one of the pamphlets. "Use force and break the racial pride of these Germanic women. Take them as your lawful booty . . ." And so *"Frau, komm!"* became the universal command.

The rampage was not open-ended. In cities such as Berlin it contin-

---

* In 1948, Mayor Ernst Reuter placed the lowest possible number of rapes in Berlin at 90,000, a figure drawn only from medical records and not including the many unreported cases.

ued for many weeks, in small towns like Liebenwalde it was over in days. Perpetrators were punished by their superiors; Ehrenburg was silenced.

Once the terror subsided in Liebenwalde, Stella settled down to wait for Heino Meissl. No word came from him. Mail, train, and phone service had collapsed. All German radio stations were silent.

Distraught but still hoping for absolution under Meissl's care (and extrication from the small-town ennui of Liebenwalde), Stella tried to force the issue. In June, five months pregnant, she marched the twenty miles to Berlin by herself. The trip took an entire day. The rapes had abated, partly in anticipation of the entry of Western Allied troops in the city. Along the way, the woods lay largely deserted. Stella hoped that pigtails, childish clothes, and a fortuitous eruption of pimples would protect her by making her look young and shabby, and that soldiers would be put off by her swollen belly.

At the home of Hertha and Georg Eichelhardt she received only terrible news. Heino Meissl had left for his mother's in Munich. No word had come from him. (Communications with Bavaria were down, but nothing was heard from him later either.) Worse, the Soviet authorities had come looking for Stella. The roundup of Nazi war criminals had begun. Jews emerging from hiding and trickling back from the East had obviously lost no time trying to track down "the blond ghost."

Stella hurried back to Liebenwalde, another day's march. In October, her daughter, baptized Yvonne Meissl, was born, but escape proved impossible for mother or daughter.

One of Frau Moschner's cronies, gossiping with the municipal nurse, the plucky Frau Müller, had disclosed that Stella was Jewish and that she had allegedly said: "The GPU (Soviet secret police) is worse than the Gestapo."

Frau Müller reported to the Liebenwalde police. They took Stella away in handcuffs while the children of Seestrasse looked on in fascination. Eventually she managed to convince the country cops that she was a persecutee, a victim of the Nazis, a hapless former inmate of Schulstrasse, but she could not save her baby.

Frau Müller appeared in Grete Moschner's house, seized the tiny Yvonne, and took her to the Liebenwalde Hospital. A few days later, Alice Safirstein, a pediatric nurse at the Jewish Hospital, was told to pick up the baby and bring her to Berlin.

Nurse Safirstein had never seen Stella and did not meet her in

Liebenwalde. She knew precisely who Stella was, however, and saw herself performing a constructive service. The baby deserved better than Stella. She was sweet, then around four months old, and slept quietly most of the way back to Berlin, and she was nicely dressed and cared for.

"I felt she should start a new life," Safirstein recalled, "and not suffer from the sins of the mother. I heard she was supposed to go to Israel."

For Stella, the loss of her baby was torture. Frau Müller had to tear the child away from the mother's arms by force. Stella screamed, she struggled, she cried, she was as inconsolable as the mothers who lost their children by separation in the death camps.

Stella herself was an inconvenience to the Liebenwalde country cops. They wanted to be rid of her. What to do? She was a Jew and they had no experience with Jews. The authorities could only guess that mistreatment under the Nazis would give way to guilt and respect in the new democratic atmosphere. They had to move carefully. Stella reinforced their caution by insisting that she had been persecuted for years and now illegally deprived of her child. She demanded to return to Berlin to fight for Yvonne's repossession and legal status as a victim.

The cops knew only rumors of Stella's crimes, no facts, certainly no evidence, and Berlin seemed an opportune destination for this unconventional prisoner. Alas, they were out of gasoline. Who might possess fuel in these catastrophic days? The authorities considered that the Berlin Jewish Community was a likely source, and a call there did indeed produce an emissary who brought twenty precious liters.

Stella realized she would face fierce opposition in Berlin. She could not guess that she was in for nearly three decades of titanic struggle.

After her stop at the Jewish Community and her enforced haircut, officials there turned her over to the city police. At the Alexanderplatz police prison she was interrogated intensively by chief of detectives Jean Blomé himself and then surrendered to the sole judicial system functioning in the area of central police headquarters: the military tribunals grinding out justice for the busy Soviet occupation authorities.

Stella would remember her "trial" as a mere blur in a courtroom deserted except for three uniformed judges sitting under an enormous poster. She understood not a word of the proceedings, which were in Russian. No matter; it was all over in a few minutes. She was guilty, sentenced to serve ten years at hard labor in Soviet camps, a verdict that forever reinforced her self-description as a victim of "concentration camps."

Like many of Stella's lies, this was not totally untrue. The Russians operated ten prison camps for Germans well into the 1950s, and in the same locations made infamous by the Nazis. Conditions were dreadful. There was no more torture, but in other respects the differences between the Nazi and the Russian keepers were not great. In late 1990, the Soviet Interior Ministry would admit to the death of 42,889 of these prisoners from disease, mostly tuberculosis, plus another 776 pursuant to death sentences by Soviet military courts.

"The losses are in truth sad," observed a commentary issued by the Soviet Foreign Ministry. "They cannot be compared, however, to the millions of dead of the Soviet people, who died without trial or investigation at the hands of the National Socialists." Vengeance lived.

Stella spent two years in Sachsenhausen, back in her old Liebenwalde neighborhood, and eight years first at Torgau, then at the notorious Hoheneck fortress prison, and finally at the Waldheim Hospital. Female fellow prisoners generally praised her conduct as comradely, but some were critical, possibly just because her notoriety as a Typhoid Mary among Berlin's Jews refused to die.

"She had the reputation of a *Spitzel*"—a stool pigeon—remembered a Hoheneck prisoner from Berlin, Eva Fischer. "She maintained friendships with the female guards. Once we ran an eight-day hunger strike and they came around to ask her who the leaders were." Fischer was not certain that Stella snitched, but she was wary. "I kept away from her," she said.

Suffering from TB and barely recovered by the time she was discharged from the German prison hospital, Stella considered herself a victim not only of the Russians but of "the Jews." If she hated Jews before, the loathing now suffused her. Throughout his career, Hitler had hammered home his slogan "The Jews are our misfortune." The Jews had surely been *her* misfortune. They were conspirators, kidnappers of her child, unspeakable. Why should she be feeling any guilt? Her only sin was survival.

Striding into court for her second trial, this time in West Berlin, a year after her release from the camps and the hospital, Stella showed no sign of poor health. She had a sturdy physique and she could mobilize plenty of grit. Let others succumb to TB or the Gestapo or Communists or—like the once mighty Dobberke—to a prosaic bacterial infection that usually endangered only very young children.

BOOK 4

AFTERMATH

21. Stella Again

I WENT THROUGH THE WINTER of 1945–46 in Berlin by courtesy of the U.S. Army and found the return to my hometown uncomfortable. Not emotionally. The word "hometown" was really a misnomer. When Germans looked at my American sergeant's uniform, heard my Berlin accent, and asked, "You're a Berliner?" I shrugged. Sure, I was a Berliner by accident of birth. But the town had ceased being home long ago. Home was above the horse stable in my mother's house, 240 East Twentieth Street in Manhattan, not in this burned-out mess of rubble. When I left here eight years earlier, I had been too young for a job, a girl, a commitment, or a mature identity. Revisiting the scene of my early years felt like an intriguing tour through rooms where I had played as a child.

Roscherstrasse, where we'd last lived, looked grayer but was untouched, amazingly. So was the villa in the Grunewald where we had spent a short while living beyond our means. The house where I was born had been bombed and burned out and soon its slender facade would be toppled to make way for a department store parking lot. Our family graves in Weissensee cemetery were neglected and overgrown. The walls of the tall loft building that once housed my father's business were barely holding up and would shortly be razed. All was only vaguely familiar, a nostalgic pilgrimage through a long-vanished past, a peek into a dusty old closet.

Nor was I moved by the complaints of the locals. They had their troubles coming to them. They hadn't hesitated to drop buzz bombs on London, to slaughter more than 20 million (million!) Russians and six million (million!) Jews, to threaten me with bodily harm in Normandy and Luxembourg and delay my normal life for three years. To hell with 'em. Their concentration camps were unspeakable and they seemed to have left Berlin *judenrein*. (Later, I learned that 1,321 Jews had survived in illegal hiding, but that winter I met none.)

I did think of Stella from time to time, but again, only vaguely, fleetingly, nostalgically, another lost souvenir. I certainly never expected to see her again. So many people had been lost in the shuffles of the war, even relatives. If Stella had not gotten out (to Shanghai? Under a new married name, irretrievably, to Los Angeles or even New York?), she had surely been lost with the millions who perished. Speculations were pointless and there were fresh realities to be dealt with.

Infuriatingly, innumerable Germans were full of stories claiming that they helped Jews during the Nazi years. I heard so many such yarns that one was entitled to wonder how harm had come to a single Jew in the Third Reich. It was the same as the magical disappearance of the Nazis. Suddenly nobody was a Nazi anymore, nobody. The hundreds of thousands of Brown- and Blackshirts—the storm troopers and the SS who had for twelve years paraded through the streets and hailed their Führer at mammoth rallies—had all been yanked offstage by some unseen producer. The fakery was too transparent to take seriously.

My personal discomfort was, first, physical. Even in defeat the Germans insisted on forcing me into an uncivilized existence. Habe had ordered me and two other Psywar men to publish the German-language newspaper that the U.S. military government had decided to put out for the Germans. Eisenhower had temporarily closed all indigenous media pending the selection of politically clean ("denazified") new publishers. My *Allgemeine Zeitung,* the American voice in Berlin, was one of a dozen local monopolies dispensing news throughout the American zone of Germany. All were different in style, in local news, and in typography; all had sprung from the head and pencil of our indefatigable press lord, Major Hans Habe. He ran the entire chain with us sergeants of the Habe Circus as his local deputies. We'd come a long way from Camp Shapiro.

In Berlin we worked, usually twelve to fourteen hours daily, in the Ullstein Haus near Tempelhof airport, the skyscraper headquarters that the Nazis had taken away from the Jewish Ullsteins, Germany's most distinguished publishing family. We were well fed at local army mess halls, but I froze all winter and cursed the Germans for it. Our working hours made it impractical to move into comfortable but distant army billets. We lived in a cold-water civilian flat heated only by little electric heaters "organized" by our supply sergeant. These gadgets heated nothing but themselves. I wore two sets of long GI underwear to bed and watched my breath puff into little clouds.

My worst discomfort was ethical. I didn't like what the occupation was doing to me and my colleagues. We were being corrupted and we were liking it. Quite a few were becoming rich—I mean truly wealthy. I knew no one who wasn't trading in the black market. American PX cigarettes (rationed but generously so) were the preferred medium of exchange. A few smokes paid for anything, including women, some of them respectable. Prices were quoted as on a stock exchange for our full inventory: GI shirts and socks, even Zagnut candy bars issued by the PX, although they seemed to consist of bone glue. Army friends stationed outside Berlin were jealous of us because they couldn't share the action. They sent us merchandise for sale on a commission basis. Anything went for preposterous prices in Berlin; among the items delivered to my office for immediate clearance were a set of used dentures and an aerial camera freshly dismounted from a Luftwaffe bomber.

The Russians were the greediest takers. Having captured the city on May 2, with 100,000 civilians killed in this last battle, they asserted their authority through waves of indiscriminate rapes. Using various lame excuses, they kept us out of the city until early July. At once Berliners told us of the raping, but we thought the stories were wildly exaggerated. Like the nonexistence of Nazis. Armies no longer raped women wholesale. We were wrong. Later, systematic research would authenticate the disgusting reports. Earliest medical estimates placed the number of rapes at a minimum of 20,000. There may have been as many as 100,000. No wonder 6,000 Berliners committed suicide at that time.

Once we were permitted to enter the city, a kind of calm had been restored. Only residual evidence of frantic Russian enterprise was visible. The ceiling-high stalls in our Ullstein printing plant, typically, were almost all stripped of presses. As in most of Berlin's industry, the machinery had been evacuated east. The Russian occupiers who greeted us in the streets were smiling, childlike, and their war cry was *"Uhri! Uhri!"*; their appetite had turned toward watches. I knew fellow GI's who got rich by selling the Russians toy Mickey Mouse timepieces for $500 that their loved ones sent them from dime stores back home. Mickey Mouse in any incarnation made our earthy allies squeal with happiness.

The bombshell exploded on my desk on the morning of March 17, 1946. My three-year indenture as a propagandist was winding down. Peace had broken out. While preparing to go home to New York, I functioned as the Berlin bureau chief for the American *Neue Zeitung,* another of Hans Habe's brainstorms. Though our original Berlin paper had been replaced by a new local German daily, as had the other outlets in Habe's chain, it would have required more than the official end of a world war to disarm my leader.

Neue Zeitung was his monument to himself. He had sold the concept of a stately national publication to the American high command as the model for that upstart he had sired, the democratic new German press. Our colonels and generals had been reluctant. We had handed the Krauts enough models. We were supposed to reduce the American operational role, not invent new gimmicks to perpetuate it. The brass had not counted on Habe's unquenchable salesmanship. I had never known him to lose an argument, and once again he closed the deal.

He was influencing American *and* German national policy. And as his Berlin ambassador, I too now dealt with generals.

The Soviets, protecting their separate and equal status, put out their own paper, *Tägliche Rundschau,* for their own territory, later to become the German Democratic Republic (GDR). Like Communist organs without exception in those days, it was a lifeless sheet bleeping out the party line with the creativity of an organ-grinder.

So I was taken aback when, leafing through this tedious competitor in my Ullstein Haus office in the line of routine duty, I came across a sizable article about a woman who didn't sound a bit dull.

"Hundreds of Jews Surrendered to the Hangman," shouted the headline. The subtitle attributed the crimes to a "Gestapo agent," one Stella Kübler, aged twenty-four. Fascinated but still in neutral gear, I read that this monster was Jewish and that she also used the names Isaaksohn and Meissl. Jews who tried to survive the war in Berlin by living illegally underground had feared her as "the blond ghost." Skillfully she manipulated her contacts and familiarity with the illegal lifestyle to hunt fellow Jews, and she made it her business to be present at the arrests.

The article's second paragraph reported that she had attended a private school before the war. Her name then had been Stella Gold-schlag. Stella! My breath stopped. It wasn't possible. Not my Stella! Instantly my old visual memory flashed through my mind. I saw her in that moment in her form-fitting gym clothes, her head high, one of the tantalizing, untouchable girls with whom I rode to the Gold-schmidt School on the No. 176 streetcar.

Stella a killer? It had to be some error, a case of mistaken identity in the confusion of the city as it attempted to dispel its anarchic recent past.

I was automatically suspicious of the article's source, the Russians. My abortive attempts to make contacts among our opposites, the Soviet press control officers, had turned me into a premature anti-Stalinist. I found the Soviets in Berlin standoffish, resistant, parroting the Communist Party as rigidly as if it were a religious cult. It was weird; they treated us like enemies. It was impossible to conduct a normal conversation with them at a cocktail party. In Normandy Nazi prisoners of war had gleefully predicted that they would shortly be our allies in a struggle against the Russians. We had laughed at them. Now it was beginning to look as if they might have been right, heaven help us!

Our notions about the world were whirling topsy-turvy, enemies turning into friends and vice versa. Icebergs were cracking—you could almost hear their crunch. It was the start of the Cold War and the Iron Curtain, although the terms had barely been invented. I was present at the creation and the tremors shook me up.

My first role in the Stella accusations, I decided, was to go back to being a reporter.

The metropolitan *Polizeipräsidium* in the block-sized municipal police headquarters at the Alexanderplatz had become part of the Soviet sector, and the police department was under strong Russian influence. Sector borders were not yet an obstacle and my uniform got me quickly into the presence of the chief of detectives.

His name was Jean Blomé, strange for a German cop. Too French.* He was a glib little dark-haired man with a pinched face. He talked too fast and was too obsequious, and I didn't like him

---

* My skepticism proved justified. Some time later, Blomé was unmasked as Johannes Blome (no accent), an ardent Nazi. Such defrockings were not uncommon. Blome was purged and became a shoemaker in Weissensee.

from the start. There weren't many Americans who spoke fluent and unaccented German, so he probably discerned that I was Jewish and a refugee, and suspected that I might have some personal interest in the Stella case.

Blomé had conducted her interrogations personally, he said. Terrible case. Unbelievable. How could she? A Jew turning on fellow Jews! Terrible! These were strange times. Yes, the article had been quite accurate. No, he was exceedingly sorry, he couldn't tell me Stella's whereabouts. She had been turned over to the Russians for trial by a Soviet military tribunal. The Russians hadn't told him where she was being held. Obviously relieved to be getting rid of me, he escorted me to the door, still dutifully muttering about the perversity of humankind.

I went back to studying the article in *Tägliche Rundschau*. Loaded with details from eyewitnesses, it described how Stella had first been betrayed by another renegade Jewish agent, one Inge Lustig; how Stella and her partner, Rolf Isaaksohn, sneaked around town trapping hidden Jews and stealing their jewels; how she was helped by other Jewish catchers, whom the article named: Bruno Goldstein, Ruth Danziger, a man named Friedlaender, and others. It sounded like a leaf out of one of Hitler's pornographic anti-Semitic hate sheets.

Many of Stalin's victims in the bloodthirsty Soviet purges of the 1930s had been Jewish. The Russian bent for anti-Semitism was long known. The Stella story could have been an inventive provocation, a roundabout maneuver to make the Russians more popular with the Germans who hated them so much. No, that was paranoid speculation. I was trying too hard to resist the obvious. The story was true. Stella of the Goldschmidt School was a murderer, a tool of Hitler's genocides, like Himmler and Göring and the others then on trial in Nürnberg.

Himmler, Göring, and their ilk hadn't been Jewish, though. Something monstrous had turned my sexy fellow traveler from the No. 176 streetcar into a cannibal who consumed her own.

Uncharacteristically, I handled my Stella dilemma quietly. I didn't mention her to my American colleagues; they would have been intrigued. I didn't write about her to my parents, who would have been scandalized. My journalistic responsibilities were not involved, because the story was out of the bag and we didn't rehash yesterday's news. I was no longer in contact with any of my fellow students from the Goldschmidt School. There was no point in contacting Jewish groups. They must have read the published account, the same as I.

No doubt they were horrified and not eager for Stella to receive greater notoriety by wider discussion.

I was perhaps less horrified. The war had thickened my skin. I had seen good people getting killed, and some of my colleagues were assigned to go into the newly liberated concentration camps as reporters. I would have found such a job exceedingly difficult and was thankful that I happened to have been spared that agony. The war had shown me that people could commit unimaginable acts upon other people.

The revelations about Stella were as revolting to me as the photos of the corpses in the camps. They were also personally upsetting. I felt dirtied by her works. To have shared the same classroom with Stella was suddenly embarrassing, like having once had a cheery dinner with a rapist. That's why I didn't want to talk about her at the time. Her unmasking was too recent, too raw a wound.

So my lifelong penchant to run interference for the maimed, to organize rescue missions, at times even when they are not wanted, ebbed away quickly on this occasion. There was no point in taking time off from my work. The secretive Russians wouldn't have uttered a word about Stella and I could hardly be expected to hire her a lawyer. The Russians would have laughed.

Suppose I had told them, "Hey, guys, you've got one of my school chums behind bars and that can't be right. Nobody from the Goldschmidt School could ever do what you're accusing her of." They would have told me to go away, that Stella was lucky she hadn't been shot outright.

Stella's problem also threatened to distract me from my own plans of the moment. Involvement could have cast me in yet another unconventional role and I was tired of playing oddball parts. I had supported my family as a stamp dealer when other kids traded baseball cards. I had startled my college instructors by appearing in their evening classes at age fifteen. In my propaganda outfit I had again come on as Mr. Precocious, the droll kid, Habe's teacher's pet.

When I took the job at *Neue Zeitung*, I had had myself discharged from the Army and had briefly gone to work as a civilian for the War (later Defense) Department. At the age of twenty-two, I was a mighty curious civilian. I advised generals on information policy. I had a tailor cut me two elegant suits in exchange for a few cartons of cigarettes. I was earning a then remarkable $7,500 a year, three times my civilian salary after I returned home. And I wouldn't own another hand-tailored suit for forty more years. It was all too bizarre. I wanted out. I hungered for the real world, for the comforts of the conventional, for life consistent with my age and status as an American, not some hybrid in Berlin.

I never filed away Stella as "out of sight, out of mind." I placed her in my mental "hold" compartment, pending her reappearance after her punishment.

22. The Trial

WITNESSES WANTED

Frau Stella Kübler, married name Isaaksohn, née Goldschlag, employed as catcher for the Gestapo during the persecutions, has returned from prison. Information is requested about her conduct during the persecution period.

T HE AD APPEARED in the thin little journal of the Berlin Jewish Community in April 1956 and the response was instant. Jews who had managed to survive the camps or the years of struggle underground remembered Stella all too vividly and were eager for revenge. The West Berlin State Court did not hesitate to promise prosecution for the second time, for the same crimes as had the Soviets. This time, thirty-two witnesses were assembled for the four-day trial. The charge was aiding and abetting an unknown number of murders, probably several hundred.

It was not surprising that relatively few witnesses could be located for the trial. The wonder was that any existed at all. Almost every eyewitness who gave testimony for or against Stella had passed through the selections in the camps. They had smelled the stench of the death ovens. Somehow they made it back to the living and to the scene of their capture, each one a walking miracle, a fugitive from almost certain cremation.

The legal proceedings commenced on June 20, 1957, in room 500 of the gloomy old block-sized courthouse with its fortresslike turrets and huge vaulted ceilings. It brooded over Turmstrasse in the Moabit area, one of the dreary downtown boroughs where Stella had pursued her hunting activities only a few years earlier.

Spectators began lining up daily by seven a.m. and they were not a passive flock. Relatives and vengeful friends of the witnesses and survivors of the camps, attracted and repelled by the haughty air and sensuous looks of the accused and the horror of wholesale fratricide, came to gape, to whistle, to hiss, and to shudder. For them the emotional scars were much too raw to have faded. They wanted retribution.

Berlin's raunchy tabloids, again recalling such wartime sobriquets as "the blond poison" and "the blond ghost," set off a predictable feeding frenzy of headlines in the customary huge red letters. "Jewess Sent All Her Friends into the Gas Chamber," screamed a banner across the front page of the *Nacht Depesche*.

Here was a trial juicier than the dry recitals of war crime horrors to which the embarrassed postwar German generation had become accustomed. Such proceedings had droned on for years without much public notice. The celebrated Nürnberg show-trial of 1945– 46 against Hermann Göring and twenty-two other Nazi principals was just the curtain raiser. Many separate trials followed to clean house among SS killer commandos, concentration camp doctors and guards, judges, cops, soldiers, Party hacks guilty of murder and torture. The hunt would continue into the 1990s.

Normally these calls to judgment tended to run a bloodless course; faceless accusers confronted faceless defendants. Sometimes a survivor pointed a finger at a torturer in court and charged: "That's him!" That was rare. The usual case might have been entitled *Anonymous* v. *Anonymous*. Not so the trial of Stella. It was most personal, a sequence of family duels, almost a case of multiple incest. There had been a great many trials (and murders and executions) of collaborators after the war. The proceeding against Stella offered the first detailed evidence showing up a system so depraved that it succeeded in turning its victims against their own.

One of the first to respond to the summons for accusers, Robert Zeiler, thirty-four, had known the defendant since they played marbles together on Sybelstrasse; he was ten and she was eleven. Zeiler, who had also known Stella's fellow catcher Rolf Isaaksohn in grade school, came from a family prominent as pacifists. He had the makings of a reformer and a daredevil, his capacity for indignation having matured at an early age.

He didn't hold it against Stella that even little boys "got the shakes" when she appeared to play; after all, she couldn't help her fabulous looks. "Once you saw her, you didn't forget her," Zeiler said. It was her skill at lying that made him mad. She fabricated tall stories so smoothly, even as a little girl, that Zeiler considered it spooky. "She was known for it," he recalled.

In the spring of 1943, when he had just turned twenty, Zeiler was still able to work under a false name in a chemical laboratory where the boss happened to be friendly to Jews. Stella's defection to the Gestapo was not yet generally known. Zeiler helped to change that. He was a congenial type, a talker, active among the remnants of the illegal Social Democratic Party, and he had a lot of friends. In June he told them what he had seen at the corner of Kurfürstendamm and Leibnizstrasse. Fourteen years later, he described the scene once more with gusto as one of the early witnesses in the spellbound courtroom.

Having rounded up a handful of Jews in nearby cafés, Stella and Isaaksohn were helping the Gestapo to load them onto a waiting truck. It was a busy intersection and a crowd of spectators collected quickly to watch the action, the way passersby become fascinated when cops catch robbers. Zeiler was in the crowd, holding his bicycle, and noticed that Stella had spotted him. Should he run? He decided to wait. It was the daredevil in him. She might let him get away. She did, though not without aiming an emphatic head motion in his direction. Her meaning was unmistakable: Get the hell out of here.

He didn't. He only withdrew from view, his curiosity aroused. He wanted to know what would happen to the arrested Jews. He watched Stella and Isaaksohn climb onto the rear door of the truck and ride off in the classic posture of officers guarding criminals to prevent escapes. Zeiler's curiosity was still not satisfied. Taking care to keep his distance, he pedaled furiously and followed the truck nearly halfway across the central city to the Grosse Hamburger Strasse collection camp. Again, the daredevil in him.

Like ghosts, other figures out of Stella's past materialized in court to reconstruct her crimes in graphic detail. These witnesses had once ridden the death trains to the East. Stella could not have expected to see any of them alive again. Facing the chorus of her accusers, her self-possession remained striking.

Closely guarded, she was led into court each morning looking like a model for a shop purveying high fashion. Her attire was expensive and flawless, her posture proud. Her glistening blond curls exuded perfection. She held her head high and clutched a pair of white gloves, by every measure the great lady. It was a breathtaking act, this stunt to nullify her past. A giant leap was needed to suspect murder beneath her stylish facade. Her very recent survival of forced labor and tuberculosis appeared to have happened to someone else.

Throughout, Stella looked upon her victims with the distance of a tourist from another continent. She peered icily at witness after witness and swore that she had never seen them before. When this was simply too farfetched, she defiantly recited other lies. Her bland front remained unbroken even when her old chum Lieselotte Streszak testified how Stella had threatened her with a pistol at Lilo's apartment door soon after their chance encounter at the milk store in 1944 had renewed their friendship.

Streszak recalled that she was holding her three-year-old son, Peter, who was sick with scarlet fever. Stella grabbed him out of the mother's arms. He was left behind in the apartment and later died. Streszak was taken to the Schulstrasse camp and managed to survive in Theresienstadt.

Questioned by defense counsel, Stella testified: "Lieselotte came to the camp voluntarily. I was only visiting her. Why not? My conscience is clear." And then archly: "This accuser was no friend of mine."

Memories, notoriously selective in court proceedings, are also flawed by absence of context. Nobody was present at the trial to recall that Stella's encounter with Lilo in 1944 took place in February, the month Stella's parents were finally deported and she turned into "a tigress."

By the fall of 1943, Stella was perfecting her *modus operandi* for trapping strangers who "looked Jewish." She could often scent the type.

Paul Regensburger, sixty, testified that Stella stopped him one afternoon around one o'clock on Kurfürstendamm at the busy intersection of Joachimstaler Strasse. It was either on September 4 or 5, the witness said, he couldn't recall precisely. He was living in hiding in Wilmersdorf, Stella's old neighborhood, and the pretty young woman looked familiar to him.

"Don't we know each other?" she asked. She looked as if she was having a difficult time.

Regensburger said, "Yes, I remember you."

"Couldn't you buy me a meal?" she asked him. "I'm so hungry."

The witness was moved by this unabashed appeal to his sense of charity and led Stella to the nearby Café Zum Klaussner. They found a small table for two. Regensburger ordered food, and Stella volunteered a sad account of her life. She said she was Jewish and in great need because she was living illegally, Regensburger testified, whereupon he told her that he was Jewish too. They chatted some more. Stella complained that she had almost nothing to wear. Regensburger sympathized. A few minutes later, Stella rose and said she had to make a call. She disappeared in the direction of the public phone booths.

"Well," asked Regensburger genially when she returned, "did you call your boyfriend?"

"No," said Stella primly, "not this time."

She was telling the truth and it made her tense. Nervously she kept glancing at the entrance door. Regensburger still suspected nothing. Less than ten minutes later, Stella left the table again. Regensburger testified that it was his impression that she didn't want to witness the ensuing scene. She was still new at her work.

Seconds after Stella left him, Regensburger was confronted by her boss, *Kommissar* Walter Dobberke, and several other Gestapo officers.

"Your papers, please," said Dobberke, and they took Regensburger to the Grosse Hamburger Strasse camp. He was one of the few prisoners able to jump off the train to Auschwitz after pounding his way through the rotting wood of his ancient freight car.

"That's an incredible defamation," said Stella when confronted by the Regensburger testimony. "I don't even know the witness."

The fate of two other witnesses, Gerda Kachel, forty, and Elly Lewkowitz, forty-two, was entwined with Stella's career over four war years. From 1940 to 1943, the three worked amicably side by side at forced labor, most of that time in the Siemens electrical defense plant. All three managed to escape arrest during the confusion of the mass Factory Action on February 27, 1943. All three went underground that day. Gerda and Elly hid in the same apartment. One October evening they wanted to visit Gerda's former Jewish landlady, a Frau Steiner at 34-35 Lothringer Strasse. They found the Steiner apartment vacant and sealed.

The next-door neighbor told them that Stella, with Isaaksohn and several regular Gestapo men, had shortly before taken twelve Jews from the apartment: Frau Steiner and her four children; a Frau Katz with two children; a Frau Gelbert and a Frau Herschendorfer, each with one child. All were deported to Auschwitz. When the witness Gerda Kachel arrived there herself shortly afterward, she learned that all had been gassed.

During daylight hours, so Gerda and Elly testified, they often found refuge in an apartment at 152 Schönhauser Allee. When they discovered in early December that Stella kept the place under surveillance from the rear courtyard, they tried to notify the occupants. It was too late. A Frau Ferber had already been arrested there with her one-and-a-half-year-old child and taken to Grosse Hamburger Strasse. Soon after that, three more Jews were led away while Stella watched. The next day, sleepless and desperate for a place where they might rest for a few hours, Gerda and Elly approached the house only to be arrested and also taken to Grosse Hamburger Strasse.

Dobberke interrogated them in Stella's presence. He told Gerda he would send her to Theresienstadt, not to the more infamous Auschwitz, if she gave him the names of three more Jews still living illegally. Gerda refused instantly, like almost every potential recruit. There was no discussion. As the two women were leaving, they overheard a collegial conversation between the commandant and Stella.

"Well, where are you headed today?" Dobberke inquired.

"To the theater," said Stella, who was wearing her customary green tailored suit and her small green hunter's hat.

"Well, here's to a big success!" Dobberke called out cheerfully.

And a macabre success the evening did become. By this time, Stella had discovered that the State Opera on Unter den Linden was a favorite place of relaxation for Jews interminably stuck in tiny hiding places.

In the middle of the war's privations it was surprisingly easy for nonsubscribers to procure tickets if they had a lot of time, as the U-boats assuredly did; and the risk was relatively low. Jews and gentiles alike were starved for music to soothe the nerves. All of the upcoming week's tickets went on sale on Sunday morning. Equipped with footstools, blankets, and pillows, opera lovers began forming a line around eleven p.m. on Saturdays. Hundreds were waiting when the box office opened the following eight a.m., and it never occurred to the Gestapo's boorish rank-and-file gumshoes that "undesirable elements" might be found among the cultured. Ever after, Jewish survivors would remind each other that they never attended so many operas as when they were on the run during the war—until the sophisticated Stella made her appearance and foreclosed yet another safe haven.

The opera house became one of her regular stops on her evening rounds, and on the night Dobberke sent her off with a special tally-ho, she was able to collar an entire family at once.

Abraham Zajdmann thought he had taken adequate precautions against just such a total catastrophe. He, his wife, and their son and daughter had watched the opera performance from widely separated seats. Stella struck when the family assembled briefly in the lobby before starting the trip home at the end of the evening. She had known the Zajdmann son, Moritz, and seized him from behind by the rear loop of his overcoat belt.

"I recognized her as 'the blond poison,' " Moritz testified. "I gave her a slap in the face and fled."

The chase was brief. Followed by Rolf Isaaksohn, Stella dashed after Moritz, shouting, "Hold him! Jew!"

That was enough for several passersby to perform what they considered their citizen's duty. They followed Stella's orders and seized Moritz until Rolf took him in tow, while Stella ran to a phone booth to notify the Gestapo. Dobberke arrived quickly and punched Moritz in the face, his usual salutation of suspects. Moritz's father could have fled. Instead, he stuck his face in Stella's and shouted: "We're Jews, not criminals!"

Wild street chases with the helpful participation of citizen volunteers were not uncommon in the daily routine of Stella and her partner. The witness Kurt Cohn, tall and burly, was crossing Rosenthaler Platz one afternoon in the fall of 1944, when he almost bumped into Rolf, whom he had once seen with Stella. Cohn turned and ran.

Indirectly, he had done business with Stella. A tailor, he had a sideline trading in fake ration cards and identity papers. When Jews came to him to plead for documents, Cohn had identity pictures taken by a Jewish photographer with whom he shared an illegal apartment. The papers were then supplied by Stella through a Jewish middleman, an old friend of Cohn's, another tailor.

Cohn realized that this tenuous connection of previous years would not help him get away from Rolf now. According to Cohn's testimony, Stella's husband had taken up the chase, yelling, "Hold him! Criminal!" Four passersby dashed after Cohn. By the time he was caught, Stella had appeared. He saw her phone the Gestapo and then Dobberke's men came and took him away to Grosse Hamburger Strasse.

In court the wave of incriminations against Stella continued relentlessly.

"I was watching personally while the Kübler woman grabbed Jews out of a café on Olivaer Platz, sometimes as many as twenty a day," testified an elderly businessman.

"I was in Auschwitz," said a forty-nine-year-old actor. "Whenever new people arrived, we asked them how they came to be there. Again and again Stella Kübler was mentioned."

A housewife, forty-three, testified that she eavesdropped on a conversation between Stella and another Gestapo undercover agent in the collection camp. "Hey, I made a wonderful catch today," Stella was heard to boast. "I dug out an entire nest of illegals."

"That's untrue," Stella testified.

"I hardly think that an encounter of this kind can ever be distorted by one's memory," replied the witness.

Only once did Stella lose her composure. That moment came when Max Reschke surfaced in court. As the officious "Jewish director" of the camps at Grosse Hamburger Strasse and Schulstrasse, this sixty-three-year-old witness had for years harassed Jewish prisoners as Dobberke's willing assistant in charge of dirty work. Trying to salvage a measure of redemption from his wartime collaboration with the Nazis, Reschke turned against his co-workers.

"Stella Kübler was permitted to enter the offices of the Gestapo at any time," he testified. "She could enter and leave the camp as she wished. Everybody knew that she was a Gestapo agent. I talked to her father and he was deeply saddened about his daughter's activities."

Stella interrupted. "Those are fairy tales!" she screamed. "I can't stand to hear any more of these lies! This witness was an agent himself!"

She broke down and cried. She had just heard her father join her accusers from the ashes of Auschwitz.

Throughout, the spectators refused to sit passively by. Catcalls and curses interrupted Stella's testimony. Cries of "Liar!" and "Beast!" were heard when she claimed that the witnesses were duped by a "mass psychosis," that she herself was the victim of enemies in the Jewish Community and "intrigues" in the collection camps, that her accusers mistook her for another woman catcher.

During one lunch break, she fled back into court to seek refuge behind the protective barrier surrounding her defendant's chair. Several spectators had tried to assault her in the hallway, and one of them, her old adversary from the opera, Moritz Zajdmann, managed to land a slap in her face. "When I meet her again, I'm still going to kill her," shouted another. And on the last day of the trial Stella's final words—"I am innocent!"—were greeted by whistles and derisive laughter.

By way of explanation, perhaps defense, some who were watching the trial invoked the context of the Nazi period. "I couldn't rid myself of the feeling that there, in the defendant's chair, Stella Kübler Isaaksohn did not sit alone," wrote one of the reporters covering the proceedings. "There, invisibly, sits the entire system of a totalitarian state . . . Everybody mistrusted everybody else. Everybody was frightened of the next person. Innumerable people were ready to sacrifice the neighbor in order to survive."

And some half-dozen defense witnesses offered good words about the defendant as a person. One woman testified that Stella smuggled food to her in the collection camp and forwarded letters to her mother. A Jewish doctor was grateful because Stella often tipped him off to impending Gestapo raids. Two of her fellow prisoners in the postwar Communist labor camps reported that she had been a loyal comrade there.

A change of heart had evidently been thrust upon Stella beginning in November 1944. She kept it secret from her Gestapo masters but made sure to receive credit from intended victims. Thus Konrad Friedlaender, forty-one, a man of Stella's acquaintance who lived in hiding, testified that he met her and Rolf near the Kempinski restaurant on Kurfürstendamm. They told him they had an order from the Gestapo to arrest a U-boat named Michaelis, who lived down the block on Fasanenstrasse. Stella told Friedlaender to warn the man, which he did.

Significantly, this was during the final days of the war, when the tide had turned against the Nazis and their bedfellows. Prosecution of the persecutors was in sight.

Stella had other such encounters when it came close to the time of reckoning. "Stella helped me a great deal," a fifty-four-year-old Jewish housewife told the court. "Under my influence, she became another person, and during the final seven months before the capitulation, she no longer picked up anyone."

"Another person"? That sounded like too radical a turnaround, quite unbelievable in the light of other testimony. Scant attention was paid to this defense witness, none other than Hertha Wolf, formerly Eichelhardt, Stella's chum and mother confessor. Hertha made an excellent impression: bright, attractive, knowledgeable, hardly a liar. But her Stella, a reformed Stella, was not on trial, if she existed at all.

Quickly the Wolf testimony was overshadowed by that of a male prisoner from the Schulstrasse camp who testified to having talked there with Stella in early 1945. Stella had tried to impress him with her efforts to protect some Jews. It was a surreal conversation. Both knew that her claim would soon be worthless. There was no way to undo what Stella had done.

The man testified: "I told her that this was all well and good, but one would be held responsible even if one had betrayed just a single person. Whereupon she told me verbatim, 'The end is in sight, so I might as well assemble my funeral pyre right now.' "

Stella was being dramatic again. She never built that pyre, never contemplated suicide. She was a fighter. Even as she sat in court, she had found a way to conduct an undercover guerrilla operation.

Realizing that she would get nowhere with any public effort to influence the trial in her favor, Stella marshaled her considerable literary skill behind the scenes to undermine the devastating case stitched together by accusers. Again and again she bombarded her prosecutors and judges with long letters pleading for mercy, citing a barrage of improbable rationalizations.

Here she posed as a victim of the bogeyman called "Eastern Bolshevism." Unjustly deprived by the Communists who sent her to concentration camps, she knew "no joys, no sky, sun, flowers, or music." She was a broken soul: "I despair."

How could society be so cruel to a pitiful woman who came across as such a devoted mother? Her child had been taken away from her at the age of four months, and she remained inconsolable. "The child is my entire life," she claimed.

Her plight stemmed from the jealousies rampant in the melancholy of the camp at Grosse Hamburger Strasse, Stella complained. "The camp was the volcano and all who tried to hold on to sanity danced on its rim," she wrote. "It wasn't my fault that I looked conspicuous, that I was different from all the others. I was not conceited and didn't try to be morally superior. I was a victim of the time."

Sounding almost like Hitler when he held Jews responsible for Germany's problems, Stella blamed her good looks for her troubles. Her beauty was "a thorn in the side of the Jewish Community," she told her judges. The Jews were persecuting her. "They still want to see my blood," she insisted. "I'm still too good-looking despite my TB."

Could Stella really have been a victim herself? Perhaps a victim of her victims? Of organized Jewry? Of "the time"? Of Bolshevism? Of her beauty? Of a mental illness?

The court commissioned a distinguished senior psychiatrist, Dr. Waldemar Weimann, to evaluate Stella's personality. Obviously intrigued, the doctor compared her persona in the courtroom to "a Roman villa in summertime"; tightly locked, all windows draped shut. Efforts to peer within are barred. The interior may hold deathly silence—or elaborate festivities; one couldn't tell.

In the examining room the highly experienced Dr. Weimann was favorably impressed with Stella's early home life. He found her physically fragile and anemic but "extremely resilient." She was a late bloomer and tended toward theatrical displays. Her above-average intelligence, her surefooted exterior, and her facile way with words enabled her to throw off restraints easily. The doctor found Stella's emotional capacity "much impoverished," her feelings "cold," her thinking "strongly egocentric."

Overall, Dr. Weimann diagnosed her as a "schizoid psychopath," probably still harboring infantile traits at the time of her crimes. However, at no time were her flaws sufficiently intense to make her psychiatrically sick. She could recognize that her activities went beyond the law. Her powers of insight were not significantly diminished. She was clinically sane.

Launching yet another public appeal, Stella tried again to paint herself in the colors of a victim. In view of her visibly impressive appearance, her self-analysis was maudlin and not credible.

"I am a cripple today," she implored. "I have only a short time to live. I have a child. I want to live for that child. I've never been allowed to live as I wish. After the inhumanity I've experienced in prison, I ask that you judge me humanely."

The spectators broke into incredulous murmurs.

In their verdict the judges made it clear that they wanted to give Stella the benefit of every reasonable doubt. They noted her immaturity during the war years; the criminal pressure exerted by the Gestapo; Stella's desire, initially, to protect her parents from deportation; and her decent conduct in the postwar labor camps. Still, the intent and intensity of her criminal conduct left the judges in no doubt.

"She knew that she was supporting Hitler's persecution of the Jews and that was what she wished to do," they wrote. "In particular, she knew that the deportation of Jews to Auschwitz would cause their death. The defendant had cited this herself as the cause for her efforts to protect her parents from deportation . . ."

Stella's drivenness left the judges in revulsion. They wrote: "She could have been expected to reject the demands of the Gestapo, as others did, or merely to simulate cooperation, as her mother had counseled. Instead, the defendant pursued her catcher activities on a large scale. In many cases she demonstrated a downright sporting zeal."

The prosecutors had asked for a prison sentence of fifteen years for this huntress. The court handed down ten years. On appeal, the sentence was remitted because of the ten years Stella had already served. Freed for the second time, she took her elegance home and, shortly, into a third marriage, leaving behind a trail of unanswered questions about her motives.

23. Stella's Daughter

"My child waits at the door daily, doesn't sleep, has no interest in school. The child is my entire life."

S O RAN STELLA'S PLEA for sympathy in one of the letters she wrote to her judges before her trial.

The judges received a second account of the daughter's status, and it did not find Yvonne pining for her mother. Investigators for the Department of Social Welfare in the district of Schöneberg reported: "The child faces a delicate situation since she can only slowly get used to the idea that she suddenly has a mother."

This version was also awry. Stella had succeeded in keeping the social workers in the dark about the volcanic impact of Yvonne's first encounter with her mother, at least in the initial stages of the family crisis. The subsequent tug-of-war between mother and daughter would keep social and judicial authorities in an uproar for a decade. The pair's polarized kinship made the hostilities unavoidable.

To Stella, the daughter did in fact mean all. During her decade of grieving in the Communist camps, the mother had been unable to learn so much as the whereabouts of the child torn away from her in Liebenwalde. The girl was the magnet that drew Stella back to Berlin and its vengeful survivors. If she had settled elsewhere, almost any-where else at all, she might have avoided renewed prosecution. In-stead, she cast herself as the righteous mother of a kidnapped off-spring and made herself a public figure, a star again—for the chance to impose her will on a child and on authorities whose consciences were still raw from the overwhelming injustices committed on all sides during the war.

To the daughter, Stella's appearance, dramatic, out of the blue, was hell.

Yvonne was at home alone in the apartment of her foster parents, the Ellmanns, doing household chores, when the doorbell rang. She asked who was there. A woman's voice replied, "Open the door!"

Yvonne said she would not open the door to a stranger. She had been instructed accordingly long ago by *Tante* Erika, her foster mother. Lately the warning had been repeated and Yvonne had picked up other signs that something scary was going on. *Tante* Erika, always tense, looked even more worried than usual. Yvonne used to enjoy reading the newspapers; now she could never find any papers in the house. Obviously, she was being protected from some-thing or someone, but she was too shy to ask what was happening.

The woman at the door became insistent. "You can open the door for *me*," she said.

Yvonne looked through the peephole in the door and was taken aback. The woman outside was elegantly dressed and extremely beautiful, more beautiful than anyone she could remember ever hav-ing seen. Mindful of *Tante* Erika's admonitions, she still refused to open the door.

The woman was becoming impatient. "You *may* open the door for me," she said again. "I am your mother."

Yvonne recoiled. No words could have hit this child harder. She had never heard of a mother. Years later, she recalled, "I felt as if someone had pierced my heart with a knife." Trembling behind her apartment door, she nevertheless managed to keep herself under remarkable control.

"You're very beautiful," she said quietly, "but I have no mother."

The woman showed no sign of budging and kept insisting that she was indeed the child's mother.

Yvonne was becoming rattled. "You're crazy!" she shouted. "And if you're crazy, go someplace else."

The woman refused to leave. The volleys of her demands and the child's refusals continued. Finally, Yvonne, her curiosity aroused and thinking that at worst nothing awful could happen to her, gave in and opened the door.

Stella marched straight into the living room, looking neither right nor left, sat down on a sofa, and ordered Yvonne: "Give me a kiss! I've been looking for you for a long time."

This incongruous demand for instant intimacy frightened the child. Making sure to keep her distance, she said again, "I have no mother!"

When Stella rose to approach Yvonne, the girl hurriedly backed away. "Don't you touch me!" she shouted. "Don't get near me!"

Stella kept coming, trying to capture her daughter. The child fought back. There was a scuffle. Muscular and made stronger by her fury, Yvonne managed to shove her mother out of the apartment.

"You'll still see that I'm your mother," Stella shot back as she headed for the stairs.

Her hair was dyed black, presumably to avoid being identified as "the blond poison," and she called herself Ingrid, the second of her two first names, which she had started using only recently.

A confused and petrified Yvonne locked the front and back doors, making certain that the locks worked. Shaking, she phoned *Tante* Erika at work and told her that a woman had just been at the apartment claiming to be her mother. "She's crazy," Yvonne said. Erika came home right away, but she couldn't decide what to tell the child. She called Siegfried Baruch, Yvonne's guardian. He and his Jewish advisers also couldn't decide how best to handle the crisis.

Yvonne had survived her first ten years through the kindness of strangers. She would always believe that Stella gave birth to her in prison—which fit the daughter's self-image—not in the Liebenwalde Hospital, which was the fact; and that she had been dangerously small for her age when she was brought to the Jewish Hospital, not healthy and happy, as she was remembered by nurse Alice Safirstein, who took her to Berlin in that awful winter of 1945.

Yvonne's memories of her next home, the Jewish Orphanage at Niederschönhausen in the Communist sector, were also *triste*. "Nobody thought I would survive," she recalled. "But there was a girl there, about fifteen or sixteen years old, who said—I was told—that if everyone thought I would die anyway, she wanted to take me to her bed and take care of me, and probably thanks to that care and warmth, I survived."

Yvonne was the youngest of the more than thirty uprooted children in the home, pretty and big-eyed, starved for love, sheltered by the others. Siegfried Baruch, the director, a dignified, psychologically sophisticated educator with fine credentials, became her legal guardian and remained her father figure for life. She would never admire anybody more. Childless and a strict disciplinarian, he had survived Auschwitz, where his wife died. Now his affections were showered on Stella's daughter.

Helmut Binnewies, one of the older boys, watched with a twinge of envy as Yvonne was taken for walks by Baruch and sometimes allowed to sit on his lap at mealtimes. On Sunday afternoons she was favored with extra helpings of pudding, and her room adjoined the director's small private apartment.

An ardent Zionist, Baruch considered it his duty to instill a sense of Jewishness in his charges. The kitchen was kept kosher. Candles were lit on Friday nights. In the small prayer room, services were held in Hebrew, not German. Palestine was prized as everyone's promised land.

In 1952, fears of new anti-Semitic persecutions, this time stirred by Communists of the German Democratic Republic, scuttled Yvonne's orphanage under traumatic circumstances. The children had to flee west in trucks late at night, with the older kids hissing "Sh . . ." to hush the younger ones like Yvonne. The scene represented another rejection to her, a life-threatening breakout much like the escapes from the Nazis she had heard about.

In the course of her stay in her next home, the Jewish Community Center in West Berlin, the other orphans gradually dispersed. Baruch was in touch less frequently. Yvonne felt alone, and her sense of abandonment would never leave her entirely, not even many years after she was no longer being "placed" somewhere, like someone's forgotten luggage.

Once no children were left in the Community Center, she lived for a spell in the quickly and efficiently reorganized Jewish Hospital, not knowing, of course, that Stella had plied her traitor's trade on those premises. While Yvonne found the environment fascinating and acquired a lifelong fondness for hospitals, the place was hardly an appropriate home for a child, so the Jewish welfare authorities moved her into the Grunewald villa of a childless refugee couple from Poland, Natan and Ursula Celnik.

Natan Celnik, then in his early forties, held a law degree and wasn't simply wealthy; he was very rich. Before the war, he had run his father's factory in Poland—its 600 employees manufactured bricks, ceramics, and roof tiles—and he had managed to transfer much of his capital to the United States.

In Berlin after the war, he imported porcelain, dealt in antiques, manufactured accordions for export, and became still more affluent. He and his wife Ursula adored little Yvonne and spoiled her with love and all the things a child might wish: the best in clothes and toys, a nurse, anything she wanted. Yvonne always considered it the most wonderful time of her life, but it had to end in a year with the Celniks' emigration to America.

And so began another placement, the years with *Tante* Erika, a loving but harassed and impecunious Jewish working-class mother of three who cooked for the Jewish Community Center, and whose life soon turned even harder. For after Yvonne rebuffed her mother's initial overture for possession, Erika Ellmann became the prime target of years of Stella's high-pressure campaigning for her daughter.

It began when Stella reappeared in the Ellmann living room on Grüntaler Strasse in the Wedding section, demanding that she be handed her daughter as if the foster parents had kidnapped the child. Frau Ellmann and her husband tried to reason with the mother, to no avail.

"How can you forbid me my daughter?" Stella screamed.

"*Raus!*" yelled Herr Ellmann.

Yvonne, shut away upstairs, heard it all and cried.

Her protectors still wanted to shield Yvonne from the truth about her mother, considering the story too horrible for someone so young and vulnerable to absorb without great trauma. They obtained a court order forbidding Stella to enter the Ellmann home and, having kept Yvonne away from the gory news accounts of Stella's murder trial, hoped that the child would continue to regard the mother as a demented housebreaker.

Stella's campaign for the possession of her daughter made that impossible. The mother appeared at Yvonne's school and demanded to see her child. School authorities managed to fend Stella off. When she returned again and again, Yvonne began to hear ugly rumors about her mother's past. The child became even moodier and more introverted than usual. Her grades dropped off precipitously. She had to be told.

The job fell to her beloved guardian, Baruch, and he managed it by sparing Yvonne some of the rawest details. She did grasp that the beautiful stranger was really her mother and that her fear of this intruder had not been misplaced. Her mother had been responsible for the death of many Jews during the war.

Yvonne felt destroyed. "It was as if a mountain had fallen on me," she said later.* The disclosure was a cataclysm from which she never fully recovered. And for the present, it was the onset of all-out hostilities with her mother—a war that, in its overt volcanic phase, was to last nearly a decade.

Sophisticated as ever, Stella tried to enlist the aid of the West Berlin courts. It was an opportune time for such moves, the jurists having recently been instructed by the American and British military occupation authorities that the civil rights of even odious murderers are sacred.

Stella's first maneuver, a lawsuit to obtain custody of the child, failed. Showing its respect for the rights of all birth mothers, the court did order Yvonne to visit Stella once a week. The judge wanted to see whether a permanent relationship might yet develop between mother and daughter.

Yvonne and her protectors were appalled. The child thought of her mother as a criminal beyond compare. Her mentors feared Stella's current intentions almost as much as her past crimes. She might kidnap Yvonne. Certainly her influence would be terrible upon a child raised as a devout Jew.

Not only had Stella turned formally toward Christianity after her return from prison, she was outspokenly anti-Semitic, volunteering insulting remarks about Jews to acquaintances on the street. She had married for the third time, and Yvonne was told that the new husband was well known as a Nazi.

His name was Friedheim Schellenberg, and the Ellmanns hated him too. "I could have made three SS men out of him," said *Tante* Erika. Conceivably, Schellenberg brought this on himself by the length of his leather overcoat. On the other hand, Stella's defection from her background and her rejection of Judaism, her dream since her days at the Goldschmidt School before the war, was demonstrable fact.

Yvonne's guardian and foster parents briefed the girl for her visits with her mother as if they were handling a boxer going into a fight. Yvonne had to take a train to Schöneberg. The "Nazi" would pick her up at the station. The visit with Stella was not to last longer than

* In Hebrew, Yvonne used an expression alluding to God on Mount Sinai *forcing* the Torah on the people of Israel.

two hours. If Yvonne wasn't back at the prearranged hour, the Ellmanns would call the police.

Yvonne's helpers had underestimated the girl's steadfastness. She confronted her mother in a state of nonstop rage. Sometimes she pretended to be ill so that a visit could be canceled. She would stall at the station and take a later train in order to shorten the visits. She wanted to refuse going altogether, but she felt that the visits were her responsibility to go through with. If she had gone on strike, the worries of the Ellmanns, Herr Baruch, and his advisers at the Jewish Community would have been further aggravated. Yvonne already felt guilty because she was causing all these good people so much trouble.

So she went on the dreaded visits month after month. The "Nazi" received her at the train station. She did not speak to him. Stella would be waiting at their apartment house, Kyffhäuser Strasse 12, sitting on a couch. Yvonne took her place at the other end and went into a demonstration of passive resistance that Mahatma Gandhi would have appreciated. She taught herself to sit on the couch without feeling that she was really there, and to stare at what was going on around her without showing that she was seeing anything.

The dialogues with her mother were always the same.

"Kiss your mother," Stella would demand.

"You're not my mother, you're a murderess!"

Stella also insisted that Yvonne call her Ingrid. The daughter refused, sensing that her mother was trying to mask her identity, to slip away from her criminal self, her past.

"You're Stella!" the girl screamed, and the name was flung out like a curse.

In time Stella's husband became furious and went to his wife's aid.

"Go to your mother or I'll break your bones!" he shouted.

"I'm not afraid," Yvonne yelled back. "You killed Jews! How many did you kill? If you want to break my bones, here I am! Make a good job of it!"

The stalemates continued. Once Stella tried to get her daughter interested in some fashion designs she had drawn. Yvonne refused to look at them. Eventually the husband took Yvonne to the train. Sometimes she was allowed to go alone. One afternoon "the Nazi" told her she would not be permitted to leave unless she embraced her mother. Yvonne invoked her passive resistance technique.

"I don't mind," she retorted. "I'll just stay." She knew that the Ellmanns would call the police if she wasn't home on time. Stella and her husband must have sensed something of that arrangement.

They let Yvonne go, and this time she ran to the station as fast as she could. At home *Tante* Erika reminded her that she needed only to scream as loudly as she could whenever she faced an emergency at her mother's house.

Yvonne, now twelve, felt that she was becoming a cause célèbre, that Jews all over Berlin had heard of her travail and were following its every turn, agonizing over her. She was touched that so many people cared, but all the fuss over her welfare violated her yearning for privacy. She hated being an isolate, having to be Stella's daughter, scrutinized, burdened by what she called the "stain" of her mother's past. She did not wish to live as a marked person.

She felt her "flaw," her "dark side," so deeply that when *Tante* Erika punished her, however mildly, Yvonne wondered whether she was being made to suffer because she was Stella's bad offspring. Erika understood what was happening. "Yvonne had only one thought," she recalled. "To make amends for what Stella did to the Jews."

It made this good woman feel helpless. She discussed her anguish with Herr Baruch, who consulted a psychologist. Nobody knew what to do.

And then the kindly Celniks showed up again on one of their periodic business trips and offered to adopt Yvonne. Everyone, including Yvonne, thought this was the best possible idea. Everyone but Stella. Weeping, she pleaded, mother to mother, with Ursula Celnik, who loved Yvonne dearly and wanted to ignore Stella, especially after Baruch came and told her, "The mother is a bad woman."

But Natan Celnik felt compelled to change his mind about the adoption. His sense of ethics was offended. "How can you even think about this?" he asked his wife. To Yvonne he said, "This is still your mother! I can't take you away from her! You can't know what happened to make her do what she did."

And there the adoption idea died, vetoed by the possessive Stella.

Wanting to end her dilemma, Yvonne took a knife to bed with her one night. Her fantasy was to bleed peacefully to death there. During her stay at the Jewish Hospital, she had seen suicide cases, so she thought she knew how to slash her wrists and end everyone's agony, including her own. Instead, she fell asleep and never could fulfill her death wish.

Stella, refusing to be put off by Yvonne's resistance to her dictatorial manner of showing affection, kept pressuring the courts. She demanded that Yvonne visit her overnight. Yvonne threatened suicide. The court refused to liberalize the visits.

Next Stella asked the judge to change Yvonne's name and religion to her own. The judge called in the girl for a private talk. A power struggle was in motion. Stella was absolutely determined to seize this child, her sole emotional asset.

For most youngsters such a squeeze play would have become an awful, possibly shattering life event. Not for Yvonne, or so it appeared. She sailed into the challenge, turned it upside down, and made it a demonstration of her hardy ego. This was a talent of her core self, the quintessential survivor—a show of the tenacity she would carry into adulthood: able to overpower hardships, emerging from strife stronger than she was before, equipped with new weapons against adversity. Inadvertently, the terrors of this child's life had prepared her for survivorhood at an age when other little girls still missed their dolls.

Yvonne had been advised that under West German law a person twelve years old had considerable say about her own status. Steeling herself for the court interview with her accustomed intensity, she decided she would be truthful, yet absolutely unswerving in remaining true to her feelings about where she belonged. She had not the slightest doubt about her identity.

Her hearing was brief. She reminded the judge that her name and religion dated back to her birth and that her family had perished in Auschwitz. She was Jewish, she said, and that was that.

"God made me Jewish and I'm going to remain Jewish," she insisted, and the judge quickly ruled in her favor.

While the court saw no reason to change her name from Meissl, Stella managed to get it changed after all. A manipulative reason was on her mind.

When Yvonne was thirteen, Stella, still the resentful rebel, the disturber of the peace, decided to sue Heino Meissl for child support. Meissl was a long reach for such a shakedown. Married to a physician and living in Munich, he had had no contact with Stella for more than a decade and had never heard of Yvonne. Indignantly he denied that he was the father, and a paternity hearing was called in Berlin.

The proceedings could have made a chapter in a Kafka novel. Yvonne was led into a large, drab office and left to sit alone with her mother and a strange man whose name, she was told, was Meissl, the same as her own. Tall and handsome, he quickly turned away from her. No one said a word to either of the two others. Yvonne felt she was on trial but could not figure out why. She did not understand what was happening except that her mother was trying to squeeze money out of this man, which wasn't surprising. Her mother was always demanding money from relatives and other prospects.

Then these three intimate strangers were led away in different directions and individually tested for a long time. Fingerprints were taken. Blood samples were drawn. Skulls and other body parts were meticulously measured; fingers and toes received particularly detailed attention. Before leaving this bizarre scene, Yvonne saw that the name Meissl had been crossed out on her court papers. She was instructed that her name was Goldschlag.

Who *was* her father? Yvonne would always insist that it didn't make much difference. She knew how to accommodate reality, having heard from an early age that Stella had slept with many men during the war. Her father might be Rolf Isaaksohn, or Walter Dobberke or one of his Gestapo compatriots, or any of the other males of many persuasions whom the chaos of the fight for survival—and Stella's turbulent psyche—had sent into this mother's bed.

Perhaps Meissl was her father after all. Since Yvonne had not understood the paternity hearing, she could not dismiss him as a possible candidate.

"Why did nobody think it appropriate to explain about my father?" she ruminated years later. She shrugged.

A long time after she underwent the court's tests, she checked the Munich phone book, found Meissl's name, and wrote him a letter politely inquiring whether she might be his daughter. He never replied.

Stella was still not finished with her tenacious quest to enlist the courts as allies. She sued for full custody of her child and once again was caught in a whopping lie. Her custody claim asserted that Yvonne was none too bright and should therefore become a helper in the supermarket near the mother's home.

Yvonne concluded that Stella was interested in pocketing her potential wages. The court decided to get at the facts and ordered a test of Yvonne's intelligence.

Feeling like the world's most analyzed guinea pig, Yvonne, by then fourteen, had to report for another all-day series of examinations. She learned that her IQ was high, whereupon the court, her foster parents, and her guardian advised her to select a career on her own and pursue her training away from Berlin, away from Stella.

Ever since her days at the Jewish Hospital, Yvonne had dreamed of becoming a doctor. A dream it would remain since there was no money for long, costly medical studies. There was enough, however, for the closest alternative, nursing, so she went off to one of the best nursing schools. It was in the village of Marl bei Recklinghausen, in rural West Germany. She was the only Jew there, again cast as an isolate, first in a preparatory course, then as a student of nursing in a hospital.

It wasn't easy to live as a Jewish adolescent, perhaps the tiniest minority in Germany. "I would meet Nazis everywhere," Yvonne recalled. "I had to work on Jewish holidays. The Jewish Community intervened, and it turned out that the supervisor who made me work on holidays had belonged to the SS."

She experienced other aftershocks of the Holocaust, scenes that would have undone a weaker person. She could never forget the Jewish woman patient who was about to be checked by a professor with whom Yvonne had been working closely. The doctor entered and introduced himself. The patient looked at him with widening eyes.

"Didn't you work in Camp . . . ?" she asked, horrified. Not waiting for an answer, she seized her clothing and ran out of the examining room.

Yvonne could not work with the professor again, but she did not lose her enthusiasm for her training, nor did she condemn the Germans collectively. Many Germans helped her. The principal of her nursing school, for example, treated her with exemplary understanding. She sympathized with Yvonne's concerns as a Jew and issued helpful instructions to her staff. The principal had been briefed on Yvonne's war with Stella, and handled this strange mother with consummate skill when Stella, inevitably, appeared in remote Marl bei Recklingshausen. She had not yet stopped trying to run her lost daughter's life.

Yvonne did not have to spend time with Stella. Still, letters kept coming from the rejected mother to the principal. Eventually even Stella grew tired of pursuing Yvonne, hammering against rock. The one-sided correspondence ceased in 1966. Yvonne never had contact with her mother again.

24. Working for Eichmann

ONLY A TRACE of a German accent offered a clue to the identity of the cheerful, tanned, slightly buxom, and bouncily energetic woman I was facing in her stylish contemporary two-story home on one of those sunny San Francisco hills near the Pacific where everybody appeared to live on a lifetime vacation.

This was Dr. Lore Weinberg Shelley, sixty-seven, an American-trained psychologist, once of Lübbecke, Westphalia, and Berlin, one of at least sixty-six self-styled "secretaries of death"* who spent a year and a half doing desk work, usually sixteen hours a day, for camp commandant Rudolf Höss and his annihilation machine in the General Staff Building at Auschwitz. Mostly they typed for him, like the fictional Sophie of *Sophie's Choice.*

I had undergone the jarring experience of reading her meticulous book describing this duty—her own and that of thirty of her colleagues. Nevertheless, sitting now at her coffee table, I felt disoriented. I could not come to terms with the reality of the smiling, exuberant Dr. Shelley's transformation. There was an element of déjà vu, as if I were seeing Stella simultaneously as my teenage heartthrob, as a Gestapo bloodhound, and as a shunned convict. Of course, an enormous and everlasting chasm divided these two Jewish employees of Adolf Eichmann, Stella and Dr. Lore, but what exactly made the difference?

---

* *Secretaries of Death* (Shengold Publishers, New York, 1988) was the title of a collection of their first-person narratives edited by Dr. Shelley.

At nineteen, having arrived at Auschwitz by train on April 20, 1943—Hitler's birthday, as she noted—Lore Weinberg survived the immediate death selection of the camp doctors by exuding the strength of physique and will of a useful slave laborer; as a tomboy, she had once been determined to become a professional circus horseback rider. In Auschwitz she was assigned to sort clothes left behind by Jews who had been gassed—had gone "up the chimney," in the Auschwitz euphemism—at the rate of up to 9,000 every twenty-four hours. Lore helped to form neat piles, shoes here, underwear there. Some of the garments were extremely small.

Out of the blue, her life became more bearable when an SS man lined up the women of her barracks and asked who could type. Lore hated the confinement of office work, but an unknown distant relative, owner of a brickworks in Sumter, South Carolina, once asked her to acquire secretarial skills when he sent her an affidavit of support toward her immigration to the United States. Lore's quota number, like Stella's, was a long way from being called up at the time of Pearl Harbor, but her secretarial training almost certainly saved her life as she stepped forward to volunteer for typing.

For the test at headquarters she was asked to complete a sentence. *Unterscharführer* Clausen dictated, "For Christmas I would like to get . . ." Feisty little Lore typed the words "my freedom," and was picked to assist in the "Political Department." She became a support of the badly overworked German staff, which numbered 7,000. Her food became somewhat more bearable and she enjoyed other privileges. The SS men were terrified of the epidemics raging through the *Lager,* so Lore and her Jewish colleagues were allowed to bathe regularly.

They had a helpful skill to offer. Skills saved Jewish lives, as I had learned from survivors who worked for the Nazis as gardeners, handymen, carpenters, housepainters—solid hands-on talents, not esoteric brainwork performed by lawyers or scientists. For the Nazis, furthermore, Lore and her co-workers served an additional cause. More than office drones, they functioned as secretaries of *Ordnung,* keepers of the System.

They kept *order* in the files, the death certificates, the interrogation transcripts. Order oiled the Eichmann machinery and gave its minions a sense of legitimacy and accomplishment. In the pervasive stench and incinerator smoke of Auschwitz, *Ordnung* remained a must.

So Lore Weinberg transferred the registration forms of the "SB" (gassed) prisoners from the files of the living to the papers of the dead. She typed daily lists of the deceased. She typed death certificates of prisoners individually executed, the cause of death always the same: "reddish-blue strangulation marks and fracture of the upper cervical vertebrae." And she took notes at interrogations by local and visiting Gestapo officers and typed the protocols.

Some prisoners who were subjected to questioning were so eager to confess, to confess to anything desired, anything at all, that torture was unnecessary; Lore greeted such cases with relief. Reluctant or helpless victims were fastened to the *Boger Schaukel*, a swinging device designed by the locally famous *Oberscharführer* Wilhelm Boger, who was proud of his nickname, "the Tiger." Prisoners were beaten on the swing until their skin flew off in strips and they "confessed," just to get off Boger's invention.

Lore Weinberg's typing pool was called a *Himmelfahrtskommando*, an ascension-to-the-sky command. Assembled in formation, they were told by *Untersturmführer* Georg Wisnitza, "At best, you'll all die here of old age. And if you ever get out, nobody will believe you." None of the secretaries expected to survive. None ever learned why they did. An oversight probably, an aberrant last-moment lapse of *Ordnung*.

The future psychologist Lore Weinberg learned to respond to calls for her tattooed inmate number in Slovakian because the original prisoners who dished out food came from Slovakia. And she wrote poetry, much poetry, verses like, "Where is that market / on which you can get / the most precious jewels / for a piece of rotten bread?"

She served Eichmann and never regretted for a moment that she did so. "It was a mode of survival," she told me on her hillside near the Pacific, matter-of-factly, without embarrassment, and with the slight suggestion of a shrug.

Her mode of survival was to type for the most notorious of the war criminals, to satisfy his yearning for order. According to my dictionary, she was a collaborator: she "cooperated with an enemy." But dictionary definitions are tone-deaf. They cannot hear the anguish of a Lore Weinberg poem. What should she have done? Refrain from volunteering for typing and deal with the final stage of Lore's Choice, to die of starvation or poison gas?

What about others who made their peace with the Eichmann system? What about Sister Elli at the Jewish Hospital in Berlin? Should she have refused to sleep with *Kommissar* Dobberke and turned him down when he offered to teach her how to ride a bicycle? Her peers, more principled or perhaps merely lacking in opportunity, did not think so.

What about Rabbi Murmelstein, the 220-pound brute who ran

the pioneering *Ordner* service in Vienna and beat fellow inmates in Theresienstadt? Why did tribunals in Czechoslovakia and Italy let him go with the consent of Jewish survivors?

What about Dr. Dr. Lustig of the Berlin Jewish Hospital who threatened to place his secretary "on transport" but did his best to sabotage and stall the Gestapo men before whom he sniveled, whether out of fear or respect or shrewdness? Should he have been put to death without trial?

I found myself confused and awed trying to wrestle with such questions. And other doubts crowded in on me, puzzles closer to home. Unquestionably, Stella had latched onto a relevant argument when, in her paranoid search for scapegoats, she blamed "the Americans" for her family's failure to escape Berlin, thereby dictating her traitorous course of action. If Franklin Roosevelt and his administrators had been more merciful about the visa quota, Stella might have sung Cole Porter for Benny Goodman instead of hunting Jews for Dobberke.

Who was culpable and to what degree? Should Assistant Secretary of State Breckenridge Long have been hanged? Should visa chief Avra Warren have been shot? Should FDR have been tried for complicity in genocide?

And what about those guardians of life itself, the doctors?

I had long known, of course, of Dr. Mengele and other Nazi physicians, the monsters who officiated at the selections and performed unspeakable experiments on prisoners. I had not known that Jewish prisoner physicians assisted such men in the death camps. They did, and their ultimate fates varied.

One such doctor with torn loyalties was Elie A. Cohen, Dutch, a "transport doctor" at the Westerbork Jewish transit camp in Holland. By his own account, he assisted at the departure of nineteen trains to the Sobibor camp in Poland. The trains were packed with 34,313 Jews, of whom nineteen survived, according to Dr. Cohen's painstaking research after the war.

He had not heard of Sobibor or of any gassings during his eight months at Westerbork. The trains were said to be headed "east." At the beginning, the fate of the deportees being at best uncertain, the doctor was liberal in granting phony certificates declaring inmates "unfit for transport," even though this usually delayed deportation for no more than a week. He was caught, and the chief doctor, Jewish, told him: "If you do it again, you and your family will have to go on transport."

Dr. Cohen remembered: "From that moment on, I worked honestly, though now and then I made some 'mistakes'; it was my egoism that led me to this decision, because I wanted to stay in the Netherlands."

The doctor was not troubled by the Jews he sent off. "After their departure I took a shower, went to bed for a rest, and in the evening went to a cabaret performance and amused myself. I was glad it had not been my turn, and for some days I forgot the next deportation train . . ."

Inevitably, Dr. Cohen's turn came. He went on transport to Auschwitz, where his wife and four-year-old son were gassed.

"My reaction was not one of grief, or despair, or there being no reason for me to carry on anymore," he recalled. "No, on the contrary, I fought for my life. I wanted to survive, and I went as far as assisting the German camp doctor with the selection."

Dr. Cohen explained how he worked with Dr. Klein in the Auschwitz hospital ward where the Jewish doctor was caring for fellow inmates:

"He would come and choose those among the Jewish patients whom he deemed no longer worthy of medical treatment, and condemned them to the gas chamber. I had to hold each one's medical card, and Klein would ask me my opinion of the patient's condition. Of course, any attempt to cover up was doomed, because Klein could see for himself what sort of state the patient was in, but the charade had to be played out. Anyone who was thought to need more than ten days' recuperation before being sent out to work again was sent to the gas. But I participated because I wanted to live. . . .

"I knuckled under. I collaborated. It is a terrible word, but I cannot escape it, although my situation was impossible; just as I cannot escape the guilt that I feel. We did the Germans' job for them."

Dr. Cohen faced no indictment after the war. He became a respected psychotherapist in Israel, specializing in helping fellow survivors.

And what, precisely, would have been the sentence for Dr. Maximilian Samuel if he, too, had left Auschwitz alive?

My friend and occasional adviser, the research psychiatrist Dr. Robert Jay Lifton, encountered traces of Dr. Samuel in the 1980s and wrote about him in his shattering work *The Nazi Doctors*. Dr. Samuel had been a prominent academic gynecologist in Cologne and a zealous nationalist, awarded the Iron Cross in World War I.

Assigned to the infamous block 10 at Auschwitz, Dr. Samuel participated in a "research project," surgically removing the cervix of numerous women. "Most prison doctors were impressed by Samuel's extreme 'diligence' in working closely with the Nazis," Dr. Lifton reported. "Furthermore, he denounced to Nazi doctors another prison physician . . ."

Some inmates insisted that Samuel had been somewhat more considerate than the Nazi doctors in the cervix removals. One woman who underwent sterilization experiments remembered him as being "kind to us." But most recalled him as "either arrogant or pathetic or both."

Pathetic? Dr. Samuel's wife had been gassed on arrival at the camp, and survivors testified that he was desperate to save the life of his nineteen-year-old daughter, who had been selected as fit for work, subject to change at whim. He even wrote a letter to Himmler personally, pleading for her to be spared in the light of his military record. Suddenly, in the midst of his experiments, Samuel was gassed, possibly because his extensive skin lesions had rendered him too repulsive to the SS, possibly because he was considered too argumentative, or for reasons even less fathomable.

What had been Dr. Samuel's crime?

"Samuel was a Jew," an acquaintance of his, a prisoner doctor from Poland, remarked to Dr. Lifton, "which meant [he was] a person 100 percent condemned to death in the camp. So he had the right to prolong his life—week by week, month by month."

And perhaps, just possibly, to save his daughter.

So what *was* the doctor's cardinal offense? His "diligence," if true? His "arrogance," if true? His repulsive eczema? Excessive loyalty to his daughter? Or, as the Polish inmate doctor thought, simply one vital statistic: he was a Jew.

At the war's end, evidence of flagrant collaboration littered Europe like the bombed-out ruins. Flooded with complaints about renegades among their own, Jewish leaders organized "Courts of Honor" to judge some of those who survived because they practiced betrayal to save their skins. The work of these tribunals-by-peers has never been studied.

Although they lacked official recognition, the courts convened secretly for years in former concentration camps such as Bergen-Belsen, lately converted into care centers for the homeless—the millions of "Displaced Persons"—as well as in major population centers: Berlin, Munich, and Rome.

These self-appointed forums were not empowered to impose punishments beyond the jurisdiction of internal Jewish affairs. Their harshest verdict was equivalent to excommunication, which meant the withholding of the modest special benefits available to Holocaust survivors. Despite their limited authority, the tribunals could easily have been conducted in the style and spirit of the kangaroo purge courts run by the Soviets, the kind that disposed of Stella's case in minutes, without hearing witnesses. Instead, the Jewish courts went to remarkable lengths to weigh judgment fairly, and their treatment of the accused was astonishingly lenient.

In Berlin the courts sat patiently for more than a decade in the Jewish Community offices, Joachimstaler Strasse 13. A lawyer survivor acted as chairman. At least one other attorney survivor assisted, as did a minimum of two lay lay jurors. All available eyewitnesses were heard, pro and con. Written testimonies, pro and con, were solicited and considered.

Even a *Kapo,* generally considered the lowest-life of traitor, received a respectful hearing and sometimes turned out to be struggling against undeserved ostracism. One such victim of postwar injustice was Harry Schwarzer, whose case was heard on January 9, 1947.

Five witnesses testified. They had been inmates with Schwarzer in one of the smaller concentration camps—Plaschow, in Poland— where, unaccountably, the accused had indeed been appointed *Kapo* by the Nazis. Allegedly, he had beaten fellow Jews.

As his collaborator history was pieced together by the Court of Honor, Schwarzer had been eighteen years old at the time, exceptionally fragile, and starved, suffering from edema of both feet. When he occasionally slapped a prisoner, which he admitted, it was to prevent the victim from being brutalized by the imminently threatened attack of a prisoner gang.

The main charge against Schwarzer was that he had stolen food and consumed it himself. It turned out that Plaschow was an unusual camp. A large portion of its prisoner laborers were Polish and gentile and these captives received vastly more nourishment than the Jews. The witnesses swore that the Poles had food to spare and that Schwarzer stole only from them, that in fact he deprived no one and mistreated no one, *Kapo* or not.

The court's decision: "It is determined that Harry Schwarzer did not abuse the interests of the Jewish Community."

For the 1956 trial of Max Reschke, for three tempestuous years the unpopular "Jewish director" of the camps at Grosse Hamburger Strasse and Schulstrasse, the court mustered three attorneys and three lay jurors. It heard eleven witnesses and received communications from ten more, including Leo Baeck, the revered former chief rabbi. The chairman was Dr. Richard Preuss, once a chief prosecutor.

Reschke, *Kommissar* Dobberke's Jewish deputy, the man who placed the fatal X on the list sending the marked victim onto the next deportation train, had not had an easy time after the war. Having made many enemies, he was denounced by one of them, and on July 18, 1945, a Soviet sergeant arrested him in a hideaway he had found in suburban Krampnitz. Without trial, he spent two years in Buchenwald under Soviet rule. Eventually he was sentenced to twenty-five years as a Gestapo collaborator, and on December 31, 1955, he was discharged without a word of explanation.

As the court got the story more than ten years after the war, even the most serious charges against Reschke were relatively nebulous. Frau Beila Wollstein testified that she applied to Reschke for permission to speak to Dobberke and the accused turned her down with "a detached, hard no." Herr Jacob Gutfeld said that Reschke had been "a bit military," and that he would have the *Ordner* stand needlessly in formation for a long time, after many hours of duty.

That was the worst of it. On his credit side, witnesses testified that Reschke warned some Jews when they were about to be arrested, that he permitted mothers from outside to visit sons, that he tried to provide "good conditions" in the camps, exercising "calm and exemplary *Ordnung*." The great Leo Baeck personally attested in writing to Reschke's good character.

The court ruled that Reschke's rule had "provided no cause for objection."

Eyewitnesses whom the court had not heard had given me a harsher view of Reschke. The court's verdict reminded me of my Shakespeare studies at De Witt Clinton High School—Portia on the quality of mercy: "It is twice blessed; it blesseth him that gives and him that takes." Who was I to judge Reschke? I wasn't there. The witnesses were. The court members were also survivors.

And who was I to second-guess the court's verdict of October 8, 1946, against Inge Reitz, née Jacoby? Inge, eighteen, had difficult days at the Grosse Hamburger Strasse camp. It was testified that Lotte Paesch, a nurse prisoner, had accused her, "You should be ashamed of yourself, one should spit at you!" To their fellow prisoners, the nurse had said, "No one is allowed to look at Inge anymore! She is responsible for getting a Jew arrested today."

Reitz had thrown herself onto her straw sack in tears, the court heard. "I've been bad," she wailed. She had led the Gestapo man

Georg Schwöbel to the apartment of an acquaintance who lived in hiding, believing he wouldn't be home. He was, and had given her "a terrible look."

Schwöbel would have been difficult to resist. He especially liked to terrorize young women. One of his routines was to throw a heavy object at a victim, usually with painful accuracy, then make her pick it up so he could throw it again.

The court held that Reitz had acted under great pressure and that her youth had to be considered. "Nevertheless," said the ruling, "she committed actions against the interests of the Jewish Community." The sentence was hardly any sentence. Reitz was denied social assistance from the Jewish Community for three months.

In Austria a Jewish "Disciplinary Commission" was created and administered by a survivor of the Mauthausen camp who was about to become famous: Simon Wiesenthal. The great hunter of Nazis was also relentless at detecting collaborators. He was especially suspicious of Jews who claimed they had "saved" someone.

"A man who had the power to save also had the power to condemn," he argued. Yet even under this stalker's tutelage, the commission pronounced only thirty Austrian Jews guilty of having worked with the Nazis.

And Wiesenthal was not shocked at their corruption. "We have our saints and our sinners," he philosophized.

The West German courts sometimes ruled more rigorously than the Jewish tribunals judged their peers, but not by much. Thus the catcher Bruno Goldstein was sentenced to seven years in 1949 but had expected worse. "If times ever change, you're probably going to chop my head off," Goldstein had told a fellow Jew on a Berlin street in 1942. Goldstein, smoking a pipe, showed off a Gestapo identity card and a set of handcuffs, along with his gun, and bragged about how many U-boats he had "delivered."

When times in fact did change, Goldstein, the former social worker, did not have his head chopped off at all, even though his was arguably the most spectacular case of collaboration next to Stella's and her partner Rolf's.

"After Dobberke, Goldstein was the most powerful man in the camp," testified an eyewitness, Inge Lefkowitz, when Goldstein was brought before the West Berlin court in 1949.

Doggedness was Goldstein's hallmark. In December 1942, Moritz Dobrin, owner of the renowned old Café Dobrin, was assigned for deportation to Theresienstadt, then considered on a par with a senior citizens' retirement center. It was Goldstein who called Dobberke's attention to the "error." Dobrin was under sixty-five, which meant deportation to Auschwitz, and the travel order was changed accordingly.

As a social worker for the Jewish Community, Goldstein had acquired a commanding acquaintance among Berlin's Jews, which made him valuable to the Gestapo. Yet when he went hunting for U-boats together with Rolf and Stella, Goldstein ranked third.

On April 21, 1944, the threesome flushed out Ida Nöcke, aged sixty, from an attic hiding place in suburban Woltersdorf. "I told them that, as Jews, they should be ashamed of themselves," Nöcke testified at Goldstein's trial.

"Ach, Sie sind ja Stella, die Ritterkreuzträgerin," Nöcke had exclaimed in recognition, before she was dragged away to the Schul strasse camp. By sardonically identifying her as a holder of the Knight's Cross decoration, this fearless old victim nominated Stella as more than a catcher, a mercenary; to Ida Nöcke, Stella was a full-fledged Nazi. Stella remained unmoved, the star.

At least one of Stella's co-workers rehabilitated himself by making good in impressive style.

Günther Abrahamson, who initiated Stella by going hunting with her for the missing forger Rogoff, had been a cheerful bumpkin from the sticks, the rural Uckermark way north of Berlin, when he joined the Gestapo forces at the Grosse Hamburger Strasse in 1943. Recruited from his first job, at the Jewish Orphanage, Günther was glib and canny for his age, "Aryan"-looking—tall, slim, and blond—and he was blessed with an ingratiating yet self-confident manner and a sonorous voice. An operator.

By 1992, Dr. Abrahamson, a Ph.D., was a professional man of many honors in his field, running his own prosperous business in a western German city. Quite a transition. He burbled at me cordially, almost uninterruptibly, and with stunning frankness.*

Günther had been one of Dobberke's first Jewish employees, starting as a scout in June 1943 after having been assigned earlier to verifying addresses of Jews in hiding. Abrahamson took pride in his handling of Dobberke, to whom he reported for orders every morning. He bribed the boss with plenty of liquor, and since he was a

---

* For the contact with this unusual eyewitness I am indebted to Nathan Stoltzfus, a Harvard University Ph.D. candidate in history and a resourceful researcher who first located Abrahamson and won his confidence in 1986.

fellow *Provinzler,* a country lad hailing from next door to Dobberke's native Pomerania, he managed to insinuate himself onto the old cop's unpolished wavelength.

Chuckling, Günther told me of a Jewish wartime associate who bragged that he stood like *soi* with Dobberke, using the Yiddish equivalent for "close" or "just like that." I suspect that Abrahamson was really talking about himself.

In tandem with his junior partner, Gottschalk, Abrahamson's first major accomplishment was the capture of Iwan Katz, fifty-four, a former Communist deputy to the Reichstag and once his party's representative in Moscow. This success gained stature for Abrahamson because Katz was expert at eluding the Gestapo. Having emerged from his first concentration camp in late 1933, he was not rearrested until 1941. Katz escaped the same year, and lived in hiding until Abrahamson and Gottschalk caused him to land in Auschwitz. He managed to survive and, in 1947, appeared in a West Berlin court as star witness against Günther.

Katz testified that Abrahamson, as Dobberke's trusty, enforced his will with a pistol and loved his work: "He got a kick out of it and felt great doing it. One look made this abundantly clear—there he was on the other side of the barbed-wire fence from Auschwitz-bound prisoners, well fed, neatly clothed, chauffeured in cars around Berlin."

The trial dragged on until 1952, when Abrahamson was sentenced to only five months in prison plus court costs.

In recent times, Stella's fellow catcher likened himself to the East German border guards who shot fugitives trying to cross the Berlin Wall in 1989. They only followed orders. He only followed orders. Abrahamson did not mention what the West Berlin judge said when he sentenced one of the soldiers to three and a half years in prison: "Not everything that is legal is right."

In his official autobiography, Abrahamson says of his war years: "Persecution and arrest by the Gestapo."

Was collaboration truly crucial for survival? Perhaps it was indeed unavoidable at times and under some circumstances. Perhaps. The fictional Sophie had no choice. At least, the alternative she was given, to pick one of her two children for the gas, was no choice. But I thought also of choices available to others, the road taken by many prisoners when they were pressured by Dobberke and his kind to join the authorities in command. Ismar Reich, for example, who told

Adolf Eichmann's men to go to hell and nevertheless made it back alive.

In my mind I began reviewing my intensive, intimate conversations with Reich and sixty-six other Berlin Jews, men and women who outwitted the Eichmann killing machine because (so I started to think) they were not the *type* to permit themselves the degradation of descent into collaboration, to go along and become either turncoats or charred corpses.

Not the type. As I went down the list of my informants, my heroes —Rogoff, Ehrlich, Behar, Linczyk, Cousin Siegfried, and the others —it dawned on me that, yes, of course, there absolutely was a type who would not bend, a U-boat type! Mentally summoning up the faces of this group, I determined in no time that a surprising number of common characteristics, nine in all, applied not only to a few but to all, to every one of my sources who imparted inside knowledge from below ground.

The element of *chutzpah* all but popped out of them. How else could they have gone boating under the nose of the Gestapo and parading in tuxedos for dinner at fancy hotels? And they were quickwitted, ready with comebacks to any suspicious inquiries fired at them from anyone, anywhere, without warning.

Their *egos* were in superb repair. They were without exception positive in outlook, optimistic, cheerful, assertive, even ebullient some of the time.

These were outgoing *people-people*, capable of adjusting quickly, chameleon-like, to new allies who might help them survive. Their constantly shifting casts of supporting characters required them to be anything but shy or standoffish; at the same time, they had to withstand the isolation of long periods alone in enemy territory.

They were consummate *role-players*, actors, forgers, liars, imaginative at creating and never forgetting details of their many cover stories, ready to run around "*heiling*" and masquerading as Hitler Youths. (By no accident, the German title of the basically nonfiction film *Europa, Europa* is *Hitler Junge Salomon.*)

They were *improvisers,* not inflexibly rutted in one script. They could switch identities to go with new papers and knew how to keep security silence in an overcrowded illegal apartment.

With the sensitivity of Charlie Chaplin, they realized that *laughter* is potent medicine for nearly all troubles. More than a sense of humor, they possessed the madcap irreverence of adventurers, nose thumbers who could pull good times, fun, out of the worst of times.

Their *luck* was nearly unbelievable again and again. Was it truly luck? My schoolmate Rudi Goldschmidt (now Goldsmith), who became wealthy doing market research in London and Chicago, thought not. He remembered that his mother, the founder of our Goldschmidt school, used to instruct him: "There's no such thing as luck. You must be well trained to convert opportunity." Which was precisely what the U-boats trained themselves to do.

Enormous *energy* was indispensable. Over the years, survival stretched into an obstacle course, winnable only by running, dodging, doing without sleep or food, and inevitably having to run some more.

"Aryan" looks helped. Gerd Ehrlich, blond and blue-eyed, had a point: *Der Stürmer* saved U-boats because Germans believed that all Jews looked like that porno sheet's caricatures. Teutonic appearance was not an essential, though. My swarthy friend Isaak Behar masqueraded for a while as a Spanish naval officer. This exotic identity kept him from telling too many risky lies. He just said, *"Nix verstehen!"*

The clustering of these similarities could hardly have been coincidental. Although it required a lot to remain one's own person under the Nazi guns, it was done. If you were the type.

Stella, insecure and rigid, was not the type. She told me so herself, and her surrender to Dobberke was proof.

25. "Dear Stella . . ."

"Our fears do make us traitors."
—Macbeth

THE SCENE WOULD HAVE BEEN fitting for a tourist poster. The hills, with their sun-flooded, terraced vineyards, nearly touched the little river flowing placidly past the park benches on my left. Increasingly puzzled, I headed out of the central city to one of the choice residential neighborhoods of the ancient little West German town. This was Beethoven country, not Hitler country.

Turning to the right into her serene and narrow street, with its huge shade trees, I stopped at No. 5, Stella's sleek beige four-story apartment house with inviting balconies, the only modern structure on the block, and wondered how she could afford such tasteful, comfortable surroundings.

She had written me that, at sixty-seven, she was subsisting on an old age pension of 238 marks a month, about $130. As I looked down her street, it occurred to me that this was but a fraction of the money she would need to rent an apartment here, not to mention other living expenses. She had also told me that she was ill, in pain, her back and legs and lungs giving her trouble. She was weak, so very weak. Her nerves were gone; she could stand no excitement, none at all. She didn't want me to visit, she wanted only to forget the past.

I had last seen her fifty-three years ago at the Goldschmidt School when she was fourteen and I was thirteen and we sang together in the chorus of Dr. Bandmann, our excitable music teacher. My memory of Stella was vivid, to state the case delicately. She was not forgettable until after one stopped breathing.

It had required considerable time and diligence for me to locate Stella in a strange new town where she lived under new names, both first and last. Her old neighbors in Berlin had refused to reveal her whereabouts because Stella wanted more than to forget her past. She wanted the anonymity afforded by her new identity as Ingrid.

The whereabouts of Stella-Ingrid Goldschlag Kübler Isaaksohn Schellenberg Pech* had been a mystery since her final abortive trial in West Berlin in 1972.** All Germans are subject to *Anmeldepflicht*; residents must register with the police whenever they move. But at the Berlin Jewish Community offices I was told that Stella had been allowed to assume a new identity. She was supposedly living in the northern suburb of Frohnau, but unidentified searchers from Israel had been unable to find her. Neither had a West Berlin author of my acquaintance, Ferdinand Kroh, who had written briefly about Stella, based on court records, in a paperback about Jews during the Holocaust.

Starting with the same records, I traced Stella to Schönwalder Strasse 98-100 in Spandau, near the city limits of West Berlin. There, a neighbor, Johanna Pürschel, said Stella had left in 1980. Frau Pürschel was closemouthed. If she was knowledgeable about Stella's past, she wouldn't admit it. She only knew, she said, that Stella had "suffered much" during the war. Frau Pürschel looked up to her beautiful and well-dressed neighbor as her heroine, something of a Joan of Arc. Neighbors made a circle around Frau Pürschel's retarded son; Stella was nice to him. When their apartment building

---

* Pech is a pseudonym.
** It was her third time in court over a quarter of a century—an unusually persistent record of prosecution, clearly an expression of the continuing fury harbored by her surviving victims. The 1972 trial was a near replay of the earlier West Berlin proceeding. It was held because the 1957 verdict was vacated on technical grounds in 1958. Since that time Stella had been medically examined seven times and declared unfit for trial each time, the doctors citing aftereffects of the tuberculosis she contracted in the postwar prison camps.

was to go co-op, Stella was the only tenant with the gumption to protest loudly. A friend of the underdog.

When I inquired of Frau Pürschel whether she was aware that her lovely neighbor had worked for the Gestapo during the war, her splutter bounced back instantly. "That's impossible!" Pause. "Well," she allowed in unmistakable Berlin worker accent, "I guess nothing is impossible." Pause. Then, softly: "Hard to believe." Recovering, she proceeded to reiterate, wistfully, her memories of Stella's grace and class, how "chic" she had been, how "modern," and those dressing gowns . . . all illusion?

A West German official of my acquaintance was eventually able (it took four months) to have the police records searched for Stella's name and her address in the picturesque southwestern corner of West Germany. He would not give me the address; he'd forward a letter from me which she could answer if she so chose. I wrote her a chatty note recalling our rides on the No. 176 streetcar to the Goldschmidt School more than fifty years ago and brought her up to date on two of our mutual school buddies, Lili in London and Edith in New York.

The response, a postcard with her address and phone number, took six weeks to reach me because it lacked airmail postage. Her message was wistful and self-pitying. She had been eager to come to the United States before the war, but her father had been too unworldly to bring off an emigration. The years she spent "in a concentration camp" had left her extremely weak and sickly. Her back, legs, and lungs gave her constant difficulties. Her husband (she mentioned just one) had died, and now "the loneliness eats you up." She was posing as a victim, a barely ambulatory catalogue of righteous complaints. No, she didn't want me to visit, she was "too weak to tolerate the excitement."

The depth of her loneliness turned out to be true, much else did not. When I had first appeared at her trim, modern apartment house, unannounced, and found nobody home, an elderly next-door neighbor confided that I could count on Stella returning around eleven a.m., because she invariably did. Seven days a week, she went by streetcar to a downtown fish restaurant, a plastic cog in a fast-food chain like McDonald's, and came straight back. Otherwise, she never seemed to leave her apartment. She never cooked at home, the neighbor lady volunteered.

"You from Berlin?" she asked, looking me over.

"I've just come from there."

"She'll be pleased."

"I guess she's been alone a lot?" I probed. At that, the woman shrugged, made a face reflecting repugnance, and quickly withdrew. Whatever she knew about her neighbor's past obviously wasn't considered fit for discussion.

Wondering whether Stella would bother to reply at all, I kept my first letter undemanding. I simply tried to establish my bona fides as a, hopefully, remembered good old guy, familiar with a long-ago part of her past that was innocent and that I had shared. Nobody here but us classmates. I didn't try to sail under fake colors. I said I was writing about Jews who had survived the war in Berlin.

My marvelous wife, Elaine, a well-mannered library director, was not entirely reconciled to habits forced on reporters and authors when, let's say, they had to talk a weeping mourner out of a photo of a loved one; she tried not to show how offended she was by what she considered my misplaced camaraderie.

I wasn't troubled, because Stella's story had mesmerized me for so long. Also, I saw myself as a representative of history. History has a right to know. I did swallow hard over two innocent words in my letter, terminology required by Emily Post etiquette. They were my salutation: "Dear Stella . . ."

Come again? What was I doing calling her "dear"?

Never mind. How *was* I supposed to address her? Killer? Scum of the Earth? No, this was a time for civility. To write "Dear Stella" as a routine overture to a letter was not to acquit her. I was eager to produce an exclusive, the dream of all writers. Nobody had written before in a meaningful way of my old chorus partner Stella, my singalong. No one had tried to understand what drove her. Would I be able to explain her? Perhaps to decipher her? I didn't know what I wanted to find. It was a professional move, an assignment, more interesting than most.

My letter worked. Postcards came from the classmate whom I had addressed as "Ingrid" on the envelope but as "Stella" within—a deliberate inconsistency I had hoped she might remark on, but she never did. Was she inattentive or accepting what looked to me like two identities?

I sent more letters. Gingerly, I began to elicit details of her past that would help me with this book, without straying into questions she could have considered threatening or too nosy. Her postcards kept coming with answers reduced to the sparsest minimum. Was she conserving her energy? Saving postage? Suspecting an ambush?

Just *schreibfaul,* too lazy to write? I couldn't tell, so I kept eliciting information with great care, concerned that any wrong move might make her lapse into permanent silence.

That was a risk I had to avoid in the interest of drawing out an accurate accounting. It was also why I planned not to confront her with deadly details, incontrovertible documentary evidence of her crimes. Nor would I express direct disapproval of her conduct. Nobody had appointed me judge or jury. Not yet anyway.

Stella seemed sufficiently intrigued or bored or flattered by the attention I was showing in her to keep responding seven times, always instantly, whenever I wrote, and later when I started phoning and asking a great many questions. Some sort of relationship was building between us, and she saw enough in it to keep it alive for two years, open-ended, seemingly indefinitely.

At first her cards netted 5 percent information, 95 percent whining. It was important to her that I recognize her as a victim to be pitied, an alumna of *Lager,* their time and sponsorship never specified. She hinted that she might be hovering on the verge of death, emotionally and physically fragile, close to paralysis. It could have been true, although I kept my mind open, my eye on her skill as an actress, remembered from our childhood.

Would she lose interest in a contact with Ridgefield, Connecticut, USA? She hinted at indifference at first: "You are there and I am here . . ." So I realized that disruption was a continuing risk. Writing postcards and having to dredge up the past—I was beginning to ask about *Kristallnacht,* unpleasant memories, if not incriminating—was an effort for her, conceivably an annoyance. I couldn't predict when I might inadvertently touch some unusually painful nerve and seal her shut.

Something more. I was dealing with the egoist of egoists; my research had already made that clear. She was bound to ask, "What's in this for me?"

I probably underestimated how bored she was, how lonely, how starved for attention. I fancy myself a sensitive negotiator, trying to feel the fit on the shoes of others, so I decided to introduce money into the relationship, such as it was. "A gift of cash is always in good taste," as has been said.

I didn't want to risk being accused—by Stella or possibly later by others—of trying to bribe her. I couldn't afford to offer her a lot of money or be accused of checkbook journalism, or to encourage some groundless legal controversy about ownership of a literary property —not that she ever performed any service except to "sit" for interviews. And so I pinned a modest $50 bill onto one of my letters, and she gushed gratitude as if I had showered $5,000 on her.

This was and remains strange. It later developed that she had been on one of her campaigns lobbying for pity when she wanted me to believe she was subsisting on 238 D-marks a month in social security. She was also getting 1,100 D-marks in monthly life insurance proceeds she was left by husband number three. She was financially fairly comfortable. Why did she display such enthusiasm over three $50 gifts I presented her over several months? I could only speculate that she wanted to string me along to keep me believing she was destitute. Why? For pity? Was I a welcome entertainment, a break in her ennui? Perhaps a final alibi, a protestation of innocence that would be immortalized in my book; a permanent record she might influence in her favor in her final days?

Or did she sense, as I prepared for my invasion, that I still hung on to remnants of doubts about the circumstances of her crimes? The initial and most damning reports of her misdeeds had appeared in the tightly censored Soviet press, nowhere else. Her trial by the Soviets had been a closed kangaroo proceeding. Hysteria (Jewish) and defensiveness (West German) could have colored her two post-war trials. The case didn't seem open-and-shut after all.

After the war, I had done my best to penetrate the curtain of secrecy that the Soviet authorities in Berlin had pulled around themselves. I might as well have tried calling the Kremlin collect. There was no way to locate a reliable source to learn what Stella had actually done during the war.

When I was sent a roster of more than 100 survivors of my own old bunch, the Goldschmidt School alumni, along with many of their life stories, I looked for a mention of Stella's fate. There was none, and so I determined to track her down and to look for answers to my questions about her guilt or innocence and about the luck (luck?) and tragedy of other fellow survivors among my group during the Hitler days.

I knew a lot about destinies of that time. Now I would discover what people do when they face the final choice: to die or to join the devil.

I wasn't entirely comfortable with the guilty verdicts of all those German judges. Assuming that they had not themselves been Nazis, their consciences had to be burdened by the guilt of their predecessors and the genocidal brand of justice practiced under the Nazis. So

I made it my business to locate several Jewish survivors who had had dealings with Stella during her alleged Gestapo employment and who had not been called as witnesses at any of her trials.

Guenther Rogoff, who had attended art school with Stella and later forged identity papers for her, was one significant figure out of Stella's past who flatly exonerated her of any wrongdoing. More than that: Rogoff was convinced that she had been unjustly railroaded by cruel ignoramuses after the war, hacks in the courts who lacked all understanding of her situation when she was still in Gestapo hands.

"I wish I could have been her defense attorney," Rogoff told me with some heat when I reached him in his Swiss advertising agency in 1990.

After the war, he tried to locate Stella but could find no trace of her. Nor did he hear of any of her three trials. It fell to me to fill him in about Stella's life with the Gestapo.

"So she's supposed to have been a witch," said Rogoff, disgusted. "She couldn't have been guilty; psychologically, she was a corpse!" *

He spluttered on: "I remember how the novelist Franz Werfel wrote: 'Not the murderer but the murdered is held guilty.' They turned Stella into a witch and really she was just a girl. People today have no idea that when you were in the claws of the Gestapo, you had to be prepared to have your teeth filed down, one by one. Stella had wonderful teeth . . ."

Rogoff's indignation would not run down. "A hundred thousand war criminals are running around loose," he fumed, matching this effrontery against the vulnerability of Stella's perfect teeth.

I gave him our mutual friend's phone number, and the two conducted a telephone reunion. Rogoff told her he had just received the number from me. "*Ach,* the great forger!" Stella said by way of cheery greeting. Why—she wanted to know—hadn't he testified for her at her trials? Rogoff was apologetic. He was terribly sorry, he simply hadn't known. The conversation was brief. He said he might come to visit her. She said that would be fine. It never happened. The thread between them had broken long ago, though not his sympathy for the blonde who had been just a girl with splendid teeth.

---

* The concept of Stella as an ambulatory cadaver had come up before. During her 1957 trial in West Berlin, the national Jewish weekly *Allgemeine* attacked an exculpatory editorial that had appeared in a Berlin tabloid. The piece had been entitled "A Dead Person in Court." The Jewish paper's response bristled: "She can't be excused by pointing to the system that 'turned humans into beasts.' What we are is within ourselves."

I wondered whether Rogoff was so ready to offer excuses for Stella because he had never seen (or suffered from) her during her tenure in action for the Gestapo. But no, eyewitnesses from her time of guilt were ready to offer alibis for her too.

One of these, Hans Oskar DeWitt Loewenstein, an inmate of the Schulstrasse to the very end, when he lived on uncooked red beets and potato peels, remembered seeing Stella there, looking well fed, and also found himself unable to hate her.

"She's a tragic person," he told me. "You mustn't forget the situation she was in. She was living on the blade of a knife! You and I would have done exactly the same thing!"

Another eyewitness who survived underground, Isaak Behar, the only fellow alumnus of my Goldschmidt School still living in Berlin, had something favorable to say about Stella as well. She had spotted him on Kurfürstendamm during a roundup of Jews. Not wearing his Star of David as required, Behar recognized her pacing on the sidewalk as he emerged from the famous Café Dobrin. He had heard that she was supposedly working for the Gestapo but couldn't quite decide whether to believe it. Like me, he had had a rampaging crush on the Goldschmidt School's most memorable blonde.

"Well, Stella," he challenged her, half serious, half joking, "should I come along with you?"

Stella did a fast double take.

"Not you!" she exclaimed. "Get out of here!"

Stella could still muster merciful instincts then, during the initial phase of her Gestapo time. Allegiance to her masters had not yet hardened, and her childhood chum Jutta Feig from Wilmersdorf thus became another beneficiary of this baptismal period.

Jutta was living illegally and had removed her yellow star, when she encountered Stella on Konstanzer Strasse at the corner of Duisburger. The two women recognized each other instantly, and as Stella approached, her old friend Jutta was sick with fear. When she was doing forced factory labor earlier, word of Stella's defection had made the rounds among her Jewish colleagues, so Jutta fully expected to be taken away on the spot. To her amazement, the danger passed in seconds.

"*Guten Tag*, Jutta," Stella said pleasantly, "how are you?"

"*Gut,*" Jutta was barely able to stammer.

"Be careful," Stella said, "and say hello at home." And she was gone.

Old friendships still counted for something at the time and were reciprocated to some degree.

Isaak Behar never did blame Stella for her betrayal as furiously as he accused her employers: "It's disgusting that they got people to do this," he summed up.

Having escaped on the run from his encounter with her, Behar kept running for the rest of the war. For months he lived with Betty, an attractive divorcée some ten years older, who had picked him up in a little shop she owned. Other times he lurked around parks and public toilets, an unwashed, unshaved vagrant, a stinking outcast, a *Penner*. Sometimes a meal consisted of very thin potato peels, nothing else. For more than three years he dodged in and out of arrest and vegetated on alert, poised like a fox for mortal trouble, never identifying his gentile helpers to each other.

"It was an hourly odyssey," he said of his life—rolling with the punches— the life he owed to Stella.

Would she recognize me in her picturesque new hometown in 1990? Would she talk to me after warning me at the start that she wanted no reminders of the past?

I had decided to surprise her, not to write or call in advance. Facing her apartment house, I determined to go a step farther. I wanted to make it difficult for her to turn me away. I would materialize directly at her doorstep.

German apartment houses make such ambush interviews difficult. The doors are almost always kept locked. One must ring the bell for a specific apartment. If the tenant answers, one must identify oneself through a loudspeaker system. It's easy to refuse an unwanted caller. No confrontation, no unpleasantness.

I didn't want to risk that possibility. Nor did I wish to disguise my identity. So I waited awhile and slipped into the house when the door opened for the inevitable elderly lady with the inevitable pooch. I simply smiled and so did she.

Upstairs, I rang Stella's apartment bell. No response. So I waited in the sleek, spotless white hallway, and then I waited some more, until someone came bounding up the steps even though the elevator was functioning. If this was Stella, what had happened to the frailty she had complained of? What about her back and leg pains? If her lungs were weak, why waste breath on the stairs?

On the other hand, if she had been dramatizing herself and told some lies, did that make her a murderess?

It was Stella all right, a faded beauty but still trim, still erect, still stylishly turned out, still perfectly coiffed, like the girl in the gym shorts of memory. She looked bouncy, cheerful, and most remarkably youthful.

"I'll be damned," she said, coming up to me after no more than a moment's hesitation, smiling and offering her left cheek to be kissed. A kiss on the cheek? How could that be? I had expected shock, fear, pain, eviction, balking, recoiling, trembling, tears, even collapse —never a kiss! Unsuspected currents had to be coursing through the prey I had stalked so carefully, almost obsessively, for so long. My amazement was, of course, followed by relief. I felt a bit like Captain Ahab, a true obsessive, finally harpooning his great white whale. That confrontation had been bloody, tragic, cataclysmic. I got a kiss on the cheek. What was this all about?

Inconsistent with her complaints, Stella looked well cared for, not a bit downtrodden when she arrived as scheduled. Her skin was sallow but the makeup flawless. Her hair, always important to Stella, looked starched—a neat, artful mix of blond and white with a reddish tinge, clearly dyed, standing stiffly away from the ears, just as on a photo taken when Stella was seven years old. Her figure had remained trim, with a mere suggestion of belly. Her plaid slacks and checkered shirt gave her a tailored British air. A severely faded beauty with great stage presence.

For the next four hours of conversation in German, Stella's flair as an actress and mimic was often on display. She imitated two teachers of our erstwhile school in Berlin: wild arm waving for the musical Dr. Bandmann, finger-shaking severity for Dr. Lewent, that feared disciplinarian.

I remembered that in their teens she and her boyfriend, later her first husband, had formed a music group of Jewish youngsters who performed at Berlin parties in the early years of the war, but I hadn't known that Stella was the vocalist. She wanted me to remember her in that role. All of a sudden, perched forward on her black leather rocker in that tiny, gloomily dark apartment, she cocked her head and began to sing Hoagy Carmichael's "Stardust." In barely accented English, she crooned of wondering why she spent the lonely night dreaming of a song. It was a haunting rendition, not an embarrassing amateur hour performance. Stella wanted me to see her as a sexy, swinging young hopeful, wanted to show me how readily she might have taken to the show business America of the 1930s. It was a wistful notion, but it was hers; it was not my imagination at work.

"If we had only made it to the States, maybe . . ." Stella said.

The starkness of her lonely nights was no melody from a reverie. It was palpable. She was a total recluse, as devoid of human contact as one can be in a lively modern city. She no longer saw old friends. The gulf between her lifestyle and her outside surroundings was striking. Her town is no bockwurst-and-beer village. The museums and theater schedules are extensive. The vineyards soften the land-scape, and more scenery and tourist attractions are minutes away.

Yet Stella told me, when I asked, that she didn't even go for an occasional walk. She lived the life of a shut-in, a fugitive, by choice, self-banished to her own island of Elba. The rote of her daily outing, the sameness of her meals day after day, the clockwork of her few other routines—everything except her attire—oozed on through the years identically, monotonously. The only ray of cheer was a group of photos showing her, all smiles, on vacation in the mountains with her last companion, whose name was still on her apartment door seven years after his death: Hans Nietsch, a train conductor.

Trains again. I wondered whether Stella had ever reflected on the mournful role of trains, those rattling executioners' tools, in the final hours of parents, her first husband, her in-laws, her victims. It was probably a foolish afterthought of mine. Stella didn't seem to reflect at all.

Most of every afternoon she spent sleeping, she told me—a blatant symptom of depression. In the evenings she gave herself to the uni-versal sedative, television. She would watch almost anything, she said, although she stayed away from *Denver Clan,* the German title for *Dynasty,* an endless series of hit shows with efficiently dubbed German voices.

Why didn't she like it?

"Too many intrigues," said Stella.

The television didn't sedate her sufficiently. She said she needed a pill or two every night to sleep adequately. I should have asked about her dreams, but I lacked the nerve. Did she need pills to avoid night-mares about her parents boarding their train, her own torture at Gestapo headquarters on Burgstrasse, a drunken Dobberke threat-ening her with deportation, the eyes of her victims as she led them away?

It was getting to be afternoon, her naptime, and for a moment or two I thought Stella might fall asleep on me. The shades seemed permanently drawn shut. The telephone never rang, and I wouldn't have been surprised if it had made no sound for days, perhaps longer.

The living room, densely cluttered, was so small that there was barely space to move one's feet. She and I sat less than three feet apart. Walls and furniture were awash with small trinkets, a very

German style. But these details hardly registered. The centerpiece, an enormous cluster of large rag dolls, gave the place the feel of a dollhouse, perhaps a child's jail cell, a place of punishment where a sentence was being served.

Because I had worried that Stella might not want to talk to me, I had come ready to pull out a photo of her forty-five-year-old daughter in Israel, with whom she had had no contact in more than twenty years, posing with the ten-year-old grandson she had never seen. Since a peace offering had not been necessary, I placed the picture in front of her, without a word, during a lull in the conversation.

She stared at it. Silence. More silence. Still more. Finally, she pointed at the dark-haired boy and asked, "Is that you?" I said "No," but nothing else.

The eerie, silent game continued. I hadn't planned this maneuvering and still don't quite know what made me do it. I certainly didn't want to tease. I suppose I could think of no other way to elicit Stella's feelings about her own kin.

Eventually she pointed at Yvonne and asked hesitantly, "Is that my daughter?" I assented. No reaction, just a poker face.

"Wouldn't you like to see her again sometime?" I asked.

"No," she said quickly. "That would finish me."

She had filed her family away; they had brought her too much pain.

I had led her gently through her prewar years, the early war years, her schools, her life with her parents, and from my questions she had obviously picked up that I was well informed.

"You know everything," she stage-whispered a bit dramatically but without sign of fear.

"I know a good bit," I said.

On the surface, that didn't appear to trouble her. Nor did she seem abashed when she inferred, correctly, that her old girlfriends Lili and Edith from our Berlin school wanted nothing to do with her.

"How do they feel about me?" she wanted to know.

"That's hard to say," I evaded, not wanting to shut Stella off. She did not press the point, just as she had not pursued her curiosity about our friends' whereabouts. She had asked for their addresses in our correspondence earlier, but I had simply ignored the question, having encountered contempt from Edith and horror from Lili. I concluded that Stella was really looking for approval or understanding for herself. She didn't ask about the health or families of her old friends. She knew she was an outcast.

Launching easily, without invitation, into a more or less chronological version of her war years, Stella stuck to the lies she had told in court a generation ago. While her parents were being held as hostages, the Gestapo asked her to track down one young Jew of her acquaintance. Just one, Rogoff, who lived illegally and forged documents. Stella said she went through the motions of trying to find this man, but that this had been an act. Although I indicated no skepticism, she seemed to sense disbelief.

"I never would have betrayed him, never, never!" she cried out, suddenly stung—touching my sleeve, reacting vehemently against an accusation I had not raised.

She did nothing else for the Gestapo, she insisted with some heat, nothing. All she did was pretend to be looking for this one man!

"The entire time?" I asked incredulously.

"The entire time."

This would have required the Gestapo to stand by patiently during a search of about two years, which was clearly absurd. Still fishing for other information, I didn't press. The obviousness of her lie did not seem to bother Stella. Nor did she seem affected by the almost certain realization that I knew she was trying to get away with a gargantuan falsehood. The credibility crisis passed as quickly and innocently as it had bubbled up.

Another emotional explosion was set off when I inquired what Heino Meissl thought she was doing at the Schulstrasse camp when they met there in the fall of 1944. She took the bait.

"He *assumed* that I worked for the Gestapo," she said.

I said nothing but offered an inquiring look. I suppose I had been lying in wait for hours to hear some sort of confession, just as her prosecutors had hoped for a self-accusation, just as her torturers on Burgstrasse had hoped she would talk, and the West Berlin police interrogators after the war. How naive! As far as I could ever discover, Stella confessed only during the pressures of the war: to Hertha Eichelhardt, her substitute mother, in Hertha's kitchen. By 1990, she may have anesthetized herself into believing she was innocent.

My Holocaust quasi-consultant Primo Levi wrote in *The Drowned and the Saved* about self-deception by survivors who "fabricate for themselves a convenient reality," describing the process from experience.

"The substitution may begin in full awareness, with an invented scenario, mendacious, restored, but less painful than the real one; they repeat the description to others but also to themselves, and the distinction between true and false progressively loses its contours, and man ends by fully believing the story he has told so many times and continues to tell . . ." Like Stella.

"Why should I confess to something I didn't do?" she demanded, again in some heat. "I was never part of it, never!"

She was clutching my arm. An appeal for me to believe her, to accept her innocence, was clearly coming.

"You know I have a conscience! I wouldn't betray anybody! You know me from childhood, I always had to be so *good,* my parents demanded that I be the *best! . . .*"

I managed to keep poker-faced.

Stella sank back in her chair, exhausted, defeated. Looking for ways to move Peter, the old classmate suddenly turned judge and jury, she fell back upon, of all things, her Jewishness. If I had not acknowledged her "conscience," as she demanded, perhaps an appeal to our joint religious origin, so long denied by her, might improve her credibility, might somehow produce—what? Sympathy? Absolution?

The entreaty came in the form of a weird non sequitur.

"My father was even related to the composer Mendelssohn-Bartholdy!" Stella flung at me, summoning the long-gone Gerhard Goldschlag, the Kaiser's unreconstructed combat veteran and German lieder composer, as witness of her suddenly useful Jewishness.

Some of her authentic attitudes did emerge in her earlier observations about Jews. In our correspondence she had volunteered that she had long ago converted to Christianity. Now she volunteered why the Jewish eyewitnesses who had testified at her trials had been "merciless" and had told only lies.

"They hated me like the plague because I was blond and pretty," she said—a theme song she had struck up before, in court and out.

This led her into an unrestrained, seemingly irrelevant attack on Joachim Prinz, the spectacularly handsome, mellifluous young rabbi of the Berlin of the 1930s who became a major Jewish leader in America. "He was the biggest swine that ever was," Stella burst out, imitating Prinz's preening. "He wore that huge ring and told all the girls to go to Palestine. I was there at the *Friedenstempel* and heard him. A beautiful guy. He proclaimed Zionism, but where did *he* go?" * Stella was tense and livid as she relived the scene. Had she

---

* Stella was not the first to remark on the apparent contradiction between the passion of Rabbi Prinz's Zionism and his destination as an emigrant. Students of his career explain that the rabbi's feelings for Palestine (and later, Israel) never

had designs on Prinz, actually or in her imagination, and had she perhaps been jilted, in reality or in her fantasies?

Or did the "beautiful" Prinz represent Judaism to her? Was he a symbol of the group that brought her only misery? That seemed most likely, for she also unleashed a sudden terrifying verbal assault on another charismatic leader, a man who had not previously come up in our conversation, Heinz Galinski.

Galinski, whom I had interviewed, was postwar Germany's most honored Jew. Nearly eighty years old, he was a Berliner who had survived Auschwitz and two other concentration camps. His mother and his wife were gassed at Auschwitz. His father died just before his scheduled deportation in Stella's section of the Schulstrasse camp. In 1949, Galinski became chairman of the Berlin Jewish Community; later, he headed the association of all German Jews and was for decades their careful, protective spokesman.

Stella detested the man because he lived. "How did *he* make it back?" she demanded angrily, insinuating favoritism, conspiracy, possibly some incredible sellout on the part of Galinski, this upstanding leader whose permanently frozen face looked like a death mask.

When I asked Stella about Walter Dobberke, responsible for the death of thousands, including her parents, she grinned and softened. To her, Dobberke, who had turned her into a catcher of Jews, was a clumsy innocent.

"Ach," she said, "he just sat around and drank. Besides, he could be bribed." Nothing more derogatory.

As our hours together went by, Stella's Berlin worker's accent turned more pronounced. The refined timbre of her upbringing faded. More expletives like "shit" peppered her talk. And as she traced her principal men for me, the curve suggested descent, a gradual vulgarization into her present life—a vacuum consisting of nothing and no one.

Her first husband, Manfred Kübler, had been a middle-class Jewish boy. Her second husband, partner in mass murder, the Gestapo catcher Rolf Isaaksohn, had come from a similar comfortable Jewish background. Her third husband, Friedheim Schellenberg, was a Nordic giant, a mechanic who had been a Luftwaffe star as a pilot

---

waned, but that his highly placed friends among the international Jewish leadership felt he could better alert the world to the needs of Jews by speaking out from a base in the United States than from the relative isolation of the promised land. It was another example of the priority attention that more or less automatically fell to the "prominent."

of Stuka dive-bombers; the couple met in a bar one New Year's Eve. Her fourth husband, the streetwise Gottfried Pech,* had run a taxi business and was twenty years younger than Stella. Her last man, Hans Nietsch, who died in 1984 although he was twelve years Stella's junior, had been a conductor of Berlin elevated trains. Stella picked him up when he punched her ticket. He was a considerable comedown in looks and manner. Even her kindly neighbor, Frau Pürschel, said so.

What was this social downward spiral about? A lowering sense of self-worth? An increasing need for self-punishment? Plain desperation for human company?

As I rose to leave, Stella seemed reluctant to let me go.

I turned toward the door; she kept talking and did not rise. In her search for continuity, for human contact, she glanced at the photo of her daughter and grandson, which I had left on the table. She had never touched it. She asked whether I had to take it with me. I shook my head. She said nothing and still did not touch it.

Why had she talked to me? I could still only guess. She was bored, lonely, homesick for Berlin and old times, and I must have looked like another of her easy male marks. When I left, she gave me a hug and stuck out her cheek for another kiss. On the phone later, she called me "Peterle," an endearment, and left me with much to think about.

What about Stella's implausible-sounding claim that she had been betrayed by her beauty, that her glamour had been a tragic liability, that the Berlin Jews, the establishment Jews, would not have turned against her so furiously if she hadn't been so good-looking?

By chance, I had acquired some familiarity with the paradox of beauty as a disadvantage. I had come across a quotation from W. B. Yeats—"Only God, my dear / Could love you for yourself alone / And not your yellow hair"—and thought immediately of Ellen, with whom I spent five years between marriages. Ellen was blond, tall, willowy, blue-eyed, and had a spectacular figure. Like Stella. In her late teens Ellen had been a model for fashion magazines. Unlike Stella, she converted her interest in clothes into a career in the fashion industry.

Her relationships with males, however, had been marred, beginning in her teen years, by her spectacular looks, she told me. She had

* A pseudonym.

been too popular for credence. Boy after boy professed to love her, but she had no trouble figuring out that they usually just wanted to go to bed with her. It was a profoundly unsettling discovery. As Yeats might have put the question: Which, if any, of these potential lovers really loved Ellen for herself, not for her body alone?

For advice on the burdens of excessive good looks I turned to Ellen S. Berscheid, a social psychologist and professor at the University of Minnesota, who had been studying and publishing papers about female beauty for more than twenty years.

I told her about Ellen and Stella, and she was not one bit puzzled by either case. Doubts about self-worth were normal in beautiful women, she reported. Such distrust could erode self-esteem and trigger emotional problems. "Experiments show that physically attractive people do indeed stand out," she said. "Some people have difficulty dealing with that."

What I hadn't thought about was how beauty can be manipulated by the beautiful. "Stella learned very early that being attractive is a very valuable weapon to survive," Professor Berscheid told me. "She knew how to capitalize on it." Still, nothing compelled her to take that route. Beauty is reversible. She chose not to change it. "If she had not wanted to be attractive, it's so easy not to be," the professor pointed out. "There are no natural beauties."

Stella did not have to be lectured on this wisdom. When she had to trek from Liebenwalde to Berlin through rape-infested territory, she knew how to make herself unattractive and did a fine job of it.

And yet Professor Berscheid was unwilling to indict her, even though, as I pointed out, Stella was no longer forced to act as a catcher to protect her parents once they had been deported. "What if she hadn't?" asked the psychologist. "Wouldn't she have been sent to a concentration camp? If I'd been in that situation, I'd have done it too. It all depends on the kind of situation we're in." And she placed emphasis on the word "situation."

Primo Levi, the Auschwitz survivor, also cited "extenuating circumstances" in passing judgment upon the "extreme experiences" created by Hitler: "An infernal order such as National Socialism exercises a frightful power of corruption, against which it is difficult to guard oneself. It degrades its victims and makes them similar to itself . . ."

Levi cited one of the "crematorium ravens" who worked on the corpses in Auschwitz. "You mustn't think that we are monsters," this raven told Levi. "We are the same as you, only much more unhappy."

The commonality of the brutalized—the slaves drawn into bonding with the slave drivers—produced bizarre scenes of camaraderie. At Auschwitz teams of crematory ravens played soccer games against SS teams, while in Stella's Gestapo world *Kommissar* Dobberke drank away dull nights playing cards with his *Ordner*. The club spirit of a joint enterprise pulled the enemy sides into togetherness and kept Eichmann's system moving. The fraternities killed together and played together.

The common ground was paved by what Sigmund Freud's psychologist daughter, Anna, who barely slipped away from the Gestapo in Vienna, called "identification with the aggressor." Another distinguished psychologist, Bruno Bettelheim, wrote about his observation of this adaptation when he was a prisoner in Dachau: *

"It was not unusual, when prisoners were in charge of others, to find old prisoners (and not only former criminals) behaving worse than the SS. Sometimes they were trying to find favor with the guards, but more often it was because they considered it the best way to treat prisoners in the camp.

"Old prisoners tended to identify with the SS not only in their goals and values, but even in appearance. They tried to arrogate to themselves old pieces of SS uniforms, and when that was not possible they tried to mend and sew their prison garb until it resembled the uniforms . . . When asked why they did it, they said it was because they wanted to look smart. To them looking smart meant to look like their enemies."

Stella's extraordinary hatred of Jews puzzled me at first. Was she plain crazy? Her outburst over Rabbi Prinz struck me as lunatic. And the notion that her father, and then she, had been persecuted by Jews for peculiarly Jewish reasons seemed to carry paranoia rather far. I should have caught on when I first learned that Benjamin Disraeli, and then his imitator, Peter Prager of my Goldschmidt School, had tried to push up their noses to escape their detested Jewishness.

* Dr. Bettelheim, who came from Vienna, was one of the most vociferous critics who denounced the submissive "ghetto mentality" of German Jewry. Following his suicide in 1991 at the age of eighty-three, patients and supervisors at his Chicago school for autistics—survivors, as it were—denounced him for beating some of his charges. I had been the doctor's editor for about two years in the 1960s when he wrote a parent-and-child column for *Ladies' Home Journal*. He couldn't have been gentler in manner, or more humane in outlook. The startling revelations about his aggressiveness toward the helpless brought to my mind the scenes he had recorded of his experiences in Dachau. Had they corrupted him forever?

I should have, but I didn't, not until I began a search to explain Stella's bizarre brand of anti-Semitism. The aberration was of significance in any attempt to explain how she could become a *Greifer*, giving expression to a demonstrably overweening hatred of her fellow Jews.

The mystery was, of course, no mystery. It was a blind spot in my education and easy to remedy. The literature on Jewish self-hatred proved to be extensive, and interestingly, it was a German-Jewish specialty. A Professor Theodor Lessing had published a book on this unpleasant subject, *Der Jüdische Selbsthass,* in Berlin in 1930, and even back then he was merely popularizing work done by German-Jewish scholars decades earlier.

Benjamin Disraeli's denial and detestation of his Jewish identity were already documented and discussed. So were similar leanings of Karl Marx and the poet Heinrich Heine and innumerable other notables, including, in modern times, the columnist Walter Lippmann and the psychoanalyst whose real name was Homburger. He called himself Erik H. Erikson and became, fittingly, an authority on the development of personal identity.

Another Jewish psychologist, Kurt Lewin, the specialist on group behavior, was among the first with a contemporary interpretation of the phenomenon rooted in "otherness"—being different from the cultural norm. Stella, Disraeli, Marx, and their fellow sufferers protested their Jewish identity because they were excluded from the privileged group, the majority of citizens who were not "other." Minorities were by definition other and were degraded for their sin, like blacks in America. Barred from the mainstream, some vulnerable victims among these groups took to hating themselves for their differentness.

Even young Jewish children were not immune. In 1990, Dr. Flora Hogman, a New York psychoanalyst, published some of her interviews with survivors who, as youngsters, were hidden by their parents with kind Catholic families.

"I started to think: if the Jews are so hated, maybe there is a reason," said Dina. "Maybe they are horrible people. I would have done anything to be just like the Christians . . . I heard so much in the Polish house that the Jews were dirty, noisy. At first I was crushed, then I started to believe it . . ."

The analyst reported on her cases:

"Renee felt Jewish and guilty; Charlotte hated the Jews; Frida disowned her Jewish identity, striving for sainthood in order not to belong to the 'cursed' people. . . ."

It made an unfortunate kind of sense for at least one girl who was expelled from high school for being Jewish and was made to wear the Star of David and tortured in the Burgstrasse to pay for an identity she had always denied. Majority rule was not invariably benign rule. And I had often found evil to be full of surprises.

If I was working toward a confession from a girl named Stella, I wasn't doing well. Valid or thin or ridiculous, her defenses were long-entrenched and sturdy: the self-hatred, the anti-Semitism, the burden of being beautiful, the guilt of survival, the threat of the deportation trains, and on and on. Nothing thus far could excuse the inhumanity of her actions. Perhaps I had been treating her with too much caution and reasonableness. A tougher, prosecutorial note might prove more productive, although I had doubts. A wilier man than I had been snowed by her: Herr Pech, the worldly cabbie, money-loving husband number four.

I chatted with Herr Pech in the cramped but comfortable two-story stone house of his most recent lover, a pleasant, thirtyish blonde, at Falkensee, across Berlin's western city limits, barely into the former German Democratic Republic—and the most intriguing upshot was what he didn't say. Stella had made nasty cracks to me about him, grousing about shabby treatment she claimed to have endured at his hands and bristling at his interest in money that she claimed was hers. Yet in an hour and a half of evidently quite candid conversation Pech never uttered a negative word about his unkind ex-wife of a generation ago.

That seemed particularly odd because this ex-husband—bearded, red-faced, quick-moving, and muscled like a featherweight boxer—turned out to be a very angry, frustrated combatant of Berlin's brawly streets—unemployed, broke, and exploding with hostility at his environment and his fate in it.

The answer was implicit in the timing sequence and, well, in affection for money. The couple met in 1971, Pech being a crony of Stella's terminally ill husband number three, Friedheim Schellenberg. They married in August 1972 and the date was significant. Stella had been wailing at her new man almost daily about her fate as a victim of conspiracies by vengeful Jews of wartime. She was obsessed and persuasive. Far from being repulsed, Pech scented opportunity. Stella's third trial was coming up on September 21. What with the waning of passions and the passing of aging witnesses, she might win acquittal this time. And then, ah then, generous compensation payments would roll in from the guilt-ridden government of the rich West Germans, indemnification due to all "victims of Fascism" under federal law.

As Pech listened to the proceedings of the six-day trial, chances of a windfall looked good to him. The trial was "a farce." The witnesses against his brand-new wife were "bloodthirsty" and "disgusting." They knew each other and were in cahoots on their testimony. Maybe Stella had indeed ratted on a few, but the witnesses had done more and worse, so it seemed to him, and if she had really sent them to their deaths, why were they alive and in court? It all added up to a gross "injustice."

The outcome was a legal and financial disappointment, of course. Before long, the couple parted, and in 1974 they were divorced. Still, this cabbie's faith in the authenticity of Stella's martyrdom was not shaken, not then and not when I caught up with him. Stella *was* terribly convincing, even to Gottfried Pech, man-of-the-streets, and even when she failed him as a meal-ticket.

Could Wyden win where Pech succumbed? I couldn't resist trying.

26. Judgment

I HAD GROWN TIRED OF OUR GAME, Stella's and mine. She was not the unjustly maligned concentration camp survivor that she pretended to be; I was not her kindly school buddy. Why keep up the pretense?

Determined to break up our charade, I appeared at her apartment for the third and final time on a hot, hazy Tuesday morning, September 3, 1991. This time I had made an appointment by phone and brought a fat black briefcase stuffed with court papers covering the decades of Stella's travail with the law.

I wanted our roles to *be* changed and to *look* changed. I was no longer the sympathetic collector of memories. I was the interrogator loaded with incontrovertible evidence of murder. She was the accused.

As the first exhibit of my carefully prepared confrontation I pulled out the transcript of an interrogation of Stella dated March 23, 1965, conducted by an investigator of the West Berlin prosecutor's office. Stella had not been on trial that time. She had been summoned as a witness in the interminable and ultimately abortive proceedings against the leaders of the Berlin Gestapo.

The interrogator was tracking *Hauptsturmführer* Erich Möller, the boss of Stella's Gestapo boss, *Kommissar* Dobberke. Yes, Stella had testified, she had met the greatly feared Möller in the summer of 1944 and remembered him well: an older man with a *Schmiss* across his face, a dueling scar. She had gone to see him at his office in the

300

Alex, the Alexanderplatz police headquarters, she said, to try to get her parents transferred from Theresienstadt to Bergen-Belsen, where she believed, erroneously, conditions were more tolerable.

Stella's manner with her interlocutor in 1965 had obviously been easy and friendly, as were her responses to me in 1991. I had selected the record of the 1965 interrogation in an attempt to establish, indirectly, Stella's coziness with the Gestapo. She seemed not to notice. Nor had her manner changed when I placed my briefcase between us or when I started reading from the transcript. It would require a lot more to derail this actress from her role as victim, uninvolved bystander, and dutiful daughter.

"Did you get Dobberke's okay so you could get in to see Möller?" I asked.

"Oh no, I went on my own."

I put on my most skeptical face. For a Jewish girl from a *Lager* to walk into the Alex off the street and be ushered in to meet with a ranking Gestapo chief was, well, totally improbable. It would have been like a bag lady being welcomed by a top man at F.B.I. or C.I.A. headquarters in Washington.

Stella rode across the incongruity with ease.

"So how did you get in to see Möller?" I demanded. "It says here in your trial transcript that you had a green Gestapo identification card with your picture on it."

"Oh no," said Stella, smiling. "I just had a pass from the camp."

"All right, so what did Möller say?"

"I wasn't there long. He told me he couldn't do anything, but that once the war was won he'd see to it that I'd be recognized as a gentile."

She smiled again and shrugged, pleased to have elicited Möller's approval as a loving daughter and squelched my effort to tar her as one of the Gestapo's valued own.

Not wanting to get bogged down in arguments over details, I didn't ask what, exactly, had moved the almighty Möller to promise her an elevation to the status of honorary Aryan. It was time to move along to the more direct tactics of my prepared plan.

Stella's face suggested that she was resigned to yet another grilling. She had endured so many of them over the decades. More than during my previous visits, the tiny, darkened room seemed like a cell, the venetian blinds like bars. A life sentence was being served here. The vacuous rag dolls in their lineup looked like guards this time.

I had announced my visit for 11:30 a.m., the time just after the cheery red-and-white streetcar would bring Stella back to her corner, back to her cell from her lonely daily outing and feeding (which seemed more than ever to resemble the exercise break in a prison routine).

What was she thinking on that streetcar? Was she at all worried about having to face me for yet another radar sweep of her past, wishing that she might have had the strength to turn me down? Could it be that she was driven into my presence by long-hidden guilt after all, that she suspected fellow passengers of staring at her reproachfully, like the woman reported by the Swedish psychiatrist long ago, the case of the mother who offered her child to be gassed and now saw accusers everywhere?

Or had her memory edited her sins and buried inconvenient sections? Memory, so I had been reading, is an intricate physiological phenomenon that experts are still working to decipher. Its selectivity, however, is established. As one authority, Dr. Elizabeth Loftus, a psychologist with a distinguished record of working with trial witnesses, has written: "We interpret the past, correcting ourselves, adding bits and pieces, deleting uncomplimentary or disturbing recollections, sweeping, dusting, tidying things up."

And as Meryl Streep spoke the lines in the film *Sophie's Choice*, remembering the lies Sophie told after the war about her past: "The truth, the truth, I don't know what is the truth."

Whatever was going on inside Stella's head, repentance was unlikely after so many years, but not inconceivable.

I leafed ostentatiously through my court documents and took a deep breath.

"I know people had to do terrible things to survive," I told her, "and you were not alone. I know about Inge Lustig and Bruno Goldstein and Heinz Behrend, and Günther Abrahamson, and Ruth Danziger . . ."

"Ja," said Stella, nodding in recognition and also diffusing the guilt, *"die* Danziger!"

"I understand how you got roped in to save your parents," I said, "and I keep asking myself what I would have done if I had come under such dreadful pressure. But it simply isn't credible that the Gestapo would have sat by for more than a year and a half while you claimed to be searching for Rogoff, one single man!"

"They kept finding more papers he'd forged," Stella offered.

"It still isn't believable!"

"Isaaksohn covered for me the entire time!"

I tried my best to summon up a look to suggest that I doubted Rolf Isaaksohn's novel role as an altruist. Stella shrugged and smiled.

"I talked to Hertha Wolf, you know," I continued. "She says you sat in her kitchen and confessed to working for the Gestapo."

"*Ach, sie spinnt,* she's making that up," exclaimed Stella, ever so slightly indignant that I'd dug up her aged confidant.

"I talked to Robert Zeiler," I said, "the one who knew you from childhood in Wilmersdorf." And I read to Stella from the court transcript about how he watched on Kurfürstendamm while Stella and Isaaksohn rounded up Jews and helped the Gestapo to load them on a truck, how she and Rolf had sat on the back platform as guards and driven off to the Grosse Hamburger Strasse collection camp, Zeiler following cautiously on his bike.

Stella waved away this graphic picture with a small show of impatience. "That never happened," she said.

"Remember the Zajdmann family?" I asked. "I found them, too. Remember how you and Rolf arrested them at the opera?"

Stella recalled the occasion with enthusiasm, betraying not a bit of surprise at my zeal for dragging skeletons out of her closet. "Rolf and I were hearing *Rigoletto,*" she related helpfully, "and Rolf said, 'Look, the Zajdmanns are sitting down there. I'm going to get them!' " She related the scene as if it had occurred the day before.

"You had nothing to do with it?"

"I only heard about it," said Stella.

And all that time Dobberke never stopped threatening her.

"I'm going to have you in Auschwitz!" he yelled at her, drunk, when Stella showed up with some black market meat in the Schulstrasse bunker during a bombardment in the final days of the war. Which was probably the truth, very probably.

I had witnessed another flawless acting job. Absolutely nothing was going to derail my old schoolmate from her role, and it was clear that she was pleased by the success of her performance. Nobody had paid attention to her for a long time, especially not a man, and what is an actress without a solid script and an audience? She had performed well again.

It was time to leave. Stella had taken off her shoes, so she looked small and childlike as she stood at the door, smiling, head slightly cocked, doll-like, still Shirley Temple.

A revealing transformation. Perhaps my interrogation had hit Stella harder than I thought. Bruno Bettelheim had written that a fellow inmate in his concentration camp would typically revert to childhood when pushed around. "If he was, like a child, unable to defend himself, this revived in him behavior patterns and psychological mechanisms he had developed when a child."

Stella conformed to Bettelheim's script.

"Don't write anything bad!" she admonished me, smiling and waggling an accusing finger, playfully, like a little girl on a playground.

She was also thumbing her nose at me for having tried and failed to crack her mask, hardened beyond thaw, frozen in place since her confession in 1944 to Hertha Eichelhardt. As victims themselves, they had credentials superior to mine and more influential than the renewed accusations of the elderly witnesses I had found and paraded against her without causing her to flinch a single time.

Few of my fellow alumni of the Goldschmidt School rushed to judge. Almost none had heard of the evil turn in Stella's life when I telephoned and wrote in search of memories about her. They received the news with incredulity, as if a relative had been unmasked as a serial killer. "My God, my God," was about all the reaction I got from the usually voluble Gerry Waldston, the owner of a business in Montreal. "What a creature!" exclaimed Alex Page, a Harvard Ph.D. and university professor. "She haunts me!"

From London, where she was a housewife and writing poetry, Stella's old chum Lili Baumann, now Lili Hart, sent a ten-page letter recalling details of her childhood attraction to the fascinating Stella, and her friend's emerging weaknesses. Reflecting on Stella's early "sangfroid," Lili responded with a survivor's cool to my account of her playmate's career with the Gestapo.

"I knew nothing of all that and am naturally deeply shocked!" she wrote. "However, I am not *too* surprised . . ."

Marion Dann Weiner, recently retired as president of her B'nai B'rith chapter on Long Island, New York, exploded when she was confronted with Stella again. "I remember her very much!" she wrote. Stella had turned in the boyfriend of her sister Eva to the Gestapo. The young man had been hidden by gentiles in a Berlin apartment. "My sister's friend survived Auschwitz and later told us the whole story," Mrs. Weiner informed me.

Several women responded much like Marion Sauerbrunn House in suburban Riverdale, New York, who had made a career of advising fellow refugees on how to manage their requests for restitution and compensation claims against the West German government. Mrs. House had sung with Stella and me in the chorus of our beloved Dr. Bandmann and had also shivered under the dictatorship of the tyrannical Herr Dr. Lewent.

"My God," she burst out, "I'm stunned!" I could hear her breathing over the phone. "I get goose pimples! No way I would have guessed!"

Mrs. House had not aspired to speak to Stella in school; she remembered her as a formidable presence and role model. "I used to admire her from afar because she was so pretty," she recalled. "So blond and vivacious, everything a girl wanted to be. Gregarious, lots of friends, just what I would have liked to have been . . ."

We talked for a long time. Like several other alumni, Mrs. House approached Stella's guilt with personal unease, self-doubt, even something close to self-accusation.

"I'm glad I was not tested," she said. "I wonder what any one of us would do. It's very easy to make judgment . . ."

Nobody said Stella should have been shot.

It seems an irony of high order that the ambivalence of the Goldschmidt alumni parallels the attitude of today's gentile Germans toward genocidal crimes committed by fellow Germans during the Nazi reign. The hunt for the culpable; the quizzing of aged witnesses scattered over every continent; the logjam tying up judicial authorities, defense attorneys, sympathizing doctors of infirm perpetrators, and postwar judges grappling to produce the wisdom of Solomon, wholesale—it all continues, massive, questioning, essentially insoluble to this day. The never-ending unreeling of horrors, of trials lasting months and years, of justice demanded, stalled, sabotaged, and very occasionally rendered—so often limply, meaninglessly—will not cease until the last defendant has died.

It is a scene impenetrable, and it has cost West German taxpayers a degree of effort and time and money that statistics can only suggest. By 1988, investigations of 91,481 suspects had been initiated; 6,482 defendants had been convicted, Stella among them. Until the death penalty was abolished, 12 were sentenced to die; 160 went to prison for life. More than 1,100 cases were pending when 17,771 new investigations were added in 1987 from files, long sheltered and suddenly released, of the United Nations War Crimes Commission.

To its credit, the Bonn government has refused to run from an overload Sisyphus might appreciate. The goading of energetic Jewish hunters like Simon Wiesenthal in Vienna helped to keep the authorities interested and funded. But I also observed independent determination not to let justice die. I talked to case investigators and was given endlessly patient help by such model prosecutors as Willi Dressen and Michael Löffler at "the Central Office," the consolidated war crimes agency in Ludwigsburg. Their patient attitude, their zeal, remained impressive—half a century after the blood has dried.

And yet and yet . . . No one denied that thousands (tens of thousands? More?) of the shooters, whippers, selectors, and gassers vanished into new identities. Not even the superb Israeli intelligence service could reach out to kidnap all war criminals and spirit them to court as they managed with Adolf Eichmann, tracking him to a shabby suburb of Buenos Aires, where he lived on Garibaldi Street under the name Ricardo Klement. Many escaped under complex statutes of limitations, many more dodged justice by legal hairsplitting or by whipping up sympathy, legitimate and not, over the failure of body parts, usually conditions of the heart—ironically, the very organ that the accused had seemed to lack in Hitler's time.

Few judicial nets proved more slippery in the end. My main familiarity was with the little-noted trial, in 1969 and 1970, of Otto Bovensiepen and several colleagues. Bovensiepen, head of the Berlin Gestapo during most of the war, was responsible for the death of 35,000 Jews, perhaps as many as 50,000, nobody knew. He was Stella's boss—the boss of Dobberke, Stella's keeper—and Stella was among the more than 700 (700!) witnesses interrogated for the proceeding. The indictment, a model of investigative ardor, took up 496 pages. I read all of them. I cannot compute how many functionaries labored how many hours during the four years required to mount this one case.

Nothing happened. Bovensiepen's doctor testified that his patient might suffer a heart attack if the trial continued, which sufficed to return the defendant to many more years of employment with a manufacturer of canned goods. The others were also dismissed or sentenced to next to nothing.

Or else they got away. One war criminal still being actively hunted twenty-five years after the war (and named in the Bovensiepen proceedings) was *Sturmbannführer* Erich Möller of the Gestapo, Dobberke's boss, by then seventy. Möller was the "mercenary" who had once graciously received Stella and promised her Aryan status after a Nazi victory; had ordered the Jews at the Jewish Hospital camp to be liquidated; and had left for Ahrensfelde to help stem the Red tide with a last stand in the battle for Berlin.

There was no last stand, although Möller would have been cast correctly if it had come to a bloodbath. He was the Führer of Ahrensfelde, commuting from his Gestapo post downtown, doubling in brass as the local Party boss, the *Ortsgruppenleiter*. Off and on, he had lived in this farming village of some 1,200 souls at the eastern city limits of Berlin since 1922. He was married to Hilde Albrecht, from one of the town's most prosperous property-owning families, although it became known during the war that he also had a lover, a foreign "guest worker," living in the old homestead at Lindenberger Strasse 1.

In the war's last weeks, Möller did his frenetic best for Hitler. He had the *Volkssturm* civil guard organized, mines planted, tank traps dug, the cemetery chapel converted into a field hospital, and the rail tracks blown up. As fleeing Wehrmacht soldiers jammed the village to overflowing, fighting seemed likely and Möller ordered all civilians to flee town. But at the climactic moment, during the night of April 20, almost everybody who was left ran off to the west. This included Möller, who stopped briefly in the Moabit apartment of his in-laws to say goodbye to his daughter, Hildetraut, age seven.

"It was rather formal," she remembered. While she maintained that she never saw or heard from her father again, the West German war crimes authorities were trying to find him as late as the 1970s.* He was declared legally dead in April 1991.

Who or what is to blame? The cleverness of the fugitives? The years of delay when the hunters pursued other prey? The ingenuity of opportunistic lawyers and overcautious doctors? Excessive loyalty to democratic procedures, the laws of evidence and other landmarks of freedom that we in the American military government foisted on the Germans in my Berlin time after the war? I shouldn't judge and I won't. Evil is a disorienting phenomenon. It has too many faces.

Some years ago, I was enjoying an excellent lunch in Barcelona with José Luis de Vilallonga, the aristocratic and flamboyant editor of *Playboy* magazine's Spanish edition. We were talking about the Spanish Civil War and Luis's first job. At sixteen, he shot "Reds," male and female civilians, in a cemetery, daily at six a.m., with a firing squad of General Francisco Franco's Fascist army, after his sergeant made him drink coffee spiked with much brandy.

The scene was quite civilized. Luis's fellow executioners were respectable white-collar people, a lawyer and a pharmacist among them. The victims moved quietly, "as if this weren't happening to

* Möller's boss, Heinrich Müller, chief of the Gestapo and known as "Gestapo Müller" because the name was so common, was also among the missing as of 1992, when he would have been ninety-two years old. Remembered as poker-faced and monosyllabic, he was last seen in Hitler's Berlin bunker on April 29, 1945, and later variously rumored to be hiding in Albania, Brazil, Argentina, and other refuges.

them." One middle-aged target, a woman, had a severe cold. A soldier offered her a handkerchief. She said thank you. The rifle felt like the shotgun Luis knew from hunting. The bodies at the wall sagged "like sacks of potatoes." There wasn't much to it.

"You and I wouldn't have been able to do it," said another handsome man, recoiling when I later told him of this encounter at his golf club in Baden-Baden. He was a retired Luftwaffe general who had fought in Spain as a lieutenant. "We would have reported sick."

Well, yes, I suppose so, although I had learned that violence can be disarming.

Almost thirty years ago, I chatted with an appealingly puppylike twenty-one-year-old fellow named Luis Moya, Jr. My first surprise was his smile. It was immediate, open, guileless. His voice was soft and cultured. He said he had been reading Hemingway and Cervantes.

My impression of Luis matched what I had heard from people who knew him well. His boss let him carry large sums of cash to the bank. His teacher remembered him as "a sweet child." His girlfriend said: "He always knew the right thing to do and say just at the time when the other person needed a lift."

It seemed to be some error that Luis and I were occupying a tiny bare visitors' cubicle on death row in San Quentin. It was no error. Luis had pleaded guilty to killing a pregnant nurse by bludgeoning her again and again with the butt of his pistol. He was sober, not on drugs, and had been hired for the job by the nurse's mother-in-law, who offered Luis and a friend $6,000, half of it payable in advance. Eventually both men were executed.

I wrote up the case, along with some others, and published it as *The Hired Killers*. The book was lavishly praised by leaders of the mental health profession and I persuaded the psychiatrist Dr. Karl Menninger to write an introduction. My last chapter was called "Speaking of the Unspeakable."

Unlike Hannah Arendt, I could never think of evil as banal, not the evil practiced as routine employment by the likes of Luis Moya or Adolf Eichmann. I agree with Dr. Robert Jay Lifton, who had this to say about the banality of the Nazi concentration camp doctors he studied: "The men were indeed banal, but the evil they did was not; nor did the men themselves, over time, remain banal."

Dr. Lifton had gone on from his psychological examination of the perpetrators and victims of the Hiroshima bombing, and of the Nazi doctors and their quarry, to consider what made their actions possible. He called the answer "the genocidal mentality."

A friend, an Auschwitz survivor, once questioned the doctor about the mentality of the concentration camp physicians:

"Were they beasts or human beings?"

Lifton replied that they were human beings, and that this was the problem.

"But it is *demonic* that they were not demonic," said the friend.

Not really, I think. Murder made its very first appearance when Cain killed Abel, his brother. Elie Wiesel reflected, "Two men, and one of them became a killer." Banal men, nonbanal deed. It has been going on since time began.

So, was Stella Goldschlag of the same mold as a thrill killer for pay like smiling Luis Moya, Jr.? Hardly. Moya acted for fun and cash—and under no pressure. Stella killed when she heard the rumble of the death trains.

"I'd guess there was a tendency in her to be calculating and uneven, and maybe limited in her capacity for love and intimacy," Dr. Lifton told me. He sensed a possible tendency toward a character disorder, but nothing psychiatrically remarkable or serious. "Under ordinary circumstances, we'd call her a bitch," the psychiatrist said.

Understandably, this interpretation would have seemed too trivial to Yvonne after nearly fifty years of living each day under the burden of Stella's deeds. "If she can live with whatever she did in the past," said the daughter, "she is either endowed with superior powers or she is out of her mind."

Dr. Lifton did not think so.

"Her potential for evil was tapped and cultivated," the psychiatrist ventured. Dobberke and his men drew her into their net by luring her into taking the first step toward becoming a recruit, promising safety for herself and her parents, and then snapping the trap shut.

"By that time she is *it,*" Dr. Lifton went on. "She's a catcher! It is a delicate coming together of evil forces."

Furthermore, living and working in lockstep with Isaaksohn, Goldstein, Danziger, and other fellow catchers, Stella gained comfort and legitimacy from the knowledge that she was not a lone black sheep. And she enjoyed security from the protection of the law. What she did was *ordered* and *authorized*—like José Luis de Vilallonga's firing squad.

Assessing the psychology of collaborators and mass killers from the Holocaust to My Lai in a study entitled "Violence Without Moral Restraint," a Harvard sociologist, Herbert C. Kelman, concluded: "The fact that such acts are authorized seems to carry automatic justification for them. Behaviorally, authorization obviates the necessity of making judgments or choices. Not only do normal moral principles become inoperative, but—particularly when the actions are explicitly ordered—a different kind of morality, linked to the duty to obey superior orders, tends to take over . . . The individual does not see himself personally responsible for the consequences of his action."

What about Stella's acting the part of a "huntress" (as the German court saw it) and becoming a "tigress" (as Heino Meissl phrased it) after her parents were deported? Was she suffering from posttraumatic stress disorder?

Dr. Lifton thought that the answer was her rage over the events. "Rage is part of grief," he explained. "At funerals such people are often angry. It's a deficiency in feeling. They can't touch their own grief."

A dissociation was at work, and it was of a piece with the genocidal mentality and what Dr. Lifton had long called "psychic numbing," an emotional deadening. Right and wrong become suspended under pressure and pain.

"There can be a radical separation of knowledge from feeling," Dr. Lifton said in a 1990 lecture, "perhaps the most malignant overall psychological tendency of our era . . ." People turn into categories, things, vermin. A psychologist friend of mine called it "thinging."

Dr. Lifton's address was directed at an appropriate audience, academics at the *Amerika Institut der Universität München*, where he was receiving an honorary doctorate. He lauded his listeners for the "commitment" of today's Germans toward a "confrontation of Nazi genocide on behalf of its victims and for the sake of both the German future and the human future."

His explanation of psychic numbing and other forms of dissociation applied to Stella, it seemed to me.

"People involved in this dissociative field are in no way abnormal in a clinical psychiatric sense," he told his Munich audience. "Indeed, the mentally ill do relatively little harm to society. It is the normal people who are dangerous . . ."

Dangerous and also evil—and, in the case of Stella and me, a mirror held up to the self.

"She came to contain for you all kinds of experience, your entire childhood," Dr. Lifton told me in New York. "Every Jew in Germany was a potential victim. Now you go back to think about your childhood in Berlin and the decisions that had to be made to your being here. Now there is this figure from your school, and your loss of innocence, the dream and the illusion of love and romance, and the dark side of woman. She becomes the vampire, sucks up your childhood, your innocence. . . ."

Is she evil?

"Yes, and it belongs to you," said Dr. Lifton, "the fact that she can fall."

And what do I have left for her?

"Residual nostalgic affection," said the doctor.

I suppose so. Perhaps that is why I cannot consign Stella to the funeral pyre where she pictured herself going up in smoke, like her parents at Auschwitz, when she considered her future as long ago as the winter of 1944. And perhaps I am an innocent even yet, at least in one crucial respect. As Marion House, my compatriot from the Goldschmidt School, reminded me: I was never tested.

Stella was forcing me to consider how I acted as a scared kid of eleven when I had to decide whether to go on heiling Hitler in my public school or to get pelted by rocks, just rocks thrown by kids. I heiled. I do not know what I would have done if I had been told by men in black uniform that I could save my parents from deportation. I just don't know, thank goodness.

"Just be glad you got out," I was advised by Lucia Weidenreich, an arch-Berliner, the new gentile wife of my round little cousin Sieg-fried. "If you hadn't, maybe she'd have gotten you, too."

Maybe. At least I had finally purged her from my life. I had man-aged to convert my childhood fascination into a biography, an ac-counting I found engrossing if grisly. For Stella's illegitimate offspring this was impossible, though she tried. For Yvonne, the blood connection hung on—the blood and its stain.

27. Mother's Shadow

In the mid-1980s, unexpectedly, Stella's daughter experienced another chilling reminder of her past. A Tel Aviv newspaper carried an article about a large contribution made to the local university by an American, Natan Celnik. Her old Berlin mentor, by then a widower, still childless, was gradually giving away slices of his many millions. The Haifa Museum of Music and Ethnology received the Natan Celnik Collection of antiques. The Israeli armed forces were given money for forty ambulances. Celnik's neighborhood hospital, Long Beach Memorial on Long Island, got $1 million to build a Celnik Pavilion.

Yvonne wrote Celnik a friendly note, and in 1986, she met with him when he was briefly in Israel. Her son called him "Uncle Natan." Yvonne kept in touch by phone, and the next year, at his repeated urging, she visited her nearly eighty-year-old friend for a month in his home near the beach, a large, lonely residence crammed with precious porcelain like a museum.

The stay quickly turned tense. Celnik was his old courtly self, but Yvonne felt confined and implicitly pressured. Her host offered no spending money and almost never let her out of his sight. They rarely left the house. She felt shy, too embarrassed to ask for anything, and she was dumbfounded when one of Celnik's friends took her aside and offered a proposition.

"Why don't you marry him and inherit his money," the friend said.

She needed no time to reply that she considered this out of the question, and her parting from the old gentleman was strained.

Back in Israel, Yvonne wrote Celnik a four-page letter. Warmly she recalled how much he and his late wife had always meant to her, how she revered him as a father and could not think of marrying him.

She received no reply and Celnik's phone calls stopped.

Stella's daughter blamed herself, as she invariably did when she experienced defeat, especially in a relationship with a man. Here was more evidence of her worthlessness, another letdown, an opportunity lost, a chance not at millions—she didn't want millions—but perhaps at escape from her studio apartment into a place with a room of his own for her boy and a new pair of eyeglasses for herself.

The pavement on her road to the promised land had been unforgiving.

Wedded to Judaism and alienated from the German scene, Stella's daughter had decided while still in her teens to be a Zionist like her guardian and role model, Siegfried Baruch. Israel was the place for a Jew to be. "As soon as you're there, you'll be on your own two feet," Baruch had told her often.

She planned to emigrate at the age of twenty-one and managed that resettlement precisely on schedule. Stella's daughter felt at once that she was among her own and mastered Hebrew in six months at a kibbutz school. Israel was home, home at last, and when the Six-Day War broke out, she volunteered immediately to tend the wounded as an army nurse.

Her assignment to the Tel Hashomer Hospital was a letdown. She had asked to be sent to the front, but the Army ruled against her choice. In Israel, the land designed to perpetuate Judaism, the precious last survivors of any family could not be exposed to the risks of frontline service. Yvonne had told the Israeli authorities that she had no family, which was the truth as she felt it. Her family had been Gerhard and Toni Goldschlag, victims of Auschwitz.

Stella was not family. Yvonne never, ever would speak of her as "mother." She tried not to have to refer to her at all. If mention of her mother was unavoidable, she called her "Stella."

The way her life as an Israeli citizen developed, Yvonne would be happy that she was drawn into the Tel Hashomer Hospital. Her war job positioned her for the hospital's postwar Project Sinai, and for the next twelve years Yvonne, always armed, tended patients in the

STELLA

Sinai desert and around El Arish, mostly Bedouins. Life was desperately primitive. Again she was alone and surrounded by strangers hostile to Jews. This time, though, she had the satisfaction of watching pain and hardships eased, lives saved, and hatreds softened.

In time she became a regional legend. Bedouin babies were named Yvonne. The government decorated her. People cried when she left, one of the last Israelis to quit the area when it was turned over to the Egyptians. The new Egyptian military governor heard about her and asked to meet this Jewish woman who served his people so devotedly.

Only a very special individual could excel at the tasks she performed for more than a decade in the Sinai. She had to get along with soldiers, Bedouins, Arabs, and splinter factions, all living in filth and direst poverty and under extreme pressure. None of her civilian clients was accustomed to dealing with a woman professional, much less a female who told them what to do. Much of her work would have required a physician in other parts of the world, and all had to be done in highly dangerous conditions.

"I go with things to the end," Stella's daughter explains. "I am not afraid of death. I would go forward without fear. I worked under military protection—either alone, with arms on me, or guarded by soldiers."

Sometimes the presence of soldiers was no help. "Once in El Arish the situation was critical," Yvonne remembers. "Parts of the Sinai were closed. The [Israeli] Army had orders to shoot at anything moving on the roads, but we were not alerted to that. We got a call and I got together an ambulance with a doctor and equipment. We drove off into a military zone and I gave the order to activate the red warning lights. Suddenly we heard shouted orders to stop—from both sides of the surrounding hills. Luckily, one of the soldiers had identified me in the ambulance."

The group was taken before the local commander and reprimanded. Yvonne heard later that the commander had in turn been dressed down by his superiors for not firing at the moving vehicle on sight, as ordered. Yvonne considered this proper procedure and was not distressed: "It did not deter me from going on."

During one stage of the Yom Kippur War, she was the sole medic in El Arish. "It was night, there was a lot of tumult, many army accidents, bazookas shooting all around, and I was alone with Arabs, Jews, wounded people, and my little Arab staff," she recalls, shrugging—the second-generation Holocaust survivor inured to trouble. Jews were no longer being wiped out by Nazis. Disease and death were Yvonne's enemy.

"I would make rounds in the homes of El Arish with my Uzi and a soldier. Most of the time I would enter a house leaving the soldier outside so as not to arouse the antagonism of the family. Besides, the soldier would be afraid. I wasn't."

Yvonne tells these stories matter-of-factly, the way a devout Jew might justify fasting during Yom Kippur. She was doing her prescribed duty, atoning, making amends for Stella, trying to cleanse herself, hoping to purge the "stain" of what she forever experienced as her "dark past," her guilty heritage, unforgivable for a Jew.

Yvonne was less than successful in her relationships with men. It could hardly have been otherwise.

Stella had been viciously exploited by men and had exploited them viciously in turn. Yvonne's very birth—she kept brooding about this since early adolescence—was the result of some loveless sexual encounter, possibly a one-night stand, certainly a temporary liaison with someone rotten, "one of Stella's kind"—that was the way a distant relative in Israel had put it to Yvonne.

In her childhood, Stella's daughter had been lucky to fall under the tutelage of her guardian, Baruch, but unlucky in encountering sexual abuse: men exposing themselves, men trying to touch her genitals, men parading their erections around the living room. She had to run away from them. Who could love without the gravest reservations?

Worse, she thought herself guilty of collusion in arousing their illicit lust. Stella had done this to her, not only by being publicly promiscuous but by casting her adrift, forcing her to live down the lonely role of "Stella's daughter." Yvonne had no trouble rationalizing her permanent status as a victim: "I said to myself, I am a person with no roof over my head and anyone thinks he can do with me what he wants."

As long as she remained in Germany, intimacy with males seemed out of the question. The atmosphere was uninviting and she was going to leave anyway. When, in Israel, she fell deeply in love with an American, it was self-evident that she had selected a man to whom she could not make a long-term commitment. He wasn't Jewish and he planned to go back home. She knew she could never marry a non-Jew and could never turn her back on her new homeland.

Until she reached her mid-thirties Yvonne wasn't certain she wanted to marry at all. Not only was a suitable prospective partner difficult to come across, marriage itself seemed a dubious state in light of her picture of the world. The view seemed bleak, beset by suffering; she had experienced more than her share of that. Even in Israel, the daily struggle to be a Jew brought little joy. There seemed no point in being married without having children. And should children be placed into Yvonne's world?

Her doubts began to weaken as soon as she met an exceptionally charming, outgoing man from a large Jewish family from Iraq. He was also in his thirties, very bright, wonderful company, well informed, an eager reader—and much in love with Yvonne. His education was limited, but his well-paid job required technical skill; he ran the computer system for the parts inventory of a manufacturing company.

It didn't trouble Yvonne that her man was dark-skinned and of a different culture. "We are all Jews here," she says, "and mixing is healthy." Her hopes ran high: "I thought, at long last I will build my own house. I will build and show the world that I have made it." She did not realize that marriage outside one's own culture is sometimes motivated less by love than by a desire to change one's identity.

The couple dated for a year, spending only weekends together: he worked in Tel Aviv, she was still a nurse in El Arish. It was a busy, happy time, seemingly without signs of the storms to come. The man's charm swept away whatever warnings might have been visible to someone not in love.

Until they were married.

The change in Yvonne's husband exploded soon and it was drastic. He turned moody and wildly argumentative, and would give her no money to help run the household. Dr. Jekyll had become Mr. Hyde. The couple fought fiercely. Before long the husband stopped working and sat idly about the house all day, demanding that Yvonne be more prompt in serving the meals.

She arrived at the only plausible conclusion: her husband was ill, a manic-depressive with very wide mood swings. For months she told no one. It didn't seem right to tattle on a sick person, much less to run out on him. She did have some good friends, and inevitably they learned of her situation. Eventually they stopped counseling and started scolding. She would absolutely have to free herself.

Detailed inquiries finally yielded the information that the husband had once been a patient in a mental hospital. His condition was chronic. Her sisters-in-law admitted that they had wanted to warn Yvonne; their husbands, hoping that the sick brother's illness was permanently controlled, forbade them to share the family secret with Yvonne.

She was beside herself. She felt duped, a victim once again. She could not get her husband out of the house. A divorce, her only hope, was unlikely. Under Jewish law, a divorce contract must be voluntarily granted by the husband to the wife. A mentally ill person is not legally competent to perform such a function. Wives in such cases are often left helplessly entrapped in their unwanted marriage. Yet for Yvonne a divorce was more than a legal technicality. A new twist of fate made it indispensable: she learned that she was pregnant. How could she raise a child with such an unfit father?

Her divorce action turned her husband's large family against her —all except one of the brothers. He stood by her and helped her with the seemingly interminable skirmishing against the bureaucracy: one year to get the husband moved out, six more years before the final decree was granted.

Yvonne's pregnancy under the attendant tensions was difficult. The birth was induced in the eighth month and she came home too weak to lift the baby. Her husband, still lounging about the house, could not or would not help out. Her financial situation was desperate, and housing in Israel is chronically in very tight supply. She felt she had to escape her four walls, no matter what, to keep from blowing up. Her solution, once she regained some strength, was to take her baby son for long, long walks and then to feed him at the house of friends. It was a demoralizing routine and at times Yvonne felt like killing herself along with her baby.

The impulse went no farther than that. In time the walks cleared her head a bit. The fresh air was obviously beneficial for the baby. She would hold on for a while, for his sake, to overcome life's hurdles for another day. And then another. She had stumbled, much in the way that saved her during past crises, on a practice that allowed survivors to hang on. She would simply hold on for another day.

The child, born in 1982, was a delicate, handsome youngster, highly intelligent, introverted, with big brown eyes and coal-black hair. He was not dark-skinned and did not have Middle Eastern features or other reminders of his sick father. At school he did well right away and was liked, although his teachers kept telling Yvonne they were concerned about his physical fragility and tendency to allergies. This didn't worry Yvonne, the nurse. He would adjust, just as he had adjusted to his closed-circuit life with his mother.

There were compensations for their isolation. Like Yvonne, Stella's grandson developed an early affinity for the excitement and achievements of hospitals. "My son also loves going with me to the hospital or on my rounds to the homes of patients," Yvonne says proudly.

Male companionship was harder to provide. Yvonne tried taking her son to see his father for two hours once a week, but the experiment failed. The father was acutely uncomfortable with his son, and the boy disliked him. As the father's condition deteriorated, Yvonne continued to bring their son to him as long as the one friendly uncle in the family—the one who helped her get the divorce—could be present. Eventually the uncle urged her to stop the visits. Instead, Yvonne occasionally took her son to see the uncle and his family.

From an early age, the boy became aware of the sadness hanging over his mother's life. He would snuggle up to her, caress her face, and cajole, "Don't be sad, smile!"

That made smiling even more difficult for Yvonne. "I would tell him that sometimes it's all right to be sad," she remembers.

Yvonne was unable to discern whether her son sensed that something more than the father's illness and the parents' divorce was causing this sadness. She told him nothing about Stella and he asked no questions. The void wasn't unusual. Israel is full of children whose grandparents perished in the Holocaust, leaving nothing behind—not even photographs, those graphic symbols of family continuity.

Yvonne maintains no photo album. She possesses no pictures of Stella or her grandparents. Furthermore, she would prefer that no photos of herself survive. She tells herself that reminders of herself and her sadness would diminish her son's chances for happiness. It is the final expression of her sadness, this wish to vanish, to leave no sad trace behind.

"I want my son to be free," she says, "not loaded with my memory. It is as if I want to destroy my part, leave no memories with him"—no reminders of Stella, none.

"Going on." Yvonne talks about that often, although it requires visible effort. For decades she avoided mention of the past. More recently, it seemed as if she was trying to kill it by letting it out. And by soldiering on. Typically, she blames herself for being trapped: "It is to a certain degree a kind of self-punishment in memory of those who are gone because of my mother."

There! In seven conversations it was the only mention of the unmentionable, the *m*-word that linked her to Stella forever.

Almost imperceptibly, the daughter was coming to terms with the works of Hitler. So, still, were friends of mine.

BOOK 5

OVERCOMING

28.
1988: Year of Endings

EXACTLY FIFTY YEARS after it all began with the fires of Crystal Night, Harry and Fredi Nomburg undertook their long planned pilgrimage to Litzmannstadt in Poland, now Lodz again, once the huge ghetto and now still almost as "Jew-free" as in the time when Eichmann dispatched his trains there.

It was 1988, a year of endings. The books were closing.

Fredi had flown from Israel, Harry from New York. I had not seen them together since January 1946, when we were all twenty-three years old and I was working for the American military government in Berlin. That was when the brothers' odyssey began, their search for final certainty, the hunt for evidence—any signs of how their parents, Georg and Lotte, had perished.

The brothers wore British khakis and jaunty berets in Berlin; I got out my best uniform. Marching past the ruins of Kurfürstendamm, the smashed Memorial Church in the background, we had our picture taken, a triumvirate of conquerors. One of us was a hero: Harry had been a paratrooper and had volunteered for several supersecret (and exceptionally precarious) night raids into Nazi-occupied France long before D-Day.

We elbowed ourselves into a British sergeants' club where sweaty Limeys were belting out "Tipperary" and the other songs they always bellow in movies as well as in reality. My friends told me of their trek to the Jewish Community offices in the Soviet sector and their hunt through the ledgers. They were large, those books, like accounting records, but the lists were not long. They were the names of Jews who had returned from camps. As Fredi and Harry had expected, their parents were not in these books and no lists existed of deaths.

In 1988, in Lodz, they found more names on more lists. After they were directed to the Jewish cemetery, it took them a long time to penetrate its stillness. It seemed to want no intruders. There was no gate, only a hidden little door. Within, they were shown some 1,000 name cards listing a tiny fraction of the dead. No Nomburgs. Had their parents perhaps died elsewhere?

Harry recalled: "I thought, maybe I'll find a grave and can put a stone there and get the care for it that it deserved." Distressingly, there were no visible burial places in this cemetery at all, for some reason—no graves, no monuments, nothing but blackened, burned-off weeds. Yet the presence of a burial ground seemed palpable.

"I knew I was on graves," Harry reported. "I thought I might be standing on my father's grave."

An aged attendant mentioned Chelmno to my friends, the death camp where so many Berliners were transported from Lodz. Harry and Fredi had never heard of the place. But when they traveled on to Kalisch, the nearby village of their grandfather, people there had heard about Chelmno—they pronounced it "Helmno"—and the relatively well fed, well clothed German Jews who had been dispatched there.

Almost certainly the elder Nomburgs had died in Chelmno. Almost. The place of their burial could never be any more certain than the death date certified by the German court after the war.

It was also in 1988 that I finally managed to locate the East Berlin apartment of my cousin Ursula Finke, my quiet playmate from my grandfather's Chanukah parties, who had fought her way back to the living through a succession of getaways dramatic enough to tax the creative resources of a Hollywood fabulist.

Poverty, usually such a grim killer, was her first savior. Her parents, squeezing a livelihood from addressing envelopes for mail order businesses, insisted in the 1930s that she learn a craft. "Ursel" became a seamstress, and as the war dragged on and people's clothes wore out, her repair skill was in great demand.

Her parents and her brother, Hans, were deported to Auschwitz during the Factory Action roundup of February 1943,* but Ursel, then twenty, was saved again. She found refuge with the Daene family, gentile resisters loyal to the dormant labor union movement, and continued life as a U-boat, strumming her sewing machine until 1944.

That August, en route home, her luck ran out. As she elbowed herself through the rush hour crowd to board the elevated at the Gesundbrunnen station, she all but ran into the arms of a fellow named Behrend, one of Stella's Jewish Gestapo colleagues. Ursel knew him and had heard through the *Mundfunk* that he had become a catcher. She bolted, determined not to be caught alive. When Behrend gave chase, Ursel sought refuge in death. She jumped in front of an oncoming train.

Again she was saved. Regaining consciousness as she was being pulled from the tracks, she felt no pain, only despair at still being alive. Bystanders, not realizing she was Jewish, were scolding her. Enraged, she shouted back: "I'd like to see what you'd do if you were being persecuted as a Jew!"

Behrend seemed momentarily conscience-stricken. "We're decent people," he blustered. "We'd have let you go."

"Go ahead," she challenged. "Let me go!"

Behrend, regaining his cool, grinned, motioned toward Ursel's left foot, and mocked, "You couldn't!"

For the first time Ursel noticed that her foot dangled from her, a seemingly shapeless bloody mass. In shock, she still felt no pain. Her sole preoccupation was her handbag, which contained the address of her courageous host family, the Daenes, and fake ration cards.

Behrend called an ambulance to take her to the Jewish Hospital. On the way, lying on a stretcher next to him, Ursel targeted him with a look so withering that he didn't dare object when she removed her address book and personal papers from her bag. Despite her pain, by then excruciating, she managed to tear everything into the tiniest possible pieces right in front of the catcher.

After suffering near mortal bouts of fever for four months, Ursel was saved yet again. The hospital's infamous medical director, Dr. Dr. Lustig, was responsible, and Ursel never ceased being grateful to him. Under the prevailing practices he would have been justified in amputating her foot, which would have resulted in her deportation

---

* The parents were gassed, but Hans, indispensable to the Nazis because he was an electrician, became one of seven survivors of the 936th *Osttransport*. He is a retired electrician in Chicago.

after the stump healed. Instead, inspired by the medical challenge of her case, the doctor decided to try to save the foot.

That required approval from the boss of *Kommissar* Dobberke: the almighty *Sturmbannführer* Erich Möller, who, miraculously, displayed a sign of humanity. The reattachment of almost separated limbs was a new art, and the big chief had once aspired to study medicine. He liked to talk shop with doctors, so Lustig talked him into allowing Ursel to be used as a guinea pig. The doctor personally bathed her foot daily, removed bone chips that kept splitting off, and maintained her two-section plaster cast, carefully replacing it in traction. Savior or devil, Lustig was a still a physician.

Immobile, Ursel suffered crying fits from pain as well as fear because fellow patients were constantly removed for transport, even those prone on stretchers. Early in 1945, Dobberke, swinging his riding crop, kept cruising through her ward and shook his head in disgust each time she insisted she was not well enough to be discharged to one of his trains.

When the Soviets moved in on the hospital, Ursel was saved for the final time. Along with Heino Meissl, Gad Beck, and the other survivors in the hospital—the strong, the lucky, and the feisty—she was presented by Dobberke with one of the discharge certificates he had signed. She was still not well enough to make use of it. It was another two months—June 1945—before she could hobble to freedom on crutches, ever to walk with a severe limp.

It was nearly fifty years of silence before I could bring myself to ask my cousin Martha, in 1988, how it was that she stayed alive after the doctors at the American consulate in Berlin pronounced themselves displeased by her husband's scars and refused him and his family a visa.

I had never forgotten that Martha's husband blamed my father for their fate; that the two men never spoke again; that Martha, my mother's most beloved kin, had made it as far as Holland with her husband and their little daughter, Lottchen; and that all three had somehow survived more than a year in the Bergen-Belsen concentration camp. But I had never dared to ask questions about the details. That was not done. Etiquette prevailed. The proper way was to wait for survivors to volunteer particulars, and in Martha's family nobody ever volunteered anything about the war. The war was forbidden ground. It was an unutterable event to be wished away.

Of course I knew about Bergen-Belsen, the barracks city on the flatlands near Celle, between Hanover and Bremen in the northwest corner of Germany. It held some 50,000 inmates of whom nearly 30,000 died in the final months. No one was gassed or incinerated in Bergen-Belsen; the technical facilities were lacking. They were not needed. By March 1945, prisoners had not bathed in five months. A piece of moldy bread was lunch. Cabbage-flavored water was dinner. Starvation, typhus, and other epidemics were doing Adolf Eichmann's work. Corpses were piled up everywhere.

"Hygienic conditions were far worse than at Auschwitz." So wrote an expert, the Auschwitz commandant Rudolf Höss, after the war. He knew because he had been called in as consultant in a hopeless effort to assist his SS colleagues run the sister camp.

In 1988, in her cozy little apartment in Amsterdam, under the watchful eye of her husband—dead for decades of natural causes but still watching sternly from his photo on the heavy credenza— Cousin Martha, seventy-seven, was still volunteering nothing. Having uneasily decided to put on my author/historian hat, I muttered inadequate-sounding pieties about not wanting to keep her grandchildren and mine forever unwarned, and began, slowly, to press questions upon her.

Martha's memory was astonishingly precise. Dryly, she recalled that it was "very hot" when Dutch soldiers arrived at five a.m. on June 20, 1943, to flush the family out of their Dutch hiding place. She remembered the day in Bergen-Belsen when her husband and daughter claimed not to be hungry and she thereupon committed a crime: "I ate the bread of my child." Often, when hunger became intolerable, Martha dealt with it by using her remarkable memory to recall recipes and write them down. Famished, she would scribble ingredients for lentil soup, for her favorite cakes, for whatever treats danced into her mind. She remembered her jaundice, her thrombosis, the pain of her open leg wound, her precise weight (seventy-five pounds), and the date, April 26, 1945, when Russian soldiers shouted, *"Raus! Raus!"* and she staggered out of the train, the train.

Martha knew that it would be a problem to convey to me, someone who did not really experience the Holocaust at all, exactly what happened to her in the final days.

She found it difficult, for instance, to describe how she left the train in which she was, freakishly, unbelievably, liberated.

"You stepped over the dead," she said matter-of-factly but stopping to search for a contemporary metaphor, "like balls littering the tennis court."

Martha remembered, all right, remembered not simply that the Russians had come for her in Tröbitz, in the province of Niederlausitz, as I subsequently read in printed accounts. From memory she wrote down for me, in German—our language, hers and mine—that the place was "Tröbitz-Torgau, Government District Frankfurt on the Oder, between Cottbus and Leipzig."

I knew that Torgau was the town where Soviet and U.S. soldiers first met and embraced and celebrated the end of all shooting.

Her train journey did tax Martha's memory in 1988. She remembered that it began April 10 and that they rode in fits and starts, evidently without plan, sometimes in circles, for two weeks. Most of the 2,500 Jews aboard had typhus. Almost all had had their heads shaved; Martha had refused this indignity and her husband combed her hair for lice three or four times a day.

Their destination was unknown, although word had made the rounds that they were headed east to be gassed. Martha remembered no air raids, no food at all, no water, only that Lottchen left the train during one stop and returned with some flour, which was useless without water.

And she remembered that when the Russians told them to take over a German farm and go looting for whatever they could hunt up, Lottchen found a wheelbarrow and went scavenging with two survivors of the train, a rabbi and his wife. Martha and her husband were too weak to move. The looters returned with a rich load of canned goods and Lottchen wanted to give her share to her parents.

The rabbi, as Martha recalled vividly, would have none of it. "That's all ours!" he said, and carted the loot away.

Lottchen had reported this to her parents. "Imagine!" Martha exclaimed in her Amsterdam home, finally managing to show indignation. "A rabbi! A child! I could have murdered him! Lottchen was beside herself!"

A fellow passenger, Abel J. Herzberg, an Amsterdam lawyer of my cousin's acquaintance, kept a daily diary of their journey. Being stronger, he remembered more.

On boarding the train April 10, he noted, he received a piece of bread, twenty-four centimeters in length, that was supposed to last eight days. Several nights later, the train was repeatedly bombed from the air, but the next morning became a "feast": the train stopped at a station and the prisoners were allowed to fetch water.

On the fourteenth, it became evident that the train's engineer was taking pity on his passengers. He walked into Lüneburg to try, in vain, to find some food, and he admitted that he had no idea where the train was heading. Six people died of typhus that day.

On the sixteenth, Herzberg noted that many passengers were too weak to move, much less to barter or loot, even less to run away from the train's SS guards. That day brought twenty-five more typhus deaths.

On the nineteenth, there were thirty deaths and the train passed through Berlin, heading southeast.

On the twenty-first, artillery fire became audible. White cloths had been fastened to many of the cars, but dive-bombers kept attacking. Herzberg was keeping himself alive on potatoes that he stole whenever the train stopped. "Many deaths," he recorded, having stopped counting corpses. "A death train."

On the twenty-sixth, the guards ordered, "All men, women and children who are able to march, form ranks!" Nobody moved. Would there be fighting? "All over the train, people were singing," recorded Herzberg. "Everyone felt we were on the eve of a holiday. Would it bring death or freedom?"

By dawn, the Russians came, handed out cigarettes, and left after telling everyone to help themselves to whatever they could loot from German homes.

Some loyalties survived the war, Martha discovered.

Her family had become friendly with Otto Frank and his daughter Anne during their time in Bergen-Belsen, and after the war, when Lottchen's father died, Mr. Frank became her guardian. He said Lottchen reminded him of Anne, his diarist.

And shortly after Cousin Martha returned to Amsterdam, they were invited to the home of Dutch neighbors, gentile friends with whom they had left their silverware and linens more than three years earlier. There, in the friends' dining room, polished and cleaned to Dutch perfection, all of Martha's possessions stood piled up, waiting for her.

I found Martha living a quiet, cozy life, but, unlike most Central Europeans, she never travels. She said her leg bothered her, though I could see no sign of it. I suspect that Martha still cannot tolerate being transported; transport meant death.

One evening she insisted on walking me to the streetcar so I wouldn't make a mistake going to my hotel. We waited at the streetcar stop, and when the little two-car Dutch train clattered toward us, Martha clutched my arm and pulled hard. Although we faced only a streetcar, there was no need for her to tell me that it reminded her of a train in the long-ago war that survivors did not wish to talk about.

I could never get Lottchen to say a word about the past.

By late September 1988, Harry and Fredi Nomburg, still tracing their
family roots across Europe, had reached their native Coburg, whence
they had fled to Berlin so early, in 1929, because the town had been
one of the first to fall under the heels of the Nazis—including the
storm troopers who torched their father's business.

A group of thirty-five onetime refugees from America, former
Coburgers and their families, had been invited by the municipality
as a gesture of reconciliation. The civic generosity was limited.
Guests paid their own travel. They were granted pocket money of
about $15 a day per person, plus free hotel accommodations with
breakfast.

The reception they were extended by *Bürgermeister* Rolf Forkel—
bald, grim, heavy, though fortunately not quite old enough to have
belonged to the Brownshirts—was friendly. But as the bespectacled
politician addressed the Jewish ex-citizens over a sparse luncheon of
bratwurst and beer and waxed eloquent about the ancient glory of
Coburg's chivalrous royal families, Harry Nomburg grew increasingly restless and finally furious.

When Mayor Forkel was done, Harry rose in his smart American
blazer and lectured him loudly about having forgotten the more
recent past. In purest high German and high agitation, he shouted:
"Let us not forget that the hands that serviced the gas chambers in
the death camps were German hands!"

His wife, Beatrice, was tugging at his blazer. Harry didn't seem to
notice. The selectivity of the mayor's history was not all that had
aroused him. He went on to give Forkel hell for having hidden away
a memorial plaque to Coburg's Holocaust victims in the outskirts of
town, in the old Jewish cemetery, where almost nobody ever went.
Why not place this reminder of shame in a downtown location,
where kids could see what Germans still had to live down vis-à-vis
inconvenient living reminders like the sons of Georg and Lotte Nomburg.

A little later, Harry and Fredi were informed that their hometown's hospitality was even more limited than announced. My
friends were not entitled to Coburg's petty visitors' stipend. The city
council's orders had been precise. The payments were available to
Jews who had emigrated directly from their hometown, not to those
who left the country from other interim stations like Berlin.

And the memorial plaque was never moved. The official explanation was that young hoodlums had been smearing graffiti all over

the town's centrally located World War I memorial. The Jewish memorial should not be similarly besmirched—or so ran the official rationale.

Both local newspapers published sympathetically worded, detailed articles about the unsavory outcome of the town's clumsy attempt to make amends for the unforgivable, quoting at length from Harry's tirade.

Did the episode embarrass people? The Nomburgs never found out, having left town promptly.

"Every time I think of Coburg, my stomach turns," Harry told me the year the books closed on Holocaust survivors—if not on their offspring.

That same year, Isaak Behar launched a new career. He was well off, had a wife and two sons, but his long siege in hiding had left traces behind. He was hyperintense, suspicious; his movements were darting; he was a walking electric charge, his memories keeping him on fire without letup. He decided to put them to constructive use—by lecturing regularly to Berlin school classes, telling today's teenagers what their parents could not or would not deal with. Soon he was booked up a year ahead.

Still the canny showman, my old schoolmate turned the Holocaust into a unique contemporary one-man survivor's show—yes, a show. He brought artifacts from his U-boat time. He scrawled the names of his family members on the blackboard and crossed them out, one by one, the way they disappeared so many years ago. Slowly, without cajoling, rebuking, pontificating, he conveyed what a miracle it was that Isaak Behar was still around.

The lesson took. Some youngsters received it stoically, some in tears; some told television reporters that only a Behar, alive, could testify convincingly about the dead, the anonymous untouchables that even the new textbooks tried to shy away from. And some people wrote wild hate letters, mostly adults, neo-Nazis, the hopeless who fantasized that the dead had been phantoms. There were not many such letters.

29. "You See, Hitler, You Didn't Win!"

SINCE HER MOTHER had been simultaneously victim as well as perpetrator of genocidal crimes, Yvonne Meissl was hardly typical of the sons and daughters of Holocaust survivors, young and middle-aged Jews throughout the world—tens of thousands, probably more, nobody knows—who inherited the Holocaust legacy and perpetuate it as "second-generation survivors."

Though Yvonne was doubly burdened, she was nevertheless representative of this postwar progeny in one surprising respect. Scarred as she was by psychological aftershocks, Yvonne could hardly have been more functional. She performed with distinction as a community nurse and, like the great majority of her peers, was actually leading a more constructive life than most people of benign parentage.

A great many other second-generation survivors, too, gravitated to the helping professions. Everywhere, they flocked to become physicians, nurses, psychologists, social workers, teachers, and crusaders of one stripe or another, all in astonishing numbers, as if heeding a call to root out the ideological virus that forced their parents and grandparents to suffer so.

The emotional fallout of the Holocaust had given rise to a crop of curiously strong, humanitarian descendants, a little-noted and paradoxical outcome.

Realization of this unexpected generational turn was slow to mature among the pertinent specialists. In the fifties and sixties, psychiatrists in the United States and Canada diagnosed a more or less gravely handicapping condition among former concentration camp inmates. They called it "survivor syndrome." One of its symptoms was "survivor guilt," an overwhelming chagrin at being alive while loved ones had perished. The horror of not having died, together with the memory of events too staggering to cope with, had led numerous sufferers into psychiatric treatment and sometimes hospitalization.

The case history evidence was convincing. "The mother of one patient had evicted each of her three children from home at age nineteen, the age at which she had been separated from her mother and interned," began a report from the Long Island Jewish–Hillside Medical Center. "Our patient was hospitalized for the first time shortly after her eviction. Her mother arranged nightly clandestine meetings with her at the hospital fence, each time throwing over a paper bag containing such items as bread and underwear." The fence, the bread, the conspiracy in the dark—all had lingered on as terrifying symbols.

Shaken by such unambiguous cases, well-meaning researchers looked for more sufferers to help, and in 1973, Dr. Norman Solkoff of New York State University at Buffalo told a symposium: "These clinicians assumed, from their psychoanalytic perspectives, that psychological damage *must* have been perpetrated upon the children, and then proceeded to search for evidence to confirm their impressions."

By the 1980s, further, more systematic studies yielded more accurate insights. The original clinicians had been misled. Survivors requiring treatment were a small minority. "Severe psychopathology in survivors is the exception rather than the norm," reported a groundbreaking study by a widely recognized authority, Dr. Eva Fogelman, a pioneering young New York psychologist and researcher, herself a daughter of survivors.

The news about the mental health of second-generation survivors was even more emphatically positive. "Systematic research conducted with nonclinical examples of children of survivors does not confirm psychological impairment of personality," Dr. Fogelman concluded. The facts showed a contrary aftermath: "Exemplary and extraordinary courage and coping abilities in children of survivors is the rule rather than the exception."

"There are effects," Fogelman conceded. The parents, often depressed, sleepless, fearful, perhaps paranoid, talked either too little or too much of past horrors. Policemen reminded them of SS oppressors. Travel to a new city prompted them to search through the phone books for lost relatives and friends or contacts with promising names. Some of the children found it difficult to relate to their troubled elders or to gentiles, to God, perhaps to subways making frightening noises—the list was vast. There were indeed "effects."

And guilt, the Jewish disease, was pervasive. My outwardly happy-go-lucky friend Gerd Ehrlich from the Goldschmidt School could thumb his nose at the Nazis as he scurried around bomb-torn Berlin and then sneaked across the Swiss frontier, but he never came to terms with the night he took his mother and sister by train to the Grosse Hamburger Strasse collection camp and left them there. His fear of trains—public traps—never ceased and he always seats himself in restaurants so that he faces the door, still alert for raiders.

"Danger came through the door," one of his fellow U-boats told me.

Gerd's daughter, Marion, one of the second-generation survivors, has never tired of combing phone books and memories of eyewitnesses for traces of her long-lost Aunt Marion, Gerd's little sister, for whom the daughter is named.

"You never know when there's been a mistake," she says, and she is hardly unworldly. She is a public interest lawyer, a prosecutor in Baltimore.

Like Yvonne, attending to her nursing duties in Israel, Gerd Ehrlich engaged for all his working life in tasks that healed. As a professor of international law, he preached justice to his university classes in suburban Towson, Maryland. In retirement, he taught the same lessons for a semester each year at Marburg University in Germany.

Trite as it may sound, Yvonne and Marion represent Holocaust descendants who became activists for a better world.

Eva Fogelman, the psychologist, who left a displaced persons camp in Germany with her parents in 1949 at the age of four months, is of the same mold. "Both my parents were fighters," she explains. When the Germans hit his village in Poland, her father, a baker, hid in an attic and then fought with the partisans for three years in the Russian woods. Her mother also got away, labored in the cotton fields, and took the lead to hunt up food for her family of seven.

Eva was a family therapist working with heroin addicts at Boston City Hospital in 1975 when she and Bella Savran, a social worker friend, also a second-generation survivor, were struck by an article in *Response,* a Jewish magazine, articulating their own pride in their Jewishness. Five second-generation people of their acquaintance had spontaneously banded together to discuss common bonds and draw upon one another for moral support.

Eva and her friend sensed a need and ran ads announcing the formation of more groups. Elie Wiesel praised the effort in his classes about the Holocaust at Boston University. By 1979, more than fifty groups were functioning. By 1987, hundreds of them were meeting throughout the country.

While traces of guilt, rage, anxiety and an occasional sense of isolation troubled these descendants of catastrophe, many of them spoke of their heritage with a note of achievement, indeed triumph. The theme kept surfacing in the support sessions, and in one of Fogelman's groups a young man expressed it with glee after sizing up his fate and that of the others in the room.

"You see, Hitler, you didn't win!" he said.

It was a moment to savor and to remember.

There were other such occasions.

It was 1983 and Sam Gejdenson, thirty-four, congressman from Connecticut—former occupation: dairy farmer—was addressing some 10,000 Holocaust survivors and their families from the rear steps of the United States Capitol in Washington—in Yiddish. As then vice president George Bush looked on, the boyish Gejdenson— small, wiry, and curly-haired—switched to English and spoke with animation and pride of his obligations as the first child of Holocaust survivors to be elected to Congress.

"I was born in Eschwege, Germany, in an American refugee camp," he began, and launched into a rundown of his parents' full names, his mother's maiden name, the names and precise locations of their native towns in Lithuania and Poland.

It happens I've long known this happy warrior who calls himself "Congressman Sam" because his last name is so hard to pronounce. He is a close friend of my son Ron, the first Jewish representative from Oregon, who is the same age, elected the same year as Sam, 1980, both Democrats.

When I asked Sam why he had gone into so much detail in announcing his family history in public, he looked surprised. "Oh, I always do that," he said. One never knows when one might run into a *landsman* or discover the final fate of a lost second cousin, or be able to render such service to a fellow survivor.

The search, the search—it could never be allowed to stop. That was another theme surviving from generation to generation.

I also knew Sam's parents, Szloma, near eighty, and Julia, in her seventies, having visited the family's little dairy farm in the mud outside of Bozrah (population 2,297) where Sam grew up and did chores. It's in the woods of his western Connecticut congressional district, the most rural in the state. With $2,000 down and three mortgages, the Gejdensons acquired their acres after they arrived from Germany in 1949. Yiddish is still their language. Papa Gejdenson, assisted by Sam's younger brother Ike, still milks the cows, and the facts and fears of the parents' survival remain fresh.

While the mother hid in the woods, the father escaped the murders of his native Parafiamovo only because of a redeemer named Serafina. It happened shortly after five a.m. on May 30, 1941, when the ghetto of the village was surrounded by *Einsatzgruppen* killer *Kommandos* and local police, as were the ghettos of hundreds of villages that year and the next.

"Everybody out!" came the shouts in German, and some 500 Jews were marched to a ravine in the outskirts and shot. The ghetto butcher barely made it, hopping on one leg; the other, wooden, had been taken from him because it was suspected that he might be using it to hide valuables.

Young Szloma Gejdenson, the lumber dealer's son, would not be led to the slaughter. He lagged behind and managed to dive into a nearby pile of wood. The only one to see him was Serafina, a gentile mother of eight, who cleaned the local synagogue. She quickly piled more wood on top of him, later hid him in her house, and helped him to flee into the woods.

The scene is never far from the thoughts of his son, Congressman Sam. "It was clear to me in early childhood that government had a direct impact on people's lives," this normally irreverent and outwardly fully Americanized legislator told me with some fervor, and thus his turning to politics came naturally.

Gregarious, full of quips, steaming with the energy of a Little Engine That Could, Sam became a habit to voters in a district known for few Jews, vanishing farmers, but a lot of political volatility. In some periods, the second district used to switch parties every two years.

Sam was different, and his Connecticut Yankee constituents took to his survivor's courage. Although his turf incorporates large defense bases and factories, he voted against significant parts of the Reagan arms buildup. And in his first term, Sam, the milk producer, dared to vote against an increase in dairy price supports. Republicans learned to live with his record as a civil libertarian and adherent of other liberal causes.

And his constituents defer to his sense of history, the displaced person's perspective that informs his politics and makes him point out the link between the luckless ships loaded with refugees in Hitler's time and the boat people from Third World countries today.

Sam's parents never wanted to burden him with their harshest memories. When they spoke to fellow survivors of the unforgettable one-legged ghetto butcher during Sam's childhood, they switched to Russian. Nevertheless, Sam learned early why so many of his relatives were missing, and when he addressed those 10,000 survivors from the steps of the Capitol, he struck, by no coincidence, a recurrent note from Eva Fogelman's support groups.

"We remember not only their deaths, but we remember their lives," Sam called out. "In doing so, we deny Hitler and his cohorts, both past and current, yet another victory!"

Survivors from my own native turf, Germany, have also fared generally well, quite a few with distinction.

Henry (Heinz) Kissinger from Fürth near Nürnberg, who lost twenty-six kinfolk at Auschwitz and never hides his emotion when he is reminded of the Holocaust in public, became, of course, the Honorable Henry Kissinger, Secretary of State, counselor to presidents.

Michael Blumenthal from Berlin-Oranienburg, home of the Sachsenhausen concentration camp, fled penniless to Shanghai, later to become a United States ambassador and Secretary of the Treasury.

Max Frankel, who remembered his home village of Weissenfels from the rear of a Gestapo truck at the age of eight, became executive editor of *The New York Times*.

Ted Koppel, whose parents escaped to England after Crystal Night, became one of the brightest of television talents.

Heinz Gruenhaus of Frankfurt turned into federal judge Harold Greene of Washington, D.C., and broke up the AT&T communications giant.

And chief rabbi Leo Baeck was granted a dignified old age in freedom. It always cheered me that an old friend of mine, Patrick Dolan, was responsible for the revered old man's rescue, and in the flamboyant style that was Pat's trademark. Hollywood missed out on a sure thing when the Mannies out there overlooked Pat's potential as hero for a thriller. He and Baeck made the oddest of couples.

Dolan was an Irish-American reporter out of Chicago in the age of Ben Hecht's *Front Page* journalism—beefy, florid-faced, fast-spoken, his ample black hair, which never grayed, glistening slickly.

I remember him as a major in our army, chain-smoking, as quick to explode in fury as in laughter. He was attached to my propaganda outfit from that gunslinging, parachuting forerunner of the C.I.A., the Office of Strategic Services (O.S.S.), and was in charge of European "morale operations," code for dirty tricks.

When I was composing respectable open propaganda at Radio Luxembourg, Pat and his pirates took over on a different wavelength after midnight, masquerading as "Radio Annie," a "black" station causing mayhem in the German lines with salvos of Pat's specialty: imaginative lies supposedly emanating from brave German "resistance" fighters. I used to stay up late so I could crack up over their carefully manicured screwball reporting.

Pat was a favorite of Major General William J. ("Wild Bill") Donovan, the head of O.S.S., who deserved his nickname and sent Pat on a 200-mile dash behind the German lines in April 1945 to scoop up Baeck. Wearing a general's greatcoat over his uniform and riding in a German staff car (I can picture it), Pat made it to Theresienstadt and forced the remaining Germans at the point of his submachine gun to take him to the startled rabbi for a greeting straight out of Stanley and Livingstone.

"Dr. Baeck?" asked Dolan.

"That is I."

"I have been sent by the President of the United States to set you free!"

Dolan took Baeck out of Prague on an American Black Widow night fighter. The rabbi was sent on to his daughter's home in London, where he became president of the World Union for Progressive Judaism and died in 1956 at the age of eighty-three.

"I don't have many heroes," Pat told Wild Bill's biographer Anthony Cave Brown, "but certainly Dr. Baeck was one of them. He was an utterly brave, decent, kind man in the midst of what can only be described as hell on earth."

The rabbi was a hero of mine as well. He married my parents in 1920. The marriage certificate is among my keepsakes.

What might perhaps have become of Stella, the soprano of Dr. Bandmann's Select Chorus of the Goldschmidt School? Just as I still see her as the sexy athlete in her gym shorts, I can picture her singing with a band on American television—if only her father had asked their St. Louis relatives sooner for the family's affidavit of support. Yvonne might then be a nurse in New York and Stella would not have to be hidden from her grandson.

The prevailing reality of the overwhelming majority of our young is, fortunately, excellent.

My wife and I had not previously met Sharon Nomburg, the thirteen-year-old daughter of Harry, my friend since elementary school in the riotous pre-Hitler Berlin of the 1920s. And here was Sharon, petite, dark blond, with a ponytail, graceful as a ballet dancer, wearing pearls and a white dress with many little ruffles, her pretty face, still a child's, glowing. She was dashing about acting as hostess at her Bas Mitzvah.

We were in the lobby of the Hebrew Tabernacle on Fort Washington Avenue on New York's Upper West Side, and these days there weren't only German refugees at home in the old Fourth Reich. Among Sharon's peers in the synagogue were quite a few black and Hispanic girls, not looking a bit uncomfortable among the many elderly Jewish parents and grandparents.

"Lest we forget our six million," said the reminder on the bronze plaque within, prominent near the front, and as the organ started up, I stopped momentarily, transported backward, backward to my childhood. The music was the ancient *"Wie schön sind deine Zelte, Jacob."* I hadn't heard the melody of "Jacob's Tents" in nearly sixty years; it isn't sung in American services. No doubt Harry had asked for it as a reminder of the long ago, forgotten by all but old-timers.

Sharon handled her transition into adulthood in style. She didn't get stuck in the several long prayers in Hebrew (as had happened to me at my Bar Mitzvah). Her talk, delivered in firm voice, dealt with a motto she had chosen for herself: "Stand upright, walk upright." She endorsed this theme gently, with warmth and loving glances at Harry beside her.

In his prayer for the departed, the rabbi made prominent mention of Harry's parents, Georg and Lotte—my parents' friends and my friends—and as we drifted slowly out, shaking hands to the right and left, the organ again took up the chant praising the tents of Jacob.

I used to sing the song at the Goldschmidt School with Stella beside me. But Stella was the past. Sharon was the future, and her prospects seemed good.

No, Hitler, you didn't win.

30. Indelible Memories

I KNEW HOW DESPERATELY the stranger who phoned me in late 1992 from Florida had fought for his survival. He and a friend of his (and mine) had jumped from their Auschwitz-bound train in 1943 after punching through the boards of their freight car under the noses of the SS.

My caller was agitated. He had read *Stella*, he said, and his memories had been stirred of his days as a "U-boat" in Berlin. Now he was incensed to learn from my account that Stella was alive and comfortably off, if depressed and lonely. Increasingly upset, he lapsed into German and it became clear that he was angry at *me*. He believed that I, too, was guilty of an offense against humanity.

"What kind of Jew are you?" he cried out, still in German. "You were in that woman's presence and you didn't strangle her!"

I was stunned, reduced to stuttering inanities. My caller kept berating my cowardice. Finally, I snapped, "I don't kill people," and hung up, thinking I had been dealing with someone uniquely overwrought.

Not so. At a lecture a few days later, an elderly man who identified himself as a Holocaust survivor said it was not enough that I had branded Stella a serial killer who survived by making a pact with the devil. He interpreted my interpretation of Stella's complex motivations as excuses for her crimes. I should have seen to her assassination, he said, and others took up his theme.

Exasperated, I finally called out, "I am not a murderer. *Hitler* murdered people!"

In Los Angeles, another questioner also accused me of being soft on Stella. He speculated that if I were asked for Stella's current address, I would withhold the information. I told him he was right. Under recent German appeals court decisions, no one was permitted to invade the privacy of a criminal whose sentence had been duly served, no matter how appalling the crime.

American military government had taught the Germans democracy, and they were living by their lessons. I saw no justice in vigilante law.

About half of my lecture audience received my views with applause. The rest sat in silence.

Shortly afterward I was invited to discuss *Stella* on national television, the "Larry King Live" program, and I brought along a partner, my friend Ismar Reich, born in Berlin, currently living in New York. Ismar was one of the U-Boats whose services as a *Greifer* had been solicited by the Gestapo but had flatly refused. I had gotten to know him fairly well and always thought of him as a peaceful soul. So I was astounded when the dialogue went like this:

KING: There are militants, Peter, who thought you should have killed her, right?
REICH: Yes.
WYDEN: Yes, yes, yes.
KING [to Reich]: Are you one of them?
REICH: Yes.
KING [amazed]: Would you have killed her?
REICH: Yes.
KING [still incredulous]: You would have killed her?
REICH: Yes. . . .
KING: When you murder, you're doing the same act she was doing, aren't you?
REICH: No, I wouldn't consider it that, because she did it in multiple fashion, and I would do it on behalf of all the others . . .

When King began taking phone calls with questions from the audience, other callers echoed my friend Ismar's view with vehemence. One called, who had survived the Holocaust in the Ukraine, said he wanted to go one step further:

KING: So you agree—if you were with Stella you would kill her?
CALLER: No question—together with this man who wrote the book.

How can this be? Won't we ever learn? Shouldn't today's neo-Nazis teach us, half a century after Stella, that the virus of violence begets further violence? that vigilante tactics are obscene, unfit to settle old scores or new? Stella's punishment, perhaps inadequate to fit her unspeakable crimes, was the product of democratically constituted courts. Who was I to supersede the rule of law and invite Nazi justice or anarchy? Was this what I'd spent three years to protect while serving in uniform abroad? Were these the values that my son Ron has been defending during his seven terms as a congressman?

Enough is enough. Let Stella's terrible crimes teach us about the evil in us all so the violence will cease at last.

It is not that simple. I still thought I was dealing with isolated outbursts. Not so.

"I get this all the time," I was told by Dr. Florabel Kinsler, a psychologist for the Jewish Family Service agency in Los Angeles, who has for decades specialized in operating support programs for former concentration-camp inmates.

All the time? Fifty years after the fact?

Yes. It is called posttraumatic stress and it will not die.

"They get it every night in their dreams," Dr. Kinsler said.

Acknowledgments

This book has been in work for forty-six years. It started out as a six-page magazine piece written when I came home to New York from World War II in 1946 after nearly three years of military service overseas. I called it "My Girl Stella" and nobody wanted it.

Leafing through it these days, with its rusty paper clip, I see that its shortcomings are obvious. It amounted to a question mark, a young man's heart spasm. It lacked the story. I had only clippings from the suspect Soviet-controlled East Berlin press with bizarre-sounding accusations against my sexy schoolmate, then only a handful of years out of sight.

As finally told now, the story required a lot of sturdy helpers.

Two research assistants stuck it out through the full three-year tour of duty: Hannelore Brenner Wonschick in Berlin (lately assisted by her husband Helmut) and the endlessly patient Ruth Winter in Tel Aviv. They located eyewitnesses thought to be dead or unfindable, befriended them, got them to talk, and left them feeling the better for the experience. Not many humans are capable of this line of work.

Among the archivists, I must give special thanks to Willi Dressen and Michael Löffler of the little-known group of German war crimes researchers at the Zentrale Stelle in Ludwigsburg, a bureaucracy deserving great praise for its devotion to national atonement; David Marwell of the encyclopedic Berlin Document Center, still operated by the United States; Frank Mecklenburg of the Leo Baeck Institute

341

in New York, the treasury of memories of German Jewry; and Steve Heims, the historian of the Goldschmidt School.

Among my family and friends, I'm most grateful to my invincible little cousin in East Berlin, Siegfried Weidenreich, and his canny new wife, Lucia; my cousins in Amsterdam, refusing to be victimized; Harry and Fredi Nomburg, my oldest pals, going back to Volksschule 21 in Berlin sixty (sixty!) years ago; my Goldschmidt schoolmates, the great and good kind: Lili Baumann Hart, Edith Latte Wendt and the extravagantly irrepressible Rudi Goldschmidt; and of course my wife, Elaine Seaton Wyden, and her staff at the Bryant Library in Roslyn, New York, sniffing out books on anything in any language—by day before yesterday.

Key eyewitnesses who were initially reluctant to help, especially Yvonne Meissl, Hertha Wolf and Heino Meissl, deserve much gratitude for overcoming their reservations.

Of the scholars, Raul Hilberg and Dr. Robert Jay Lifton were the most indispensable.

The Bibliography contains any number of works that aren't merely books but experiences so shattering that some of them can hardly be coped with, certainly not dry-eyed. In addition, three books of facts served me unusually well: *Die Juden in Deutschland 1933–1945*, edited by Wolfgang Benz; *Wer War Wer im Dritten Reich?* the remarkable Who's Who by Robert Wistrich of London; and David Wyman's ground-breaking study, *The Abandonment of the Jews*.

The level of editorial support from my publishers, Simon and Schuster, is invariably of the best. These people really edit books, an art rarely practiced nowadays. Michael Korda, editor-in-chief and my editor now for the fifth project, stuck his neck way out by committing himself to *Stella* before I even knew she was still alive, much less that she would see me—which makes him a profile in publishing courage not much seen anymore. And my initial manuscript elicited a ream of suggestions, line by line, from him and from his excellent associate Chuck Adams. Both documents are probably of higher grade than anything taught in publishing courses. *Prosit,* gentlemen!

What about Stella, whose assistance saddled me with so many questions of ethics and protocol? Without her willingness to participate, for whatever reason, with full knowledge of what was involved, this obviously would be a vastly less informed book. How do you thank a chronic perjurer, enmeshed in murderous conspiracies, responsible for countless deaths, yet opening herself up to a remarkable degree? I guess I must steel myself and put down the words: "Thank you, Stella. It could not have been easy for you."

What more goes on inside her pretty head? A psychologist friend asked me about her dreams. I said I'd not had the nerve to inquire, but I'll hazard a guess here. I remember the terror that descended on her when Stella told me of taking her parents to the train, the train east, one of those countless death trains that she feared so, for herself as well. Yes, I'm quite certain: Stella dreams of trains.

P.W.
Ridgefield, Connecticut
June 1992

The Interviewees

STELLA, HER RELATIVES, FRIENDS, SCHOOLMATES, AND VICTIMS

Abrahamson, Günther (Western Germany)
Beevers, Inge (Los Angeles)
Behar, Isaak (Berlin)
Binnewies, Helmut (Berlin)
Celnik, Natan (Long Beach, New York)
Cohn, Kurt (Berlin)
Ehrlich, Gerd (Towson, Maryland)
Eisner, Henry (Baltimore)
Ellmann, Erika (Berlin)
Goldschlag, Klaus (Toronto)
Goldschlag, Stella (Kübler, Isaaksohn, Schellenberg, Pech) * (Western Germany)
Goldsmith, Rudolph (London)
Gutermann, Regina (Berlin)

Hart, Lili Baumann (London)
House, Marion Sauerbrunn (New York)
Isaaksohn, Dorothy (Philadelphia)
Linczyk, Margot (London)
Meissl, Heino (Munich)
Meissl, Yvonne (Tel Aviv)
Page, Alex (Amherst, Massachusetts)
Pech, Gottfried ** (Falkensee)
Pürschel, Johanna (Berlin)
Reizes, Sonia (Lexington, Massachusetts)
Rogoff, Guenther (Switzerland)
Roos, Gerd (Berlin)
Salinger, Fred (Baltimore)

* Correspondence with Stella commenced October 26, 1989. Interviews were on May 3 and August 24, 1990, and September 3, 1991. The last of five telephone interviews was on November 14, 1991. Of the surnames listed here, only Pech is fictitious.
** A pseudonym.

Schuster, Eva *(Massapequa, New York)*
Schwerin, Ursula Tarnowski *(Westport, Connecticut)*
Stannett, Suzanne *(Raleigh, North Carolina)*
Waldston, Gerry *(Willowdale, Ontario)*
Wendt, Edith Latte *(Forest Hills, New York)*
Wolf, Herta Eichelhardt *(Berlin)*
Woolley, Philip *(Landau, Germany)*
Zajdmann (Seidman), Esther *(New York)*
Zajdmann (Seidman), Moritz *(New York)*
Zeiler, Robert W. *(Berlin)*

HISTORIANS, RESEARCHERS, AND ARCHIVISTS

Alter, Henry *(Dobbs Ferry, New York)*
Bachmann, Claus-Henning *(Berlin)*
Berscheid, Dr. Ellen *(Minneapolis)*
Brenner, Hannelore *(Berlin)*
Caplan, Sophie *(Sydney, Australia)*
Dallin, Alexander *(Palo Alto, California)*
Dressen, Willi *(Ludwigsburg, Germany)*
Felstiner, Mary *(Palo Alto, California)*
Fleming, Gerald *(London)*
Fogelman, Eva *(New York)*
Frei, Alfred *(Singen, Germany)*
Geisel, Eike *(Berlin)*
Gellately, Robert *(Bonn)*
Gross, Leonard *(Los Angeles)*
Gross, Dr. Ruth *(Berlin)*
Hartung, Dagmar von Doetinchem *(Berlin)*
Heims, Steve *(Cambridge, Massachusetts)*
Hermann, Klaus *(Montreal)*
Hilberg, Raul *(Burlington, Vermont)*
Hirschmüller, Christina *(Ahrensfelde, Germany)*
Insdorf, Annette *(New York)*
Karas, Joza *(Hartford, Connecticut)*
Kempner, Robert M. W. *(Frankfurt)*
Kroh, Ferdinand *(Berlin)*
Kuby, Alfred H. *(Edenkoben, Germany)*
Kwiet, Konrad *(Sydney, Australia)*
Laqueur, Walter *(Washington, D.C.)*
Lifton, Dr. Robert Jay *(New York)*
Löffler, Michael *(Ludwigsburg, Germany)*
Luckmann, Gert *(Liebenwalde, Germany)*
Marwell, David *(Berlin)*
Mecklenburg, Frank *(New York)*
Milton, Sybil *(Washington, D.C.)*
Oldenhage, Klaus *(Potsdam, Germany)*
Pailthorp, Bellamy *(Berlin)*
Papadatos, Caroline *(Toronto)*
Peterson, Agnes *(Palo Alto, California)*

Richarz, Monika *(Cologne)*
Richter, John Henry *(Ann Arbor)*
Rudof, Joanne *(New Haven, Connecticut)*
Scheffler, Wolfgang *(Berlin)*
Schieb, Barbara *(Berlin)*
Schmidt, Franz *(Edenkoben)*
Simon, Hermann *(Berlin)*

Stoltzfus, Nathan *(Cambridge, Massachusetts)*
Strauss, Herbert A. *(New York and Berlin)*
Welles, Elliott *(New York)*
Wichmann, Christa *(London)*
Winter, Ruth *(Tel Aviv)*
Wyman, David *(Amherst, Massachusetts)*

EYEWITNESSES

Abelson, Ulrike *(New York)*
Arndt, Ellen *(Rochester, New York)*
Aron, Anne Ellenburg *(West Orange, New Jersey)*
Barzel, Monika *(Ramat Hashoron, Israel)*
Beck, Gad *((New York)*
Beigel, Bert *(Sarasota, Florida)*
Collin, Ilse *(New York)*
Cramer, Ernst *(Berlin)*
Deutschkron, Inge *(Berlin)*
Edvardson, Cordelia *(Jerusalem)*
Ehrlich, Ernst Ludwig *(Basel)*
Eisenberg, Fanny *(Albuquerque, New Mexico)*
Erdberg, Sophie *(Amherst, Virginia)*
Faust, Hans *(Berlin)*
Fischer, Eva *(Lexington, Massachusetts)*
Fontheim, Ernest *(Ann Arbor, Michigan)*
Friedlaender, Martin *(Berlin)*
Friedmann, Edith *(Lugano, Switzerland)*
Galinski, Heinz *(Berlin)*
Gay, Peter *(New Haven, Connecticut)*
Hallermann, Ernst *(Cologne)*
Heilbrunn, Gunther *(Berlin)*

Herman-Friede, Eugen *(Western Germany)*
Hilton, Werner *(Berlin)*
Hollaky, Peter von *(Berlin)*
Hottelet, Richard C. *(Wilton, Connecticut)*
Hyman, Marjorie Ellenburg *(St. Louis)*
Issermann, Fred *(Thompson, Connecticut)*
Jacobs, Helene *(Berlin)*
Joseph, Rolf *(Berlin)*
Karski, Jan *(Washington, D.C.)*
Kaufmann, Ilse *(New York)*
Kern, Fred *(Atlanta)*
Klappenmacher, Else *(Liebenwalde)*
Levy, Margot *(Rockville Center, New York)*
Lewkowitz, Inge *(New York)*
Lingenfelder, Norbert *(Edenkoben, Germany)*
Loewenstein, Hans Oskar DeWitt *(Berlin)*
Löwenthal, Gerhard *(Wiesbaden, Germany)*
Maltzan, Maria Gräfin von *(Berlin)*
Mamlock, Helga *(New York)*
Mayer, Heinz *(Edenkoben, Germany)*

Metzger, Rabbi Kurt *(Monroe, New York)*
Meyer, Howard *(Little Neck, New York)*
Neumann, John von *(Monaco)*
Nussbaum, Ruth *(Sherman Oaks, California)*
Perl, William *(Beltsville, Maryland)*
Peters, C. Brooks *(New York)*
Reich, Ismar *(New York)*
Riegner, Gerhart *(Geneva)*
Rischowsky, Günther *(Northport, New York)*
Ruschin, Günther *(Berlin)*
Safirstein, Alice *(Ridgefield, New Jersey)*
Safirstein, Markus *(Queens, New York)*

Safirstein, Paul *(Ridgefield, New Jersey)*
Scheurenberg, Klaus *(Berlin)*
Schott, Bulli *(Sydney, Australia)*
Schwerin, Ernst *(Westport, Connecticut)*
Schwersenz, Jitzchak *(Berlin)*
Shelley, Lore *(San Francisco)*
Sherfield, Lord (Roger Makins) *(London)*
Steinitz, Regina *(Tel Aviv)*
Storozum, Walter *(Amherst, Virginia)*
Wolff, Edith *(Haifa)*
Wolfsohn, Eva *(New York)*
Wollheim, Norbert *(New York)*

PETER WYDEN:
FAMILY AND FRIENDS

Brahn, Ursula *(Bern, Switzerland)*
Fink, John *(Chicago)*
Finke, Ursula *(Berlin)*
Gejdenson, Sam *(Washington, D.C.)*
Nomburg, Fredi (Yair Noam) *(Givatayim, Israel)*

Nomburg, Harry *(New York)*
Weidenreich, Lucia *(Berlin)*
Weidenreich, Siegfried *(Berlin)*
Lottchen (cousin) *(Amsterdam)*
Martha (cousin) *(Amsterdam)*

Notes on Sources

1 · THE MEMORY

Lieselotte Streszak told her story to the Berlin newspaper *Nacht Depesche* of March 31, and April 4, 1956. She emigrated to America the same year, but I was unable to locate her. The article about the New York reunion of Goldschmidt alumni appeared in *The New York Times,* November 11, 1985. A rich and moving biographical collection by Goldschmidt alumni, *Passages from Berlin,* was edited and privately published by Steven J. Heims in 1987. The Snorre Wohlfahrt case history is in Erwin Leiser's *Leben nach dem Überleben,* p. 68.

PRINCIPAL INTERVIEWS: Steven J. Heims, Rudi Goldsmith, Ernst Schwerin.

2 · STELLA

A brilliant evocation of Berlin in the 1920s is my friend Otto Friedrich's *Before the Deluge.* The most accessible work on Jews *in Germany* during Hitler's time is *Die Juden in Deutschland 1933–1945,* edited by Wolfgang Benz. True to its title, it doesn't deal with mass murders to the East. Peter Gay's memorial lecture "The Berlin-Jewish Spirit—A Dogma in Search of Some Doubts" is flavorful. Work on newsreels is sparse; the Nazi view is in Hans-Joachim Giese, *Die Film-Wochenschau im Dienste der Politik.* For Gaumont history I used Raymond Fielding's *The American Newsreel 1911–1967.* Literature exists for the *Jüdische Kulturbund,* the writings of Eike Geisel being the most thorough. The culture/arts offices in the town halls of most Berlin boroughs have recently encouraged a remarkable subliterature about Jewish ex-citizens; some of this work comes combined with research on local anti-Nazi resistance. The excellent *Juden in Kreuzberg,* edited by Berliner Geschichtswerkstatt, runs 436 pages. For Stella Goldschlag's Wilmersdorf, the booklet *Wilmersdorf: Alltag und Widerstand im Faschismus* by Peter Dimitrijevic et al. is useful, as is *Berlin Wil-*

mersdorf—Die Juden: Leben und Leiden, edited by Udo Christoffel (Berlin: Kunstamt Wilmersdorf, 1987). Gerhard Goldschlag is something of a nonperson, in documents as in life. Fragments of his final financial history (provided by the Oberfinanzpräsident Berlin-Brandenburg) are in the Landesarchiv, Berlin.

Principal interviews: Harry and Fredi Nomburg, Peter Gay, Ursula Brahn.

3 · Berlin Boy

Die Juden in Edenkoben, by my friend, Mayor Franz Schmidt, is another model example of today's gentile scholarship, painstaking if belated, about local Jewish history in German communities. Biographical material about my great-uncle Franz is in Schmidt's book and in much of the basic literature on anthropology, in the Columbia Encyclopedia, etc. Franz Weidenreich's most famous work was *The Skull of sinanthropus pekinensis* (1943).

Principal interviews: Jutta Feig, Klaus Goldschlag, U. Tarnowsky, Stella Goldschlag, Lili Hart, Walter Laqueur.

4 · School for Refugees

A history of the Goldschmidt School is in Steven J. Heims, *Passages from Berlin.* For a history of five Jewish schools in Wilmersdorf, see "Hier ist kein Bleiben länger," Wilmersdorf Museum.

Principal interviews: Rudi Goldsmith, Stella Goldschlag, Lili Hart, Isaak Behar, Gerd Ehrlich.

5 · Exit

Minutiae of emigration from Berlin and elsewhere in Germany are widely covered, notably by Wolfgang Benz, *Die Juden in Deutschland 1933–1945,* Walter Laqueur, *Heimkehr,* Bella Fromm, *Blood and Banquets,* Anthony Heilbut, *Exiled in Paradise,* in the files for the relevant years of the New York weekly *Aufbau,* and in the oral histories and other reports of the Leo Baeck Institute (New York and London) and the Wiener Library (New York and Tel Aviv). The passivity of German Jews is challenged by Bruno Bettelheim in "The Ignored Lesson of Anne Frank," p. 246, and "Eichmann, the System, the Victims," p. 258, of *Surviving and Other Essays.*

6 · 1938: The Year the End Began

From the mountainous literature on Adolf Eichmann, I relied mostly on his relatively cooperative 1961 pretrial testimony, as selected by Jochen von Lang in *Eichmann Interrogated,* and Gideon Hausner's *Justice in Jerusalem. Eichmann in My Hands* by Peter Z. Malkin and Harry Stein is excellent on the capture and first interrogations. Alois Brunner's crucial and little-noted idea to force Jewish collaborators to do much of the horrid labor of annihilating Jews is documented in Simon Wiesenthal, *Recht, nicht Rache,* pp. 293–5, and in Bruno Bettelheim's *Surviving and Other Essays,* pp. 268–9. By far the best biography of Brunner is Mary Felstiner's 1986 treatment, "Alois Brunner: Eichmann's Best Tool." William Shirer's and Edward Murrow's Vienna days are in Shirer's *Berlin Diary*. The early Eichmann career and Rabbi Murmelstein in Vienna are in Herbert Rosenkranz, *Verfolgung und Selbstbehauptung: Die Juden in Österreich, 1938–1945*. For the badly neglected Evian Conference see Shirer's *Berlin Diary*, Vincent Sheehan, *Not Peace But the Sword*, S. Adler-Rudel, "The Evian Conference and the Refugee Question," *Year Book 13*, and the Bibliography entries for Hans Habe. The Freud section is based on Peter Gay's readable *Freud*.

PRINCIPAL INTERVIEWS: John von Neumann, Mary Felstiner, Elliot Welles, Henry Alter, Eric and Susanne Winters.

7 · THE THIRD FIRE

Crystal Night spawned a formidable literature, but even sympathetic German authors fail to do justice to the haunting personal and the multiple political dimensions of this event. The arguably most accessible treatment in English is *Kristallnacht: The Tragedy of the Nazi Night of Terror* by two British authors, Anthony Read and David Fisher. Numerous excellent eyewitness accounts are easily retrievable in the superbly organized Fortunoff videotape archive at Yale University. The Goldschmidt School accounts are largely taken from Heims, *Passages from Berlin*. The Nussbaum family section is based on Ruth Nussbaum's unpublished autobiographical chapters. Wilhelm Krützfeld's role is in Heinz Knobloch's *Der beherzte Reviervorsteher*. Karol Siegel Westheimer ("Dr. Ruth") wrote about herself in *All in a Lifetime: An Autobiography*. Ernst Cramer's recollections are in *Die Welt*. Louis P. Lochner's hiding of Jews is in *What About Germany?* Events in Edenkoben are in Franz Schmidt's *Die Juden in Edenkoben*. The public relations boomerang effect against the Nazis is discussed by several authors in *Western Society After the Holocaust*, edited by Lyman I. Legters. Ian Kershaw and Detlev J. K. Peukert have investigated public opinion under the Nazis in several works.

PRINCIPAL INTERVIEWS: Stella Goldschlag, Gerd Ehrlich, Heinz Mayer, Richard Hottelet, C. Brooks Peters, Anne Ellenburg Aron, Franz Schmidt, Peter Gay.

8 · TRYING TO ESCAPE

Herr Hitman and other jazz fans appear in Mike Zwerin's *La Tristesse de St. Louis: Jazz Under the Nazis*. Statistics on the dwindling number of Berlin Jews are in Benz (op. cit.). The history of illegal Palestine transports is in William R. Perl's *The Four-Front War*. Rabbi Nussbaum's visa experience is in Leonard Baker's *Days of Sorrow and Pain*. The State Department record on visas is spelled out in David S. Wyman's painstaking works, *Paper Walls* and *The Abandonment of the Jews;* in Henry L. Feingold's *The Politics of Rescue;* and in Varian Fry's "Our Consuls at Work." Professor Wyman kindly lent me a copy of the Margaret E. Jones (American Friends Service Committee) memo about Avra Warren. Background on Avra Warren is in *Current Biography*, 1955. A rundown on Berlin deportations is in Matthias Schmidt's *Albert Speer: The End of a Myth*. The vicissitudes of the *St. Louis* are in Gordon Thomas's *Voyage of the Damned* and Hans Herlin's *Die Reise der Verdammten;* the latter also contains details on visa problems. The Kübler family involvements were tracked by John Henry Richter, a relative. Rabbi Nussbaum's farewell is in *Gegenwart im Rückblick*. Bella Fromm's memories are in her *Blood and Banquets*.

PRINCIPAL INTERVIEWS: Stella Goldschlag, Harry Nomburg, Guenther Rogoff, Regina Gutermann, William R. Perl, Ruth Nussbaum, Gerhart Riegner.

9 · LAST STOPOVER TO FREEDOM

The history of *Casablanca* is in *You Must Remember This: The Filming of Casablanca* (New York: Prentice Hall, 1980). About Lisbon I used Remarque's *Die Nacht von Lissabon,* but for the psychology of refugees every one of this author's postwar novels is insightful. Habe tells about Lisbon in *Ich stelle mich.* Shirer and Murrow are in Shirer's *Berlin Diary.* Varian Fry relates his rescue efforts in *Surrender on Demand.*

PRINCIPAL INTERVIEWS: Stella Goldschlag, Ruth Nussbaum.

10 · ON THE BRINK

Klaus Scheurenberg described his story vividly in *Ich will leben.* Inge Deutsch-kron evokes the lot of Berlin's Jews in *Ich trug den Gelben Stern.* The Levetzow-strasse and other synagogues are chronicled in Nikolai, *Wegweiser durch das jüdische Berlin.* The apartment evictions are in *Albert Speer: The End of a Myth.* The Herbert Baum resisters and "armaments Jews" are in Benz, Eric Brothers, *On the Anti-Fascist Resistance of German Jews,* and much specialized literature. The Hilde Miekley vignette is in *Wir haben es gesehen,* edited by Gerhard Schoenberner. Herta Pincas's recollections are in her Oral History (New York: Leo Baeck Institute, May 1954). It includes data about suicides, for which also see the Martha Mosse testimony in Gideon Hausner's *Justice in Jerusalem;* Konrad Kwiet, "Suicide in the Jewish Community," in materials of the Leo Baeck Institute, an outstanding compilation; Dagmar Hartung von Doetinchem's history of the Jewish hospital, *Zerstörte Fortschritte;* and Benz (op. cit.).

PRINCIPAL INTERVIEWS: Stella Goldschlag, Klaus Scheurenberg, Inge Deutsch-kron, Margot Levy, Ernst Fontheim, Heino Meissl.

11 · "EVERYTHING IS BEING SURROUNDED BY THE SS!"

While Alois Brunner's impact on Berlin's Jews was devastating, his presence was so brief (October 1941 to January 1942) that specifics on his activities are scant. The best account happens to be in *Synagogen in Berlin, Teil 2,* p. 105, edited by Rolf Bothe. The evacuation and "Community Action" schemes are in Baker, *Days of Sorrow and Pain: Leo Baeck and the Berlin Jews.* Population and train statistics are in Benz and in *Sonderzüge nach Auschwitz,* edited by Raul Hilberg. Accounts of the "Factory Action" are fragmentary and thus not too satisfactory. Benz has highlights (pp. 592–595); the account edited by Bothe is vivid but fleeting; the same holds true for reports by Eva Wagner (Yad Vashem Oral History, 1947) and by an anonymous Jewish nurse in Schoenberner (pp. 313–317); the remarkable experience of Ruthen, including the full text of his complaint, is reconstructed by Robert Kempner in *Gegenwart im Rückblick*, pp. 199–202.

Principal interview: Stella Goldschlag.

12 · "To the Bath"

Dobroszycki's *Chronicle of the Lodz Ghetto, 1941–1945* is encyclopedic and shattering. Chelmno and the gas vans are documented in Rückerl's *Nationalsozialistische Vernichtungslager im Spiegel deutscher Strafprozesse;* also Mathias Beer's "Die Entwicklung der Gaswagen"; and *Schöne Zeiten* by Ernst Klee and Willi Dressen. Jan Karski, Felix Frankfurter, and the deafness of the American media are dealt with by Walter Laqueur in *The Terrible Secret*. The McCloy episode is in Martin Gilbert's *Auschwitz and the Allies*. Reporting on the top-secret Wannsee Conference has been spongy, in part because its purpose —putting in place the grand plan for genocide—went unrecognized for years. Euphemisms poured out by Heydrich, the organizer, dominate many accounts and camouflage the cover-up: following the relatively bland formal proceedings, liquor loosened tongues for talk of mass killings. A new compilation of documents and notes, *Tagesordnung: Judenmord* by Kurt Pätzold and Erika Schwarz adds little of value except for its careful biographies of the participants. John Toland's *Adolf Hitler* reports the dancing on tables, but the meeting's true thrust and texture emerges only in Adolf Eichmann's 1960 and 1961 pretrial and trial testimony. Gerald Fleming's groundbreaking discovery of the personal link between Hitler and the Rovno killings is in his brilliant *Hitler and the Final Solution*. Hitler's vision of his "thousand-year Reich" is quoted in Robert Harris, *Selling Hitler*.

Principal interviews: Harry and Fredi Nomburg, Jan Karski, Stella Goldschlag.

13 · Life as a U-boat

This is based on interviews with Guenther Rogoff, Stella Goldschlag, and my cousin Siegfried Weidenreich. Rogoff had already found his way into the literature through an oral history given by one of his extraordinary gentile protectors, Helene Jacobs, in *Frauen leisten Widerstand: 1933–1945*, edited by Gerda Szepansky.

14 · The Decision: Making the Deal with the Devil

The Burgstrasse Gestapo headquarters is another black hole in Holocaust research. The histories fail even to mention the existence of this local outpost. Stella Goldschlag's account of her torture is in *David kämpft* by Ferdinand Kroh, as is her stay at the Bessemer Strasse barracks. Gerhard Löwenthal's experience is in his *Ich bin geblieben*. The Adelberg torture account was contributed by my friend Nathan Stoltzfus (Harvard University), a by-product of his research into the women's riot at Rosenstrasse jail, around the corner from Burgstrasse. Rolf Joseph's experience is partially recorded in "Illegal in Berlin," his chapter in *Wir haben es gesehen*, edited by Gerhard Schoenberner. The extensive coverage of the air war against Berlin includes *The New York Times* of August 25, 1943, et seq; Werner Girbig, . . . *im Anflug auf die Reichshauptstadt;* Hans-Georg von Studnitz, *Als Berlin brannte;* Jean-Claude Favez, *War der Holocaust aufzuhalten?* Gerd Ehrlich's recollections are in his war diary. The Edward Murrow experience is in Alexander Kendrick, *Prime Time,* and A. M. Sperber, *Murrow: His Life and Times.*

PRINCIPAL INTERVIEWS: Stella Goldschlag, Dorothy Isaaksohn, Rolf Joseph, Esther Zajdmann (Seidman), Günther Abrahamson, Edith Wolff, Ernst Hallermann, Gerhard Löwenthal.

15 · FIRST BLOOD

Gerd Ehrlich described his underground days in his wartime diary. Luise Meier's Oral History is in the Wiener Library (see Bibliography). Dr. Edith Kramer-Freund testified for Anton Gill in his *The Journey Back from Hell,* and in her Oral History at the Wiener Library.

PRINCIPAL INTERVIEWS: Sophie Erdberg, Günther Abrahamson, Herta Goldstein, Margot Levy, Heinz Meyer, Margot Linczyk, Ismar Reich, Regina Gutermann, Isaak Behar, Kurt Cohn, Rolf Joseph.

16 · THE KEEPER AND THE CATCHER

Walter Dobberke was perhaps best known to his late assistant, Johanna Heym, who testified about him at length (see bibliography). Among Dobberke victims who wrote about him, the most perceptive were the tireless diarist Bruno Blau (in his Oral History); Gerhard Löwenthal; and Klaus Scheurenberg. I was able to interview some of Dobberke's most perceptive targets, especially the canny Gad Beck. The rich literature on Theresienstadt includes a solid overall sketch in the *Encyclopedia of the Holocaust* and the authoritative *Theresienstadt 1941–1945* by H. G. Adler. The exceptional treatment of music at Theresienstadt is described in *Music in Terezín* by the indefatigable Joža Karas of Bloomfield, CT. The role of music in concentration camps is mentioned in most relevant histories. (The Freund-Eichmann encounter is in Gill, op. cit.) Eugen Herman-Friede's encounters with Dobberke are in his autobiographical *Für Freudensprünge keine Zeit* and in Dagmar Hartung von Doetinchem's history of the Jewish Hospital in *Zerstörte Fortschritte.* The Manfred Guttmann material is taken from his 1957 and 1968 testimony.

PRINCIPAL INTERVIEWS: Stella Goldschlag, Sister Elli, Klaus Scheurenberg, Hans Faust, Eugen Herman-Friede, Rolf Joseph, Norbert Wollheim, Heino Meissl, Gad Beck.

17 · THE CATCHER AND THE LOVER

Literature about the daily life of U-boats includes *The Last Jews in Berlin* by Leonard Gross; *Die versteckte Gruppe* by Jizchak Schwersenz; Ferdinand Kroh's *David kämpft; Der Schattenmann* by Ruth Andreas-Friedrich; Gerhard Löwenthal, op. cit.; Klaus Scheurenberg, op. cit.; Eugen Herman-Friede, op. cit.; Robert Darnton's *Berlin Journal 1989–1990* re Isaak Behar; Joel König's

David; Edith Ehrlich's haunting "Bericht einer, die im Berlin des Dritten Reiches untertauchte und überlebte" in Nelki, *Geschichten aus dem Umbruch der deutschen Geschichte;* and, notably, by Inge Deutschkron (op. cit.). Details of Stella Goldschlag's and Rolf Isaaksohn's catcher operations are drawn from the records of Stella's 1957 trial (*see* Bibliography under Generalstaatsanwalt bei dem Landgericht Berlin).

PRINCIPAL INTERVIEWS: Morris and Esther Zajdmann (Seidman), Heino Meissl, Dorothy Isaaksohn, Gad Beck.

18 · THE HERTHA TRIANGLE

The Hertha/Stella story is based on three interviews with Hertha by my Berlin research associate, Hannelore Brenner Wonschick, and one lengthy phone interview I conducted with Hertha. The Herman-Friede material is based on Dagmar Hartung von Doetinchem's history of the Jewish Hospital.

OTHER INTERVIEWS: Hans Faust, Heino Meissl.

19 · THE HEINO TRIANGLE

Hospital scenes are drawn largely from Hartung von Doetinchem history; the Bruno Blau Oral History; Eugen Herman-Friede, op. cit.; the Heino Meissl, Erika Miethling and Fritz Wöhrn police and court testimonies.

PRINCIPAL INTERVIEWS: Gad Beck, Günther Rischowsky, Heino Meissl, Hertha Eichelhardt Wolf, Inge Lewkowitz, Edith Friedmann, Klaus J. Herrmann.

20 · FINAL DAYS

Berlin's final war days are thoroughly covered in Cornelius Ryan's *The Last Battle,* which includes the still best available reporting on the epidemic of rapes; *see* also: John Toland, *The Last 100 Days;* James P. O'Donnell, *The Bunker;* Peter Padfield, *Himmler;* and numerous fragmentary German accounts. Some scenes in the Jewish Hospital are in Hartung von Doetinchem and Blau. The Erich Möller story is from his personnel files in the Berlin Document Center (U.S.) and 1992 investigations conducted in Ahrensfelde and Berlin on my behalf by Bellamy Pailthorp. Sophie Caplan in Sydney, Australia, was my principal source on Dobberke's capture; I also talked to Bulli Schott by phone. Dobberke's death is in Manfred Guttmann's 1968 *Landgericht* testimony. The Gerhard Löwenthal scene is taken from his memoir, *Ich bin geblieben.* The end of Karinhall is in Leonard Mosley, *The Reich Marshal.* The Liebenwalde story is largely based on two intensive on-scene reporting trips made for me in 1991 by Hannelore Brenner Wonschick and her husband Helmut. Henry Orenstein wrote his horror tale in *I Shall Live.* Wolfgang Szepansky's account is in *Niemand und nichts vergessen.* Rudolf Höss's memories are in Martin Broszat, *Kommandant in Auschwitz.*

PRINCIPAL INTERVIEWS: Stella Goldschlag, Walter Storozum, Günther Ruschin, Markus Safirstein, Heino Meissl, Gad Beck (interviewed by Hannelore Brenner

Wonschick), Sophie Caplan, Bulli Schott, Alice Safirstein, Eva Fischer, Christina Hirschmüller, Gert Luckmann, Bert Beigel, Peter von Hollaky, Else Kappenmacher.

21 · STELLA AGAIN

The *Tägliche Rundschau* article on Stella appeared March 17, 1946, the year I also interviewed Jean Blomé.

22 · THE TRIAL

Trial records are in Generalstaatsanwalt bei dem Landgericht Berlin, 1957. For news accounts see *Der Abend, Berliner Morgenpost, Berliner Zeitung,* Heinz Deilke, Heinz Elsberg, and *Nacht Depesche.* Ferdinand Kroh has additional details.

PRINCIPAL INTERVIEWS: Stella Goldschlag, Kurt Cohn, Robert Zeiler, Moritz Zajdmann (Seidman), Heino Meissl, Herta Eichelhardt Wolf.

23 · STELLA'S DAUGHTER

This information is based entirely on interviews. Ruth Winter, a most empathic social worker, conducted seven lengthy emotion-laden conversations on my behalf with the patient, long-suffering Yvonne Meissl, in Tel Aviv. Ms. Winter also met Stella's grandson. I spoke with Tante Erika Ellmann in Berlin and Natan Celnick in Long Beach, NY. Helmut Binnewies, a fellow orphan with Yvonne in Berlin, became a friend.

24 · WORKING FOR EICHMANN

Dr. Lore Weinberg Shelley's *Secretaries of Death* is meticulous and shattering direct testimony. Dr. Elie A. Cohen's self-accusations are in Anton Gill's *The Journey Back from Hell,* also in Dr. Robert Jay Lifton's *The Nazi Doctors,* and Dr. Cohen's own *Human Behavior in the Concentration Camp,* published in the United States as *The Abyss.* Dr. Samuel's horror story is in Lifton. For proceedings against Harry Schwarzer, Max Reschke, Inge Reitz, Bruno Goldstein, and Günther Abrahamson, see Bibliography.

PRINCIPAL INTERVIEWS: Lore Shelley, Heinz Galinski, Günther Abrahamson.

25 · "DEAR STELLA"

This is based almost entirely on interviews with Stella Goldschlag, Guenther Rogoff, Hans Oskar DeWitt Loewenstein, Isaak Behar, Jutta Feig, Johanna Pürschel (interviewed by Hannelore Brenner Wonschick as well as myself), and Ellen Berscheid. For Stella's 1972 trial, see court record (Bibliography: Schwurgericht bei dem Landgericht Berlin, 1972) and *Die Welt.* Jewish self-hate is treated in Theodor Lessing's *Der jüdische Selbsthass;* Sander L. Gilman in *Jewish Self-Hatred,* which also contains exhaustive bibliographical material;

and Kurt Lewin in *Resolving Social Conflicts*. For Flora Hogman's work, see Bibliography.

26 · JUDGMENT

This is based on interviews with Stella Goldschlag, Lili Baumann Hart, Marion Dann Weiner, Marion Sauerbrunn House, Alex Page, Jerry Waldston, Willi Dressen, Michael Löffler, Hildetraut Möller, and Robert Jay Lifton. Up-to-date information on German war crimes is at the Zentrale Stelle archives in Ludwigsburg, Germany. The extraordinary indictment preparatory to the abortive Otto Bovensiepen trial is at the Leo Baeck Institute, New York. Simon Wiesenthal and Robert Kempner are among Nazi hunters who consistently complain about foot-dragging in war crimes prosecutions. My interview with José Luis de Villallonga is in my book *The Passionate War;* for my encounter with Luis Moya, Jr., see my *The Hired Killers*.

27 · MOTHER'S SHADOW

This originated in Ruth Winter's extensive talks with Yvonne Meissl in Tel Aviv.

28 · 1988: YEAR OF ENDINGS

This is based on my interviews with Harry and Fredi Nomburg; my Dutch relatives in Amsterdam; and my cousin Ursel Finke in East Berlin. The Abel Herzberg dairy is in Eberhard Kolb's relentless and heartbreaking history *Bergen Belsen*. Ursel's suicide attempt and medical treatment are mentioned in Wolfgang Benz.

29 · "YOU SEE, HITLER, YOU DIDN'T WIN!"

Of the extensive literature on second-generation Holocaust survivors, the arguably most insightful overall treatment is in *Response* magazine, "Five Children of Survivors, a Conversation." Eva Fogelman's publications bring solid new good sense to the subject, as does the entire special issue of *The Psychoanalytic Review*. The case history from the Long Island Jewish Hospital is by Sylvia Axelrod et al, *Bulletin of the Menninger Clinic*. Wolf Blitzer's "In Congress, the Memory Lives" is valuable on Representative Sam Gejdenson and his congressional Holocaust survivor colleagues. Pat Dolan's liberation of Rabbi Baeck is in Anthony Cave Brown's *The Last Hero—Wild Bill Donovan*. Dolan's rich life is capsuled by his old comrade-in-arms and mine, H. Peter Hart, in *The Independent*. The standard work on second-generation problems is the very accessible *Children of the Holocaust* by Helen Epstein.

PRINCIPAL INTERVIEWS: Yvonne Meissl, Gerd Ehrlich, Marion Ehrlich, Eva Fogelman, Sam, Szloma, Julia, and Ike Gejdenson, Harry Nomburg.

Select Bibliography

Mrs. A. "Jewish Hospital in Berlin." Wiener Library (Tel Aviv) (November 1954), Index no. P.III.a.No.4.

Der Abend (Berlin). "Durch Verrat das eigene Leben gerettet?" (June 21, 1957).

Der Abend (Berlin). "Tumulte um Stella Kübler." (June 25, 1957).

Abrahamson, Günther. Landgericht Berlin, 1 PKLs 7/52 (1952). Trial record from notes by Nathan Stoltzfus.

Adler, H. G. Theresienstadt 1941–1945. Tübingen: Mohr, 1960.

Adler-Rudel, S. "The Evian Conference and the Refugee Question." Year Book 13. London: Publications of the Leon Baeck Institute, 1968.

Allgemeine (Frankfurt Jewish Weekly). "Prozess gegen Gestapo-Greiferin." (June 25, 1957).

Ambrose, Stephen E. Eisenhower, Vol. 1. New York: Touchstone, 1985.

Andreas-Friedrich, Ruth. Der Schattenmann. Frankfurt am Main: Suhrkamp, 1983.

Arendt, Hannah. Eichmann in Jerusalem. New York: Viking, 1963.

Ashman, Charles, and Robert J. Wagman. The Nazi Hunters. New York: Pharos Books, 1988.

Associated Press. "Noch gegen mehr als 1,100 Personen NS-Verfahren anhängig." Tagesspiegel (Berlin) (March 9, 1988).

Axelrod, Sylvia, Ofelia L. Schnipper, and John H. Rau. "Hospitalized Offspring of Holocaust Survivors." Bulletin of the Menninger Clinic (Topeka) 44, no. 1 (January 1980).

Bachmann, Claus-Henning. "Eine Reise nach Theresienstadt." Aufbau (New York) (January 3, 1992) p. 3.

Baedeker, Karl. Der grosse Baedeker: Berlin. Freiburg: Karl Baedeker, 1986.

Baker, Leonard. Days of Sorrow and Pain: Leo Baeck and the Berlin Jews. New York: Macmillan, 1978.

Bar-On, Dan. Legacy of Silence. Cambridge: Harvard University Press, 1989.

SELECT BIBLIOGRAPHY

Bar-On, Dan, G. Beiner, and M. Brusten, eds. *Der Holocaust: Familiale und Gesellschaftliche Folgen.* Wuppertal: Universität Wuppertal, 1988.

Baumer, Franz. *Erich Maria Remarque.* Berlin: Colloquium, 1984.

Beer, Mathias. "Die Entwicklung der Gaswagen beim Mord an den Juden." *Vierteljahreshefte für Zeitgeschichte.* Munich: Oldenburg, 1987, 403–18.

Behrend-Rosenfeld, Else R. *Ich stand nicht allein.* Munich: Beck, 1988.

Benz, Wolfgang, ed. *Dimension des Völkermords.* Munich: Oldenburg, 1991.

———. *Die Juden in Deutschland 1933–1945.* Munich: Beck, 1988.

Berlin, Isaiah. *Against the Current.* New York: Viking, 1980.

Berliner Geschichtswerkstatt, ed. *Juden in Kreuzberg.* Berlin: Hentrich, 1991.

Berliner Morgenpost. "Heftige Tumulte um Stella Kübler. (June 25, 1957).

Berliner Morgenpost. "10 Jahre Zuchthaus für Stella Kübler." (June 30, 1957).

Berliner Zeitung (BZ). "Staatsanwalt fordert für Stella Kübler: 15 Jahre Zuchthaus." (June 28, 1957).

Berman, Marshall. "Life History and the Historical Moment" (Review of Erik H. Erikson). *New York Times Book Review* (March 30, 1973).

Bettelheim, Bruno. *The Informed Heart.* New York: Avon, 1960.

———. *Surviving and Other Essays.* New York: Knopf, 1979.

Bild (Hamburg). "10 Jahre für die Greiferin der Gestapo." (October 10, 1972).

Blasius, Dirk, and Dan Diner. *Zerbrochene Geschichte.* Frankfurt am Main: Fischer, 1991.

Blau, Bruno. "Der Geiselmord vom 2. Dezember 1942." *Aufbau* (New York) (December 19, 1952): 9.

———. "Vierzehn Jahre Not und Schrecken." Oral History. New York: Leo Baeck Institute, n.d.

Blitzer, Wolf. "In Congress, the Memory Lives." *Hadassah* (New York) (April 1984).

Blumenthal, Ralph. "Decades after Helping Jews Escape, a Psychologist Gains Honor as a Hero" (re William R. Perl). *The New York Times* (November 18, 1990).

Boehm, Eric H. *We Survived.* New Haven: Yale, 1949.

Bothe, Rolf, ed. *Synagogen in Berlin, Teil 2.* Berlin: Wilmuth Arenhövel/Berlin Museum, 1983.

Bovensiepen, Otto. Landgericht Berlin, 1 Js 9/65 Stapoleit. Bln., 500/10/69 and 1 Ks 2/69, Stapoleit. Bln. Indictment in Berlin Gestapo trial. New York: Leo Baeck Institute.

Brahn, Ursula. "Max Brahn." Biography, Bern, n.d.

Breitman, Richard. *The Architect of Genocide.* New York: Knopf, 1991.

Brewster, Eva. *Vanished in Darkness: An Auschwitz Memoir.* Edmonton, CD: NeWest, 1984.

Broszat, Martin, ed. *Kommandant in Auschwitz* (Rudolf Höss diaries). Munich: DTV, 1963.

Brothers, Eric. "On the Anti-Fascist Resistance of German Jews." *Year Book 13.* London: Leo Baeck Institute/Secker & Warburg, 1987.

Brown, Anthony Cave. *The Last Hero—Wild Bill Donovan.* New York: Vintage, 1982.

Browning, Christopher R. "The Development and Production of the Nazi Gas Vans." *Fateful Months.* New York: Holmes and Meier, 1985, 57–67.

Carey, John, ed. "The Fall of Berlin." *Eyewitness to History.* New York: Avon, 1987, 625–30.

Carroll, Donald. "Escape from Vichy" (Varian Fry). *American Heritage,* vol. 34, June/July 1983, p. 82.

Clark, Ronald W. *Einstein.* New York: Avon, 1972.

Cohen, Elie A. *The Abyss.* New York: Norton, 1973.

Conot, Robert E. *Judgment at Nuremberg.* New York: Harper, 1983.

Cornelsen, Horst. "Mord ohne Sühne." *Allgemeine* (May 7, 1957).

Cramer, Ernst. "Ein Amerikaner in Buchenwald." *Die Welt* (Hamburg) (November 9, 1978).

——. "Epitaph auf meinen Bruder Erwin." *Die Welt* (Hamburg) (August 1, 1981).

Darnton, Robert. *Berlin Journal 1989–1990.* New York: Norton, 1991.

Deilke. Heinz. "Eine Tote vor Gericht." *Berliner Zeitung* (June 21, 1957).

——. "Das sind Märchen!" (Stella Kübler testimony). *Berliner Zeitung* (June 25, 1957).

——. "10 Jahre Zuchthaus." *Berliner Zeitung* (July 1, 1957).

Dershowitz, Alan M. *Chutzpah.* Boston: Little, Brown, 1991.

Deuerlein, Ernst. *Der Aufstieg der NSDAP 1919–1933 in Augenzeugenberichten.* Düsseldorf: Karl Rauch, 1968.

Deutsche Volkszeitung (Berlin). "Agentin Himmlers verhaftet." (March 4, 1946).

Deutsche Volkszeitung (Berlin). "Das 'blonde Gespenst.' " (March 13, 1946).

Deutschkron, Inge. *Ich trug den Gelben Stern.* Munich: DTV, 1987.

Dietrich, Marlene. *Nehmt nur mein Leben.* Munich: Goldmann, 1981.

Dimitrijevic, Peter, Maria Paulsen, Norbert Weitel, Laura von Wimmersperg, and Peter Wollenweber. *Wilmersdorf: Alltag und Widerstand im Faschismus.* Berlin: Arbeitsgruppe der Friedensinitiative Wilmersdorf, Verband der Antifaschisten, n.d. [c. 1985].

Dobroszycki, Lucjan, ed. *The Chronicle of the Lodz Ghetto, 1941–1944.* New Haven: Yale, 1984.

Duncan, Scott. "Reunion" (Goldschmidt School). *Baltimore Evening Sun* (November 8, 1985).

Dyck, Richard. "Stella Kübler, Menschenjägerin." *Aufbau* (New York) (April 13, 1956), 28.

Eckardt, Wolf von, and Sander L. Gilman. *Bertolt Brecht's Berlin.* New York: Anchor/Doubleday, 1975.

Edvardson, Cordelia. *Gebranntes Kind sucht das Feuer.* Munich: DTV, 1989.

Ehrlich, Ernst Ludwig. Oral History, London, September 1959, Wiener Library P III d (Berlin) No.1141/Yad Vashem 02/1067.

Ehrlich, Gerd W. "Mein Leben in Nazi-Deutschland." Manuscript, Geneva, 1945.

——. "Reflections on Berlin Jews." *Gegenwart im Rückblick.* Herbert A. Strauss and Kurt R. Grossmann, eds. Heidelberg: Lothar Stiehm, 1970.

Elsberg, Heinz. "Stella Kübler freigelassen." *Aufbau* (New York) (July 12, 1957), 1.

Encyclopedia of the Holocaust, 4 vols., Yisrael Gutman, ed. New York: Macmillan, 1989.

Epstein, Helen. *Children of the Holocaust.* New York: Putnam, 1979.

Favez, Jean-Claude. *War der Holocaust aufzuhalten?* Zürich: Verlag Neue Zürcher Zeitung, 1989.

Feingold, Harry L. *The Politics of Rescue.* New Brunswick, NJ: Rutgers, 1968.
Felstiner, Mary. "Alois Brunner: Eichmann's Best Tool." *Simon Wiesenthal Center Annual* 3. White Plains, NY: Kraus International, 1986, 1–46.
Fénelon, Fania. *Playing for Time.* New York: Berkley, 1979.
Fielding, Raymond. *The American Newsreel 1911–1967.* Norman, OK: University of Oklahoma, 1972.
Finke, John. "Das jüdische landwirtschaftliche Umschulungslager Gut Neuendorf, 1939–1943." Manuscript, n.d.
Fittko, Lisa. *Mein Weg über die Pyrenäen.* Munich: DTV, 1989.
Fleming, Gerald. *Hitler and the Final Solution.* Los Angeles: University of California Press, 1984.
Fogelman, Eva. "Intergenerational Group Therapy: Child Survivors of the Holocaust and Offspring of Survivors." *The Psychoanalytic Review* (New York), 75, no. 4 (Winter 1988), 619–40.
———. "Therapeutic Alternatives for Holocaust Survivors and Second Generation." R.L. Branam, ed. *The Psychological Perspectives of the Holocaust and Its Aftermath.* New York: Columbia University Press, 1988, 79–108.
Frankel, Max. "You Can't Go Home to Weissenfels." *New York Times Magazine* (January 10, 1965).
Frankl, Viktor E. *Man's Search for Meaning.* New York: Pocket Books, 1984.
Frei, Alfred G., and Jens Runge. *Erinnern Bedenken Lernen.* Sigmaringen: Thorbecke, 1990.
Freud, Anna. *The Ego and the Mechanisms of Defense* ("Identification with the Aggressor"). New York: International Universities, 1966.
Friedlaender, Bernard, and Martin Friedlaender. Testimony re Walter Dobberke and other Gestapo personnel, before Landgericht Berlin, 1-A-KI3, November 3, 1965.
Friedman, Philip. "Aspects of the Jewish Communal Crisis in the Period of the Nazi Regime in Germany, Austria, and Czechoslovakia." Re Rabbi Benjamin Murmelstein. *Essays on Jewish Life and Thought.* New York: Columbia University Press, 1959.
Friedrich, Jörg. *Die kalte Amnestie.* Frankfurt am Main: Fischer, 1988.
Friedrich, Otto. *Before the Deluge.* New York: Harper, 1972.
Fromm, Bella. *Blood and Banquets.* New York: Harper, 1942.
Fry, Varian. "Our Consuls at Work." *Nation* (May 2, 1942).
———. *Surrender on Demand.* New York: Random House, 1945.
Galante, Pierre, and Eugene Silianoff. *Voices from the Bunker.* New York: Anchor, 1989.
Gay, Peter. "The Berlin-Jewish Spirit—A Dogma in Search of Some Doubts." Leo Baeck Memorial Lecture. New York: Leo Baeck Institute, 1972.
———. *Freud.* New York: Norton, 1989.
———. *Freud, Jews and Other Germans.* New York: Oxford, 1978.
Gegenwart im Rückblick. Herbert A. Strauss and Kurt Grossmann, eds. Heidelberg: Lothar Stiehm, 1970.
Geiger, Ludwig. *Geschichte der Juden in Berlin.* Berlin: Arani, n.d.
Gellately, Robert. *The Gestapo and German Society.* Oxford: Clarendon, 1990.
Generalstaatsanwalt bei dem Landgericht Berlin. Indictment re Stella Ingrid Kübler Isaaksohn, née Goldschlag, (500) 1 P Js 855/56 (9.57), Berlin, April 10, 1957.

Generalstaatsanwalt bei dem Landgericht Berlin. Trial record re Stella Ingrid Kübler Isaaksohn, née Goldschlag, (500) 1 P Ks 1 57 (p. 57), Berlin, July 30, 1957.

Gies, Miep, with Alison Leslie Gold. *Anne Frank Remembered*. New York: Simon & Schuster, 1987.

Giese, Hans-Joachim. *Die Film-Wochenschau im Dienste der Politik*. Dresden: Dittert, 1940.

Gilbert, G. M. *Nürnberger Tagebuch*. Frankfurt am Main: Fischer 1962.

Gilbert, Martin. *Auschwitz and the Allies*. New York: Holt, 1981.

———. *The Holocaust*. New York: Holt, 1985.

Gill, Anton. *The Journey Back from Hell*. New York: Avon, 1988.

Gilman, Sander L. *Jewish Self-Hatred*. Baltimore: Johns Hopkins, 1986.

Giordano, Ralph. *Die Zweite Schuld*. Munich: Knaur, 1990.

Girbig, Werner. *. . . im Anflug auf die Reichshauptstadt*. Stuttgart: Motorbuch, 1970.

Gisevius, Hans Bernd. *Bis zum bitteren Ende*. Hamburg; Rütten & Loening, n.d.

Goldstein, Bruno. Testimony re Berlin Gestapo, Berlin, I-A-KI 3, 1 J9/65 (Stapol. Bln) E13, November 30, 1965.

Gosztony, Peter, ed. *Der Kampf um Berlin in Augenzeugenberichten*. Munich: DTV, 1985.

Gross, Leonard. *The Last Jews in Berlin*. New York: Bantam, 1983.

Grossmann, Kurt R. *Die unbesungenen Helden*. Berlin: Ullstein, 1984.

Günther-Kaminski and Michael Weiss. *Juden am Ku'damm*. Berlin: Berliner Geschichtswerkstatt, 1989.

Guttmann, Manfred. Testimony before Ehrengericht der Jüdischen Gemeinde zu Berlin, July 3, 1957. Zentrale Stelle, Ludwigsburg.

———. Testimony before Landgericht Berlin, re Walter Dobberke et al., 1-A-KI 3, June 10, 1968.

Guttmann, Oskar. "Kompositionsabend Gerhard Goldschlag" (concert review). *Familien Blatt* (Berlin), (May 26, 1936).

Habe, Hans. "Prof. Neumann's Mission." Evian Conference. *Prager Tagblatt* (July 12, 1938).

———. *Ich stelle mich*. Autobiography. Munich: Desch, 1954.

———. *Die Mission*. Munich: Desch, 1965.

———. "Evian: Secret Conference." *ADL Bulletin* (New York) June 1966. Vol. 23, No. 6.

———. *Erfahrungen*. Olten: Walter, 1973 (Evian Conference).

———. *Leben für den Journalismus,* Vol. 1. Munich: Knaur, 1976, 192–7.

Hanach, Else. Oral History re Berlin 1939–1944, dated July 1944. Yad Vashem, 01/58, 891/55.

Harris, Robert. *Selling Hitler*. New York: Penguin, 1987.

Hart, Peter. "Patrick Dolan" (obituary). *The Independent* (London), (January 11, 1988).

Hartung von Doetinchem, Dagmar, and Rolf Winau, eds. *Zerstörte Fortschritte*. History of Jewish Hospital, Berlin. Berlin: Hentrich, 1989.

Hass, Aaron. *In the Shadow of the Holocaust*. Ithaca: Cornell, 1991.

Hausner, Gideon. *Justice in Jerusalem*. New York: Harper, 1966.

Heenen Wolff, Susanne. *Im Haus des Henkers*. Frankfurt: Dvorah, 1992.

Heilbut, Anthony. *Exiled in Paradise*. New York: Knopf, 1983.

Heims, Steven J., ed. *Passages from Berlin*. (Privately published history of the Goldschmidt School, 1987).

Hellman, Peter. "Stalking the Last Nazi" (Alois Brunner). *New York* magazine (January 13, 1992).

Henry, Frances. *Victims and Neighbors*. Boston: Bergin & Garvey, 1984.

Herlin, Hans. *Die Reise der Verdammten*. SS *St. Louis*. Hamburg: Kabel, 1984.

Herman-Friede, Eugen, and Barbara Schieb-Samizadeh. *Für Freudensprünge keine Zeit*. Berlin: Metropol, 1991.

Heym, Johanna, née Mühle. Landgericht Berlin, testimony (re Walter Dobberke and other Gestapo personnel) June 5, 1967, 1 Js 9/65 (StL.Bln) E 13.

————. Kammergericht Berlin, testimony (re Walter Dobberke and other Gestapo personnel) June 14, 1966, Braunschweig 1 Js 9/65 Stapoleit. Bln.

Hilberg, Raul. *The Destruction of the European Jews*. New York: Holmes and Meier, 1985.

————. *Documents of Destruction*. New York: Quadrangle, 1971.

————. *Sonderzüge nach Auschwitz*. Berlin: Ullstein, 1987.

Hogman, Flora. "The Experience of Catholicism for Jewish Children During World War II." *The Psychoanalytic Review* (New York) 75, no. 4 (Winter 1988), 511–22.

Höhne, Heinz. *Der Order unter dem Totenkopf* (History of the SS). Gütersloh: Mohn, 1967.

Insdorf, Annette. *Indelible Shadows: Film and the Holocaust*, second edition. Cambridge & New York: Cambridge University Press, 1989.

International Committee of the Red Cross. "German Concentration Camps" (Sachsenhausen death march). Report. Geneva, 1975.

Jäckel, Eberhard. "Die Konferenz am Wannsee." *Die Zeit* (Hamburg) (January 17, 1992).

Kaduri, Kurt Jakob Ball. "Berlin wird Judenfrei." *Jahrbuch für die Geschichte Mittel- und Ostdeutschlands*, Vol. 22. Berlin: Colloquium, 1973.

Karas, Joža. *Music in Terezín*. Stuyvesant, NY: Pendragon, 1985.

Kardorff, Ursula von. *Aufzeichnungen aus den Jahren 1942–1945*. Munich: DTV, 1982.

Kee, Robert. *1945: The World We Fought For*. London: Sphere, 1990.

Kelman, Herbert C. "Violence Without Moral Restraint: Reflections on the Dehumanization of Victims and Victimizers." *The Journal of Social Issues*, 29, no. 4 (1973), 25–61.

Kempner, Robert M. W. *Ankläger einer Epoche*. Berlin: Ullstein, 1986.

Kendrick, Alexander. *Prime Time*. Biography of Edward R. Murrow. Boston: Little, Brown, 1969.

Kennan, George. *Sketches from a Life*. New York: Pantheon, 1989.

Kiezgeschichte Berlin 1933, ed. *Wer sich nicht erinnern will*. Berlin: Elefanten Presse, 1983.

Klee, Ernst, and Willi Dressen. *Schöne Zeiten*. Frankfurt am Main: Fischer, 1988.

Klingaman, William K. *1941*. New York: Harper, 1988.

Knobloch, Heinz. *Der beherzte Reviervorsteher*. Berlin: Morgenbuch, 1990.

Kogon, Eugen. *The Theory and Practice of Hell*. New York: Berkley, 1980.

Kolb, Eberhard. *Bergen-Belsen*. (Re Abel Herzberg diary.) Hannover: Verlag für Literatur und Zeitgeschehen, 1962, 155–6, 282–92.

König, Joel. *David*. Frankfurt: Fischer, 1983.

Kramer-Freund, Edith. "Hell and Rebirth" (autobiographical manuscript). Wiener Library, Vienna, WL 587a, 1976.

Kroh, Ferdinand. *David kämpft*. Hamburg: Rowohlt, 1988.

Kwiet, Konrad, and Helmut Eschwege. *Selbstbehauptung und Widerstand*. Hamburg: Christians, 1984.

———. "The Ultimate Refuge: Suicide in the Jewish Community Under the Nazis," in Yearbook 29 of the Leo Baeck Institute, 1984, 135–67.

Landau, Anneliese. "Junge jüdische Komponisten." *C.V. Zeitung* (Berlin), n.d. [c. 1936].

Landgericht Berlin. (500) 1 Ks 1/69 (RSHA) 51/70, Testimony against Fritz Wöhrn, Berlin Gestapo, see Dr. Walter Lustig, March/April 1971.

Lang, Jochen von, ed. *Eichmann Interrogated*. New York: Farrar, Straus & Giroux, 1983.

Langer, Lawrence L. *Holocaust Testimonies*. New Haven: Yale, 1991.

Lapides, Robert, and Alan Adelson, eds. *Lodz Ghetto*. New York: Viking, 1989.

Laqueur, Walter. *Heimkehr*. Berlin: Propyläen, 1964.

———. *The Missing Years*. Boston: Little, Brown, 1980.

———. *The Terrible Secret*. New York: Penguin, 1980.

Leasor, James. *Code Name Nimrod* (Harry Nomburg). Boston: Houghton Mifflin, 1981.

Legters, Lymant I., ed. "The *Kristallnacht* As Turning Point." *Western Society After the Holocaust*. Boulder, CO: Westview, 1983, 39–90.

Leiser, Erwin. *"Deutschland, Erwache!"* Hamburg: Rowohlt, 1989.

———. *Leben nach dem Überleben*. Königstein: Athenäum, 1982.

Lessing, Theodor. *Der jüdische Selbsthass*. Berlin: Jüdischer Verlag, 1930.

Levi, Primo. *The Drowned and the Saved*. New York: Vintage, 1989.

———. *Survival in Auschwitz*. New York: Collier, 1961.

Lewin, Kurt. *Resolving Social Conflicts*. New York: Harper, 1948.

Lifton, Robert Jay. "The Genocidal Mentality." *Tikkun* (May/June 1990), 29.

———. *The Nazi Doctors*. New York: Basic, 1986.

Lochner, Louis P. *What About Germany?* New York: Dodd Mead, 1942.

Lookstein, Haskel. *Were We Our Brothers' Keepers?* New York: Vintage, 1985.

Löwenthal, Gerhard. *Ich bin geblieben*. Munich: Herbig, 1987.

Mahler-Werfel, Alma. *Mein Leben*. Frankfurt am Main: Fischer, 1989.

Malkin, Peter Z., and Harry Stein. *Eichmann in My Hands*. New York: Warner, 1990.

Maltzan, Maria, Gräfin von. *Schlage die Trommel und fürchte Dich nicht*. Berlin: Ullstein, 1986.

Manvell, Roger, and Heinrich Fraenkel. *Dr. Goebbels*. New York: Simon and Schuster, 1960.

———. *The Terrible Secret*. New York: Putnam, 1967, 149.

Meier, Luise. Oral History, Berlin, November 1955. Wiener Library, London and Tel Aviv, P.III f (Berlin) No. 193/02/188.

Meissl, Heino. Testimony before prosecutor, Berlin Kammergericht. Munich, June 12, 1967.

Meissl, Heino. Testimony before prosecutor, Berlin Kammergericht, 1 Js 1/65 (RSHA), Munich, February 2, 1968.

Melcher, Peter. *Weissensee*. Berlin: Haude und Spener, 1986.

Metcalfe, Philip. *1933*. New York: Perennial, 1989.

Miethling, Erika. Testimony before prosecutor, Berlin Kammergericht, 1 Js 1/65 (RSHA). Berlin, October 24, 1967.

Möller, Erich. Nazi Party personnel files, 1926–1945. Berlin Document Center (U.S.).

Der Morgen (Berlin). "Das blonde Gespenst." (March 14, 1946).

Morgenpost (Berlin). "Verriet sie Juden an die Gestapo?" Third Stella Kübler trial. (September 26, 1972).

Morgenpost (Berlin). "Stella Kübler durch Zeugen belastet." (September 29, 1972).

Morse, Arthur D. While Six Million Died. New York: Random House, 1967.

Mosley, Leonard. The Reich Marshal. New York: Doubleday, 1974.

Mosse, Martha. Testimony re Alois Brunner in Bovensiepen trial, Untersuchungs-richter IV bei dem Landgericht Berlin, IV VU 2.67, July 11, 1967.

Müller-Münch, Ingrid. "Nur keine Eile, dann erledigt sich der Prozess fast ganz von selbst." Frankfurter Rundschau (January 3, 1990).

Nacht Depesche (Berlin). "Jüdin schickte alle ihre Freunde in die Gaskammer." (March 31, 1956).

Nacht Depesche (Berlin). " 'Jüdische Lorelei' wollte Unterstützung." (April 4, 1956).

Nelki, Erna, and Wolfgang Nelki. Geschichten aus dem Umbruch der Deutschen Geschichte. Hannover: Revonnah, 1991.

Nicolai, publ. Wegweiser durch das jüdische Berlin. Berlin: Nicolaische Verlags-buchhandlung, 1987.

Nussbaum, Ruth. Autobiographical chapters, n.p., n.d.

O'Connor, John J. "Remembering Anne Frank, Holocaust's Witness" (TV review). The New York Times (June 12, 1989).

O'Donnell, James P. The Bunker. Boston: Houghton Mifflin, 1978.

Orenstein, Henry. I Shall Live. New York: Touchstone, 1987.

Overy, R.J. Hermann Göring. Munich: Heyne, 1986.

Padfield, Peter. Himmler. New York: Holt, 1990.

Pätzold, Kurt, and Erika Schwarz. Tagesordnung: Judenmord (Documents on Wann-see Conference). Berlin: Metropol, 1992.

Peck, Abraham J., ed. The German-Jewish Legacy in America 1938–1988. Detroit: Wayne State, 1989.

Perl, William R. The Four-Front War. New York: Crown, 1979.

Pineas, Herrmann, and Herta Pineas. "Unsere Schicksale seit dem 30. Januar 1933," Oral History, Leo Baeck Institute, May 1954.

Prinz, Joachim. Biography. Current Biography. New York: W. H. Wilson, 1963.

Prinz, Joachim. Obituary. The New York Times (October 1, 1988).

"Procontra" (pseud.). "Sie verfolgten Stella Kübler." Berliner Zeitung (June 31, 1947).

Read, Anthony, and David Fisher. Kristallnacht: The Tragedy of the Night of Terror. New York: Times Books, 1989.

Reinerova, Lenka. Der Ausflug zum Schwanensee. Berlin: Aufbau, 1983.

Reitlinger, Gerald. The Final Solution. New York: Thomas Yoseloff, 1968.

Reitz, Inge. Testimony before Ehrengericht der Jüdischen Gemeinde zu Berlin, October 8, 1946. Zentrale Stelle, Ludwigsburg.

Remarque, Erich Maria. Die Nacht von Lissabon. Berlin: Ullstein, 1978.

Reschke, Max. Testimony before Ehrengericht der Jüdischen Gemeinde zu Berlin, April 5, 1956. Zentrale Stelle, Ludwigsburg.

Response (Boston). "Five Children of Survivors: A Conversation." 9, no. 1 (Spring 1975).

Rewald, Ilse. "Berliner, die uns halfen, die Hitlerdiktatur zu überleben" (Pamphlet). Informationszentrum Berlin, Gedenk- und Bildungsstätte Stauffenbergstrasse, *Beiträge zum Widerstand*, no. 6 (1975).

Riesenburger, Martin. *Das Licht verlöscht nicht.* Berlin: Union, 1984.

Riess, Curt. *Ascona.* (Erich Maria Remarque and Hans Habe) Zürich: Europa, 1964.

Rimer, Sara. "Reunion Recalls Schools for Jews in Nazi Germany" (Goldschmidt School). *The New York Times* (November 11, 1985).

Roazen, Paul. *Erik Erikson.* New York: Free Press, 1976.

Rosenkranz, Herbert. *Verfolgung und Selbstbehauptung: Die Juden in Österreich, 1938–1945.* Vienna: Herold, 1978.

Rosenstrauch, Hazel, ed. *Aus Nachbarn wurden Juden.* Berlin: Transit, 1988.

Rosenthal, Hans. *Zwei Leben in Deutschland.* Bergisch Gladbach: Lübbe, 1987.

Rückerl, Adalbert. *Nationalsozialistische Vernichtungslager im Spiegel deutscher Strafprozesse* (Chelmno war crimes trials). Munich: DTV, 1977, 243–346.

Runge, Irene. *Onkel Max ist Jüdisch.* Berlin: Dietz, 1991.

Rürop, Reinhard, ed. *Topographie des Terrors.* Berlin: Arenhövel, 1987.

Ryan, Cornelius. *The Last Battle.* New York: Simon and Schuster, 1966.

Sanders, Ronald. *Shores of Refuge.* New York: Holt, 1988.

Sanford, Ralph. Punishment Without Crime. Oral History (Buchenwald after Crystal Night), New York, Leo Baeck Institute, n.d.

Schäfer, Hans Dieter, ed. *Berlin im zweiten Weltkrieg.* Munich: Piper, 1991.

Scheffler, Wolfgang. "Der Brandanschlag im Berliner Lustgarten im Mai 1942 und seine Folgen." *Jahrbuch des Landesarchivs* (Berlin, 1984); 91–118.

Scheurenberg, Klaus. *Ich will leben.* Berlin: Verlagsbüro Charlottenburg, 1982.

Schmidt, Franz. *Die Juden in Edenkoben.* Landau: Sparkasse Südliche Weinstrasse, 1990.

Schmidt, Matthias. *Albert Speer: The End of a Myth.* New York: St. Martin's, 1984.

Schnapp, Harry. Testimony before Landgericht Berlin, Untersuchungsrichter IV, June 20, 1967.

Schoenberner, Gerhard. *Der Gelbe Stern.* Frankfurt: Fischer, 1991.

———, ed. *Wir haben es gesehen.* Wiesbaden: Fourier, 1988.

Schubert, Helga. *Judasfrauen.* Frankfurt: Luchterhand, 1990.

Schwarzer, Harry. Testimony before Ehrengericht der Jüdischen Gemeinde zu Berlin, February 12, 1947. Zentrale Stelle, Ludwigsburg.

Schwersenz, Jizchak. *Die versteckte Gruppe.* Berlin: Wichern, 1988.

Schwurgericht bei dem Landgericht Berlin. Record of re-trial re Stella Ingrid Goldschlag, (500) 1 P Ks 1/57 (42/72) Berlin, September 21, 1972.

Sellenthin, H. G. "Wir meinen: Es liegt am Einzelnen." *Allgemeine* (Frankfurt Jewish weekly) (May 7, 1957).

Sheehan, Vincent. *Not Peace But the Sword.* New York: Doubleday, 1939.

Shelley, Lore, ed. *Secretaries of Death: Accounts by Former Prisoners Who Worked in the Administrative Offices of Auschwitz.* New York: Shengold, 1986.

Shepherd, Naomi. *Wilfrid Israel.* Berlin: Siedler, 1985.

Shirer, William L. *Berlin Diary.* New York: Penguin, 1979.

——. *The Rise and Fall of the Third Reich.* New York: Fawcett, 1959.

Short, K. R. M., and Stephan Dolezel, eds. *Hitler's Fall—The Newsreel Witness.* London: Croom Helm, 1988.

Simon, Hermann. *Die Neue Synagoge Berlin.* Berlin: Hentrich, n.d.

Sperber, A. M. *Murrow: His Life and Times.* New York: Freundlich, 1986.

Der Spiegel (Hamburg). "Voll Blut und Wunden." (music in concentration camps) (No. 47/199, 1992).

Spoto, Donald. *Lenya: A Life.* New York: Ballantine, 1989.

Staatliche Kriminalpolizei. Kriminalpolizeileitstelle Berlin (Bundesarchiv Potsdam), Personalakte F5-1619/46 Mi, Stella Kübler Isaaksohn, East Berlin police files, 1946.

Staatliche Kriminalpolizei. Kriminalpolizeileitstelle Berlin (Bundesarchiv Potsdam), Personalakte 2Ast K167 J34, Rolf Isaaksohn, East Berlin police files, 1946.

Stoltzfus, Nathan. *The Protest in the Rosenstrasse.* Manuscript. Cambridge, MA, n.d.

Studnitz, Hans-Georg von. *Als Berlin brannte.* Stuttgart: Kohlhammer, 1963.

Styron, William. *Sophie's Choice.* New York: Bantam, 1980.

Szepansky, Gerda. *Frauen leisten Widerstand: 1933–1945.* Frankfurt am Main: Fischer, 1989.

Szepansky, Wolfgang. "Todesmarsch" (Sachsenhausen death march). *Niemand und Nichts Vergessen.* Berlin: Elefanten, 1984.

Tagesspiegel (Berlin). "Eine jüdische Agentin Himmlers." (March 10, 1946).

Tagesspiegel (Berlin). "Der Schrecken der 'U-Boote.' " (March 17, 1946).

Tagesspiegel (Berlin). "Ein Gehilfe von Stella Kübler" (Trial of catcher Bruno Goldstein). (May 15, 1949). Staatanwaltschaft Berlin file P Ks 9/48.

Tägliche Rundschau (Soviet Military Government newspaper, Berlin). "Hunderte von Juden dem Henker ausgeliefert." (March 17, 1946).

Thomas, Gordon, and Max M. Witts. *Voyage of the Damned.* New York: Stein and Day, 1974.

Toland, John. *Adolf Hitler.* New York: Ballantine, 1976.

——. *The Last 100 Days.* New York: Bantam, 1967.

Urrows, Henry, and Elizabeth Urrows. "Varian Fry." *Harvard Magazine* (March/April 1990).

USSR Interior Ministry. Denkschrift zu den Sonderlagern in der ehemaligen Sowietischen Besetzungszone, quotes in *Neues Deutschland* (Berlin) (July 27, 1990).

Vassiltchikov, Marie. *Berlin Diaries 1940–1945.* New York: Vintage, 1988.

Das Volk (Berlin). "Ein Scheusal in Weibsgestalt." (March 13, 1946).

Wagner, Eva. Oral History, Berlin to 1944. Jerusalem: Yad Vashem, 605/55 Inv. Nr. 0169, 1947.

Weber, Hermann. "Katz, Iwan." *Neue Deutsche Biographie* 11. Berlin: Duncker & Humboldt, n.d., 333–34.

Die Welt (Hamburg). "Gestapo-'Greiferin' wieder vor Gericht" (Third Stella Kübler trial). (September 22, 1972).

Westheimer, Ruth K. *All in a Lifetime.* New York: Warner, 1987.

Whelan, Richard. *Robert Capa.* New York: Ballantine, 1985.

Wiesel, Elie. *Night.* Autobiography. New York: Bantam, 1982.

Wiesenthal, Simon. *The Murderers Among Us.* New York: McGraw, 1967.

——. *Recht, nicht Rache.* Berlin: Ullstein, 1991.

Wilmersdorf Museum. "Hier ist kein Bleiben länger." Exhibition catalogue re Jewish schools. Berlin: Bezirksamt Wilmersdorf, 1992.

Wipperman, Wolfgang. "Die Berliner Gruppe Baum und der jüdische Widerstand." Berlin: Informationszentrum Berlin, Gedenk- und Bildungsstätte Stauffenbergstrasse, 1981.

Wistrich, Robert. *Wer war wer im Dritten Reich?* Frankfurt: Fischer, 1987.

Wöhrn, Fritz. Schwurgericht bei dem Landgericht Berlin, (500) 1 Ks 1/69 (RSHA) (51/70), trial record, March 9 to April 6, 1971, re Jewish Hospital and Dr. Walter Lustig.

Wolf, Naomi. *The Beauty Myth.* New York: Morrow, 1991.

Wolff, Edith. Oral History re Berlin, 1933–1943, dated 1955. Yad Vashem, 752/41–1, 01/247.

Wollenberg, Jörg, ed. *Niemand war dabei und keiner hat's gewusst.* Munich: Piper, 1989.

Wyden, Peter. *The Hired Killers.* New York: Morrow, 1963.

———. *The Passionate War.* New York: Simon & Schuster, 1983.

Wyman, David S. *The Abandonment of the Jews.* New York: Pantheon, 1984.

———. *Paper Walls.* Boston: University of Massachusetts, 1968.

Young-Bruehl, Elisabeth. *Hannah Arendt.* New Haven: Yale, 1982.

Zivier, Georg. *Deutschland und seine Juden.* Wiesbaden: VMA, n.d.

Zwerin, Mike. *La Tristesse de Saint Louis: Jazz Under the Nazis.* New York: Morrow, 1985.

Index

Auschwitz (*cont.*)
  survivors of, 211, 258, 276, 293,
    295, 304, 309
  transports to, 108–9, 122, 166, 167,
    174, 189–90*n*
Austria
  anti-Semitism in, 56, 124
  Nazi annexation of, 55, 64
Authors Society, 28

Baeck, Rabbi Leo, 63, 106, 107, 113,
    179, 273, 335, 336
Baker, Josephine, 20, 78
Bandmann, Dr., 15–16, 42–43, 160,
    280, 288, 304, 336
Bartered Bride, The (Smetana), 180
Baruch, Bernard, 64
Baruch, Siegfried, 257–62, 313, 317
Bassani (author), 43
Bauhaus architecture, 20
Baum, Herbert, 99
Baumann, Lili, 26–28, 45, 304
Baumann, Renate, 45
Bayer pharmaceutical company, 201*n*
BBC, 115, 148, 191
Bechuanaland, 88
Beck, Gad, 170, 172, 200–1, 213, 217,
    324
Beck, Margot, 200–1
Beer Hall Putsch, 29, 38
Beethoven, Ludwig van, 22, 43
Before the Deluge (Friedrich), 22*n*
Behar, Isaak, 164, 166*n*, 219, 277, 278,
    286–87, 329
Behrend, Heinz, 302, 323
Bekessy, Jansci, *see* Habe, Hans
Belgium, 132
  refugees in, 88
  resistance in, 145
Belzec, 122, 180
Benz, Wolfgang, 172*n*
Bergen-Belsen, 18, 51, 108, 116, 181,
    271, 301, 324–25, 328
Bergman, Ingrid, 91
Berlin Academy of Arts, 123
Berlin Diary (Shirer), 59, 65, 93, 95, 96
Berlin Hot Club, 78
Berlin Jewish Community, 34, 70, 143,
    162, 230, 250, 252, 280, 293,
    321

and concentration camp survivors,
    211–12, 243
  courts of, 271–74
  and deportations, 102, 103, 106–7,
    177
  and Factory Action, 111
  Yvonne and, 258, 261, 265
Berlin Stories (Isherwood), 20
Berlin Technical University, Center for
    the Study of Anti-Semitism at,
    127*n*
Berlin University, 28*n*
Berscheid, Ellen S., 295
Berzel, Monika, 207
Bettelheim, Bruno, 296, 303–4
Binnewies, Helmut, 258
Black market, 89, 237
Blau, Bruno, 201, 215, 216
Blomé, Jean, 230, 239–40
Blue Angel, The (film), 20
Blue Note Records, 78
Blumenthal, Michael, 335
B'nai Brith, Anti-Defamation League of,
    56
Bogart, Humphrey, 91
Boger, Wilhelm, 268
Boldt, Captain Gerhard, 219
Book burnings, 28, 49, 67
Borinski, Anneliese-Ora, 164
Bormann, Martin, 128, 203, 219
Bosel, Siegmund, 56
Boston City Hospital, 332
Boston University, 333
Bovensiepen, Otto, 306
Bradfisch, Otto, 125
Brahn, Max, 34, 53, 116, 180
Braun, Eva, 226
British Royal Navy, 84
Brown, Anthony Cave, 336
Brundibar (Krásas), 181
Brunner, Alois, 55–56, 58, 105–7, 109,
    111, 163
Brunner, Anton, 55*n*
Buchenwald, 72, 221, 273
Bulge, Battle of the, 199
Bullitt, William C., 64
Buna, 180
Burmeister, Walter, 120
Bush, George, 333
Buthner, Hans, 78

Nussbaum, Rabbi Max, 69, 85, 89–90, 94
Nussbaum, Ruth, 69, 85, 94

Office of Strategic Services (O.S.S.), 336
Olympic Games, 78
Opel Motors, 147
Operation Seraglio, 215
Ordner, 105–6, 141n, 145, 155, 163, 165–66, 172, 177, 187, 188, 210, 220, 273, 298
in Vienna, 56–58, 269
Orenstein, Henry, 224
Organization of Jewish Displaced Persons, 58n
Ostjuden (Eastern Jews), 22, 33
Owens, Jesse, 78

Paedagogische Hochschule, 44
Paesch, Lotte, 273
Page, Alex, 304
Palestine, 83–84, 88, 95, 132, 258, 292
Panama, 87
Paraguay, 87, 88
Pearl Harbor, 52, 88
Pech, Gottfried, 294, 298–99
Peking man, 33
People's Court, 161
Perl, William R., 83, 95
Pineas, Hermann, 103
Pineas, Herta, 103, 104
Plaschow, 272
Playboy magazine, 307
Playing for Time (Fénelon), 180n
Pogroms, 22
Poland, 33, 42
concentration camps in, 55; see also names of specific camps
deportations to, 101
government-in-exile of, 122
Nazi invasion of, 80
postwar borders of, 122
Porter, Cole, 77, 269
Posttraumatic stress disorder, 159n, 177, 190, 310, 340
Prager, Peter, 67–68
Prager Tagblatt (newspaper), 62
Preuss, Richard, 273

Princeton University, Institute for Advanced Study at, 21
Prinz, Rabbi Joachim, 22–23, 35, 69, 292–93, 296
Prokop, Party Comrade, 171–72
Propaganda Ministry, 23, 73, 189
Prüfer, Franz Wilhelm, 143n
Psychic numbing, 310
Psychoanalysis, 20, 64
Pürschel, Johanna, 280–81, 294

Quakers, 85
Queen Mary (ship), 88

Race theory, 67
Radio Luxembourg, 336
Rape, 228–29, 237
Reagan, Ronald, 334
Red Army, 129
in Berlin, 208–9, 214–16, 219–22, 237
rapes by soldiers of, 228–29, 237
Redgrave, Vanessa, 180n
Regensburger, Paul, 246–47
Reich, Ismar, 161–62, 166n, 174, 276–77, 339
Reich Flight Tax, 88
Reich Labor Front, 71
Reichstag fire, 37, 67
Reiffenberg, Jean, 217n
Reinhardt, Max, 21
Reitz, Inge Jacoby, 273–74
Remarque, Erich Maria, 28n, 30, 87–88, 91–92
Republican Party, 334
Reschke, Max, 170, 179, 187, 250, 272–73
Resettlement Division, 102
Resistance, 99–100, 132, 134, 135, 145, 209–10, 323
revenge on collaborators by, 212
Response (magazine), 332
Reuter, Ernst, 228n
Rewald, Ilse, 102
Rischowsky, Günther, 201
Rockefeller Foundation, 33
Rogers, Ginger, 79